Lecture Notes in Computer Science 3412

Commenced Publication in 1973
Founding and Former Series Editors:
Gerhard Goos, Juris Hartmanis, and Jan van Leeuwen

Xavier Franch Dan Port (Eds.)

COTS-Based Software Systems

4th International Conference, ICCBSS 2005
Bilbao, Spain, February 7-11, 2005
Proceedings

Volume Editors

Xavier Franch
Universitat Politècnica de Catalunya (UPC)
Jordi Girona 1 - 3, 08034 Barcelona, Spain
E-mail: franch@lsi.upc.edu

Dan Port
University of Hawaii at Manoa
Department of Information Technology Management
Honolulu, HI, USA
E-mail: dport@hawaii.edu

Library of Congress Control Number: 20044118380

CR Subject Classification (1998): K.6.3, D.2, J.1

ISSN 0302-9743
ISBN 3-540-24548-0 Springer Berlin Heidelberg New York

Springer is a part of Springer Science+Business Media

springeronline.com

Printed in Germany

Typesetting: Camera-ready by author, data conversion by Scientific Publishing Services, Chennai, India
Printed on acid-free paper SPIN: 11386254 06/3142 5 4 3 2 1 0

Foreword

The theme "Build and Conquer" chosen for this year's conference fully represents what we (the organizers) want to put across to the software community: software development is an engineering discipline, and not an artistic expression. Once we are ready to "build" our software systems using pieces previously builtin (similar to any other technology manufacturer), we will be able to "conquer" the software engineering process. If we take a look at other engineering disciplines such as car manufacturing, house appliances or aeronautics, we see that the final products are built through the integration of multiprovider commercial components. These components are successfully integrated and constitute an important part of the final product. Most software-related organizations still build software from scratch, omitting thousands of ready-built commercially available software components that could be used very effectively during the development phase.

This year ICCBSS moves to Europe for the first time since the first conference took place in Orlando, FL, USA in 2002. The conference scope has enlarged over the years to include the Open Source community and Web Services technologies. The reason for this is that I believe both are considered components-off-the-shelf, so many of the characteristics of COTS are also applied to Open Source and Web Services. Due to this, we will enjoy the presence of keynote speakers and researchers presenting on these two topics for the first time.

The conference program is divided into three different tracks comprising research and experience presentations, panels of discussion with renowned experts, tutorials in which to expand the knowledge of the field, poster presentations, and keynote presentations. The conference is preceded by two additional workshops, in which attendees may interact with COTS experts face-to-face to solve certain COTS-related issues. Moreover, due to the fact that this is the first time to host the conference in Europe, there is an introductory course on "Building Software Systems with Commercial Components (COTS)" for those who are new to this area.

Last but not least, I would like to express my thanks to all the members of the ICCBSS 2005 Planning Committee for volunteering their time to make the fourth conference a reality. I would also like to thank the Program Committee for their excellent work in reviewing and selecting the papers that will be presented here.

Again, welcome to the proceedings of ICCBSS 2005, and I hope you find this conference interesting for your own needs, and you find the solutions needed to "conquer" your software systems.

February 2005

David Morera

Preface

On behalf of the ICCBSS 2005 Planning and Program Committees, we would like to welcome you to the proceedings of this year's conference, the fourth in the series. All of the previous ICCBSS conferences indicated a growing interest in the issues of COTS, and this year's conference continues this trend: the number and excellence of the papers we received for this year's conference attest to the continuing interest throughout the world in the use of commercial software in almost every domain.

Our original hope for this year's conference was to emphasize those issues that mark the growing maturity of COTS in the world: consolidating the COTS market, dealing with the many legal issues, and finding and publicizing COTS success stories. While not all of the papers in the conference are reflections of these goals, there are many that do. We believe that at least some of the impetus for this growing maturity about COTS issues is a reflection of the hard work and perseverance that has marked the three previous ICCBSS conferences.

This year's conference is the first to be held in Europe, and the papers that will be presented reflect this fact. They represent a very broad, multinational community that spans the globe, and it can truly be said that ICCBSS is an international conference.

We would especially like to thank the members of the Program Committee and the referees for their great contribution of time, talent, and wisdom in choosing the papers you will hear. We would also like to thank our hosts, the members of the European Software Institute, for their generous work in organizing the conference. We look forward to a truly memorable conference in Bilbao.

David Carney
Jean-Christophe Mielnik

International
Conference
on COTS-Based
Software Systems

Planning Committee

General Chair	David Morera (European Software Institute)
Program Chairs	David Carney (Software Engineering Institute)
	Jean-Christophe Mielnik (Thales Research & Technology)
Proceedings Chairs	Xavier Franch (Universitat Politècnica de Catalunya)
	Dan Port (University of Hawaii)
Tutorials Chair	Lisa Brownsword (Software Engineering Institute)
Panels Chair	Ljerka Beus-Dukic (University of Westminster)
Posters Chair	Mark Vigder (National Research Council Canada)
Publicity Chairs	Jason Mansell (European Software Institute)
	Sylvia Illieva (Sofia University)
	Paul Mason (Asian University of Science and Technology)
	Ashraf Saad (Georgia Tech Savannah)
Finance and Local Arrangements	Miren Ojinaga (European Software Institute)
Secretariat	Piergiorgio Di Giacomo (European Software Institute)
Chair Emeritus	Barry Boehm (University of Southern California)

Program Committee

Chris Abts	Texas A&M
Cecilia C. Albert	Software Engineering Institute
Carina Alves	University College London
Divya Atkins	Parvat Infotech Private Limited
Sally J.F. Baron	Management Consulting Services
Gorka Benguría	European Software Institute
David P. Bentley	South Carolina Research Authority
Lisa Brownsword	Software Engineering Institute
Ignacio Delgado	Martin & Lawson
Anne Dourgnon-Hanoune	EDF R&D (Électricité de France)
Anthony Earl	Sun Microsystems Inc.
Shadia Elgazzar	National Research Council Canada
Rose F. Gamble	University of Tulsa
Göran V. Grahn	Volvo Information Technology
Pedro Gutiérrez	European Software Institute
Renya Inagaki	C3IS Corporation
Anatol Kark	National Research Council Canada
Judy Kerner	The Aerospace Corporation
Neil Maiden	Centre for HCI Design, City University London
Diane Mularz	MITRE Corp.
Michael Ochs	Fraunhofer Institute for Experiment Software Engineering
Fernando Piera	INDRA Sistemas
Peter Popov	City University London
Dan Port	University of Hawaii
José María Salvatierra	Vodafone, CDS Zamudio
Mark Vigder	National Research Council Canada
Ye Yang	University of Southern California

Conference Organizers

The European Software Institute (ESI) has now established itself as one of the world's major centers for software process improvement. Our strength lies in our close partnership with industry. ESI's business-driven approach focuses on issues that result in a genuine commercial impact, such as reduction of costs and improving productivity.

The European Software Institute's technical work is driven by the philosophy of bringing measurable business improvements in the management and development of software-intensive systems for both individual companies and the software-related industry as a whole. In partnership with its patrons, ESI identifies relevant emerging process-improvement technologies. We then mature these methodologies through research, trials and close collaboration with business. Finally, we help companies to adapt the methodologies to their own organization or industry.

Within this overall framework, ESI's work is divided into four key technology areas: software process improvement, measurement, system engineering, and product-line based reuse where COTS research is allocated.

Learn more about the ESI at http://www.esi.es

The Software Engineering Institute (SEI) provides leadership in advancing the state of software engineering practice. We collaborate with industry, academia, and the government to learn about the best technical and management practices and then use what we learn to benefit the software engineering community.

The SEI program of work consists of initiatives grouped into three areas of software engineering: technical practices (especially product engineering principles and methods), management practices, and independent research and development (IRAD) activities. The COTS-Based Systems Initiative is grouped with other technical practice initiatives like Performance Critical Systems, Product Line Practice, Architecture Tradeoff Analysis, and Survivable Systems.

The institute is based at Carnegie Mellon University and is sponsored by the US Office of the Under Secretary of Defense for Acquisition, Technology, and Logistics [OUSD (AT&L)].

Learn more about the SEI at http://www.sei.cmu.edu

National Research Council Canada | Conseil national de recherches Canada

The National Research Council (NRC), Canada's premier science and technology research organization, is a leader in scientific and technical research, the diffusion of technology, and the dissemination of scientific and technical information.

Working in partnership with innovative companies, universities and research organizations worldwide, NRC enhances Canada's social and economic well-being and creates new opportunities for Canadians. Through knowledge, research and innovation, NRC and its partners are expanding the frontiers of science and technology. The Institute for Information Technology is one of the National Research Council's research institutes. Its mission is to assist industry through collaborative research and development projects.

Learn more about the NRC at http://www.nrc-cnrc.gc.ca/.

ICCBSS 2005 Sponsors

Bizkaiko Foru Aldundia

Berrikuntza eta Ekonomi Sustapen Saila

Diputación Foral de Bizkaia

Departamento de Innovación y Promoción Económica

Keynote Speakers

Mr. John Kemp
Technical Architect
Web Services Technologies, Nokia

Mobile Web Services – Bridging Fixed and Mobile Networks with COTS Software

The traditional fixed Internet has offered a wide variety of services and content to the general Web-browsing public. The mobile network has been seen quite differently, offering several challenges to the provision of Internet-based software and services. Web services technologies aim to overcome these challenges, and provide a world of new and exciting software-based services to mobile users. How will COTS software support mobile Web services, and what are some of the issues in bringing Web services support to COTS software?

Prof. Patrice Degoulet
Head of Medical Informatics
Pompidou Hospital

Building a COTS-Based Hospital Medical System

Pompidou Hospital is one of the first hospitals to implement an EPR (Electronic Patient Record). This is a not-too-old medical ideal where everyday operations and record-keeping are carried out and maintained almost exclusively with computers. The idea behind it is to make all patients' medical reports, lab results, and images electronically available to clinicians, instantaneously, wherever they are and using only a laptop. Patrice Degoulet chose a commercial solution, a collection of the most effective COTS already existing in the market, in constructing the entire Pompidou's Medical System. He will present how the new system was designed and how the integration was carried out with so many different commercial components from different COTS vendors.

Mr. Tom Glover
President and Chairman of the Web Services Interoperability Organization (WSI)
Senior Program Manager – Web Services Standards at IBM

Evolving COTS and GOTS Software into the 21st Century

Throughout the world today the drive towards ubiquitous interoperability has become a critical step towards meeting the need for flexible configuration of software solutions. Web services has emerged as the standards-based component model with the potential to deliver this broad interoperability, and the Services-Oriented Architecture model is hailed as the architecture within which these services will be deployed. We'll look at the synergies between these emerging technologies and the "off-the-shelf software" movement and discuss the synergies between the two initiatives which, if exploited, may empower new software users.

Table of Contents

Panels

COTS Component-Based Embedded Systems – A Dream or Reality?
Ivica Crnkovic, Jakob Axelsson, Susanne Graf, Magnus Larsson, Rob van Ommering, Kurt Wallnau 1

Free and Proprietary Software in COTS-Based Software Development
Bernard Lang, Jean-François Abramatic, Jesús M. González-Barahona, Fernando Piera Gómez, Mogens Kühn Pedersen 2

Workshops

2nd International Workshop on Incorporating COTS into Software Systems: Assessment and Prediction of Behavior and QoS Attributes of COTS Software Components and Systems
Franck Barbier, Goiuria Sagarduy, Xabier Aretxandieta 3

Challenges of COTS IV & V
Dan Port, Haruka Nakao, Masafumi Katahira, Christina Motes 4

Tutorials

The COTS Product Market: An EU Legal Perspective
Ignacio Delgado González, Carlos Arias-Chausson 5

Composable Spiral Processes for COTS-Based Application Development
Barry Boehm, Ye Yang, Jesal Bhuta, Dan Port 6

Posters

Heterogeneous COTS Product Integration to Allow the Comprehensive Development of Image Processing Systems
Cristina Vicente Chicote, Ana Toledo Moreo, Carlos Fernández Andrés 8

A Contextualized Study of COTS-Based E-Service Projects
Ye Yang, Barry Boehm 9

Quality of Service Profiles in Web Service Discovery
Barry Norton 10

Decision on Replacing Components of Security Functions in COTS-Based Information Systems
Myeonggil Choi, Hyunwoo Kim, Eunhye Kim, Sehun Kim 11

Best Papers

Best Paper Award 2004: Characterization of a Taxonomy for Business Applications and the Relationships Among Them
Juan P. Carvallo, Xavier Franch, Carme Quer, Marco Torchiano 12

Best Paper Award 2005: Using Earned Value Management for COTS-Based Systems: Issues and Recommendations
Lisa Brownsword, Jim Smith 13

COTS at Business

Business Process Definition Languages Versus Traditional Methods Towards Interoperability
Leire Bastida Merino, Gorka Benguria Elguezabal 25

The Necessary Legal Approach to COTS Safety and COTS Liability in European Single Market
Carlos Arias-Chausson 36

COTS Acquisition: Getting a Good Contract
Shadia Elgazzar, Anatol Kark, Erik Putrycz, Mark Vigder 43

Integration and Interoperability

Specifying Interaction Constraints of Software Components for Better Understandability and Interoperability
Yan Jin, Jun Han 54

Resolving COTS System Assessment Clashes
Daniel Port, Haruka Nakao, Hideki Nomoto, Hitoshi Mamiya, Masafumi Katahira 65

COTS Components and DB Interoperability
Radmila Juric, Ljerka Beus-Dukic 77

Evaluation and Requirements

On Goal-Oriented COTS Taxonomies Construction
Claudia P. Ayala, Pere Botella, Xavier Franch 90

Assets and Liabilities of Organizational Trust: COTS Software Adoption in Government Projects
Sally J. F. Baron 101

Filtering COTS Components Through an Improvement-Based Process
Alejandra Cechich, Mario Piattini 112

Enabling the Selection of COTS Components
Sudipto Ghosh, John L. Kelly, Roopashree P. Shankar 122

A Method for Compatible COTS Component Selection
Jesal Bhuta, Barry Boehm 132

One Global COTS-Based System to Replace 20+ Local Legacy Systems
Elisabeth Hansson, Göran V. Grahn 144

Using Goals and Quality Models to Support the Matching Analysis During COTS Selection
Carina Alves, Xavier Franch, Juan P. Carvallo, Anthony Finkelstein 146

Safety and Dependability

Addressing Malicious Code in COTS : A Protection Framework
Donald J. Reifer, Pranjali Baxi, Fabio Hirata, Jonathan Schifman, Ricky Tsao 157

Protective Wrapping of Off-the-Shelf Components
Meine van der Meulen, Steve Riddle, Lorenzo Strigini, Nigel Jefferson 168

An Automated Dependability Analysis Method for COTS-Based Systems
Lars Grunske, Bernhard Kaiser 178

Integration and Interoperability

Loose Integration of COTS Tools for the Development of Real Time Distributed Control Systems
Javier Portillo, Oskar Casquero, Marga Marcos 191

Managing Dependencies Between Software Products
Mark Northcott, Mark Vigder 201

Architecture and Design

Analysing the Impact of Change in COTS-Based Systems
Gerald Kotonya, John Hutchinson 212

Considering Variability in a System Family's Architecture During COTS Evaluation
Nelufar Ulfat-Bunyadi, Erik Kamsties, Klaus Pohl 223

An Approach to Analysis and Design for COTS-Based Systems
Grace A. Lewis 236

Resolving Architectural Mismatches of COTS Through Architectural Reconciliation
Paris Avgeriou, Nicolas Guelfi 248

COTS Management

Reuse of Existing Software in Space Projects — Proposed Approach and Extensions to Product Assurance and Software Engineering Standards
Manuel Rodríguez, João Gabriel Silva, Patricia Rodríguez-Dapena, Han van Loon, Fernando Aldea-Montero 258

Ten Signs of a Good Reuse Management Plan
Edwin Morris, Wm B. Anderson, Mary Catherine Ward, Dennis Smith 268

Preliminary Results from a State-of-the-Practice Survey on Risk Management in Off-the-Shelf Component-Based Development
Jingyue Li, Reidar Conradi, Odd Petter N. Slyngstad, Marco Torchiano, Maurizio Morisio, Christian Bunse 278

Open Source Software (OSS)

Managerial and Technical Barriers to the Adoption of Open Source Software
Jesper Holck, Michael Holm Larsen, Mogens Kühn Pedersen 289

COTS and Open Source Software Components: Are They Really Different on the Battlefield?
Piergiorgio Di Giacomo 301

Author Index 311

COTS Component-Based Embedded Systems – A Dream or Reality?

Ivica Crnkovic[1], Jakob Axelsson[2], Susanne Graf[3], Magnus Larsson[4], Rob van Ommering[5], and Kurt Wallnau[6]

[1] ivica.crnkovic@mdh.se, [2] jaxelss5@volvocars.com, [3] Susanne.Graf@imag.fr, [4] magnus.larsson@se.abb.com, [5] rob.van.ommering@philips.com, [6] kcw@sei.cmu.edu

Embedded systems cover a range of computer systems from ultra small computer-based devices to large, possibly distributed, systems monitoring and controlling complex processes. COTS-based development in embedded systems, with electronic and mechanical components has a long tradition. However component-based development (CBD) with software components, in particular COTS components, is utilized to a lesser degree. A major reason is the inability of component technologies to cope with specific requirements of embedded systems. In general, component-based technologies do not address timing issues, QoS, dependability, resource constraints, and other extra-functional properties of crucial importance for embedded systems. This raises the question whether Component-based and COTS-based approach is beneficial for development of embedded systems, and which are the specifics to be addressed to make such an approach feasible.

The aim of this panel is to discuss the needs and problems with respect to a component based approach in the context of embedded systems and come to some conclusion about the feasibility of COTS and CBD approaches for embedded systems. The following questions will be in the focus of the discussion:

- Will COTS and CBD be the dominant approaches in the future, or will these approaches never overcome the problems of today?
- Which are the crucial factors and the main challenges for a successful adoption of COTS component-based development of embedded systems?

The panelists are reputed researchers and experienced industrial experts in different application domains of embedded systems (automotive, consumer electronics, and automation industries) and component-based software engineering. The statements will include the following topics:

- Ivica Crnkovic, Prof., Mälardalen University, moderator: An overview of embedded systems. State of the art and practice of CBD in embedded systems.
- Jakob Axelsson, Program Manager, Volvo Cars: Using COTS in automotive industry; main requirements and constraints and their impact on the development.
- Susanne Graf, Senior Researcher, Verimag: Modeling component-based real-time systems.
- Magnus Larsson, Research Manager, ABB: Using COTS in process automation industry. Main concerns and requirements and their impact in using COTS.
- Rob van Ommering, Senior Researcher, Philips: Product-line approach and CBD. Feasibility of using COTS components in consumer electronics industry.
- Kurt Wallnau, Senior Researcher, Software Engineering Institute/CMU: Achieving predictable composition of COTS components.

X. Franch and D. Port (Eds.): ICCBSS 2005, LNCS 3412, p. 1, 2005.

Free and Proprietary Software in COTS-Based Software Development

Bernard Lang[1], Jean-François Abramatic[2], Jesús M. González-Barahona[3], Fernando Piera Gómez[4], and Mogens Kühn Pedersen[5]

[1] Bernard.Lang@inria.fr, [2] jfa@ilog.fr,
[3] jgb@gsyc.escet.urjc.es, [4] fpiera@indra.es, [5] kuehnp@mac.com

Free software, also known as Open-Source, is a new player in the software world. Though it is mostly popularized by the Linux operating system, it is not limited to it. More and more software applications, tools and libraries are available as free software, for free as well as proprietary platforms. In the COTS business, this raises a host of issues regarding both COTS producers and COTS users, issues that can be technical, economic or legal. From the point of view of producers, it is important to understand where the competition between free and proprietary production of COTS is heading, and what are the natural techno-economic niches for both. From the point of view of COTS-based development, one has to understand issues such as (this list is not limited in any way):

- legal constraints implied by the different types of licences,
- legal liabilities for the software (regarding reliability and fitness, or intellectual property violations),
- long-term availability and adaptability,
- interoperability and adherence to standard,
- technical quality and performances,
- implied costs (maintenance, licenses, ...)

The panelists will address these issues from their own experiences, positions and points of view.

- Bernard Lang, Senior Investigator, INRIA, France: moderator
- Jean-François Abramatic, Chief Product Officer, ILOG, France: proprietary COTS producer
- Jesús M. González-Barahona, Professor, University Rey Juan Carlos, Madrid, Spain: free software specialist
- Fernando Piera Gómez, R&D Manager, INDRA Sistemas, Spain: legal view
- Mogens Kühn Pedersen, Professor, Copenhagen Business School, Denmark, economic view

X. Franch and D. Port (Eds.): ICCBSS 2005, LNCS 3412, p. 2, 2005.

2nd International Workshop on Incorporating COTS into Software Systems: Assessment and Prediction of Behavior and QoS Attributes of COTS Software Components and Systems

Franck Barbier[1], Goiuria Sagarduy[2], and Xabier Aretxandieta[3]

[1] Université de Pau et des Pays de l'Adour, France
[2] Universidad de Mondragón, Spain
[3] Universidad de Mondragón, Spain

The complexity and heterogeneity of COTS-based software products are increasing rapidly. In contrast to in-house software, COTS components and systems are close entities and, as such, hide many parts of their implementation. Even if this is safe with regard to the principles of encapsulation, high-cohesion and low-coupling, one expects to determine how these external entities may behave in user's deployment environments which are often different from vendor's development environments. "Assessment and prediction of behaviors and QoS attributes of COTS software components and systems" means here that if COTS components and systems are not built/prepared for the assessment and the prediction of their properties, they may not be qualified as high-confidence software entities. The proposed workshop mainly stresses the design of COTS software, in other words how to create trustworthy software in order to better instrument, support and organize a COTS software market.

For more information, please visit the workshop webpage, at:
http://www.eps.mondragon.edu/webeps/ingsw/

X. Franch and D. Port (Eds.): ICCBSS 2005, LNCS 3412, p. 3, 2005.

Challenges of COTS IV & V

Dan Port[1], Haruka Nakao[2], Masafumi Katahira[3], and Christina Motes[4]

[1] University of Hawaii, USA
[2] Japan Manned Space Systems Corp, Japan
[3] Japan Aerospace Exploration Agency, Japan
[4] NASA IV&V facility, USA

COTS can significantly complicate the independent verification and validation (IV&V) process. The necessarily pessimistic culture of IV&V has a perspective on COTS that greatly differs from a developer's generally optimistic, success-oriented perspective. For example, there is no basis for assuming that the COTS assessments made by developers will ultimately be consistent or even compatible with those made by an IV&V group. This frequently results in higher project risk and uncertainty. This workshop seeks to illuminate these and other COTS and IV&V related challenges

The workshops topics are:

- Safety critical V&V of COTS
- V&V of COTS "dormant" code
- Reconciling developer and IV&V COTS assessments
- Tactical IV&V response to COTS problems
- Strategic planning of IV&V COTS activities
- Rationalizing the cost of COTS IV&V
- Black box COTS IV&V
- How much is enough COTS IV&V?

X. Franch and D. Port (Eds.): ICCBSS 2005, LNCS 3412, p. 4, 2005.

The COTS Product Market: An EU Legal Perspective

Ignacio Delgado González and Carlos Arias-Chausson

Martin & Lawson, c/ Alameda Urquijo, 28 – 2°C, 48010 – Bilbao, Spain
{idg, cach}@martinlawson.com

This tutorial introduces the legal information that both software developers and COTS purchasers have to consider when buying and selling in the European Union (EU) marketplace. After 1 May 2004, the EU has enlarged up to 25 Member States. In principle this means one legal system but recognizes different Member States rules and legal cultures. Despite the efforts made to unify the regulations, an American COTS product seller whose products are or may be sold in the EU, will find a different legal environment than back at home.

To clarify the legal situation in the EU, this tutorial will present the information with examples in simple and clear language. The challenges in the EU legislation are how to protect the software developers and their final results, and at the same time how to protect the interest of the consumers and end users of the COTS software products. The current situation and future developments on the way such us the software patentability will be discussed during the tutorial with the participants. The tutorial aims to provide up-to-date legal information. If you are a business manager, software developer, COTS buyer or end user decision maker, or interested in legal issues concerning COTS software products then you should attend this tutorial.

X. Franch and D. Port (Eds.): ICCBSS 2005, LNCS 3412, p. 5, 2005.

Composable Spiral Processes for COTS-Based Application Development

Barry Boehm[1], Ye Yang[1], Jesal Bhuta[1], and Dan Port[2]

[1] University of Southern California, Center for Software Engineering,
941 W. 37th Place, SAL Room 328, Los Angeles, CA 90089-0781, USA
{boehm, yangy, jesal}@cse.usc.edu
[2] University of Hawaii, Information Technology Management,
2404 Maile Way, CBA E601k, Honolulu, HI 96822, USA
dport@hawaii.edu

Empirical studies show that the activities conducted while developing COTS-Based Applications (CBA) differ greatly from those conducted while developing non-COTS. The challenges go beyond the need to acquire new expertise and managing uncertainty and volatile risk profiles and demand an entirely new development paradigm. This shift of development paradigm, if not appropriately planned and monitored, can lead an apparently simple CBA development project into disaster.

The objective of this tutorial is to provide prospective and existing managers, architects, and developers of CBA's with a "composable" collection of spiral-based processes and techniques found to be useful for successfully developing a wide range of CBA's and acquire some experience in using them in within a participatory exercise. The elements of the tutorial will be:

Motivation. Why traditional waterfall, V-Model, or risk-insensitive development do not work for CBA development. The tutorial will begin with examining how these models fail to or only partially address the critical issues within CBA development by discussing problems within several representative projects, and then introduce briefly how spiral-based development anticipates and avoids potential problems.

Approach. The tutorial will summarize the key aspects of the recursive, re-entrant Spiral-based Framework of primary activities and decisions within CBA development to guide the CBA developers through each development Spiral cycle. The composable process elements for this framework will be elaborated including COTS assessment and system definition, COTS tailoring, glue code development, custom code development and integration. It will show how these are dynamically composed within a Spiral development cycle according risk and context sensitive patterns in response to rapidly changing project circumstances.

Techniques. Four categories of techniques will be addressed. First, the role of risk management in CBA development will be summarized and illustrated, including the use of risk analysis to determine how much is enough of activities such as COTS evaluation [Port]. Second, guidelines for executing the process elements, such as the COTS Assessment Background (CAB), COTS Assessment Plan (CAP), and COTS

X. Franch and D. Port (Eds.): ICCBSS 2005, LNCS 3412, pp. 6–7, 2005.

Assessment Report (CAR) for performing COTS assessment, are defined in a minimum-essential, tailoring-up fashion rather than in an exhaustive, tailoring-down fashion [Yang]. Third, cost and schedule estimation models, such as the COCOMO II and COCOTS, are used to scope projects and perform tradeoff analyses [Yang]. Fourth, examples of techniques for effective COTS tailoring, applications scoping and architecting, and glue code development and integration.

Examples. Two non-trivial, real-project representative case studies will be included to illustrate the application of above techniques. One is from the multimedia archive domain, and the other is from the e-commerce domain.

Participatory Exercise. The tutorial will also provide a project case study with points at which attendees will apply the techniques such as prioritizing objectives, filtering COTS candidates, identifying risk-driven assessment priorities, performing cost tradeoff analyses. Attendees will also gain experience determining and discussing strategies for smoothly navigating through the process framework, and early identification and avoidance of unnecessary go-backs which typically causes unnecessary rework, waste of resources, and schedule delays.

Heterogeneous COTS Product Integration to Allow the Comprehensive Development of Image Processing Systems

Cristina Vicente Chicote[1], Ana Toledo Moreo[2], and Carlos Fernández Andrés[1]

[1] Departamento de Tecnologías de la Información y Comunicaciones
E. T. S. Ingeniería de Telecomunicación
[2] Departamento de Tecnología Electrónica
E. T. S. Ingeniería Industrial
Universidad Politécnica de Cartagena
Campus Muralla del Mar S/N, 30.202 Cartagena, Spain
{Cristina.Vicente, Ana.Toledo, Carlos.Fernandez}@upct.es

Image processing techniques are applied in a wide range of products. Automated visual inspection of industrial products, medical imaging or biometric person authentication are only a few examples. In order to process the great amount of data contained in images highly complex and time-consuming algorithms are needed. Furthermore, many of these applications require real-time performance making specific hardware devices indispensable. Currently, there exist several Commercial Off-The-Shelf (COTS) component libraries that help to implement these hybrid software/hardware systems. In addition, some powerful tools are available that allow prototyping and simulating image processing applications prior to their implementation. However, none of these tools allows to realistically coprototype and co-simulate both software and hardware simultaneously. This work presents a new approach to the development of image processing applications that tackles the question of how to fill the gap between design and implementation. A new graphical component-based tool has been implemented that allows building image processing applications from functional and architectural prototyping stages to software/hardware co-simulation and final code generation. Building this tool has been possible thanks to the synergy that arises from the integration of several preexistent software and hardware COTS components and tools.

X. Franch and D. Port (Eds.): ICCBSS 2005, LNCS 3412, p. 8, 2005.

A Contextualized Study of COTS-Based E-Service Projects

Ye Yang and Barry Boehm

Center for Software Engineering, University of Southern California,
Los Angeles, California 90089, USA
{yey, boehm}@cse.usc.edu

Properly recording the context factors of empirical results is essential for comparison and integration of results from different studies and for assessing the relevance of a given result to one's own environment. COTS-based application (CBA) developers need both empirical data and context data for choosing among current and newly-emerging candidate technologies based on solid evidence that they will work cost effectively under the conditions of their particular projects. Previous empirical research on COTS-based development (CBD) has produced various insights on the critical success factors of CBD. Such accumulations also produce various experience/knowledge bases on which the contextualized longitudinal analysis of CBA can be performed. This poster presents an initial contextualized longitudinal analysis of CBA's by identifying a set of project context factors as contextualizing meta-data which represent the characteristics of the project, process, product, and personnel perspectives of the system being developed. It provides comparative contextualization analysis among different CBA types, and also presents a comparison of two CBA's from different domains, and then shows how the different contexts lead to different CBA process, products, and economic decisions.

X. Franch and D. Port (Eds.): ICCBSS 2005, LNCS 3412, p. 9, 2005.

Quality of Service Profiles in Web Service Discovery

Barry Norton

Department of Computer Science, University of Sheffield, UK
B.Norton@dcs.shef.ac.uk

Standardization of the description and delivery of XML-based *web services* has opened up a market in 'commercial off-the-shelf' (COTS) software components. As a result, standardization efforts are being made towards the assembly of systems from web services where the coordination is defined by *workflow* languages. With several potential implementations for many of the tasks within such a system an automated *discovery* process is required. With many functional equivalents, it is necessary to discriminate between these on the basis of cost and performance.

Cardoso and Sheth propose a useful set of Quality of Service measurements [1] and a framework to apply such considerations within web service discovery [2] [3]. Unfortunately the 'fitness' metric [2] contains mathematical flaws that have been propagated to other work [3]. In particular:

- Metrics are defined, and claimed normalized, but these can take negative values (and even undefined values due to division by zero);
- Combinations of these are defined using the geometric mean (even though this doesn't fit their informal claims) and so combined metrics can also be undefined;
- Under- and over-performance are not distinguished and are equally penalized.

In proposing corrections for these problems [4] we have found alternative solutions to the latter issue that accommodate different design strategies. We present the resulting system as an advance in the technique.

References

1. Cardoso J., Sheth A., Miller J.: Workflow Quality of Service. In *Proc. Int. Conf. on Enterprise Integration and Modeling Technology and International Enterprise Modeling Conference (ICEIMT/IEMC'02)*, Kluwer (2002) 303-311
2. Cardoso J., Sheth A.: Semantic E-Workflow Composition. In *J. Intell. Inf. Syst.*, 21(3): 191-225 (2003)
3. Cardoso J.: Quality of Service and Semantic Composition of Workflows. PhD Thesis, Department of Computer Science, University of Georgia (2002)
4. Norton B.: A Sound Mathematical Basis for Quality of Service Profiles in Web Service Discovery. Technical Report, Department of Computer Science, University of Sheffield, CS-04-11 (2004)

X. Franch and D. Port (Eds.): ICCBSS 2005, LNCS 3412, p. 10, 2005.

Decision on Replacing Components of Security Functions in COTS-Based Information Systems

Myeonggil Choi[1], Hyunwoo Kim[2], Eunhye Kim[2], and Sehun Kim[2]

[1] National Security Research Institute
161, Kajong-dong, Yuseong-gu, Daejeon, 305-350, Korea
mgchoi@etri.re.kr
[2] Department of Industrial Engineering, KAIST
373-1, Guseong-dong, Yuseong-gu, Daejeon, 305-701, Korea
{hwkim, ehkim, shkim}@tmlab.kaist.ac.kr

As governments and enterprises adopt COTS-based information systems, COTS components must be selected to satisfy the security requirements of applied systems. However, the selection of security components is a trade-off between the confidence level in the components and the cost of replacing components. The higher confidence required of the security components leads to a higher cost in the selection process. Particularly, as governments take into account the confidence-level of COTS-based information systems, they must replace security functional components by their own developing components in high security environment. A decision method is needed to solve the trade-off between security and costs. This paper focuses on decision making to solve the problem of replacing the security functional components in COTS-based systems. This paper suggests an appropriate adaptation level and a cost-effective priority to replace security functional components in security environment. To make a cost effective decision on adapting security functional components, we develop a hierarchical model of information security technologies. Based on this, we determine the priority among security functional components using AHP (Analytic Hierarchy Process).

Acknowledgements. This work was sponsored in part by the Korean Ministry of Information and Communication in the context of University IT Research Center Project.

X. Franch and D. Port (Eds.): ICCBSS 2005, LNCS 3412, p. 11, 2005.

Best Paper Award 2004: Characterization of a Taxonomy for Business Applications and the Relationships Among Them*

Juan P. Carvallo[1], Xavier Franch[1], Carme Quer[1], and Marco Torchiano[2]

[1] Universitat Politècnica de Catalunya, UPC-Campus Nord (C6),
08034 Barcelona, Catalunya, Spain
{carvallo, franch, cquer}@lsi.upc.es
http://www.lsi.upc.es/~gessi
[2] Politecnico di Torino, C.so Duca degli Abruzzi, 24,
10129 Torino, Italy
torchiano@polito.it
http://softeng.polito.it/torchiano

Abstract. In the paper [1] we propose a taxonomy for classifying COTS business applications, i.e. products that are used in the daily functioning of all types of organizations worldwide, such as ERP systems and document management tools. We propose the identification of characterization attributes to arrange the domains which these products belong to, and also we group these domains into categories. We define questions and answers as a means for browsing the taxonomy during COTS selection. We show the need of identifying and recording the relationships among the domains and propose the use of actor-oriented models for expressing these relationships as dependencies. Last, we explore the definition of quality models for the domains, to be used in COTS selection, focusing on their reusability and stepwise definition downwards the hierarchy.

Reference

1. Carvallo, J.P., Franch, X., Quer, C., Torchiano, M.: Characterization of a Taxonomy for Business Applications and the Relationships among them. In: Kazman, R., Port, D. (eds.): Proceedings of the 3rd International Conference on COTS-Based Software Systems (ICCBSS'04). Lecture Notes in Computer Science, Vol. 2959. Springer-Verlag, Berlin Heidelberg New York (2004) 221 – 231†

* This work is partly supported by CICYT TIC2001-2165 and WISE IST-2000-30028.

† Due to an error in the process, this paper was not included in the printed proceedings and therefore it is available on-line only.

X. Franch and D. Port (Eds.): ICCBSS 2005, LNCS 3412, p. 12, 2005.

Using Earned Value Management for COTS-Based Systems: Issues and Recommendations

Lisa Brownsword and Jim Smith

Carnegie Mellon Software Engineering Institute,
4301 Wilson Blvd, Suite 200, Arlington, VA 22203, USA
{llb, jds}@sei.cmu.edu

Abstract. Earned value management (EVM) has long been used by organizations to plan, monitor, and control the development and evolution of custom developed systems. EVM was developed for managing such projects, and assumes a waterfall development model. COTS-based systems (CBS), on the other hand, are formed and evolved through the selection and composition of pre-existing, off-the-shelf packages or components with potentially some number of custom components. Experience indicates that a spiral or iterative development process is a key to success with CBS. While EVM has been applied to CBS projects, the results have not been uniformly satisfying. This paper explores the fundamental challenges in using EVM with CBS, and proposes adaptations to some of the principals of EVM to render it more suitable for CBS development.

1 Introduction

Earned value management (EVM) is a recognized technique that integrates the technical, schedule, and cost parameters of a project [1]. EVM has been around since the 1960's, and has seen extensive use in projects ranging from very large, complex systems to small-scale development efforts [2]. Properly applied, EVM allows project managers to answer the fundamental question, "How much progress have I made against my original plan?" The validity of the plan, and the means to objectively measure against that plan are paramount to the success of EVM on any project.

As the use of commercial-off-the-shelf (COTS) products to provide significant capability in our delivered systems has grown, managers have found that the approaches traditionally used in custom software development to define, build, acquire, field, and evolve these systems require fundamental changes [3], [4], [5].

The key difference between the development of custom software systems and COTS-based systems (CBS) is the need to simultaneously define and make tradeoff between competing *spheres of influence,* such as stakeholder needs, current and target business processes, architecture, available COTS products, interfaces to legacy systems, ability of end-user community to accommodate operational changes, cost, schedule, and risk [6]. Practical experience has shown that a spiral or iterative development approach is necessary to facilitate the required discovery and negotiation to reconcile what users want and what the commercial marketplace can provide.

It is this requirement to use an iterative or spiral development process for CBS which gives rise to several challenges in applying EVM in their development, including:

X. Franch and D. Port (Eds.): ICCBSS 2005, LNCS 3412, pp. 13 – 24, 2005.

- Conflict between the *product-oriented* work breakdown structure (WBS), which forms the basis for EVM, and a *process-oriented* WBS suitable for spiral development
- Difficulty in accommodating a high degree of uncertainty, in terms of cost, schedule, product selection, architecture, etc. within the constraints of a product-oriented WBS
- Inability to relate product-oriented earned value measurements to a process-oriented WBS

Published experience in using EVM has focused primarily on projects using a conventional waterfall development approach, but there has been some research into using EVM for spiral COTS development. An earlier report by Staley, Oberndorf, and Sledge offered an example of EVM applied to a small CBS, along with several promising adaptation strategies [7]. This paper provides an overview of some of the key aspects of EVM and CBS development, and briefly explores how the mismatch between their respective development models affects the use of EVM for CBS development. Building upon the earlier work by Staley and associates, this paper proposes further adaptations of EVM to improve its applicability to CBS development.

2 EVM Overview

EVM projects are managed through the establishment of a *performance management baseline* that represents the work that needs to be performed along with the needed resources and schedule. As Alexander notes, the fundamental requirement for using EVM on a project is to plan <u>all</u> work prior to beginning development [8]. Project progress is measured as *earned value* against the baseline.

EVM focuses a project manager on answering five essential questions:

1. What is the value of the work planned? – Budgeted Cost for Work Scheduled (BCWS)
2. What is the value of the work accomplished? – Budgeted Cost for Work Performed (BCWP)
3. How much did the work cost? – Actual Cost of Work Performed (ACWP)
4. What was the total budget? – Budget at Completion (BAC)
5. What do we now expect the total job to cost? – Estimate at Completion (EAC)

To use EVM, work to complete the project is arranged into a tree structure where the "leaves" of the tree are the individual *work packages* and *planning packages*. Near-term effort is divided into manageable work packages that can be planned in detail, covering technical content, budget, and schedule. Far-term effort is divided into planning packages that have less detail; over the course of the project, planning packages are refined into work packages which are then planned in detail. Work and planning packages are assigned start and end dates and arranged across the project time line. Thus, a WBS identifies all significant work and provides a framework to assign responsibilities, schedule, and budget. The performance measurement baseline (BCWS) is simply the sum of all work packages and planning packages over time.

Progress against the plan is determined by comparing the earned value to the baseline at any point in time. Numerous methods exist to determine the earned value of a work package, such as:

- Weighted milestones, interim milestones, or per cent complete for discrete tasks with a end product or result
- Apportioned effort for tasks such as quality control or peer reviews
- Level of effort (LOE) for non-discrete tasks such as coordination that have no specified end product or result

The baseline is thus the plan against which the value of the work performed (BCWP) and actual cost (ACWP) are compared. A negative cost variance results when ACWP is greater than the BCWP at a given point in time, and indicates that a project is overrunning its development budget. Correspondingly, an unfavorable schedule variance results when the BCWP is less than the value of the work planned to that point (BCWS).

For EVM to work effectively, the following must be true:

- Time phasing of the work packages must be accurate.
- The performance baseline must be objective and verifiable.
- Earned value (BCWP) must accurately represent progress.
- The relation of work packages to a project's life cycle approach must be appropriate.
- The performance baseline must deal with the reality that there is a high degree of uncertainty in the plans earlier in a project, where EVM assumes you know rather precisely what will be done and when and what it will cost.

EVM was designed for, and has been used primarily with, "waterfall development processes. As such, it assumes that the requirements can be defined prior to the start of a project (or very soon thereafter) and, with good requirements management, they will not change significantly. It is also assumed that the high-level structure or architecture for the system can be defined prior to the start of the project. Further, the activities necessary to define, build, field, and evolve the system can also be well defined—with much of their definition in the early project planning phases of a project. The conventional WBS structure used by many projects further reflects these assumptions.

3 CBS Development Overview

Tyson and others identified a number of key elements or drivers required for the management and engineering processes needed to build, field, and support CBS [9]. These include:

- Simultaneous definition and trades between the CBS spheres of influence continue throughout the life of the solution.
- Concurrent engineering of enterprise processes are coordinated with the engineering of the solution. The end-user community must be willing and able to modify its enterprise processes to align with those assumptions.
- Requirements definition depends on understanding opportunities and limitations of available off-the-shelf products.

- Continuous marketplace awareness is required throughout the life of the solution.
- A flexible architecture—developed early and maintained throughout the life of the solution—is an asset.
- An effective, disciplined spiral or iterative practices, with frequent executable representations of the solution allows for the discovery of the critical attributes of the solution through an evolutionary exploration of the highest risk elements [10].
- Direct, active involvement of all stakeholders throughout the life of the solution.

4 Challenges Using EVM with CBS

The previous sections discussed the relevant characteristics of EVM and CBS development, and how they are closely tied to their respective life cycle models: waterfall and spiral development. This section will focus on how the fundamental differences between these two life cycle models give rise to problems when EVM is applied "as-is" to a CBS development.

4.1 Differences Between Waterfall and Spiral Development Models

Understanding the distinction between the waterfall and spiral development models is important because the way a project manager plans and monitors progress are subtly different. Table 1 captures a number of these critical differences.

Table 1. Key differences between waterfall and spiral development models

Waterfall Development Model [10]	***Spiral Development Model***
Requirements knowable in advance of development	High-level/generic requirements known prior to development—but requirements are discovered & refined *during* the development process.
Requirements have no unresolved high-risk implications	Risks continually discovered during development; risks *drive* the development process, and are used to determine "how much" engineering, design artifacts, etc. are needed.
Nature of requirements will not change very much	Acknowledges that requirements, and stakeholders' understanding of them, will change throughout the development—and for very good, legitimate reasons.
Requirements compatible with all key system stakeholders' expectations	All key stakeholders remain committed throughout the development/evolution of the system. Executable representations & anchor point milestones are mechanisms to gain & validate stakeholder agreements.
"Right" architecture for implementing requirements is understood	"Right" architecture is incrementally formed and validated through executable representations.
Sufficient calendar time to proceed sequentially	"Time as an independent variable" (TAIV). Program cost/schedule is continually refined; as a result, plans are continually refined.

To demonstrate how these differences affect the use of EVM, the following sections provide a simple example.

4.2 Waterfall Requirements Management

First, consider requirements management in a waterfall development. Within a product-oriented WBS, there are work packages for requirements definition in each system, subsystem, and lower-level component which comprises the developed solution. The earned value of these work packages is based on the portion of the total requirements which have been finalized or allocated, often a straight percentage. This earned value is then, in turn, tied to various engineering and management review exit criteria (e.g., 80% of the requirements definition completed prior to preliminary design review, etc.). If you accept that the requirements can be unambiguously defined prior to the start of development, that there are no unforeseen risks, and that the system architecture will remain constant—in other words, that you have a stable program management baseline—then this approach results in a reasonable definition of earned value.

4.3 Spiral Requirements Management

On the other hand, if you are developing a CBS using a spiral development method, then this approach to requirements management is inappropriate because one **cannot** (and should not) define all of the requirements "up front." Attempts to use the same approach for determining the earned value of the requirements management WBS elements as in the waterfall development (i.e., percentage of requirements defined and/or allocated) results in endless cycling between high earned value (as requirements are defined) and low earned value (as it is discovered that the requirements thus defined are incorrect, inadequately understood, or not agreed-to by all of the stakeholders).

To be meaningful in this context, earned value needs to be based on a WBS which reflects the spiral development processes, and is tied to the exit criteria for each anchor point milestone in the spiral development process [11]. For the purposes of this paper, the phases and anchor point milestones of a spiral or iterative development process will follow the terminology and characterizations of Boehm and Kruchten [11], [12]. The phases are denoted as inception, elaboration, construction, and transition. The corresponding phase milestones are life cycle objectives (LCO), life cycle architecture (LCA), initial operational capability (IOC), and production releases. The next section will discuss the characteristics of such a WBS, and make some recommendations about how one could make meaningful measurements of earned value.

5 Recommendations

For a CBS project using a spiral or iterative life cycle approach, the early phases are characterized by discovery and negotiation involving the broad range of stakeholders to form a feasible scope for the project (LCO milestone), and select and validate an architecture that includes the selection of the COTS product(s) (LCA milestone). The later phases of the project are then characterized by the creation of production quality releases. Also, as the project progresses, consensus of the stakeholder groups regarding the scope and solution architecture is obtained (and maintained); estimates of cost and schedule for the production phases typically improve.

5.1 An Alternative Work Breakdown Structure

Royce proposed a WBS structure that is process-oriented [13]. Using this general WBS structure, Staley and associates proposed additions to further tailor the Royce WBS for CBS development where:

- Level 1 indicated a major development discipline, usually allocated to a single team such as management, requirements, analysis and design, or implementation
- Level 2 indicated a phase of the life cycle, such as inception, elaboration, construction, or transition
- Level 3 indicated key tasks, including CBS activities, that produced principal artifacts within a given phase and discipline, such as use cases in the inception phase for the requirements discipline
- Level 4 indicated additional tasks or activities required to execute a level 3 task, including CBS activities

While both the Royce and Staley WBS approaches infer that the elements in the WBS support the attainment of phase milestones, neither directly links the objectives nor exit criteria for a phase with the WBS elements. Thus it is difficult for project managers to judge the efficacy of the WBS tasks toward meeting the project's goals. Our proposed structure seeks to rectify this situation in two ways. First, as did Royce and Staley, we propose to change the structure of the WBS such that level 1 is the phase and milestone with level 2 indicating the development disciplines [12]. Secondly, we propose the addition of explicit WBS elements at levels 3 and 4 that capture essential phase exit criteria. A partial outline of our revised WBS for CBS projects is summarized in Table 2. For the purposes of this paper, the table only provides details in the WBS outline for selected level 3 elements.

Table 2. Partial outline of a spiral development, phase-oriented WBS. Notional level 3 detailed breakouts only provided for selected CBS-related activities

1. Inception demonstrating feasible scope
- 1.1. Business modeling
- 1.2. Requirements
  - 1.2.1. CBS market survey/initial product identification & characterization
  - 1.2.2. Vision specification
  - 1.2.3. Critical use cases modeling with candidate COTS product(s)
  - 1.2.4. Critical non-functional (quality attributes) identified with consensus
- 1.3. Analysis and design
  - 1.3.1. Candidate alternative CBS solutions formed (skeletal)
- 1.4. Implementation
- 1.5. Test
- 1.6. Deployment
- 1.7. Configuration and change management
- 1.8. Project management
- 1.9. Environment

Table 2. (*Continued*)

2. Elaboration demonstrating valid architecture
2.1. Business modeling 2.2. Requirements 2.2.1. COTS product in-depth characterization and experimentation 2.2.2. Significant use cases modeling with candidate COTS product(s) in detail 2.2.3. Significant non-functional (quality attributes) identified with consensus 2.3. Analysis and design 2.3.1. Refine CBS solutions with stakeholder negotiations 2.3.2. Refine & expand architecture prototype(s) for CBS solution(s) 2.4. Implementation 2.5. Test 2.6. Deployment 2.7. Configuration and change management 2.8. Project management 2.9. Environment
3. Construction demonstrating initial production release
3.1. Business modeling 3.2. Requirements 3.2.1. Continue COTS product/marketplace monitoring & impact analysis 3.2.2. Remaining use cases modeling incorporating COTS product(s) 3.2.3. Monitor attainment of non-functional or quality attributes 3.3. Analysis and design 3.3.1. Design custom components 3.4. Implementation 3.4.1. Build production integration mechanism/interfaces 3.4.2. Build production tailoring of COTS products 3.4.3. Build custom components 3.5. Test 3.6. Deployment 3.7. Configuration and change management 3.8. Project management 3.9. Environment
4. Transition demonstrating full deployment releases
4.1. Business modeling 4.2. Requirements 4.2.1. Continue COTS product/marketplace monitoring & impact analysis 4.2.2. Update use cases as COTS product(s) change 4.2.3. Monitor attainment of non-functional or quality attributes 4.3. Analysis and design 4.4. Implementation 4.4.1. Build solution update releases (with COTS product patches, minor releases) 4.5. Test 4.6. Deployment 4.7. Configuration and change management 4.8. Project management 4.9. Environment

The first item to note from the table is the reflection of the phase goal directly in the level 1 identifier. The intent is to provide constant and visible awareness of what all sub-elements should be focused on achieving. For example, the primary goal for the Inception phase is the formation of the scope for the project that is demonstrated to be feasible and that all relevant stakeholders concur. The level 2 elements then represent the typical system development disciplines (similar to the Royce and Staley WBS). The level 3 (and 4 where needed) elements are focused on activities and tasks in support of the phase goal for the specified level 2 discipline. Continuing with the Inception phase example, under the requirements discipline, one of the level 3 elements is modeling the critical use cases, including negotiated tradeoffs based on understanding the application of the candidate COTS products. In the Inception phase the focus is on the critical functional and non-functional requirements that impact the eventual architecture (and thus the product selection). In contrast, the Royce and Staley WBS elements make no distinction about which requirements should be addressed. Identifying the critical requirements (and gaining consensus on their priority) is an essential risk mitigation approach and is the basis of an iterative or spiral development approach.

5.2 Another Interpretation of Earned Value

The previous section described an alternative WBS structure which we assert provides a more rational basis for planning and managing a CBS development effort. Just as this WBS ties the activities to the phase objectives and exit criteria, the definition of earned value must be linked to progress towards attaining those goals. This section will introduce residual risk as a way to measure progress, and illustrate its use in constructing a risk-oriented baseline and measuring earned value.

As shown in Figure 1 the emphasis during the Inception and Elaboration phases is on reducing the unknowns associated with the scope for delivered capability, achievable

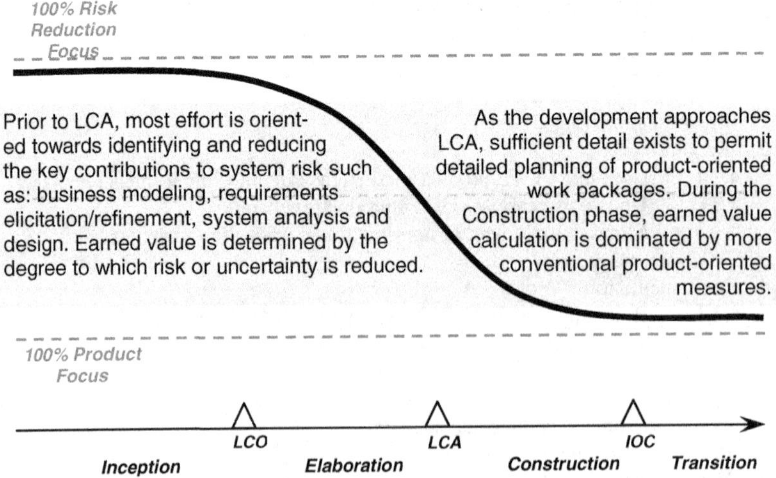

Fig. 1. Notional depiction of how the relative proportion of development effort—and, hence, method of determining earned value—changes throughout the spiral phases

requirements, and feasibility. Armour notes that the focus of the development effort is not on the software product itself but, rather, on knowledge acquisition and "ignorance reduction" [14]. Essential to this is understanding and agreeing on the priorities for resolving these unknowns: not all risks are equally important. Boehm uses the term "value-based software engineering" to describe this process of incorporating value considerations into all aspects of software development [15].

Successful completion of the Inception phase occurs with the Life Cycle Objective (LCO) milestone. The Inception phase is characterized by stakeholder negotiations to identify and prioritize key system risks. This includes defining the development scope, identifying critical mismatches between stakeholder needs and CBS components' capabilities, and ensuring that there is at least one feasible solution. The degree to which there is consensus on these goals represents progress towards LCO. Lack of consensus is represented by "residual risk."

Risk-Oriented Earned Value. To measure progress, there needs to be something to measure progress against: a baseline. As previously discussed, a conventional EVM baseline is determined by summing the value (i.e., cost) of the WBS elements over time. By analogy, a risk-oriented baseline should reflect the cumulative residual risk reduction of the WBS elements over time. However, instead of simply imputing the value of a work package as its cost, relating progress within individual WBS elements to the entire program requires that *total* development risk be allocable across the WBS elements in some fashion that reflects the relative contributions of individual activities to the total development risk. This is an inexact science, but techniques such as Boehm's Wideband Delphi technique provide a structured, consensus-driven process for making reasoned judgments in the absence of quantifiable data [16].

Once the total development risk has been allocated down to the WBS element level, a "normalized" value for each task within an element may be defined as its BCWS (i.e., cost) adjusted by a factor that represents that element's contribution to the total development risk:

$$\left|BCWS_i\right| = \left(BCWS_i \cdot eRisk_i\right) \cdot \frac{\sum_{j=1}^{n} BCWS_j}{\sum_{k=1}^{n}\left(BCWS_k \cdot eRisk_k\right)} \tag{1}$$

Next, the earned value of each work package is determined over time based on the reduction in residual risk obtained throughout the performance of the activity, as shown:

$$EV_T = \left|BCWS_i\right| \times \left(\frac{1 - rRisk_T}{1}\right),\ rRisk_T \xrightarrow{\lim} 0 \tag{2}$$

To complete the baseline, the normalized work package earned values are summed over time:

$$BCWS_T = \sum_{j=0}^{T} \sum_{i=1}^{n} EV_{ij} \tag{3}$$

Example Application. These concepts can best be illustrated with a simple example. Suppose there is a task in WBS element 1.2.2 (vision specification) that is planned to last three weeks and cost $50,000 to complete. Assume that the risk allocated to this element is 0.3 (i.e., 30% of the total development risk), and the total development cost is $500,000. Considering the allocation of risk to the other tasks (which is beyond the scope of this paper), the normalized BCWS for this task is calculated as $55,600. Furthermore, it was determined that the appropriate definition of residual risk was the degree to which consensus among the stakeholders on the vision, consisting of the high-level requirements (functional and non-functional) and constraints such as cost, schedule, etc. was not achieved. These values are shown in Table 3.

Table 3. Definition of residual risk

Residual Risk	Definition	Estimated Time to Achieve
100%	Task initiation, $\neg\exists$ consensus	0
30%	$\exists$ consensus • 1 feasible solution	1 week
0%	$\exists$ consensus • > 1 feasible solutions	3 weeks

After one week, it is determined that the stakeholders have only made 50% progress towards a consensus on one feasible solution, but that $21,000 had been spent. Thus, the earned value is $19,250, against a baseline of $38,500. This would be a clear signal that this task was seriously behind schedule after only one week. Since $21,000 was spent to accomplish $19,250 worth of work, the task is also slightly over budget (by $1,750).

By way of contrast, the more conventional EVM approach (using LOE as the baseline) would still lead to the conclusion that the task is slightly over budget, but the earned value would equal the baseline, so there would not be any apparent schedule slip.

6 Summary

While EVM has proven to be an effective tool for managing software development projects, it is dependent on an objective, accurate program management baseline. The baseline, in turn, depends on an understandable WBS. We have shown how structuring the WBS around the system design, as is typically done with conventional projects, makes it much more difficult to change the plan as the system architecture changes, and renders the WBS unusable as a baseline against which to measure progress for spiral CBS developments. The alternative WBS proposed in this paper addresses these weaknesses. Coupled with a new interpretation of earned value, this approach has the potential to lead to a more incisive answer to the program manager's age-old question: "How much progress have I made against my original plan?" At the same time, other factors, such as technical performance metrics, provide additional insight into the progress (or lack thereof) in a development effort, and will also have to be reinterpreted for spiral CBS development.

Just as projects need a revised EVM approach to better accommodate the realities of a COTS-based system, oversight and governance staff, such as financial managers or senior executives, must also understand the issues with EVM and a project's revised approach. Often, this responsibility falls on the insightful program manager.

Finally, lest we get too impressed with our ability to organize, prioritize, measure, and interpret, we should remember this dictum from Albert Einstein: "Not everything that can be counted counts, and not everything that counts can be counted."

References

1. Wilkins, T. "Earned Value, Clear and Simple" April 1999. Paper online at http://www.acq.osd.mil/pm/paperpres/wilkins_art.pdf
2. Abba, W. *Earned Value Management: Reconciling Government and Commercial Practices.* DSMC Earned Value Management Center, 1997. Article online at http://www.acq.osd.mil/pm/paperpres/abbapmmag.htm
3. United States Air Force Science Advisory Board report on *Ensuring Successful Implementation of Commercial Items in Air Force Systems*, SAB-TR-99-03, http://www.sab.hq.af.mil/archives/reports/1999/COTS/COTS_Report_Final_Public_Relea se .pdf (April 2000).
4. Adams, R. and Eslinger, S. "Lessons Learned From Using COTS Software on Space Systems" *CrossTalk.* June 2001.
5. Boehm, B. & Abts, C. "COTS Integration: Plug and Pray?" *IEEE Computer*, *32*, 1 (January 1999) 135-140.
6. Albert, C. and Brownsword, L. *Evolutionary Process for Integrating COTS-Based Systems (EPIC)*; (CMU/SEI-2002-TR-005). Pittsburgh, PA: Software Engineering Institute, Carnegie Mellon University, 2002.
7. Staley, M.; Oberndorf, T.; & Sledge, C. *Using EVMS with COTS-Based Systems*, (CMU/SEI-2002-TR-022). Pittsburgh, PA: Software Engineering Institute, Carnegie Mellon University, 2002.
8. Alexander, S. Earned Value Management Systems (EVMS): Basic Concepts. Presented at Project Management Institute, Washington, DC Chapter, available online at http://www.acq.osd.mil/pm/paperpres/sean_alex/sld001.htm
9. Tyson, B.; Albert, C.; and Brownsword, L. *Interpreting CMMI for COTS-Based Systems*; (CMU/SEI-2003-TR-022). Pittsburgh, PA: Software Engineering Institute, Carnegie Mellon University, 2003.
10. Boehm, B. "Spiral Development and Evolutionary Acquisition: Where Are We Today?" Presented at SEI-CSE Spiral Development and Evolutionary Acquisition. September 2000.
11. Boehm, B. "Anchoring the Software Process." *IEEE Software*, 13 (4) (July 1996) 73-82.
12. Kruchten, P. *The Rational Unified Process: An Introduction*, 2nd ed. New York, NY: Addison-Wesley Object Technology Series, March 2000.

13. Walker, R. *Software Project Management: A Unified Framework.* Addison-Wesley. 1998.
14. Armour, P. "The Five Orders of Ignorance." *Communications of the ACM, 43,* 10 (October 2000) 17-20.
15. Boehm, B. "Value-Based Software Engineering." *Software Engineering Notes, 28,* 2 (March 2003).
16. Boehm, B. *Software Engineering Economics*, Prentice Hall, 1981

Business Process Definition Languages Versus Traditional Methods Towards Interoperability

Leire Bastida Merino and Gorka Benguria Elguezabal

European Software Institute,
Parque Tecnológico de Zamudio, 204
E-48170 Zamudio, Spain
Tel: +34 94 420 9519, Fax: +34 94 420 9420
http://www.esi.es
{Leire.Bastida, Gorka.Benguria}@esi.es

Abstract. A business process is a collection of activities that are required to achieve a business goal and it is represented with an activity flow that specifies the orchestration needed to complete the goal. The definition of these processes allows business people to easily integrate the functionalities of the COTS in the company to support the business objectives. This activity flow can be implemented in two ways, using traditional methods or using a Business Process Definition Language (BPDL). Traditional methods encode the activity flow using state of the art programming languages such as Java, C#, etc. BPDLs describe the activity flow with a specific language that is directly interpreted by a BPDL engine. This paper analyses the use of BPDLs and traditional methods to develop solutions for services-based architectures. It presents a case study where the results obtained using a BPDL and a traditional method are compared.

1 Introduction

Nowadays organisations are evolving to *networked* organisations whose Information Systems, mainly composed by COTS, need to be interoperable in order to facilitate the interactions inside and outside their organisational limits. Web Services identify an emerging technology for integrating enterprise applications. Some technical and engineering aspects have been solved to achieve the wide use of Web Services. Others are still under Research & Development pursuing to make the *plug and do business* vision a reality.

Standardisation is a key element to achieve interoperability and to describe interoperable business processes. It is necessary to use high level modelling languages such as Business Process Definition Languages (BPDL) in order to facilitate the definition of business processes that orchestrate internal and external services through services-based technology such as Web Services to achieve the business goals.

New specifications are continuously emerging to define how Web Services are composed and deployed to achieve business goals through the interoperation among internal and external services. Most of those specifications have become or are in the process of becoming standards. Examples of these specifications are BPEL, WSCI,

X. Franch and D. Port (Eds.): ICCBSS 2005, LNCS 3412, pp. 25 – 35, 2005.

WS-Choreography, BPML, etc. There is no clear winner yet, but the availability of development tools and the industrial background will be some of the drivers to faster standard adoption.

BPDLs are interesting as Domain Specific Languages (DSL) for the specific domain of business process modelling and execution. They deal with services composition by abstracting the mechanisms of communication and the control flow. A DSL should be specific to a problem domain and provide a set of useful abstractions for working in that problem domain.

Other application domains where several DSLs have been developed, are industrial automation or graphical user interface development. For industrial automation, we have a DSL with the objective of standardising the development of control and monitoring applications for several industrial sectors such as metal processing lines or car assembly lines. This DSL is the IEC1131, which is an international standard. For graphical user interface development we have Struts. Struts define a specification language for specifying structure of views (web forms) and the interaction among them.

In recent years, there has been a growing interest in BPDL as a way to orchestrate the existing services to implement new business functionalities. But, why should we use these new BPDLs instead of using traditional programming languages that are also valid to build new applications based on existing services? This paper compares both methods to provide an explicit evidence on the advantages and disadvantages of each of those approaches to support business interoperability.

2 State of the Art on BPDL

Relevant organisations, such as W3C [1], OASIS [2], OMG [11], have recently formed groups to examine and contribute to the emerging standards in this area. W3C has formed the Web Services Choreography working group [3], OASIS has created the Business Process Execution Language Technical Committee [4] and the OMG has formed the Business Enterprise Integration Domain Task Force (BEI). Other organisations working on this subject are BPMI.org, [12] which promotes and develops the use of Business Process Management (BPM) through the establishment of standards, or WfMC, [13] that has 'Interoperability' as a core value. Figure 1 puts in context the different issues worked out by the standardisation initiatives.

The standardisation efforts in this area are trying to give a solution to issues such as how to specify the processes flow textually and graphically, how to model the relationship between several business entities, how to specify the interface of a web service implementing a process, how to use specific business protocols, …

The following list summarises the most relevant standards and emerging specifications:

- *Business Process Execution Language for Web Services* (BPEL) [5] from OASIS [2]: This is a standard that provides a XML based programming language to define a business process. This language allows to define a process that implements a new service gathering inputs from actors and invoking other available services. Once the service is defined, it can be also used by other processes. The only interface that BPEL supports is SOAP and XML messages. BPEL allows users to define an understandable business process used directly to execute the process. This standard is supported by several and big organisations such as IBM and Microsoft, so it has sufficient industry backing to become an important standard.

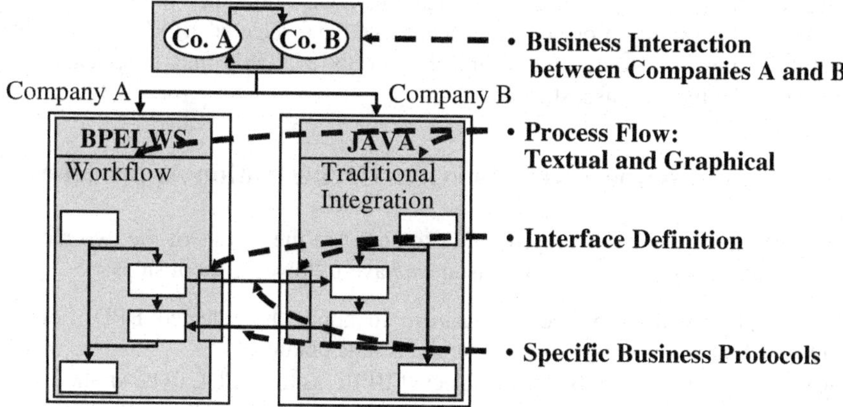

Fig. 1. Issues for Business Process Definition & Interoperability

- *ebXML Business Process Schema Specification* (BPSS) [8] from OASIS [2]: This standard provides a XML based specification language to define both the choreography and communication protocols between Web-based business partners. It allows to specify business transaction between two partners, but it only describes public processes.
- *Business Process Definition Metamodel* (BPDM) from OMG [11]: This standard defines a metamodel to support the graphical specification of a business process. Its objective is to define a common notation for business process definition in the same way that UML is a common notation for software system definition.
- *Business Process Modelling Language* (BPML) **Error! Reference source not found.** from BPMI.org [12]: It is a XML based language for modelling business processes. BPML is similar to BPEL in its objective and in the solution approach.
- *Business Process Modelling Notation* (BPMN) [15] from BPMI.org [12]: It is a metamodel that allows the graphical specification of business processes. It is the graphical representation of the BPML.
- *Web Service Choreography Interface* (WSCI) [6] [12] from W3C [1]: It is an XML based interface description language that describes the flow of messages exchanged by a Web Service participating in choreographed interactions with other services. The goal of WSCI is to describe the observable behaviour of a Web Service by means of a message-flow oriented interface.
- *Web Service Choreography Description Language* (WS-CDL) [9] from W3C [1]: It is a XML based language that allows to specify the interaction between entities that collaborate in a business choreography. It describes the participants, the messages exchanged, the interaction, and other elements necessary to completely specify the choreography.

- *XML Process Definition Language* (XPDL) [14] from WfMC [13]: It is a XML based language dedicated to model business processes. It is similar to BPML and BPEL.

From all these specifications only BPEL, BPML, BPDM, BPMN and XPDL could be consider as BPDLs, the rest of the specifications makes reference to other issues for business interoperability. For our experiments we have selected BPEL because there are multiple low-cost tools and technical tutorials available and it appears to be extending in the industry as a standard.

3 Process to Compare Web Services Orchestration Approaches

We have to develop a case study in order to compare the results of the two methods implementation. To make this comparison we have followed a set of steps:

- First of all, we have defined a *scenario* to apply the selected BPDL and the traditional method in order to compare the results obtained.
- Once the scenario was defined, we selected BPEL as the BPDL to be applied.
- Then the case study was *implemented* using *BPEL* and the *traditional* method.
- After implementing the case study using the two methods, the *results* were compared from 3 points of view: development results, impact of changes on the results and efficiency of implementation.

The following sections describe and provide our analysis of each of these steps.

4 The Scenario

Suppose a scenario where users want to get an evaluation questionnaire depending on a set of parameters and latter on get the results obtained after answering it. There is a system called eQuestionnaire system that provides this service through Web Services.

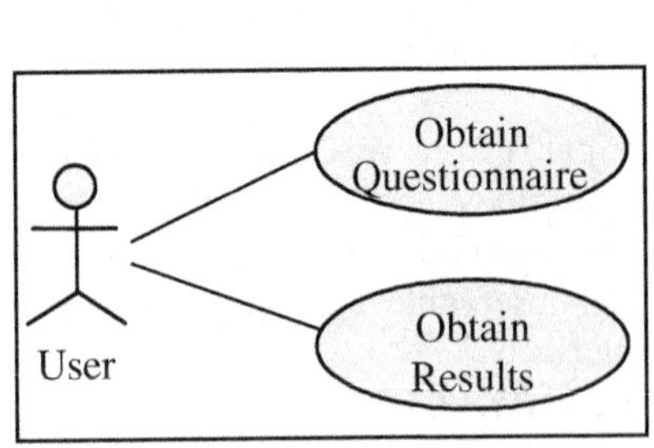

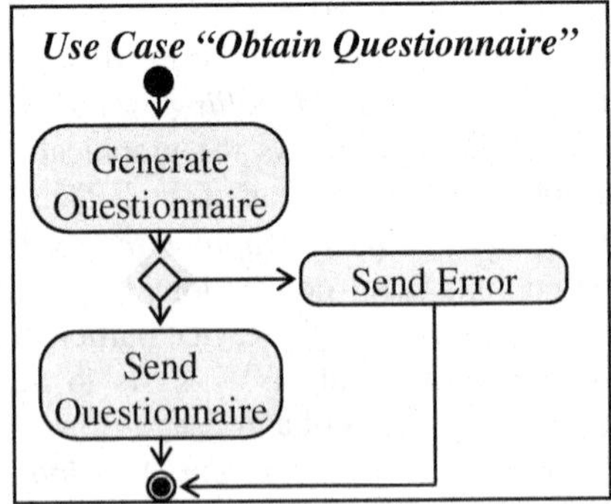

Fig. 2. Use Case and Activity Diagram

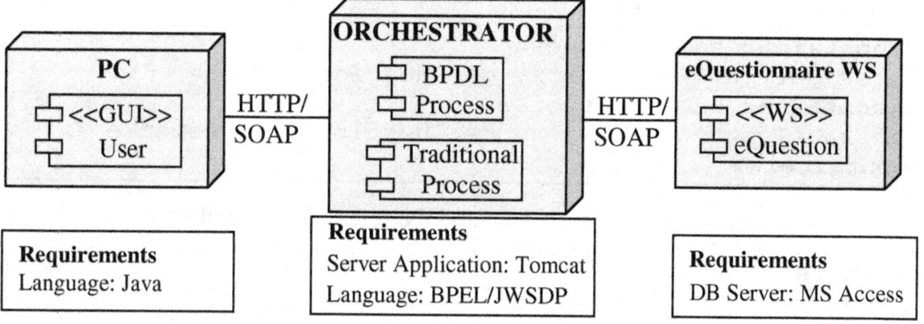

Fig. 3. Deployment Diagram and requirements for each node

The following figures show some UML diagrams such as Use Case, Activity and Deployment diagrams, which define the scenario described. The Deployment diagram identifies the hardware nodes and the software components that run on those nodes; the development environment for each node, for example Java language; and the middleware used to connect the disparate machines to each other, such as Internet to access to Web Services of eQuestionnaire system.

5 Implementation with a Business Process Definition Language

Business Process Execution Language (BPEL) has been chosen as the BPDL which is going to be used. In the figure 3, *BPDL Process* is the component that implements the business process using BPEL.

To develop a business process using BPEL it is necessary to follow four steps [10]:

- Create the BPEL file and its corresponding WSDL file. The WSDL document describes the interfaces that the business process will present to the external users.
- Find the WSDL locations of the services used. If the BPEL process invokes another external Web Service, then it must be included the WSDL file that describes this service invoked. In this case, the business process invokes a service on the *eQuestionnaire* system through Web Services so we need the location of its WSDL.
- Deploy the BPEL and WSDL files. To do this, it is necessary to specify the files developed in the first steps and if the BPEL process invokes external services, it must be specified the WSDL location too.
- Create the SOAP client with any SOAP implementation. The client interaction with the service is defined by the process WSDL document specified in the first step.

A BPEL code represents a complete process and it contains three main parts:

- The containers for holding messages that define the type of messages used in the process.

```
<containers>
  <container name="request"
  messageType="wsd:WSProxy_getQuestionnaire"/>
  <container name="response"
  messageType="wsd:WSProxy_getQuestionnaireResponse"/>
</containers>
```

– The partners involved in the interaction and the role that they will play.

```
<partners>
  <partner name="User"
  serviceLinkType="tns:Obtain_eQuestionnaireSLT"/>
  <partner name="provider"
  serviceLinkType="tns:Obtain_eQuestionnaireSLT"/>
</partners>
```

– The process activity that, in our case, consists of getting a message, then invoking the *eQuestionnaire* through Web Services, and finally replying to the user. These three actions are defined in BPEL using the <receive>, <invoke>, and <reply> activities. Additionally, the process defines how and when to run each activity by using structured activities. In this example, we want the three activities to occur one after the other and this ordering may be achieved in BPEL using a <sequence> activity.

```
<sequence name="sequence">
  <receive name="receive" partner="User"
  portType="tns:WSProxy" operation="getQuestionnaire"
  container="request" createInstance="yes"/>
  <invoke name="invoke" partner="provider"
  portType="wsd:WSProxy" operation="getQuestionnaire"
  inputContainer="request" outputContainer="response"/>
  [...]
  <reply name="reply" partner="User"
  portType="tns:WSProxy" operation="getQuestionnaire"
  container="response"/>
</sequence>
```

With regard to code, this BPEL file has 10 statements that enclose only 8 different instruction types from around 20 possible types that are defined in the BPEL standard.

6 Implementation with a Traditional Method

The traditional method encodes the activity flow using state of the art programming languages. In this case, the programming language that is going to be used is Java language and the Java Web Service Development Pack (JWSDP) that allows to use Web Services with Java language based on the developer's experience in this programming area with Web Services technology.

We have chosen a Web Service to represent the activity flow using Java language in order to facilitate the comparison with the BPEL implementation. *Traditional Process* is the component that implements this Web Service using Java Language.

Before implementing the activity flow, it is fundamental as a preliminary step to develop the interface that provides the services exposed identifying the parameters of each service. In this case, this interface will be represented with a Java class.

Using a programming language implies to implement the SOAP calls that invoke the Web Service. This is not a trivial work and it is necessary to have a certain knowledge about the usage of the selected programming language with Web Services technology.

The Java code implements the SOAP call to invoke the eQuestionnaire service.

- First, the SOAP message is created with the name of the service and its parameters.

```
[...]
bodyName = envelope.createName("getQuestionnaire",
"wsd", "http://com.test/wsdl/WS_Demonstrator ");
SOAPBodyElement gltp = body.addBodyElement(bodyName);
Name name = envelope.createName("String_1");
SOAPElement symbol = gltp.addChildElement(name);
symbol.addTextNode(parameter);
message.saveChanges();
```

- Once the SOAP message is created, it is sent to the location of the Web Service in order to get the answer.

```
URLEndpoint destination;
destination = new
URLEndpoint("http://localhost:8080/WS_Demonstrator/WS_
Demonstrator");
reply = con.call(message, destination);
[...]
```

With regard to code, the entire program has 44 code statements that enclose 6 different instruction types. These statements make use of 14 different classes and 21 methods from the huge number of possible objects and methods included in the JWSDP.

7 Analysis of Results

To compare the results obtained from applying BPEL and Java programming language, the analysis is going to be performed from 3 perspectives: development, modifications and efficiency.

7.1 Development Perspective

First, the development is going to be analysed by measuring the size, development complexity and deployment process steps of the result.

- *Size*: Using the following table, we can observe that both methods have a similar size in code statements but BPEL requires less statements than Java. The reduced number of code statements in BPEL is due to the fact that BPEL is specialized to represent business processes while Java is a general purpose programming language.

- *Complexity*: It can be measured with the number of instruction types, external classes and functions *used* in the case study and it can be compared with the set of instruction types, external classes and functions *available* in the language used: BPEL and JWSDP.
- BPEL doesn't need to use external classes, it only needs the BPEL engine that can interpret it. On the other hand, using a programming language as Java it is necessary to apply libraries that allow to use Web Services technology such as SOAP calls.
- *Deployment*: Using BPEL we have to upload the BPEL file and all the needed WSDL files to a server. With Java, first we have to compile and package the code and then upload that package to a server. Using current BPEL engines, such as the IBM Business Process Execution Language for Web Services Java Runtime, changes on the BPEL file or WSDL locations imply to undeploy all files and deploy the new ones again. With Java, it is only deployed one package that includes all necessary files so changes imply to recompile and redeploy the whole package again.

Table 1. Number of statements, using BPEL and Java Language

	Statements
BPEL	10
Java Language	44

Table 2. Number of instruction types, classes, and functions used in the case study

USED	Inst. types	Classes	Functions	Total
BPEL	8	0	0	*8*
Java Language (JWSDP)	6	14	21	*41*

Table 3. Number of instruction types, classes, and functions available in BPEL and JWSDP

AVAILABLE	Inst. types	Classes	Functions	Total
BPEL	20	0	0	20
Java Language (JWSDP)	52[1]	385	3850[2]	4287

7.2 Modification Perspective

It is also important to check how modifications could impact on the business process implementation. A modification could be adding a new functionality, removing an existing activity or modifying it.

[1] Keywords + assignation and declaration

[2] Supposing 10 functions per class

We have added a new activity to the case study presented. Now, before requesting a questionnaire, the user has to provide the username and password to the system in order to verify its access to the eQuestionnaire service. Checking the user identity rights is implemented by an external system that provides this functionality through Web Services so we only have to integrate it in the eQuestionnaire system.

The following Activity diagram shows this new activity that checks the user identity rights to access to the questionnaire service.

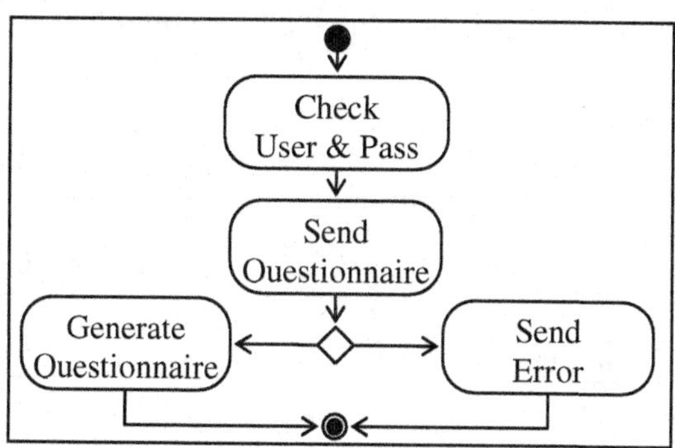

Fig. 4. Activity Diagram with a new activity to check username and password

Using traditional methods it is necessary to implement again the SOAP calls to invoke the new service and use the result to grant access to the eQuestionnaire, then we have to uninstall the previous version, compile the new one, pack it, and finally launch it in the server. Using the BPDL, it is only necessary to modify the process described in the BPEL, add the WSDL location of that new Web Service used and upload it to the server.

The following table shows the number of statements and complexity before and after adding the new activity. We can observe that the more complex and bigger the activity flow, the more effective and simpler BPEL is versus Java code.

Table 4. Number of code lines and instructions using BPEL and Java Language after adding a new activity

	Before		After	
	Statements	Complexity	Statements	Complexity
BPEL	10	8	16	8
Java Language	44	41	60	41

Therefore taking into account the data in the *Table 4* and the deployment complexity explained above, we can conclude that the modification of the business process implemented through the traditional method is more complex and bigger.

7.3 Efficiency Perspective

Additionally, it is important to analyse the efficiency of implementation at runtime. For doing this, we have developed a client that measures the time elapsed between the beginning and the end of the activity flow with both implementations.

We could think that the efficiency depends on the complexity of the activity flow and the number of activities required. For this reason we can measure the time spent with two additional activity flows: one that adds a new activity (in this case it is the activity flow used in the previous section) and other that adds three more activities.

Table 5. Number of seconds at runtime spent between the beginning and the end of activity flows composed of three, four and six activities

	3 activities	4 activities	6 activities
BPEL	30.8	34.8	59.73
Java Language	20.32	22.91	36.09

Observing the *Table 5* we can deduce that the more complex the flow, the more time spent with both methods but with BPEL the time elapsed increases almost a 100%, while with Java the time increases only a 75%. So, the efficiency at runtime is bigger using a traditional method such as Java than a BPDL. When considering these figures we should also take into account that the domain of java engines is more mature than the domain of BPDL execution engines. Surely as the BPDL execution engines evolve this performance gap will be reduced.

8 Conclusion

Current organisations are crowded with a multitude of Information systems, where most of them are usually COTS. Some examples could be ERP, CRM and Communications systems. In order to increase the performance of the organisation managers frequently envision new ways to mix the functionalities provided by the different systems to better achieve the business goals. In most of the cases this mixture consists on integrating those systems in a business process that specifies the orchestration needed to complete the business goals.

A business process is represented with an activity flow that can be implemented in two ways, using traditional methods or using Business Process Definition Languages (BPDL). Traditional methods encode the activity flow using programming languages such as Java, while the BPDLs describe the activity flow with a specific language that is directly interpreted by a BPDL engine.

This paper analyses the results from the comparison of BPEL (as a specific BPDL) and Java (as a specific traditional method) to develop solutions for services-based architectures to support business interoperability. These are the main conclusions:

- Using a traditional method such as Java language implies more effort and more time to perform modifications in the activity flow but its efficiency is bigger than using a BPDL, such as BPEL This performance gap relies in the BPDL execution engine and it will be improved as the BPDL domain gets more mature.
- The BPDL is easier for the development as it is a specialised language. It has a reduced set of instructions (20 instructions) specifically selected for the business process definition. This advantage is more relevant for big activity flows because it allows to make modifications in a simpler way and then easily deploy the process.
- BPDLs enable the automatic interpretation of the business process. The computer is aware of the business entities involved in the process and the activities carried out from the parsing of the business process definition document. This is not possible using a traditional programming language such as Java or C# because how the activities are encoded depends too much on the programmer style, and the automatic interpretation of the code as a business activity is quite complicated.

References

1. World Wide Web Consortium (W3C), http://www.w3.org, June 2004
2. Organization for the Advanced of Structured Information Standards (OASIS), http://www.oasis-open.org, June 2004
3. Web Services Choreography Working Group, http://www.w3.org/2002/ws/chor/, June 2004
4. OASIS Web Services Business Process Execution Language Technical Committee, http://www.oasis-open.org/committees/tc_home.php?wg_abbrev=wsbpel, May 2004
5. Business Process Execution Language for Web Services (BPEL), BPEL TC of OASIS, http://www.oasis-open.org/committees/tc_home.php?wg_abbrev=wsbpel, May 2004
6. Web Service Choreography Interface (WSCI), W3C Note 8 August 2002, http://www.w3.org/TR/wsci/, May 2004
7. Business Process Modelling Language (BPML), Business Process Management Initiative, http://www.bpmi.org/bpml.esp, May 2004
8. ebXML Business Process Specification Schema (BPSS), http://www.ebxml. org/specs/eb BPSS.pdf, May 2004
9. Web Services Choreography Description Language (WS-CDL), W3C Draft April 2004, http://www.w3.org/TR/2004/WD-ws-cdl-10-20040427/, June 2004
10. IBM Business Process Execution Language for Web Services Java, IBM August 2002, http://www.alphaworks.ibm.com/tech/bpws4j, May 2004
11. Object Management Group (OMG), http://www.omg.org, June 2004
12. Business Process Management Initiative (BPMI.org), http://www.bpmi.org, June 2004
13. Work Flow Management Coalition (WfMC), http://www.wfmc.org/, June 2004
14. XML Process Definition Language (XPDL), http://www.wfmc.org/, June 2004
15. Business Process Modelling Notation (BPMN), Business Process Management Initiative, http://www.bpmi.org/bpmn.esp, May 2004

The Necessary Legal Approach to COTS Safety and COTS Liability in European Single Market

Carlos Arias-Chausson

Martin & Lawson, c/ Alameda Urquijo,
28 – 2ºC 48010 – Bilbao, Spain
cach@martinlawson.com
www.martinlawson.com

Abstract. Nowadays, we can take the European single market for granted. With old barriers gone, people, goods, services and money move around Europe as freely as within one country. However, single market is not possible just sweeping away the technical, regulatory, legal, bureaucratic, idiomatic, cultural and protectionist barriers, but it has been essential to work hardly to defend fair competition as a simple and efficient means of guaranteeing consumers a level of excellence in terms of the quality and price of products and services, and to grant consumer protection to improve the quality of life of all European citizens. In this paper, we analyse the impact of these areas EU legislation on the COTS industry, how the COTS single market is forming and what *safe COTS* and *COTS defective* mean and imply.

1 Introduction

1.1 Single Market in Europe

The European internal market is one of the essential cornerstones of the European Union. It makes a significant contribution to European prosperity by stimulating intra-Community trade, reducing its costs (elimination of customs formalities, fall in prices as a result of greater competition, etc.), increasing productivity and reinforcing requirements to market safe products. Harmonized national laws prevent competition distortion, facilitate the free movement of goods and allow the internal market to operate smoothly. As result, we have a coherent, high level of protection for the health and safety of persons in the EU against damage caused to health or property by a defective product.

Some Figures. At the moment, European Market is formed by 25 states and firms selling in the single market know they have unrestricted access to more than 450 million consumers. EU Gross National Product means 30% world and Per Capita Income raises 30,000 $. There are 45,000 companies developing software and European software market is 124 billion $ approximately.

Outline. The four freedoms of movement —for goods, services, people and capital— are underpinned by a range of supporting policies. Relating to freedom movement for goods, we can find:

X. Franch and D. Port (Eds.): ICCBSS 2005, LNCS 3412, pp. 36 – 42, 2005.

- remove technical barriers to trade
- ensure that healthy competition is not hindered by anticompetitive practices on the part of companies or national authorities
- adopt policies designed to protect the specific interests of consumers
- reinforce the general requirement to market safe products and improve product safety measures
- ensure a high level of consumer protection against damage caused to health or property by a defective product
- eliminate unfair terms from contracts drawn up between a professional and a consumer
- strengthen consumer confidence in cross-border shopping by laying down a common set of minimum rules valid no matter where the goods are purchased

1.2 COTS as a Product

There is a legal definition to "product". In European Single Market, product means all movables, with the exception of primary agricultural products and game, even though incorporated into another movable or into an immovable, including gas and electricity. So, COTS are considered products from European Law point of view. Certainly, there are some products that enjoy of specific regulation, but it's not the case: Software products, developers and sellers have to observe product general regulation.

1.3 Securing Consumers' Safety

The advantages of the Single market in facilitating the availability in all member States of a wide range of products from all corners of the Union must be made available within a framework which assures citizens of the safety of those products and the possibility to claim compensation in case of damages caused by defective products. Consumer policy is a core component of the European Commission strategy objective of improving the quality of life of all EU citizens, who play a key economic and political role in society.

Investing consumers with a certain number of fundamental rights, the Member States have put in place policies designed to reduce inequalities, abolish unfair practices, promote safety and health and improve living standards in general. For the market to work effectively it should be competitive and deliver a fair deal for consumers, whose rights established at Europe level derive more benefit from the internal market.

2 COTS Safety

COTS software products are most often "black boxes" to the end users, who can only surmise the safety or security of the software by examining the system behavior.

The UK Health and Safety Executive (HSE) commissioned research from Adelard into how pre-existing software components may be safely used in safety-related programmable electronic systems in a way that complies with the IEC 61508 standard Two reports resulted from this work: the first report summaries the evidence that is likely to be available in practice relating to a software component to assist in assessing the safety integrity of a safety function that depends on that component [1]; the second report considers how the available evidence can best be used within the framework of the IEC 61508 safety lifecycle to support an argument for the safety integrity achieved by a safety function [2].

European Parliament and Council have adopted the Directive 2001/95/EC on general product safety, which is to be applied if there are no specific provisions among the Community regulations governing the safety of products concerned or if sectional legislation is insufficient. This Act establishes at Community level a general safety requirement for any product placed on the market, or otherwise supplied or made available to consumers, intended for consumers, or likely to be used by consumers under reasonably foreseeable conditions even if not intended for them, including those products that are supplied or made available to consumers in the context of service provision for use by them. Products which are designed exclusively for professional use but have subsequently migrated to the consumer market should be subject to the requirements of this Directive because they can pose risks to consumer health and safety when used under reasonably foreseeable conditions, too.

As mentioned, COTS are considered products; just as software item commercially available not to be customized but to be integrated into an application system; and there is no specific regulation to software products. Therefore, the Product Safety Directive should apply to COTS, irrespective of the selling techniques and of the identity and nationality of the developer.

Safe Software. Safe COTS are those which poses no threat or only a reduced threat in accordance with the nature of its use and which is acceptable in view of maintaining a high level of protection for the health and safety of persons. COTS are deemed safe once they conform to the specific Community provisions governing its safety. In the absence of such provisions, they must comply with the specific national regulations of the Member State in which they are being marketed or sold, or with the voluntary national standards which transpose the European standards. In the absence of these, the COTS's compliance is determined according to the following:

- the voluntary national standards which transpose other relevant European standards and the Commission recommendations which set out guidelines on the assessment of product safety
- the standards of the Member State in which the product is being marketed or sold
- the codes of good practice as regards health and safety
- the current state of the art
- the consumers' safety expectations

Developers and Distributors Obligations. The developers must put on the market COTS which comply with the general safety requirement. In addition, they must provide consumers with the necessary information in order to assess a COTS's inherent threat, particularly when this is not directly obvious, and take the necessary measures to avoid such threats (e.g. withdraw COTS from the market, inform consumers, recall products which have already been supplied to consumers, etc.) Distributors are also obliged to supply COTS which comply with the general safety requirement, to monitor the safety of COTS on the market and to provide the necessary documents ensuring that the COTS can be traced. If the manufacturers or the distributors discover that a COTS is dangerous, they must notify the competent authorities and, if necessary, cooperate with them.

It's important to clarify when the developer is not based in the EU, this obligation applies to his representative in the EU or, in the absence of a representative, to the importer or to the distributor who had marketed that COTS into the European Market. So, European consumers always have someone in the EU to claim.

3 COTS Liability

In a June 2002 article titled "Buggy Whipped," The Economist weighs into the debate over software quality, reporting that most of the industry responding to its survey agreed on the magnitude of the problem (responses were mainly from the software industry itself), most felt that product liability laws were not the answer. Why? This immature industry has no quality[1] or reliability baseline upon which to evaluate performance and render judgments.

The Directive 85/374/EEC on liability for defective products introduced in the EU the principle of objective liability or liability without fault. According to it, any producer of a defective movable must compensate any damage caused to the physical well-being or property of individuals, independently whether or not there is negligence on the part of the producer

Bjective Liability. COTS developers are liable of damage caused by defective COTS. This liability includes objective liability or liability without fault and it is not necessary to prove the negligence or fault of the developer or importer.

COTS Developer. COTS developer has a wide meaning including any participant in the production process, the importer of the defective COTS, any person putting their name, trade mark or other distinguishing feature on the COTS, and any person supplying a product whose developer cannot be identified.

COTS developer is freed from all liability if he proves

- that he did not put the COTS into circulation
- that the defect causing the damage came into being after the COTS was put into circulation by him
- that the COTS was not manufactured for profit-making sale
- that the COTS was neither manufactured nor distributed in the course of his business
- that the defect is due to compliance of the COTS with mandatory regulations issued by the public authorities
- that the state of scientific and technical knowledge at the time when the COTS was put into circulation was not such as to enable the defect to be discovered
- in the case of a manufacturer of a component of the final product, that the defect is attributable to the design of the product or to the instructions given by the product manufacturer

[1] Paul Strassmann, NASA's acting chief information officer, once proclaimed software to be "one of the most poorly constructed, unreliable and least maintainable technological artifacts ever invented by man".

The developer's liability is not altered when the damage is caused both by a defect in the product and by the act or omission of a third party. However, when the injured person is at fault, the producer's liability may be reduced.

In order to reduce liability probability the producer can use several measures. Firstly, a COTS developer can do all things possible to prevent the software from being or becoming unsafe. Secondly insurance can be subscribed for the liability of software. In general, this insurance can have one of two forms, general corporate liability insurance or professional liability insurance.

COTS Supplier. COTS Suppliers are considered as developers, so their obligation can be divided into four aspects. These obligations are related to each other.

Information obligation. In the first place the supplier will inform the client in a clear and complete way about the consequences of using the new COTS. The information must not be misleading. If there are any failures in the tool the supplier has to inform the client soon as possible.

Warning obligation. In line with the obligation above the supplier has to warn for risks and possible failures with the new software component.

Research obligation. The supplier has to provide necessary information about the COTS. The supplier can decide on his own how much he will provide. The obligation to provide information will increase with a layman in the software industry. The supplier has to investigate if his software component is suitable with the rest of the software tool.

Advice obligation. If there is a relation based on advice the supplier has to provide correct advices.

COTS Users. COTS users are protected by Law when they enter into a contract with any supplier[2]. When they contract with a COTS developer or supplier, they have to check the wording of the contract by an expert. Some recommendations are [3]:

Specifying the Work In general contracting practice, the information that defines or specifies the work of the contract can take one of several forms:

- Functional Specification
- Performance Specification
- Technical Specification
- Some combination of all three types of specifications provided that the instructions are not in conflict

Negotiating the Contract. Once you receive and evaluate proposals in response to a solicitation, you select the highest-ranking supplier or suppliers to develop a contract that best fulfills your needs. This is not an easy process; and especially for large contracts, you must conduct this process with the utmost ethical integrity. The following measures can help ensure high standards:

---

[2] In Europe, next clause is void: "*Under no circumstances, including, but not limited to, negligence, shall XXXX Inc. be liable for any special or consequential damages that result from the use of, or the inability to use, the materials in this site, even if XXXX Inc. or its representative has been advised of the possibility of such damages*"

- Plan and prepare carefully for negotiations; get internal consensus on what you want as an organization.
- Technical capability, previous experiences and guarantees.
- Ask for product and professional liability insurance policy.
- Conduct meetings formally and stick to an agenda.
- Follow up promptly and translate terms of agreement into writing as soon as possible.
- Conduct an in-house, post-negotiation review to capture lessons learned.

Administering the Contract and Controlling the Supplier's Work. In all but the simplest of agreements, the acquirer has certain technical responsibilities with respect to the contract. How well you perform these responsibilities will have a significant effect on the supplier's performance. Your overriding aim should be to maximize the likelihood of meeting all the contract objectives on both sides. Therefore, you should pay close attention to fulfilling the following responsibilities.

- Provide technical clarifications quickly.
- Respond as soon as possible to supplier requests for information, or reviews and approvals, relating to schematics, architecture, interface configurations, use of subcontractors, and so forth.
- Coordinate, or ensure coordination, among suppliers if the project involves multiple contracts.
- Promptly exercise quality control acceptance, waiver, or rejection; if you reject something, quickly request correction of defects and certify progress when the correction is complete.
- Resolve disputes and/or claims early by forewarning the supplier of potential difficulties, initiating fact-finding activities for potential or registered disputes, and initiating a change order process if appropriate.
- Show interest by monitoring and tracking the supplier's progress and expediting roadblocks.
- Process changes expeditiously.
- Abide by the terms of the contract.
- Above all, pay progress payments promptly. Nothing discourages a
- Supplier more than leaning on his 30-, 60-, or 90-day line of credit!

Contract Control. As we noted earlier, the type of contract you select largely determines the degree of control you have over the supplier's work; the firmer the price, the lower the acquirer's level of control over contract performance. Nevertheless, even in fixed-price situations you still have levers, short of extreme actions such as termination and lawsuits. Of course, you must make sure to write these control procedures into the contract. You cannot expect to unilaterally assume these privileges after the contract is signed, at least not without risk of legal action by the supplier!

4 Conclusions

There is no regulation establishing standard safety in COTS. That does not mean COTS are excluded from general requirement of safety, but the standard safety will be stated following indeterminate criteria as current state of the art and consumer's safety expectations.

Analysing the experience developed by other industries, the recommendation to COTS developers and distributors must focus on self-regulation and technical harmonisation. Consumers are demanding safe products and COTS industry has to make an effort to satisfy them and elaborates essential technical and safety requirements. Governments are giving to consumers the necessary instruments to protect their interests and rights, and have created the procedures for economic agents into the COTS market to be able to start a certification and conformity marking system.

In the United States market, today the DO-178B standard has been adopted as a method of software component approval in many critical aerospace, defense and other environments, including military, nuclear, medical and communications applications. As a result, such disparate groups as the Society of Automotive Engineers (SAE), the Department of Defense (DoD), and even the Food & Drug Administration (FDA) give DO- 178B their blessing.

The consequences that product liability has for the producer of software containing defects, are not very unfavorable relative to other forms of liability. An unsatisfied customer can hold not only the producer accountable, but also the importer or even a person presenting himself as the producer. Some cases even allow for the supplier to be accused for defects in the software.

References

1. UK Health and Safety Executive (HSE) commissioned research. "Methods for assessing the safety integrity of safety-related software of uncertain pedigree (SOUP)". Report No: CRR337 HSE Books 2001 ISBN 0 7176 2011 5, 2001 http://www.hse.gov.uk/research/crr_pdf/2001/crr01337.pdf
2. UK Health and Safety Executive (HSE) commissioned research. "Justifying the use of software of uncertain pedigree (SOUP) in safety-related applications". Report No: CRR336 HSE Books 2001 ISBN 0 7176 2010 7, 2001 http://www.hse.gov.uk/research/crr_pdf/2001/crr01336.pdf
3. R. Max Wideman. "Progressive Acquisition and the Rational Unified Process". The Rational Edge, by IBM, 2002.

COTS Acquisition: Getting a Good Contract

Shadia Elgazzar, Anatol Kark, Erik Putrycz, and Mark Vigder

National Research Council of Canada,
Institute for Information Technology, Ottawa, Canada K1A 0R6
{Shadia.Elgazzar, Anatol.Kark, Erik.Putrycz, Mark.Vigder}@nrc.ca

Abstract. Organizations that are acquiring a COTS based system must adapt many of their acquisition process activities that are traditionally used for acquiring non-COTS based systems. Much of this adaptation becomes quite difficult within government environments where the process is often constrained by government rules and regulations. This paper provides an experience report on COTS based acquisition for a government agency during the early stages of the process. The impact on requirements engineering and the steps for developing the Request For Proposal (RFP) and evaluating the proposals are outlined. The parties involved in the acquisition process are identified, and their relationship within a project governance structure are discussed. The final discussion provides some guidance as to how the early stages of the acquisition process should be adapted to minimize risk through the project.

1 Introduction

Acquisition agencies responsible for acquiring software systems typically use a process that involves creating a Request for Proposal (RFP), distributing the request to potential developers, and receiving the resulting proposals. Once the proposals have been received, the acquisition agency can evaluate the proposals according to a predetermined set of criteria and award a contract to the winning bidder.

Many of the activities of this process are similar whether the system being acquired is completely custom-built or a COTS-based system. However, when the organization is specifically targeting a COTS-based solution, there are differences in the approach that must be used.

This paper provides an experience report on an acquisition process with which we are currently involved and which is targeted towards a COTS-based acquisition. The activities described in this paper are those involved in developing the RFP. In particular, this paper will describe the overall strategy used to develop the RFP, including the requirements, and show the impact of targeting a COTS-based system.

The authors intend to monitor the project progress and report on the upcoming results.

X. Franch and D. Port (Eds.): ICCBSS 2005, LNCS 3412, pp. 43 – 53, 2005.

2 Background

The acquisition discussed in this paper is a major government acquisition for a complex information processing system which will serve about 600 000 accounts accessed by different stakeholders.

Given the complexity of the business rules involved in the system, a COTS-based solution is more flexible (in terms of support, maintenance) than a custom-build solution.

The system consists of

- Several core functions relating to legislation, contracts, privacy and security; and
- Support functions: users services, users communications, periodic reporting, employer services and sponsor services.

Prior to issuing the RFP, a study has been commissioned to explore alternatives for modernizing the applications. The study considered modernizing and enhancing the existing systems or replacing them with a COTS product. The alternatives were evaluated against a large set of criteria (implementation and operation costs, business and technical risks, time, service and several types of impacts). The resulting evaluation indicated a preference to replace the legacy system based mainly on cost and service.

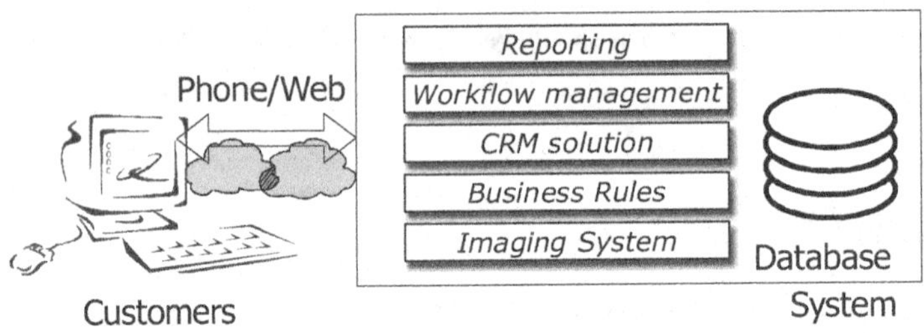

Fig. 1. Description of the system architecture

The new system will consist of one or several COTS products that need to cover these main requirements (Figure 1):

- A large set of business rules (with many exceptions and special processing)
- Imaging functions to transform physical media to digital format and permit storage and retrieval, integrity, and annotation of images.
- Workflow functions: to track physical and electronic files;
- Reporting functions; and
- Customer-Relationship Management functions for communications between the stakeholders involved.

Most of these COTS products are "database-centric" and rely on existing databases for storing and accessing all data. As a consequence, many technical requirements (such as scalability, backup, recovery, etc.) can be delegated to the underlying database product.

In addition to COTS products, the contract will involve a System Integrator who will be in charge of customizing and connecting the COTS products, bringing solutions for the missing functionalities, and communicating with external systems.

3 Acquisition Process

3.1 Description

The acquisition process by government's organizations starts with the preparation of a Request for Proposals (RFP). At this stage, the government's organizations can communicate with any vendors to learn about their products.

Some of the items described in the RFP are

- Instructions to bidders/contractors;
- Requirements definition;
- Pricing requirements; and
- Model contract.

This includes information related to proposal preparation and evaluation including evaluation criteria, relative weights and methods of marking.

The preparation of the RFP itself (requirements and governance) is detailed in sections 4 and 5.

The RFP is issued through the Canadian Government Electronic Tender Service. If the bidders have any questions they have to submit them in writing. Questions and answers are then provided to all bidders (without differentiation).

In the next step, all bidders proposal are evaluated using the agreed upon evaluation methodology. The bidder who gets the highest score is the winner. Unsuccessful bidders have the right to be debriefed following the award of the contract. This will typically involve a review of the strengths and weaknesses of their proposal.

3.2 Procurement Strategy

There were two significant requirements concerning this acquisition. First, it was decided that the system being acquired would be COTS-based. The organization was expecting a *COTS-solution* as defined by the SEI[3]. A COTS-solution is a system that is dominated by a single COTS product. Although there may be other COTS products in the delivered system, they play a secondary role to the primary COTS product that dictates the overall architecture and capabilities of the system.

The second major requirements is that the acquisition must conform to the policies and procedures of the government procurement process. Government procurements can be significantly different from commercial procurements because of the regulations and legal constraints under which they operate. Among the constraints imposed by the government process are the following:

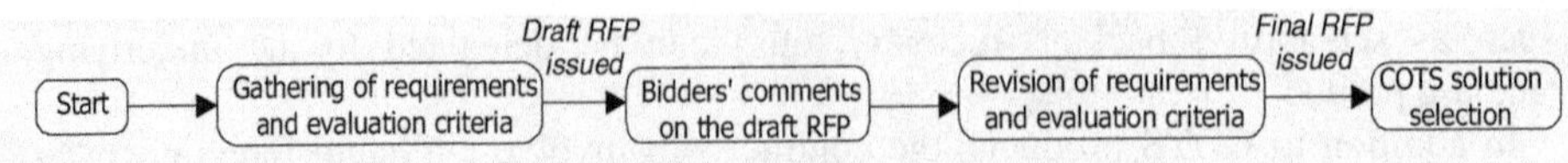

Fig. 2. The procurement process

- The process must be open, with all information available to all bidders.
- The procurement is subject to requirements of various trade agreements such as the North American Free Trade Agreement (NAFTA). If these requirements are not adhered to, then the government may be subject to formal complaints to the Canadian International Trade Tribunal (CITT). This, in turn, may lead to rulings that include the requirement to re-issue the RFP and/or pay other penalties.
- In evaluating proposals, the government must follow the procedures that it has set out in the RFP. For example, a proposal must meet any requirement listed as "mandatory" within the RFP or it will be rejected. The government cannot consider factors to evaluate that were not included in the RFP
- Once the evaluation has been completed based on the criteria set out in the RFP, the government has constraints in negotiating the final contract with the selected bidder. In summary, the government may not negotiate and award a final contract that includes any term that deviates from the RFP requirements or includes work that is materially outside the scope of RFP requirements.

The procurement process involves the following different roles from both the procurement side and the supplier side. These roles, and their responsibilities are defined as follows:

- *Business expert.* The business expert is responsible for the knowledge about the business services of the acquisition organization. During the procurement process, they have primary responsibility for defining the functional requirements of the system.
- *Technical expert.* Technical experts are the part of the acquisition organization responsible for the IT infrastructure. During the procurement process, they have primary responsibility for providing the technical requirements of the system, as for example, the constraint that the existing legacy system might impose (interfaces, existing networks, etc).
- *Procurement officer.* The role within the acquisition organization that is responsible for the procurement process. This includes making sure that all policies and procedures are followed and that the process is open and legally correct.
- *System integrator.* Responsible for proposing a solution to the acquisition agency that is based on COTS products.
- *COTS Product Vendor.* Owner and developer of the COTS product and responsible for its ongoing maintenance of the COTS product. The COTS product developer is usually a member of the bidding team headed up by the system integrator.

Because of the constraints upon the process, there is minimal opportunity for the iterative development suggested by most COTS acquisition processes [2,4]. Once the final contract has been published and the evaluation criteria have been established, the contract must be awarded to the bidder who best satisfies the criteria with no further iteration allowed at this stage. To overcome some of these limitations, and to allow at least a single level of iteration, the process that is followed, as illustrated in Figure 2, includes a draft RFP. This is not legally binding, but allows potential system integrators the opportunity to view and respond to the contract, and permits the acquisition organization to consider all input and to modify the RFP as necessary before issuing the legally binding version.

3.3 Impact on the Acquisition Process

One of the major issues that arose during the early discussion of the acquisition was about the perception of the goals of the acquisition process. Was the result of the acquisition process the acquisition of a COTS product, or was the result the acquisition of a solution to a business need? The answer to this problem should be obvious i.e., the acquisition is being driven by the need to find a solution to a business problem not simply the need to acquire a COTS product. However, particularly during the early stages of developing the RFP, participants would focus discussion on details of "out-of-the-box" functionality of different products, rather than trying to focus discussion on the real business needs of the organization.

The view of "buying a COTS product" versus "acquiring a solution to a business need" impacts the requirements gathering, evaluation criteria, and contracting structure.

When organizations opt for a COTS-based solution there is a temptation to begin the acquisition process by studying the products in the marketplace and trying to compare their relative merits. Although studying the available COTS products is necessary, the focus should always be on defining the fundamental business needs of the organization and evaluating where and how COTS-based solutions support the business needs. The business needs must also be formulated in such a specific manner that they do not preclude the use of viable COTS products that do not fit into particular business processes.

3.3.1 Evaluation Criteria Impact

A challenging issue that arose was how to develop a set of criteria for evaluating the proposed solutions. Two opposing views can be argued. First, the evaluation criteria could be based primarily on COTS-product features. Secondly, evaluation criteria could look at the design of the proposed solution. In fact, evaluation must be done from both perspectives. The goal and challenge for this project was to develop an objective and open set of evaluation criteria that could be applied in an open, objective, and non-iterative manner, and would result in the best solution being acquired.

Given the size of the project and the potential products involved, a major issue for the evaluation is customization. Customization can be divided into tailoring and modifications. Tailoring consists of changes to COTS software product functions along parameters that are predetermined by the vendor. In particular, tailoring is distinguished from modification, as it does not change the basic product or its capabilities in any way unintended by the vendor[3]. Potentially, this system will require many customizations. In order to maintain and upgrade the system, these customizations have to be properly engineered: for several existing COTS products, certified developers can only perform certain types of customizations.

There are many techniques that have been developed for evaluating COTS products[4][1]. There is much less work that has been done on evaluating bid proposals that include solutions built from COTS products. Moreover, most COTS-based procurement processes suggest a highly iterative approach involving extensive interaction with individual solution providers.[2] However, under the government procurement approach, all potential Bidders must be given a formal, equal opportunity to participate in the process. It was decided not to take a relatively long-term, complex, multi-phased procurement to support this type of interactive approach with multiple vendors.

The suggested approach to this problem includes the following guidelines:

- Evaluate the level of customization required for meeting the business requirements. This criterion requires a precise definition of the possible customization involved. As a consequence, this criterion has a high impact on the maintenance and possible upgrades of the system.
- Focus on how the solution, not the COTS product satisfies business needs.
- Identify the business requirements from which the criteria will be derived. For example, requirements that could impact evaluation criteria include the following:
  - The system must be able to update the different calculations in a cost-effective manner. Cost-effective may imply that the update can be done by in-house personnel who have not gone through an expensive certification process by the COTS vendor.
  - The tailoring and configuration must be guaranteed to be compatible with updated versions of the COTS product.
  - Implementing the core set of requirements must involve the minimum cost and risk possible. This type of requirement would require looking at a fit-gap analysis between the core requirements and the proposed product. Where there is a gap between the product and the requirements, the method of filling the gap would have to be evaluated as to the level of effort and the risk level.

3.3.2 Contracting Impact

When contracting for a COTS-based solution, there are two general strategies that can be considered. The first is to have a single contract with a system integrator that delivers a solution that includes COTS products. Bidders propose a solution that includes the COTS products of their choice. The second approach is to use two RFPs and two contracts, one for purchasing the primary COTS software, and one to contract with a system integrator to build a solution from the selected COTS product. In this case, system integrators must show how they can build a solution from a COTS product that has already been purchased by the acquisition organization.

Arguments can be made for using either a one-contract or a two-contract approach to acquisition. The primary argument for using the two-contract approach is that since the product and the system integrator are not tied together in a single proposal, the acquisition agency is free to choose what they consider to be the best product and the best system integrator. An evaluation can first be performed on products to determine which of the proposed products is the closest match to the needs of the organization. After purchasing the product, the acquisition agency can evaluate the proposals from system integrators to determine the best proposal for building a solution from the product.

The acquisition discussed in this paper decided on using a single RFP and a single contract for the system. There are two arguments for this approach. First, it was felt that a single contract could be done in a more expeditious and timely manner. Furthermore, this requirement was focused on getting best-of-breed COTS products to meet business requirements. The approach of considering COTS products separately would have caused a significant degree of complexity to considering all of the potential combinations of COTS products being offered. Perhaps a more significant result of the single contract approach is that the acquisition agency is focused from the start on buying a solution rather than buying a product. Although the two-contract approach has been very successful[5], in our particular circumstances the single contract helped to focus our requirements and evaluation criteria on the business solution needed, rather than on the COTS products being purchased.

4 Requirements Gathering

Requirements' gathering concentrated on the business requirements. A conscious effort was made to stay at the business level and not to include technical requirements (other than the constraint imposed by the legacy systems to which the new system interfaces). This allows maximum flexibility to the bidder to come up with the most flexible and conforming solution. For this reason the requirements were gathered by an integrated team, led by business experts and including technical representation. This gave the technical staff the knowledge required to produce the supporting documentation for the RFP, as for example, the description of the different legacy system that the system will need to interface to. Requirements' gathering was approached from the following perspectives:

- The core business the requirements had to be very precise and restrictive.
- The requirements were written in a way that should accommodate a certain level of business process re-design; the concentration was on the "what" and not the "how".
- The non-core requirements are clearly divided into "mandatory" requirements that must be fulfilled by the solution for it to qualify, and "rated" requirements that can be used to differentiate between solutions.
- The ultimate goal is a solution, and the requirements are focused on not eliminating interesting solution by being too specific.

4.1 Process for Gathering Requirements

For this project the following process to gather requirements was used:

- Creating a business model for the system including its interaction with existing legacy system and the takeholders.

- Developing the "business activities". A business activity is defined as a logical grouping of work. It has a definite beginning, with a well-defined trigger, and a definite end. Since members of the team were domain specific experts, it was relatively easy to come up with the list of activities. Each activity included
    - A reference to its location in the Table of Content
    - A business activity name
    - A business activity scope
    - A business activity explanation
    - A reference to the relevant business rules
    - A reference to the required data
    - A list of results (outputs)
- While working on the business activities, the team started producing a list of business processes. Every business process is formed of a sequence of business activities that are executed due to a certain trigger or event, as for example creating and changing the state of an account. These allow the team to discover any missed, or may be not used anymore, business activities. Also, having all the business processes well-defined help the bidders understand the system and will help the team in scripting the different scenarios that the successful bidders will demonstrate.
- The last step in the process was to derive the requirements from the business activities and to classify them as "mandatory" and "rated". A large set of business requirements was derived for the core requirements of the system and also for reporting, Workflow Management, Customer Relationship Management and imaging. Many of the core business requirements and a small number of the non-core requirements were identified as mandatory. An effort is made to keep the mandatory requirements to a minimum so that no possible solutions are eliminated.

4.2 Impact of COTS on Requirements

Targeting a COTS-based system did not impact the approach or the result of requirements gathering. It does impact the way the requirements are used in evaluating bids.

For each individual requirement, factors that influences the evaluation include:

- The level of effort required to build a solution from the proposed COTS product;
- The risk associated with the implementation of the requirement. This was determined by looking at the complexity of the change and the type of change, e.g., a change to configuration files was assumed to be lower risk than modification to the COTS software; and
- The ongoing maintenance effort associated with the requirement. This includes the effect on the requirement implementation of upgrading the underlying COTS product.

5 Governance Structure

Proper management structure for the development of the large, COTS-based products is critical to the successful delivery of the product. It would therefore be required that the *customer (end user)* has the responsibility for the overall project. In the case of a large COTS-based product there are two other players involved - COTS product supplier and System Integrator. Based on our understanding of the relations among those players, we are recommending that an *Integrated Project Team* be created with the structure for the governance of the project illustrated in Figure 3.

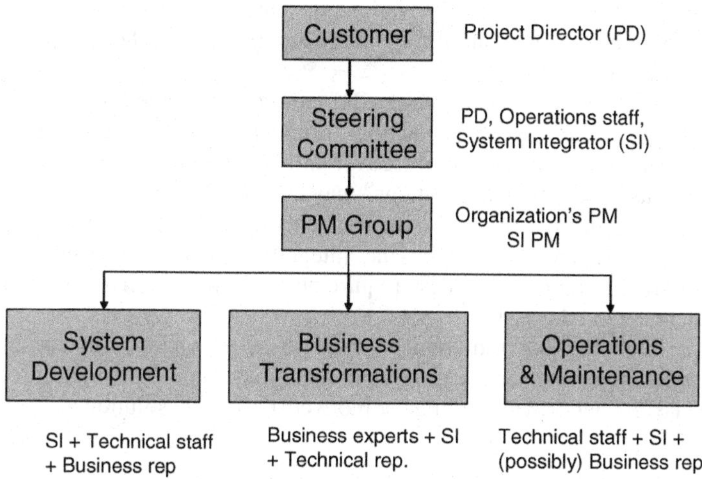

Fig. 3. Project Governance Structure

The customer organisation should form an *alliance* with a System Integrator and create a Steering Committee comprised from the senior representatives of the project, the organisation's operations, which will most likely be responsible for delivering services to the clients, and System Integrator, with all three parties having equal influence. This Steering Committee would oversee a Project Management Group having overall responsibility for execution of the project. Three Integrated Project Teams would be then created to deliver the system and to implement the business transformations, including training and eventual Operation and Management for the system. Composition of these teams will vary with time and depending on eventual contract arrangements might include only the organisation staff. It is foreseen that COTS product suppliers will have contracts with the organization, however it will be the System Integrator dealing directly with them.

We are of the opinion that a governance structure has to be established prior to the issuing of the RFP, as the potential System Integrator needs to understand relations, which might be imposed on him. We expect that the Systems Integrators might propose different governance structure, which will be rated as part of the evaluations process. At the time of writing of this paper, this proposed governance structure is still under discussion.

6 Discussion

Many lessons have been learned from the requirements gathering and the acquisition process.

The first lesson concerns the requirements gathering: requirements that may eliminate viable COTS products must be avoided. The restrictiveness or looseness of each requirement must be carefully weighted. Once the RFP is issued, the requirements cannot be changed and if they are overly restrictive, they may eliminate cost-effective solutions.

Being aware of existing products during the requirements gathering may lead to requirements being driven by the potential products' capabilities: focusing on products capabilities doesn't necessarily cover all the business needs. Looking at separate products as being separate "systems" may even lead to mistakes. An example was found in the Imaging system: many requirements focused on the capabilities of a potential imaging software suite while the integration with the system was not mentioned. Looking at the core business requirements of the imaging system and its role in the system solved this issue.

A challenge while writing requirements was to avoid taking into account the business processes involved. Some COTS products may impose business processes re-engineering (BPR) but provide a better or more cost effective solution.

7 Conclusions

This paper presented lessons learned in the acquisition of a new system for the Canadian government. After several studies, it was decided that a COTS-based solution has been chosen to replace the current system. The government procurements and several choices lead to the decision of acquiring a full COTS-based solution (a central COTS solution and a system integrator) rather than only a product. These conditions have many impacts on the usual COTS acquisition process: evaluation of the products, contracting, the requirement gathering and the governance structure have to be focused on the whole solution rather than products.

The main lesson learned in this experience has been changing the view of participants (working in the requirements gathering and RFP preparation) from a COTS product vision to a whole solution view. In the early stages of the RFP preparation people tended to focus on "out-of-the-box" products features rather than focusing only on their business needs.

Work is currently ongoing on this project on preparing an evaluation method. The evaluation method should rate the functional and design aspects of the whole solution instead of only the product. Further steps in the project after the RFP is issued will help us to learn on the effectiveness of requirements and evaluation method.

Acknowledgements

We would like to thank all the members of the organization involved for their help and support on this paper.

References

[1] Annotated Bibliography of COTS Software Evaluation, Software Engineering Institute, 1999, http://www.sei.cmu.edu/cbs/papers/eval_bib.html.

[2] Maiden N.A.M., Ncube C.: Acquiring Requirements for Commercial Off-The-Shelf Package Selection, IEEE Software, 15(2), (1998) 46-56.

[3] SEI COTS bibliography.

[4] Solberg, H., Dahl, K.M.: COTS Software Evaluation and Integration issues, Norwegian University of Technology and Science, Software Engineering Project, (2001) Trondheim, Norway.

[5] Commonwealth of Pennsylvania, ImaginPA project, http://www.imaginepa.state.pa.us/imaginepa/site/default.asp

Specifying Interaction Constraints of Software Components for Better Understandability and Interoperability

Yan Jin and Jun Han

Faculty of ICT, Swinburne University of Technology, Hawthorn, VIC 3122, Australia
{yjin, jhan}@swin.edu.au

Abstract. A vital issue in the correct use of commercial-off-the-shelf (COTS) components is the proper understanding of their functionality, quality attributes and ways of operation. Traditionally, COTS component vendors provide some of this information in accompanying documentation. However, the documentation is often informal and likely contains ambiguous and inconsistent statements. Even equipped with interface descriptions clearly defining the basic aspects of component use, such as operation signatures and operating platforms, this documentation does not provide a mathematically sound means for addressing the behavioural interoperability issues in component-based system design. In this paper, we propose a formal but user-friendly component specification approach which augments commercial IDLs with the capability of capturing component interoperability requirements. This approach uses unambiguous temporal operators to define sequencing and concurrency constraints between component operation invocations. Accordingly, it enables precise specifications of how a component provides its services and the correct way in which its services should be used.

1 Introduction

A key feature of component-based software engineering is that it allows the use of independently developed components, especially commercial-off-the-shelf (COTS) components, in constructing software systems. Underlying this independence is the common understanding of a component's capability and ways of operation between the component developer and the component user. Component interface definitions facilitate this understanding and serve as contracts between service provider components and service consumer components. A service consumer component will be able to use the services of a provider component based on its interface definition without knowing its implementation details. On the other hand, the service provider component can be implemented based on its interface definition without knowing the potential users or consumers. As such, component interface definitions play a vital role in ensuring the compatibility between the components of a composite system [7].

Commercial interface definition languages such as CORBA IDL primarily address the signature aspects of software component interfaces, *i.e.* the names, parameters and data types of the provided operations. They do not provide support for capturing the

X. Franch and D. Port (Eds.): ICCBSS 2005, LNCS 3412, pp. 54–64, 2005.

semantic or behavioural aspects of a component, including its usage, capabilities and interaction behaviour. This often poses significant problems in enforcing behavioural interoperability between components when designing component-based systems, especially COTS-based systems. That is, incorrect assumptions about the services of components often lead to incorrect usage, and therefore system failure.

Informal documentation usually accompanies the interface definition to provide supplementary information about component services and their usage. However, informal documentation is often ambiguous and sometimes contains inconsistency. This leads to difficulties in properly understanding and deploying COTS components, automating the component selection process, and developing CASE tools for automated system analysis.

To provide a sound support for component interoperability, richer and unambiguous interface descriptions are required. In addition to operation signatures, they should include service semantics, service qualities and service usage protocols [8]. In particular, the usage protocols describe the rules that govern the component interactions, including the order in which a component's operations are to be invoked so as to facilitate the proper use of the component's services. The specification of these protocols is the focus of this paper.

A body of work has been proposed to explicitly and precisely describe component interaction protocols, including [1, 2, 3, 4, 5, 8, 9, 16, 17, 18]. Most of these approaches employ formalisms with a strong mathematical flavour. This limits their use among software engineers or component developers who usually do not have the required background.

In this paper, we extend our previous work in [8, 9] and present a specification approach to component interoperability requirements. The approach builds on a formal foundation but employs a user-friendly language as the front-end. The component interaction protocol is specified in the form of constraints, using a set of intuitive temporal operators. Each constraint states a sequencing or concurrency relationship between operation invocations, representing a partial view of the protocol on the invocations. As such, this approach allows incremental specification of the interaction protocol. It also supports the run-time validation of component interactions against each individual constraint.

The remainder of this paper is organized as follows. section 2 motivates our work. section 3 presents our specification approach to component interaction. Then, section 4 discusses some relevant issues and ways to address them. This is followed by a presentation of the related work in section 5. Finally, section 6 contains the conclusions and future work.

2 Motivation

In this section, we present an example to highlight the need for the precise specification of component interaction protocols. In the subsequent sections, we shall use it to illustrate our approach. This example is an auctioneer component, drawn and adapted from the distributed auction system in [4]. The auctioneer communicates with a number of sellers and bidders. It is able to accept registrations from the bidders, handle auction requests

```
interface Auctioneer {
  void register(in Bidder b);
  void unregister(in Bidder b);
  long sell(in string itemDesc, in float minPrice, in float maxPrice);
}
```

Fig. 1. An auctioneer IDL definition

from the sellers, set up and hold auctions upon request. The CORBA IDL definition for the auctioneer is shown in Fig. 1, where an invocation to *sell* represents a selling/auction request and will return a reference number to the corresponding auction.

From this figure, one can hardly know what operations the user (in this case, sellers and bidders) should provide in order to properly use the auction services. Therefore, as widely recognised in the literature, the explicit declaration of required operations is also needed. For example, the auctioneer requires each bidder to provide three operations for bidding inquiry, settlement notification and announcement. It also requires each seller to provide an operation for notifying the auction outcome. Furthermore, the auctioneer communicates with sellers and bidders through two sets of operations. It is thus conceptually simpler to introduce local scopes for them in the interface definition. We call them *ports*, *e.g.* *A2B* for bidders and *A2S* for sellers. Fig. 2 shows the extended interface definition for the auctioneer with required operations and ports.

```
interface Auctioneer {
  port A2B {
    provides
      void register(in Bidder b);
      void unregister(in Bidder b);
    requires
      boolean wannaBid(in long refNo, in string itemDesc, in float price);
      void youGotIt(in long refNo, in float price);
      void itemSold(in long refNo);
  }
  port A2S {
    provides
      long sell(in string itemDesc, in float minPrice, in float maxPrice);
    requires
      void notify(in long refNo, in boolean isSold, in float finalPrice);
  }
}
```

Fig. 2. An auctioneer interface definition with ports and required operations

Even with the above enhancement, the interface definition as shown in Fig. 2 still cannot convey the semantic information about the auctioneer component.In order for the system designer to deploy this component properly, additional information, *e.g.* its interoperability requirements, has to be sought. This may describe how the component provides its services, how the provided services can be utilised, and what are the obligations of the clients in using the services. For example, does a bidder need to register before the auctioneer can query its interest in an auction? Can the auctioneer conduct multiple auctions at the same time? Does the auctioneer assume a "request-and-wait" policy for each seller? Will the auctioneer always notify the seller of the outcome of each auction? What is the relation between selling requests and bidding inquiries?

Without clear answers to the above questions, the system designer using the component may need to make certain assumptions. False assumptions will eventually lead to malfunction of the system or even system failure. For instance, an auction system may run into deadlock if sellers assume that the auctioneer always notifies them of the auction outcome, while in fact the auctioneer's implementation only notifies successful auctions.

Usually, informal documentation is attached with components to help resolve such problems. However, this is not satisfactory due to the ambiguity and inconsistency that is often associated with such documentation. One can hardly be sure that the component implementation actually behaves as the documentation describes [13]. Also, it is difficult or sometimes impossible to utilise the documentation for tool-supported automated system analysis. This highlights the need to devise sound principles and techniques for the component developer to explicitly and precisely specify the interoperability requirements of components, so as to assist the system designer in using the provided services in an appropriate manner as well as enforcing the interoperability of components in the system.

3 Extending Interface Specifications with Interaction Constraints

In this section, we present an approach to addressing the problems identified above. We extend the interface specification with protocol information which describes the rules governing the interaction of a component with others and accordingly captures its behavioural interoperability requirements. In particular, the protocol specifies the temporal or sequencing constraints between operation invocations[1]. Such constraints are called *interaction constraints* in this paper.

The main techniques we propose to specify interaction constraints are as follows:

- Assume that by default a component can engage in any interaction scenario. That is, it can concurrently accept any operation invocation and invoke any operation at any time. This is to avoid unnecessary constraints on the nature of components.
- Employ intuitive temporal operators to define interaction constraints, each of which represents a partial view on the component's interaction rules. This helps separate concerns and introduces a natural way of thinking for the user.

[1] For simplicity, we do not consider asynchronous message passing or event notifications here. Details about this can be found in [11].

- Make use of operation parameters and return values in defining interaction constraints and thus gain more expressiveness than many other approaches such as [9, 17, 18].
- Distinguish the beginning (or call event) of an operation invocation from its termination (or return event), and then use interleavings of these events to model the nesting and concurrency between operation invocations. Compared with existing approaches such as [9, 17] which consider operation invocations to be atomic units of control, this distinction leads to more accurate specifications of the relative sequencing between operation invocations.

In the following, we first illustrate with the auctioneer component our specification approach to interaction constraints in section 3.1. We then present the underlying semantic basis in section 3.2, and demonstrate how the overall component protocol can be derived from individual interaction constraints in section 3.3.

3.1 Specifying Interaction Constraints

In this section, we study three example interaction constraints of the auctioneer. First, the auctioneer can only query registered bidders for their interests in a particular auction. In other words, the $wannaBid$ invocations to any given bidder must occur between its registration and unregistration. Second, to avoid confusion, the reference number has to be unique for each auction. Third, a bidding inquiry always results from a selling request. That is, the auctioneer cannot autonomously set up auctions without being requested.

These constraints are sequentially specified in Fig. 3 using temporal operators. The operators will be elaborated in the next section. As shown, an operation can be customized with a partial evaluation of the parameters and the return result, for example $sell(*, *, *, refNo)$. Such a customization specifies a group of related operation invocations and later named an *invocation template*. For descriptive convenience, we append the return value, if any, to the parameter list. A name in the parameter list represents that the constraint *concerns* the value of the corresponding parameter or return result, while the symbol "$*$" represents the otherwise. One may consider such a name represents a local variable in the constraint, which ranges over the domain of the corresponding parameter/result type. For the sake of brevity, we refer to an operation with only $*$ in its parameter list by its name. For instance, we write $wannaBid$ for $wannaBid(*, *, *, *)$.

As each of the example constraints applies to a different set of neighbouring components, they are declared in Fig. 3 at three different levels: *peer-level*, *port-level*, and *component-level*. A peer-level constraint is to constrain the interactions with a particular neighbour. For example, constraint (1) applies to every individual bidder, a neighbour communicating with the auctioneer via port $A2B$. It is thus declared at the peer level in this port. For a given bidder, this constraint ensures the relative sequencing among $register$, $wannaBid$ and $unregister$, regardless of their parameter values. Note that $wannaBid$ may be invoked several times between the other two operations. Further, a port-level constraint concerns all neighbours interacting via a specific port. For instance, constraint (2) concerns the interactions with all the sellers, and is thus associated with port $A2S$. In essence, this constraint claims that, for any used auction reference number, a *sell* invocation concerning it occurs only once. In other words, such a number

interface $Auctioneer$ {
  port $A2B$ {
    ...
    peer-constraint: $wannaBid$ between $register$ and $unregister$; (1)
  }
  port $A2S$ {
    ...
    constraint: once $sell(*, *, *, refNo)$; (2)
  }
  constraint: $wannaBid(refNo, *, *)$ causedby $sell(*, *, *, refNo)$; (3)
}

Fig. 3. An Auctioneer Interface Definition with Interaction Constraints

is returned once by $sell$. In addition, a component-level constraint concerns about the neighbours communicating via multiple ports. For example, constraint (3) relates the operation invocations in two ports and is thus placed at the component level. It indicates that any $wannaBid$ inquiry about an auction $refNo$ must have its cause, *i.e.* a selling request acknowledged with $refNo$.

The above constraints present a partial set of rules governing the interaction of the auctioneer. It is, however, easy to add more constraints so as to make its interaction behaviour more predictable. For instance, due to its default chaotic/omnipotent behaviour as we assumed previously, the auctioneer so far is able to conduct multiple auctions at the same time with respect to each seller. That is, it does not assume a "request-and-wait" protocol for each seller. To enforce such a protocol, one can add a peer-level constraint at port $A2S$, saying that invocations to $sell$ and $notify$ happen alternately. One can also add a constraint requiring that a selling request $sell$ associated with $refNo$ eventually lead to a notification with $refNo$ (before the component terminates). For the sake of brevity, the details about how to state these constraints are omitted here. Interested readers are referred to [11].

From the above, one can see that the addition of an interaction constraint involves two key steps: determine the appropriate level and specify the relationships using a suitable temporal operator. With the ability to easily add or remove constraints, the component developer is given the freedom to determine the extent to which the component's interaction logic is made available to the user (or system designer) in order to facilitate its proper use while protecting its proprietary implementation techniques. Also, the developer can make use of the protocol specification as a communication tool to facilitate the component development.

3.2 The Semantic Basis

We have informally presented our interface specification approach using the auctioneer example and described what each example interaction constraint specification means. In this section, we present a semantic basis for this approach, clarifying the basic concepts such as invocation templates and temporal operators. This semantic basis will be utilised in section 3.3 to give a semantics to each constraint specification and the overall component protocol.

Invocation Templates. Invocation templates are defined to capture the key constituents of operation invocations and provide a grouping mechanism for related invocations. They are also defined to facilitate the specification of the operation parameters and return result that have a great impact on the interaction of a component. One may consider an invocation template defines a type of operation invocations.

As noted earlier, an invocation template includes an operation and a partial evaluation to its parameters and return result. Since generally an operation parameter may be of both input and output types, we associate two parameter evaluation functions to an invocation template. Additionally, in a system, components communicate and collaborate to achieve the overall functionality of the system. This implies that the interaction of a component depends on not only its internal logic but also its neighbouring components. Therefore, in defining invocation templates, we also need to consider the identities of its neighbours. In summary, for a given component, say "this", we define an *invocation template (IT)* as a quadruple:

$$\langle N, op, f_i, f_o \rangle$$

where N is a set of neighbouring components of this, *op* is an operation either provided or required by this, f_i and f_o are (possibly partial) input and output parameter evaluation functions of *op*, respectively. More specifically, f_i assigns values to some input parameters of *op*. Parameters not constrained by f_i may take arbitrary values. The same applies to f_o except that f_o assigns values to some output parameters of *op*, which may include the return result.

In essence, an IT defines a set of call and return events for an operation. A call event of an IT is a call event of *op* from/to a neighbour in N with the input parameters actualised by f_i. Similarly, a return event of an IT is a return event of *op* from/to a neighbour in N with the input and output parameters actualised by f_i and f_o, respectively.

Taking into account the level at which they are declared, it is straightforward to interpret interaction constraint specifications as in Fig. 3 in terms of ITs. For instance, $sell(*, *, *, refNo)$ in constraint (2) corresponds to an IT, $\langle S, sell, \emptyset, f_o \rangle$, such that S is the set of sellers in the system and $f_o = \{\text{"return"} \mapsto refNo\}$. Here we let keyword "return" represent the return result.

Temporal Operators. Temporal operators are defined to describe recurring patterns of temporal or sequencing relationships between call and return events of operation invocations. For the sake of space, we shall only define the three temporal operators used in the auctioneer example, *i.e.* once, causedby and between. Other temporal operators, however, can be found in [11].

Given an IT it, constraint statement "once it" requires that the return events associated with it occur at most once. This implies that the call event of it occur at most once. This statement is often used to ensure the uniqueness of some identifier, *e.g.* the auction reference number $refNo$ in the auctioneer. The event sequences acceptable by the constraint are depicted by the labelled transition system (LTS) in Fig. 4, where grey circles represent states, the circle pointed to by an arrow with no source represents the initial state, and arcs between states represent transitions. The LTS transits between states when any event in a labelling set of a transition occurs. There, C stands for the set of call events of it, R the set of return events of it, and O the set of all the other events.

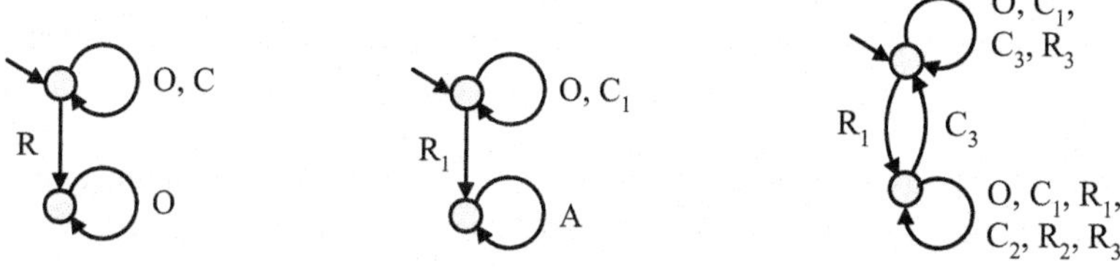

Fig. 4. once it **Fig. 5.** it_2 causedby it_1 **Fig. 6.** it_2 between it_1 and it_3

As shown, any event occurrence from C when the LTS is at the lower state results in a violation to this constraint.

Given two ITs it_1 and it_2, constraint statement "it_2 causedby it_1" indicates the causality between a return event in it_1 and a call event in it_2. In other words, a call event in it_2 cannot occur before an occurrence of any return event in it_1. The acceptable event sequences are depicted by the LTS in Fig. 5, where C_1, R_1, O are as above and A is the set of all events. As shown, any event occurrence from C_2 and R_2 when the LTS is at the upper state is a violation to this constraint.

Given ITs it_1, it_2 and it_3, constraint statement "it_2 between it_1 and it_3" restricts the possibility of event occurrences from it_2 relative to it_1 and it_3, where it_1 is the "on" switch and it_3 is the "off" switch. More specifically, any occurrence of call/return events of it_2 is possible only when a return event in it_1 has occurred but any call event in it_3 has not yet occurred afterwards. The acceptable event sequences are described by Fig. 6, where any event occurrence from C_2 and R_2 is prohibited at the upper state.

3.3 Formalising Interaction Constraints

As noted earlier, interaction constraints are declared at three levels depending on the group of neighbours under consideration. In formalising them, we need to take their levels into account. Furthermore, we stated that each interaction constraint represents a partial view on the component's interaction rules. It is thus important to be able to derive the overall component protocol from individual interaction constraints. In this work, we interpret interaction constraints as predicates and the overall protocol as their conjunction.

Take the auctioneer as an example. For a given system, let S be the set of sellers and B the set of bidders, then the predicates corresponding to the constraints and the overall protocol are shown in Fig. 7.

During the formalisation, constraints at different levels are handled differently. In particular, a peel-level constraint applies to each communicating peer. Hence all the

$$
\begin{aligned}
&(\forall b \in B, \langle\{b\}, wannaBid, \emptyset, \emptyset\rangle \text{ between } \langle\{b\}, register, \emptyset, \emptyset\rangle && (1)\\
&\qquad\qquad \text{and } \langle\{b\}, unregister, \emptyset, \emptyset\rangle)\\
&\wedge (\forall refNo \in \text{long}, \text{once } \langle S, sell, \emptyset, \{\text{"return"} \mapsto refNo\}\rangle) && (2)\\
&\wedge (\forall refNo \in \text{long}, \langle B, wannaBid, \{\text{"refNo"} \mapsto refNo\}, \emptyset\rangle && (3)\\
&\qquad\qquad \text{causedby } \langle S, sell, \emptyset, \{\text{"return"} \mapsto refNo\}\rangle)
\end{aligned}
$$

Fig. 7. The Component Protocol for the Auctioneer

corresponding invocation templates will involve the same neighbouring component which in turn ranges over all neighbours communicating through the associated port. For example, constraint (1) iteratively applies to every individual bidder with all its ITs involving the same bidder.

In contrast, a port-level constraint applies to all neighbours communicating via a port and accordingly contains invocation templates with each involving a set of all these neighbours. For example, in constraint (2), the whole set of sellers S is associated with $sell$. Also, the auction reference number $refNo$ is universally qualified over the long integer domain. This means that this constraint must hold for any reference number. This rule generally applies to every parameter variable involved in a constraint.

For a component-level constraint, each of its invocation templates needs to contain all neighbours using or providing the operation. For instance, in constraint (3), the $wannaBid$ IT now includes the set of bidder B and the $sell$ IT includes the set of sellers S.

The overall protocol of a component is obtained by combining all its interaction constraints. Logically, it is the conjunction of all predicates representing the constraints. Hence the three constraints for the auctioneer join together to form its protocol. Any additional constraint will become another conjunct in the protocol. This implies that a violation to any constituent constraint will yield a violation to the protocol.

4 Discussion

As noted earlier, an interaction constraint represents a partial view on the interaction behaviour of a component. A set of constraints collectively infer a complete view on the interaction. This conforms well to the usual process of understanding, that is, comprehending the whole from the parts.

On the other hand, we need to make sure that the collective inference produces a consistent view of the component interaction. This is an issue of detecting and eliminating potential conflicts between interaction constraints. A simple solution is to reason about the conjunction of the corresponding predicates and detect the negative outcome. A more efficient solution would analyse only relevant constraints at each step. As the semantics of our temporal operators is defined in terms of labelled transition systems, we will need to build such transition systems for each constraint and compute the language intersection of the transition systems for all or relevant constraints. An empty intersection implies the existence of conflicting constraints.

A similar approach can be applied to detect constraint conflicts between components and ensure their interoperability when designing a system. A hurdle for applying such reasoning is that operation parameters often range over infinite or very large domains. Accordingly, the language automata for constraints become too large to handle. The techniques for alleviating such a problem, *e.g.* data abstraction, are the focus of our ongoing research.

Complementary to such design time reasoning is the ability to validate at runtime the interaction constraints of each component for ensuring the system interoperability. Basically, an automated tool is needed to intercept messages received or sent by components and check their sequencing relationships against the predefined interaction constraints.

When a constraint violation is detected, the tool then issues an error message to the user or executes error recovery operations. Our preliminary investigations on this issue have been reported in [9].

5 Related Work

Our work builds on the previous work in [8, 9] and extends it with the ability to capture complex sequencing relationships between operation invocations, *e.g.* parameter value correspondence, invocation nesting and concurrency.

There have been a number of other efforts in introducing protocol information into component interface definitions, *e.g.* [1, 2, 3, 4, 5, 16, 17, 18]. Most of them require that the user have an expertise or sound knowledge in formal languages, *e.g.* finite state machines (FSMs) [5, 17, 18], regular expressions [16], process algebra [1, 4], Petri nets [2], or description logics [3]. On the contrary, our specification approach assumes little of such knowledge from the user. In particular, our approach differs from [5, 17, 18] in that these approaches assume atomic executions of operation invocations, which limits their ability to capture the relationships between nested or concurrent invocations; it differs from [1, 4, 16] in its ability to support incremental protocol specification and runtime validation of partial interaction protocols [9]; it differs from [2] in its ability to hide the internal semantics of components from their external behaviour. A more extensive comparison with these approaches can be found in [9].

Also related to our work is the work based on Design by Contract [14]. Examples include [6, 12, 15]. The semantic information of components (or classes) are specified in terms of contracts, which cover the internal consistency conditions (or invariants) and the pre- and post-conditions of operations. However, the specification is usually tied with a particular implementation language such as Eiffel or Java and contracts are interleaved with source code [13].

6 Conclusion

The proper use of software components in a distributed system is critical to the correct functioning of the system. This is especially the case when COTS components are used. To facilitate their proper use, unambiguous specifications of interaction protocols of the components are needed.

In this paper, we have presented an approach to the protocol specification. It has a formal semantic basis and a user-friendly front-end. It employs intuitive temporal operators and promotes an incremental means to capture, at a sufficient level of abstraction, component interoperability requirements in terms of interaction constraints. These constraints collectively describe how components provide their services, what is required for such provision, and how the client components are supposed to use these services. Based on this information, a better understanding of software components can be achieved and the component interoperability in a system can be ensured either by design time reasoning or runtime validation.

Currently, we are investigating the development of tool support for automatic *consistency checking* of component interaction constraints as well as design-time *interop-*

erability checking. We are also extending a validation tool called RIDLMON [9] for validating runtime inter-component communications against the components' interaction constraints.

References

1. R. Allen and D. Garlan. A formal basis for architectural connection. *ACM Transactions on Software Engineering and Methodology*, 6(3):213–249, July 1997.
2. R. Bastide, O. Sy, and P. Palanque. Formal specification and prototyping of CORBA systems. In *Proc. 13th European Conference on Object-Oriented Programming (ECOOP)*, pages 474–494, 1999.
3. A. Borgida and P. Devanbu. Adding more "DL" to IDL: Towards more knowledgeable component inter-operability. In *Proc. 21th Int'l Conference on Software Engineering (ICSE)*, pages 378–387, 1999.
4. C. Canal, E. Pimentel, J.M. Troya, and A. Vallecillo. Extending CORBA interfaces with protocols. *The Computer Journal*, 44(5):448–462, October 2001.
5. I Cho. A framework for the specification and testing of the interoperation aspect of components. In *[10]*, pages 53–64.
6. C. Cicalese and S. Rotenstreich. Behavioral specification of distributed software component interfaces. *IEEE Computer*, pages 46–53, July 1999.
7. D. Garlan, R. Allen, and J. Ockerbloom. Architectural mismatch — why it's hard to build systems out of existing parts. In *Proc. 17th Int'l Conference on Software Engineering (ICSE)*, pages 179–185, 1995.
8. J. Han. A comprehensive interface definition framework for software components. In *Proc. Asia-Pacific Software Engineering Conference (APSEC)*, pages 110–117, 1998.
9. J. Han and K.K. Ker. Ensuring compatible interactions within component-based software systems. In *Proc. Asia-Pacific Software Engineering Conference (APSEC)*, pages 436–445, 2003.
10. J. Hernández, A. Vallecillo, and J. Troya, editors. *Proc.* ECOOP Workshop on Object Interoperability, 2000.
11. Y. Jin and J. Han. PEIDL: An interaction protocol specification language for software components. Technical Report SUTIT-TR2004.02/SUT.CeCSES-TR002, Centre for Component Software and Enterprise Systems, Swinburne University of Technology, June 2004. *http://www.it.swin.edu.au/centres/cecses/trs/2004/SUT.CeCSES-TR002.pdf*.
12. R. Kramer. iContract — the Java Design by Contract tool. In *Proc. TOOLS*, 1998.
13. R. McKegney and T. Shepard. Techniques for embedding executable specifications in software component interfaces. In *Proc. Int'l Conference on COTS-based Software Systems (ICCBSS)*, LNCS 2193, pages 143–156, 2003.
14. B. Meyer. *Object-Oriented Software Construction*. 1988.
15. B. Meyer. *Eiffel: the Language*. Prentice Hall, 1992.
16. F. Plasil and W. Visnovsky. Behaviour protocols for software components. *IEEE Transactions on Software Engineering*, 28(11):1056–1076, November 2002.
17. R.H. Reussner. An enhanced model for component interfaces to support automatic and dynamic adaption. In *[10]*, pages 33–42.
18. D.M. Yellin and R.E. Strom. Protocol specifications and component adaptors. *ACM Transactions on Programming Languages and Systems*, 19(2):292–333, March 1997.

Resolving COTS System Assessment Clashes

Daniel Port[1], Haruka Nakao[2], Hideki Nomoto[2], Hitoshi Mamiya[2], and Masafumi Katahira[3]

[1] University of Hawaii at Manoa, College of Business Administration, Department of Information Technology Management, Honolulu, Hawaii, USA
dport@hwaii.edu
[2] Japan Manned Space Systems Corporation, Tsukuba, Japan
{haruka, nomo, mamuya}@jamss.co.jp
[3] Japan Aerospace Exploration Agency, Tsukuba, Japan
katahira@computer.org

Abstract. COTS significantly complicates the IV&V process. The necessarily pessimistic culture of IV&V has a perspective on which COTS assessment attributes and techniques are relevant that differs greatly from developer's typically optimistic, success-oriented perspective. There is no basis to assume that the COTS assessments made by developers will ultimately be consistent with IV&V COTS assessments. The result frequently results in a "lose-lose" situation where either large re-work costs are incurred to replace existing COTS with IV&V approved COTS, or higher risk and uncertainty must be tolerated (from the IV&V perspective) to continue with the COTS the developers chose. This work seeks to remedy this "culture clash" of COTS assessment perspectives by integrating IV&V and developers system level COTS assessments that provides a result that is both consistent and cost-effective.

1 Introduction

Exploding costs and shrinking budgets have necessitated the use of COTS (Commercial Off The Shelf products) in the development of new safety critical systems such as satellites and spacecraft ground system [1]. Enthusiasm for COTS use has faded after recent high-profile space-mission failures underscored the need for highly reliable software in safety critical systems [1]. COTS and safety has become a critical issue [2, 3] and along with it the challenges of performing Independent Verification and validation (IV&V) on COTS based systems [4]. Remarkably, many of these challenges have yet to be addressed [1].

In the development of satellite and ground control systems at the Japan Aerospace Exploration Association (JAXA) we have observed that the traditional IV&V approach for safety critical systems has not been effective when these systems critically rely on COTS. In particular, we have had trouble selecting a mutually acceptable (from the developers and IV&V risk perspectives) COTS system architecture among numerous architecture options. Our selections have been beset with late-term COTS "black box" effects that have run IV&V efforts aground. Efforts to increase or make our COTS assessment more rigorous have had little impact.

X. Franch and D. Port (Eds.): ICCBSS 2005, LNCS 3412, pp. 65–76, 2005.

Restricting developers to "pre-approved" COTS has not proven an effective remedy. As a result, the cost-effective IV&V of COTS based systems has become a major problem.

A contributor to this problem has been traced to *contradictory developer and IV&V COTS system assessment results*. When such a misalignment is present, it is difficult to judge which assessment results should be used, the developers or IV&V? In our experience, choosing one over the other has resulted in long-term problems. In this paper we will elaborate on the problem of developer and IV&V COTS system assessment conflicts with an actual case study from a COTS based space system currently under development at JAXA. This case study will also present a new approach to resolving this conflict to aid in making strategic risk reducing choices of COTS systems architecture options.

2 COTS System Assessments: Different Perspectives, Different Results

Of the many challenges of COTS and IV&V, this paper considers the particularly frustrating challenge of conflicting developer and IV&V COTS system assessment results. Here we differentiate "COTS system assessment" from "COTS assessment" in that the assessment is of the system that uses the COTS rather than for individual COTS products. A phenomenon we have observed in this is an unintentional "one hand doesn't know what the other hand is doing" problem. On one hand, a developer's assessment perspective is necessarily *optimistic* and success-oriented. The attributes developers are concerned with and the techniques they might use to assess such attributes are chosen to reduce overall *risk with respect to project development* cost, schedule, and the satisfaction of quality requirements. That is, potential losses that may occur in the *development* of the system. On the other hand, the IV&V perspective is necessarily *pessimistic*. A system is assumed to have risky defects until there is evidence that it does not. The attributes and techniques chosen by IV&V are to mitigate a systems' overall *deployment risk* (i.e. potential losses incurred during the operation of the system).

Both the IV&V and the systems developers COTS assessments must be done well in advance of system implementation in order to identify and avoid potentially critical deployment risks before committing to a particular COTS-based architecture. Failure to do so may result in costly re-work or unacceptable system quality or risk. In this regard, it is ideal if IV&V assessments are performed simultaneously with the developers assessments. However, an IV&V assessment cannot be done outside the context of the system development due to the risk of developers committing too early to COTS products that may be inappropriate, mismatched, or too risky for use within a system.

One suggested approach to this problem is to simply restrict developers to utilize only "IV&V pre-approved" COTS products. Unfortunately, this approach cannot provide the system-specific risk assurance required by rigorous IV&V (e.g. safety critical). Even without this consideration, this approach is generally infeasible as IV&V teams cannot provide a sufficiently large and diverse collection of "approved" COTS products for developers to utilize in the face of rapidly evolving COTS products and COTS marketplace. For very good reasons, developers will desire to have as many COTS options as possible in order to satisfy their cost, schedule, and quality requirements. Frequently developers desire to make use of the newest, most powerful, most comprehensive and cost-effective COTS products. Limiting their choices may actually **increase** overall risk as developers try to work around limitations (either perceived or real) in their COTS options.

Within this context, what remains is to have both developers and IV&V each make their own COTS system assessments. Unfortunately, there is no basis for assuming that the assessments made by the IV&V team (usually done long after the developers COTS choices have been made) will be consistent. Both assessments are vital, and from our experience, inconstant assessments have can result in tangible (but often avoidable) complications and risk. To remedy this, both IV&V and developer COTS system assessments must somehow be integrated to provide a single, consistent and view.

In this paper we elaborate on these concerns and describe our continuing efforts in developing practical approaches to reconciling developer and IV&V COTS system assessments early within the development cycle.

2 Different Perspectives in COTS System Assessments

As discussed previously, developers have a COTS assessment perspective that is optimistic and oriented towards developing a system successfully. When faced with choosing COTS system architectures, developers must assess the risk of system attributes that may adversely affect development cost, schedule, and quality and their ability to satisfy project requirements. IV&V takes a notably different perspective. The concern is to provide assurance that the system will operate as expected and to mitigate risks from the operation of the system (including loss of the system itself). Table 1 provides a selection of COTS system assessment attributes. Both developers and IV&V share concern for many of the same attributes. However the degree to which assessment mitigates risk associated with these attributes may vary considerably. For example, a developer concern for the "Fail Safe" attribute of a system might focus on the existence of fail safe capabilities within COTS candidates. The risk from this perspective might be that the capability does not exist or is insufficient and would have to be custom built. This risk may easily be reduced to negligible if the developer prototypes the desired fail safe capabilities. The IV&V perspective might be more concerned that in some exceptional case, the COTS product may not perform its fail safe as required. Without access to the code for careful analysis (such as with formal methods), even with extensive exception testing, risk due to uncertainty may remain. For example how can it be assured that there will not be a mis-operation of the fail safe capabilities given some unanticipated internal state of the COTS product (it is generally not possible to exhaustively test all possible internal and external states in a complex system)? Table 1 indicates some example developer and IV&V COTS assessment attributes that were used in our Launch Tracking system case study project.

In addition to different choices of assessment attributes, there are differences in choice of techniques used to perform the assessments. There are many assessment techniques that developers and IV&V both make use of, and some that are exclusive to one or the other. Exclusive here means that a technique is used frequently by one, and infrequently or is disallowed (or is deemed infeasible) by the other. For example, "Model Checking" requires significant specialized knowledge and skill and generally is costly and effort intensive. As a result, Model Checking is usually exclusive to IV&V. Different techniques provide different levels of risk reduction with different costs. Developers and IV&V will select which technique will be used to assess a given attribute based on the degree of risk present for that attribute, the potential of the technique to reduce this risk (due to uncertainty), and cost/effort. Table 2 provides some examples of exclusive IV&V and Developer assessment techniques used within the case study.

Table 1. Developer and IV&V Assessment Attributes for Launch Tracking System

IA1:SingleFailure Point	*DA4:Real time performance*
IA2: Requirement Consistency and Completeness	DA5:Development Schedule
IA3: Understandability	DA6:Cost
IA4:Code Quality	DA7:Portability/ Replace
IA5:Message Queue Overflow	DA8:Maintenability
IA6:Realtime performance	DA9:Scalability
IA7:Resouce Utilization	DA10:Testability
DA1:Priority Inversion	DA11:Access to Code
DA2:Code Quality	*DA12:Resource Utilization*
DA3:Message Queue Overflow	DA13:Vender Support

Table 2. Launch Tracking System Assessment Techniques

Technique	**Who**
IT1:Analysis Using Model	IV&V
IT2:API TEST	IV&V
IT3:Model Checking	IV&V
IT4:IV&V code review	IV&V
IT5:Lessons Learned	IV&V
DT1 Test Suites	Developer
DT2:Developer code review	Developer
DT3:Static Analysis of code	Developer
DT4:Estimation	Developer
DT5:Interview Vendor	Developer
DT6:Investigation of past data	Developer
DT7:Test on Emulator	Developer
DT8:Benchmark test	Developer
DT9:Simulation	Developer

3 A Clash of Perspectives

Traditional IV&V is usually predicated on having a fully developed system. The IV&V team performs an assessment to assure the system meets requirements and quality standards (e.g. safety critical). However, waiting until after a system has been implemented is generally too late to take action on IV&V COTS assessment results. This presents a dilemma – either have the developers re-work the system until assurance can be achieved, or "gamble" and ignore the IV&V assessment results. The former may incur unreasonable and unanticipated development costs and unexpected risks in addition to additional IV&V effort to assure the re-worked system. In the latter, the "gamble" may prove to have unacceptable risk levels leading to operational disasters. We have experienced both scenarios and Table 3 summarizes our ongoing challenges with IV&V within some of our COTS based space systems.

Table 3. COTS IV&V Challenges at JAXA

System	Phase	COTS IV&V Problem
G (A)	RDM	Inability to balance COTS, legacy, and development items
G (B)	TI	Over 1,000 bug reports
OBS (A)	TI	Integration test OBS and sensor S/W failed
OBS (B)	A	Incoherent documentation quality
OBS (C)	A	Inability to integrate COTS and legacy

RDM = Requirements Definition and Management

TI = Test and Integration G = Ground Control Syst.

A = Architecting OBS = On Board Software

Some of the factors that contribute to the developer and IV&V COTS system assessment clash problem include:

- A fully developed system may obscure potentially fatal COTS risks such as "dormant code" by making it difficult to access or uncover [5].
- It is difficult to determine potential risks with limited access to system internals.
- If problems within the COTS are found after they are integrated into the system, there is limited means of addressing them within the COTS without introducing collateral risks (e.g. side-effects) and subsequently additional IV&V effort.
- COTS that are intimately integrated within a system or depend on intimately (e.g. proprietary API's, protocols, etc.) are generally not "exchangeable" with other COTS. It is often difficult to find alternative COTS to replace problematic or difficult to validate COTS components.

The above indicates that a traditional IV&V approach to COTS system assessment may result in unacceptably high uncertainty and difficult to mitigate risks. Some have attempted to address the above problems by "pre-assessing" individual COTS products well in advance of system development and then require developers to use only these COTS products. Aside from severely limiting the COTS choices (perhaps to the extent that none are actually deemed suitable for the system under consideration), this approach has also proven risky as it fails to adequately assess the COTS products for the particular system [6, 7]. This may include particular system safety requirements that a general purpose individual COTS product IV&V assessment may not have considered. As noted by Ronald Stroup, FAA Safety & Certification Lead, "An unwise [advance] purchase of a COTS product could doom your program to cost and schedule overruns and more importantly induce safety instability that in all likelihood will never be adequately mitigated."

The only remaining viable option is to have both developers and IV&V perform assessments of the COTS system (i.e. not just the individual COTS products within the system) *prior* to committing to a particular architecture. Given the significantly different developer and IV&V perspectives, a-priori we have no basis to assume that the two assessments will be consistent. In our own experience and through anecdotal interviews with other organizations we have observed that the two assessments frequently are at odds with each other even when both are done before architecture commitments are made. We will show an explicit example of this in the next section's case study.

4 The JAXA Ground System Case Study

We now consider a particular example of developer and IV&V COTS system assessments from a current project at JAXA. For privacy considerations, the description will be general and omits many specific (and are irrelevant for this discussion) details.

Target System Description:

The top left corner of Figure 1 is an illustration of the Launch Tracking system and three COTS options A,B,C. This system calculates data distributed from multiple ground tracking stations and provides operators a real-time display of launch vehicle information. The ground tracking data is collected on Machine 1 then distributed to machines 2,3, and 4 which process the data in to a variety of launch monitoring and control information. This system must be reliable without a single failure point and provide a redundant data processing string. This system must also display the data in real time (50msec network synchronization) with the maximum CPU operating rate to be 30% .

The COTS in question are the operating systems used for all the machines. System A uses HP UNIX for all the machines, System B uses HP UNIX on all but the main data collection machine 1 which uses TimeSys, and system C uses all TimeSys. The developers prefer System A since they are very experienced with HP-UNIX and have a large amount of well-tested code that can be reused for the current system. The developers are highly confident that they could develop the system rapidly and inexpensively and that the resulting system will meet all performance reliability requirements. While HP-UNIX has exceptionally good performance, it does not have real-time execution guarantees. To address this, System C replaces HP-UNIX with the real-time operating system Timesys. The IV&V team prefers this option because the execution times can be assured throughout the system. They note that no amount of testing could provide the same level of assurance with HP-UNIX and thus is risky. The developers are concerned about their lack of experience with Timesys (or any real-time OS), increased the cost of the OS, and delay in the implementation of the system as they cannot reuse their existing code base. Furthermore, the execution time for Timesys is over 500ms which exceeds 200ms and 250ms requirements from machine 1 to machines 2 and 1 respectively. To the developers, this system is risky. System B is a compromise making use of Timesys only for the main time critical data collection and distribution machine. In theory, with this system both performance and execution times can be assured but there is additional risk due to the mixing of technologies. Integration of HP-UNIX and Timesys may pose unforeseen problems and challenges and the amount of additional development effort is unclear.

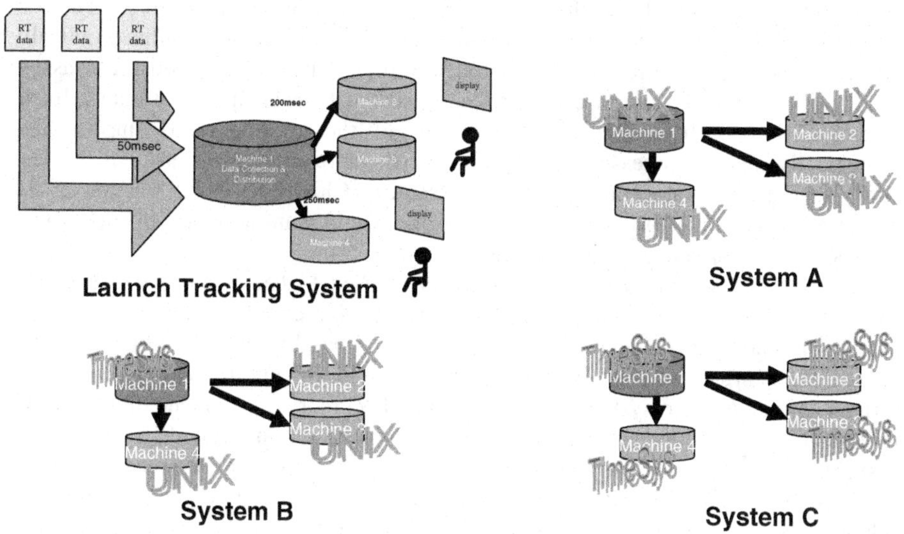

Fig. 1. Launch Tracking System

Table 1 indicates that the IV&V team focuses on 7 attributes while the developers are concerned with 13. This difference illustrates the difference in perspectives (as described in a previous section) between the two groups. There are four attributes (listed in italics) that both are concerned with.

5 Developer and IV&V COTS System Assessments

The developers and IV&V team are not in consensus as to which COTS system architecture to implement for the Launch Tracking system. Even if there was consensus, the developers and IV&V team must still assess carefully which of system choices A, B, and C would be best with respect to their risk considerations. As discussed in a previous section, these assessments must be made before commitment (either deliberate or de-facto) to a particular system architecture is made. In our case study, these assessments have been planned according to the Strategic COTS Assessment method described in [6]. A strategic assessment plan is one that chooses the assessment techniques to use for each particular assessment attribute and the order in which to perform the assessment in such as way that the most risky attributes are assessed first with respect to cost considerations. This is so called "cost-effective" risk assessment where high risk attributes with high assessment costs but low risk reduction potential are prioritized downward proportional to their cost relative to other attributes.

There are two important reasons assessment efforts should be strategically planned. First, it is rarely feasible to expend arbitrarily large amounts of cost (sometimes in terms of effort rather than dollars) to exhaustively assess the risk for all possible attributes using the most effective techniques. As a result, only a fraction of a possible assessment is performed and the limiting factor is usually economic resources (i.e. budget, schedule). The second reason is that assessment strategies can have radically different risk reduction profiles (as illustrated in [6]). For example, choosing to assess attributes in order of "lowest cost" or "least risk" will result in worse than a linear reduction in risk [6]. Accounting for both of the considerations implies that strategically planned assessment will reduce risk more effectively and will be less costly than a non-strategically planned assessment. Clearly if only a fraction of the possible assessment effort is expended then one would want to assess in such a way that the largest risk reductions are achieved first.

For our purposes the assessments have been used to help choose which COTS architecture option is expected to be less risky. In this case it is important that the assessments are performed in a consistent and comparable manner without bias or uncontrolled influences. For example it would not be reliable to compare a careful, formal assessment for system A to an informal, cursory assessment of system C. Performing strategic assessments for all three system options provide a meaningful basis of comparison. Although some might argue that cost-effectiveness is not the best basis for comparison, it has been shown in [6] that risk based cost-effectiveness achieves the "ideal" risk-reduction profile of a "highest risk first" approach (not that they are equal, but they approximately reduce the risk at the same rates). Table 4 shows the particular developer and IV&V strategic assessments planned for systems A,B,C with respect to the desired attributes listed in Table 1 and available techniques listed in Table 2.

In Figure 2 we see the expected results of the assessments. Analysis the developers assessments in figure 2a indicates that if arbitrarily large effort is expended then the risk for systems B or C would be about tied for lowest. However, the rate of risk reduction is clearly greater for system A and the ultimate risk level is not significantly higher than for systems B and C. The developers believe that it is risky to assume that the full assessment will be performed for all the systems and that the outcomes of these assessments will turn out exactly as hoped. Based on this perspective, system A presents the overall lowest risk from their perspectives. The IV&V assessment expectations in Figure 2b tell a different story. System B has a considerably better risk reduction profile. The ultimate expected risk level is significantly lower and even if only half the assessment effort is made, clearly system B has lower risk than system A. The result concluded by the IV&V team is that system B provides the lowest overall risk.

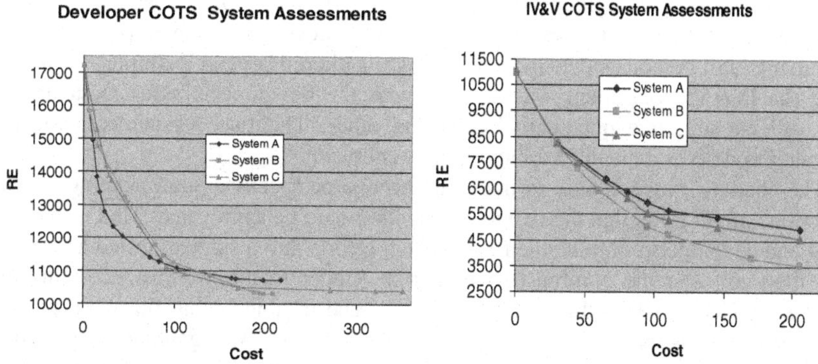

Fig. 2. (a) Developer Assessment Risk Reduction (b) IV&V Assessment Risk Reduction

Here we see the fundamental clash of perspectives problem. Simultaneous, pre-architecture commitment assessments cannot resolve this clash. Both assessments are valid and important to the success of the system. The next section will discuss a method for integrating the assessments to provide a meaningful and consistent view of lowest overall project and system risk.

Table 4. Developer and IV&V Strategic Assessments for Systems A,B,C

	Sys-A Dev		Sys-B Dev		Sys-B Dev		Sys-A IV&V		Sys-B IV&V		Sys-B IV&V	
Step	A_i	T_i	A_i	T_i	A_i	T_i	A_i	T_i	A_i	T_i	A_i	T_i
T_1	DA12	DT7	DA12	DT4	DA12	DT1	IA3	IT1	IA3	IT1	IA3	IT1
T_2	DA5	DT4	DA10	DT4	DA5	DT4	IA1	IT4	IA6	IT5	IA6	IT5
T_3	DA6	DT5	DA4	DT1	DA4	DT1	IA6	IT5	IA5	IT5	IA1	IT4
T_4	DA10	DT9	DA2	DT3	DA6	DT5	IA5	IT5	IA1	IT4	IA5	IT5
T_5	DA2	DT1	DA6	DT5	DA10	DT4	IA2	IT5	IA2	IT5	IA2	IT5
T_6	DA4	DT1	DA3	DT8	DA2	DT3	IA4	IT4	IA7	IT2	IA4	IT4
T_7	DA3	DT8	DA13	DT5	DA3	DT8	IA7	IT2	IA4	IT4	IA7	IT2
T_8	DA7	DT5	DA11	DT5	DA11	DT5						
T_9	DA13	DT6	DA5	DT6	DA13	DT5						
T_10	DA1	DT7	DA1	DT1	DA1	DT7						
T_11	DA8	DT4	DA9	DT4	DA9	DT9						
T_12	DA9	DT8	DA8	DT4	DA8	DT6						
T_13	DA11	DT6	DA7	DT5	DA7	DT8						

6 Integrating Developer and IV&V COTS Assessments

In the previous section we saw that in our case study the developers assessment clashed with the IV&V assessment in regards to lowest risk choice of COTS system architecture. In this particular case the assessments were not obviously contradictory. They were, however, ambiguous and not clearly compatible. That is, the developers did not have compelling rationale to choose system B over system A given the IV&V

teams assessments. Through anecdotal interviews for other projects, we found that our basic premise holds – that there is no basis for believing that developer and IV&V assessments will be consistent. Indeed, we have gathered several examples of projects where the IV&V assessment was at odds with the developer's assessment and the result of choosing one perspective over the other. The two perspectives must be integrated to deliver a meaningful and consistent result.

The challenge here is how to integrate the two perspectives in a meaningful way? At first one might think that the two assessments should be aggregated. That is, have the IV&V and developers combine their assessment efforts into a single, unified assessment effort then consider the combined overall risk. Under many circumstances this may indeed be a viable option, but not in this case. The trouble is that the main point of IV&V is that they provide an independent perspective. An aggregated assessment strategy will remove the "I" from IV&V. For comparison with other approaches, the graph of the aggregation assessment for our case study is shown in Figure 3.

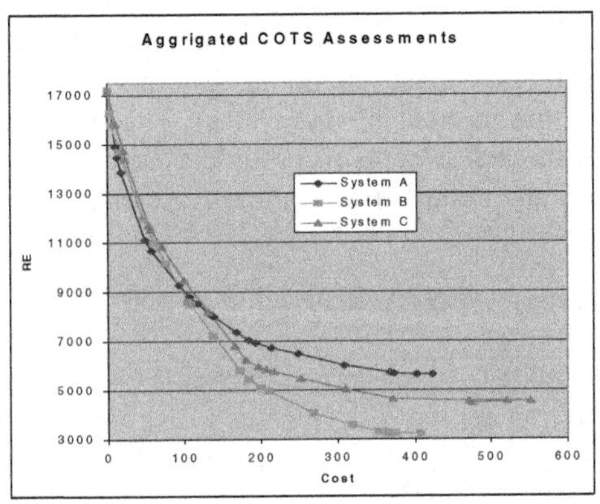

Fig. 3. Aggregation of Assessments

Another approach one might consider is to sum developer and IV&V risk exposures for each particular system. The difficulty with this approach is that assessing a system twice (even in different ways) does not imply the system has actual risk that is the sum of the risk assessments. There will likely be overlap that is difficult to account for. As a result, the risk assessed is often greater than the actual amount of risk present!

Inspired by cooperative game-theory, we propose to integrate the two assessments using what we call the "Max-Min" strategy. Say that the developers have assessment steps DS1,DS2,DS3,…,DSn and IV&V have steps IS1, IS2, IS3,…,ISm. Consider the risk reduction profiles generated by min(DSi, ISi) and max(DSi, ISi) i=0…max(n,m). If n>m, use ISm for IS(m+1), …, ISn (and similarly is n<m). The idea for the strategy is that the most pessimistic risk level we might expect given the two perspectives will be approximately the min(DSi, ISi) curve, while the most optimistic will be max(DSi, ISi). The "true" risk level will fall somewhere in between. We note that we use "assessment steps" rather than cost for the Min-Max

curves. While these approximate cost, it is unknown if the assessment steps are actually performed side-by-side. However, it is the end risk values that are of most interest, but the step by step trend also may provide useful information. The Min-Max profiles for system A,B,C are shown in figure 4.

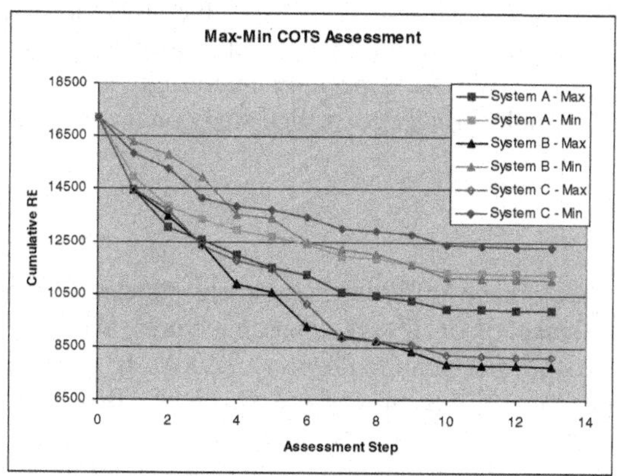

Fig. 4. Max-Min Assessments

The ideal Min-Max assessment profile will have its min curve below all other curves (both min and max). This would imply that the highest risk level expected for that system is smaller than the lowest expected for any of the others and thus has overall lower risk. Another case is when a max profile curve is lower than all others max curves and its min curve is lower than all other min curves. The case where the Max-Min curves are entirely contained within another Max-Min curve is somewhat ambiguous. The Max-Min containing the other curve has the potential for a lower risk level, but it also has the potential for a higher risk level. In this case it is best to try to eliminate the options by pair wise comparison with another option that does not have the same containment issue. If this cannot be done, then the decision must be based on risk tolerance and the relative size and position of the containment relations. If the contained curve's min curve is near the max for the curve that contains it, then this might be the overall lower risk choice. In general, the following test may be used to select an option A over option B:

If (A_max – B_max)(A_min-B_min) > 0 select A
If (A_max – B_max) =0 and (A_min-B_min) > 0 or
(A_max – B_max) > 0 and (A_min-B_min) = 0 then select B

Analysis of the Max-Min curves in Figure 4 indicate that system B is the overall lowest risk option. Option A is out because its max curve is above option B's and it's min curve is about he same as B's. This implies that while option A can do no worse than B, option B has the potential to do much better. Option C is out because its min curve is much higher than option B's while its max curve is about the same. This implies that option C can do no better than option B but may do much worse.

7 Ongoing and Future Research

We have described the phenomenon of developer and IV&V COTS system assessment clashes. We would like to more rigorously document this phenomenon though a number of case studies across different organizations and industries. We further would like to study the effects of using the strategic assessment method for COTS architecture selection. Do the theoretically lower risk choices actually lead to lower risk in practice? We are especially interested in empirically validating the Max-Min strategy. A multi-project controlled study on this is in the planning stage.

8 Conclusions

Developers and IV&V have different assessment perspectives resulting in possible clashes in the assessment of COTS system architectures. We have observed many real examples of this on projects undertaken at JAXA. It is clear that this must be addressed through some form of early assessment. Both the optimistic, project oriented assessments of developers and the pessimistic, operation oriented assessments of IV&V provide important contributions to the overall COTS system risk management. Choosing one perspective over the other is risky and it is unclear on what a sensible weighting scheme would be. The clash problem cannot be resolved by summing the assessments, aggregating assessments, or by restricting COTS choices (e.g. IV&V pre-approved COTS). A strategy must be used that integrates both developer and IV&V assessments in a meaningful way. The Max-Min strategy provides a means of selecting a COTS system option that lowers overall expected risk with respect to cooperative game theory and presents a viable integrated approach.

References

1. M. Rahmatipour, IV&V of COTS RTOS for Space Flight Project, The 1st NASA OSMA SAS, 2000
2. RTCA Inc., "Final Report for Clarification of DO-178B 'Software Considerations in Airborne Systems and Equipment Certification'," Washington, D.C. RTCA/DO-248B, October 12, 2001.
3. G. Brower, Validation of Commercial Off the Shelf Software, Journal of Validation Technology, 1999
4. R. Kohl, IV&V of COTS Dormant Cord: Challenge and Issues, GSAW, 1999
5. C. Abts, B. Boehm, and E. Bailey Clark, COCOTS: A Software COTS-Based System (CBS) Cost Model, Proceedings, ESCOM, 2001
6. D. Port, S. Chen, Assessing COTS Assessment: How much is enough?, Proceedings, ICCBSS, 2004
7. B. Boehm, Software Risk Management: Principles and Practices, IEEE Software, 1991

COTS Components and DB Interoperability

Radmila Juric and Ljerka Beus-Dukic

Cavendish School of Computer Science, University of Westminster,
115 New Cavendish Street, London W1W 6UW, United Kingdom
R.Juric@wmin.ac.uk, L.Beus-Dukic@wmin.ac.uk

Abstract. The paper addresses the specific issue of interoperability in heterogeneous databases (DBs) and the possible use of COTS components that may alleviate the DB interoperability problem. A component-based software Architectural Style (AS) for interoperable DBs has been used, and an example of its application given, to identify which role the COTS components may play when populating the architecture. We discuss the characteristics of such COTS components and advocate that such COTS components should be developed with a specific component platform in mind, interoperate within a certain context, and adhere to constraints of our AS.

1 Introduction

DB systems have experienced vigorous change in the last decade because of the strong pull of commercial applications and the incessant push of technology and research advances. Heterogeneity and distribution have become main characteristics of DB systems, placing the question of interoperability in the focus of interests in both academia and industry. The increasing complexity of software systems and infrastructures, have pushed forward component-based software engineering practices, aiming to develop software from pre-produced reusable software components. Capitalising on third-party expertise and synthesising component technologies with commercial-of-the-shelf (COTS) components might bring new answers to problems of interoperability when building today's software systems.

This work merges long-term research in the DB interoperability field with component technologies and COTS components. We use a component based AS for interoperable DBs and identify the characteristics of COTS components that may populate the AS and alleviate the DB interoperability problem.

There are many interoperability perspectives in today's software systems, ranging from interoperability across domains and systems, to software architecture composability of components and their interactions. In our definition of DB interoperability [12], interoperable DBs exhibit communication and use of each others' data and functionality, despite their heterogeneities. Hence the works on components' interoperability such as [11], or on interoperability between software systems and system of systems from [14], or on software multi-operability from [23], are not discussed in this paper. Our work is *solution-specific*, i.e. it addresses a specific issue of DB interoperability and the use of COTS components. This is close to works of [33, 22], where

X. Franch and D. Port (Eds.): ICCBSS 2005, LNCS 3412, pp. 77–89, 2005.

COTS are used for addressing heterogeneity and interoperability in GIS and web information systems. Our AS for interoperable DBs fits within the Universal Systems layer for enterprise-wide shared system of the Levels of Information System Interoperability (LISI) model [21]. We also conform to the Seamless Sharing of Information of the structured data interchange degree in the NC3TA Reference Model for Interoperability (NMI) [25].

Tightly coupled with the term interoperability is the concept of integration. Integration is very important in COTS-based systems development and the idea of "focusing on integration to achieve interoperability" is at the core of the COTS-Based Systems Initiative Group tasks [10]. However, integration per se does not always bring interoperation in multiple DBs, because it affects individual DB's autonomy and evolution, and might have an impact on their distribution [12,16]. A technical initiative [6] points out that many heterogeneous systems might be perceived as integrated, but from the perspectives of their individual constituent elements, they actually inter-operate with each other. Consequently, we use both terms carefully and leave discussion on using integration and interoperation interchangeably outside the scope of this paper.

Section 2 comments on related research. Section 3 defines our layered reference model and the building blocks of the AS for interoperable DBs. Section 4 introduces a motivating example, designed as an EJB [28] application. Section 5 outlines characteristics of COTS components that can partially populate our AS. Section 6 gives conclusions and a brief outline of our future work.

2 Related Background

The numerous works related to the semantics of DB interoperability, which have intrigued researchers from the DB community since the early 1990s, range from

(a) migration between various DB systems [29] and
(b) multidatabase and federated architectures [13] to
(c) the mediator paradigm [35] which has culminated in many research projects from the 90s, such as [7], some of its applications on the Internet [26] and their counterparts emerging from industry [31].

Each of these approaches to DB interoperability, and particularly various levels of integration have drawbacks [12,16], and today's trend is to

i. allow the individual DB to evolve naturally within its own environment, and
ii. build/offer services, i.e. to use service-oriented technologies that will provide transparent facilities across different DB systems.

Thus current solutions should move away from known ideas of integration of data/applications, centralisation of data structures, federation architectures and multidatabase languages when addressing the heterogeneity of data centric applications and their interoperability. We have used a layered software architecture as defined in [4] and have proposed a component-based AS for interoperable DBs, given in Fig. 1 and 2, which should allow interoperation amongst multiple DBs and a certain level of evolution and autonomy of individual DBs [12,16]. Our architectural model has been described in terms of its building blocks, where components offer/require services through specified interfaces. We have also contextualised [30] such components in order to ease their implementation and binding complexity [18].

We are not aware of any work involving COTS components and the interoperability of heterogeneous DBs. We chose to comment on two works, which point to COTS components deployment in certain application domains. The work of Lu and Mylopoulus [22] shows how automatic generation of the EJB code from legacy SQL-like queries can address the DB interoperability problem by exploiting the fact that many methods in EJBs can be seen as view definitions of the underlying DBs. Their automation may fit within the components of our AS (e.g. our ***A*** component can be their EJB-SQL mediator). However, their vision of using the EJB technology because "it addresses the object-relational interface" is common but it is not what we would use the same technology for, i.e. the assumption that all legacy systems are to be sheltered by a relational environment is a concern of ours [19]. Their EJB-SQL mediator is a perfect candidate for a COTS component built to fit within the EJB platform that may address one sector of DB interoperability.

Tu et al. [33] also use the EJB technology to address the interoperability of data-centric applications by integrating the COTS GIS components into the J2EE framework and making them J2EE-CA [27] compliant. The J2EE-CA specification is used as a protocol for accessing non-relational data sources. We do not use the J2EE-CA standard when deploying our software architecture: we shift its role towards functionalities implemented in components that comprise our own software AS for interoperable DBs. Our motivating example from Section 4 makes two heterogeneous DBs interoperable by coordinating their services through a J2EE server.

3 Software Architectural Style for Interoperable DBs

3.1 A Layered Reference Model

The five-layered reference architectural model for interoperable DBs in Fig. 1 proposes layering based on how specific/general to our problem each component is.

The *application specific layer* contains components that encapsulate user/application specific code, which may be distinct and not re-usable in, or interoperable with, any other applications. These components manage value added services, such as querying metadata, accessing ontology, or adding user's intervention when resolving heterogeneity problems in multiple DB systems.

The *translation layer* has components responsible for translating the user's request to a targeted DB environment. For example, we may translate a relational SQL query into a set of different joint queries that range from object to XML data retrieval; or we can translate an existing relational schema declaration into class declarations of an object DB. Components from this layer encapsulate a code that can be shared by a family of related applications.

The *domain specific* layer has components responsible for implementing the functionality of users' requests and applying them to domain specific components derived from general-purpose persistent components from the *data source* layer. Components from this layer encapsulate a code that may be used from different places within the same application and by a family of related applications. For example, these components may implement functionality of (a) joining a relational table and XML document for retrieval or (b) executing a family of data definition statements in order to create various data structures or schemas simultaneously across multiple DBs.

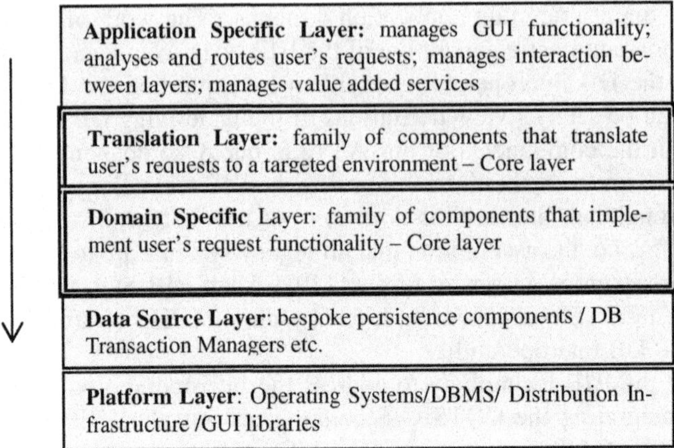

Application Specific Layer: manages GUI functionality; analyses and routes user's requests; manages interaction between layers; manages value added services
Translation Layer: family of components that translate user's requests to a targeted environment – Core layer
Domain Specific Layer: family of components that implement user's request functionality – Core layer
Data Source Layer: bespoke persistence components / DB Transaction Managers etc.
Platform Layer: Operating Systems/DBMS/ Distribution Infrastructure /GUI libraries

Fig. 1. Layered reference model for interoperable DBs

The *data source layer* contains components that provide persistence and programming infrastructure services for general-purpose persistent components. They encapsulate potentially reusable code across many application domains.

The *platform layer* accommodates components that underpin the application, which include operating systems, DB Management Systems, GUI class libraries etc.

3.2 Building Blocks of Our Architectural Style

The building blocks of our AS are given in Fig.2. Component ***A*** (Analyse User's Request) determines:

- The *translation* needs of the user's request (e.g. we might need to translate the request in order to fit it within the targeted DB environment)
- The *functionality* of the user's request (e.g. it could be the *creation* of a new structure or DB element, or *manipulation* of existing DB, or *entering* new data).

The translation is required from components Tr_i only if the user's request is executed outside the environment from which it originates. Translated requests are then routed towards the appropriate D'_i component that implements required functionality. If the received request needs **no** translation, it is routed towards an appropriate D'_i.

Components Tr_i belong to a family of primitive components each of them implementing a different algorithm for translation of user's requests to a targeted DB environment. In other words, each Tr_i component provides different implementations of the same behaviour, where the received request and user's understanding of the problem decide the most suitable implementation. We deal with semantic and schematic heterogeneity in multiple DB systems at the topmost layer: the implementation of component **A** might require user's intervention through value added services, the involvement of metadata, access to possible taxonomies/ontology etc. Our AS resembles mediator architectures, where mediator software modules are placed in between data resources and applications, provide intermediate services in heterogeneous, autonomous, distributed and evolving information systems [35,7]. For discussion on mediation systems we refer reader to our earlier works [16,17,18].

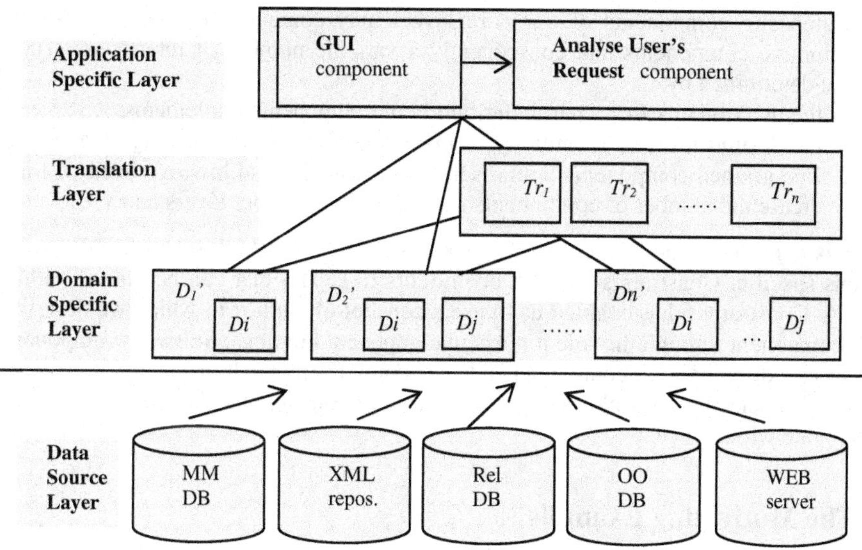

Fig. 2. Architectural style building blocks

Components D_i' belong to a family of D_i' components where each D_i' component may encapsulate any combination of D_i components. Each primitive D_i component is a subset of general-purpose persistent component from the data source layer. Each D_i' implements a certain functionality, required by the application specific layer, which can be performed on any combination $(D_1, D_2, \ldots, D_n)$ of persistent data components.

3.3 Characteristics of Chosen Architectural Style

We summarise the characteristics and constraints of our architectural style below:

1. Components are separated into layers according to their specificity within the application. Layer ordering is based on compile time dependencies. The higher a component in the model is, the more specific it is and the more dependent on other components, i.e. it is less reusable.
2. Our layered architecture allows components from a particular layer to use services of components from any other layer and not only from adjacent layers. Components within a particular layer can also use each other's services.

3. When binding services we allow that an intuitive *many:one* relationship between requirements and provisions is extended towards *many:many*, i.e. each required service may be bound to more than one provided service.
4. The content of a particular component may be decided by which layer it is appropriate to reside upon, i.e. knowing the layer in which the component resides, we know which services it offers.
5. There is a possibility of extending families of core layer components without affecting existing components in the same and adjacent layers. In addition, we may generate in advance core layer components to suit new requirements/applications.
6. Composite components of our core layers may contain a variable number of primitive components and consequently a variable number of interfaces. They are determined by:
   i. the functionality that a particular family of components implements;
   ii. the desired level of granularity of primitive components. Aiming to generate fine-grained components with discrete functionality and low overhead will increase the number of components needed within the core layers and v.v..

Constraints 1, 2, and 3 represent the essence of our AS, which makes it DB applications specific. Constraints 4 and 5 open doors to COTS that can be placed within our SA. Constraint 6 has enabled us to use a concept of *context* in which we describe each component through the role it plays in component bindings. Software component interfaces exhibit explicit context dependencies only [30], which means that for a specific component there should be a set of other components that the components can collaborate with.

4 The Motivating Example

The example below gives an illustration of our proposal and helps in determining which role COTS components may play within our AS. The example scenario is a heterogeneous DB system within a university with two nodes: (a) the legacy system on students' data, which is a relational DB *student* db_1, and (b) the object DB *registry* db_2 with data from all functional areas (teaching/ registry/ administration). Let us assume that we want to create one new data structure **COURSE** and place it within both nodes, which means that we create a new table in $\boldsymbol{db_1}$, and new class in $\boldsymbol{db_2}$, as below:

```
create table COURSE (
course_no             number(5) Primary Key,
course_name           varchar(10),
course_desc           varchar(10),
course_level          number(2);

class Course type tupple
(course_id: integer; course_name: string; course_desc:
string, course_level: integer) end;
```

To demonstrate the interoperability between these two nodes we require that a user's request for creating a relational table, written in a relational SQL, must result in simultaneous creation of two data structures: relational table **COURSE** (D_1) for a relational schema of db_1, and a class Course (D_2) for the object DB db_2. This means that we should be able to create a class for an object DB db_2 with an SQL request create table **COURSE**. Thus users in the relational environment will not have to learn how to write a class declaration and they might not be aware that translation between the relational SQL create table and the class declaration might have taken place. Fig. 3 deploys the components that implement this functionality within our architectural model.

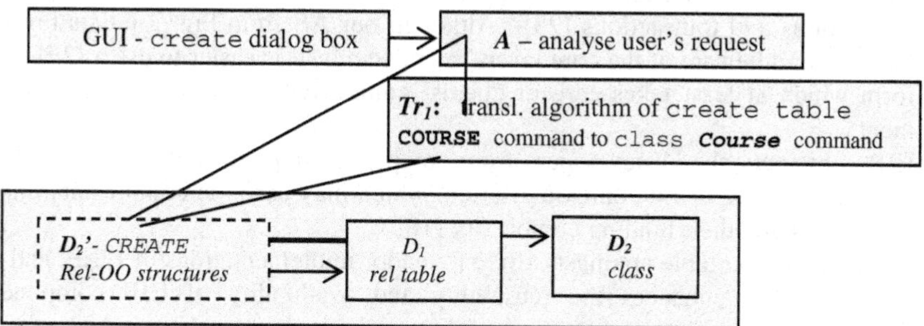

Fig. 3. The motivating example: creating the two data structures

The triviality of this example is needed in order to (i) move away from the complexity of the DB interoperability problem and concentrate on the role that COTS components may play within our AS and (ii) eliminate discussion on the role of the ***A*** component, which may replace mediators/wrappers in mediation based systems. Consequently component ***A*** determines that after issuing an SQL create table **COURSE** statement, a relational table **COURSE** will be created; the create table **COURSE** command will be translated into the class ***Course*** type tupple command and finally a class ***Course*** will be created. The translation layer from Fig. 3 contains only one component, which implements an algorithm Tr_1 for translation of the SQL create table **COURSE** into the class ***Course*** type tupple command. The domain specific layer contains D'_2 component called *CREATE* Rel-OO, which is responsible for creating the two data structures simultaneously: a relational table ***COURSE*** and a class declaration ***Course***. Our Tr_1 and D'_2 components interoperate in the context of creating two DB structures [18].

4.1 Modelling an EJB Application

For deploying our example, we need a component infrastructure that will allow the implementation of the above functionality, guarantee that our independently designed components can be integrated in a certain way, and permit flexible composition of such components. Component standards allow implementation of reusable components' functionality, accessed via an interface and generally implemented by a particular technology, such as CORBA, COM or J2EE. In such cases a technology's standard communication infrastructure and its interaction complexities are encapsulated in components and compromise components' independence [8,15]. Our decision to design the example as an EJB application has been based on:

i. The EJB standard has become the backbone of a set of technologies for developing component-based distributed system. Its client-focused and client-type component models and server-side portability for Java applications, based on open standards such as XML, Java and JNDI, have already been adopted by a number of vendors in order to provide EJB-compliant servers.
ii. Working with EJB implies working with DBs, where multiple clients' interactions are supported by mechanisms for management of system resources such as DB connections and transactions [28]. Although our AS from Fig. 2 points towards our own middleware of the core layers' components, it is easier to use a J2EE platform which at least takes care of clients' connectivity and transaction management.
iii. EJB containers shield developers from component implementation complexities. They allow component contextualisation, which may ease the components implementations and their binding complexity [18].
iv. The EJBs are portable amongst different vendor implementations of J2EE, and the platform itself enhances the reusability and availability of EJB components through their remote interfaces, which list methods that can be invoked on each component. This is the ideal environment for deciding which component will be used in which applications, particularly if they are prepared in advance. In addition, the number of commercial implementations of EJB specifications is substantial, which makes them quite reliable software modules.

A design of our multi-tier EJB application is shown in Fig. 4. The GUI components from the application specific layer are represented by an <<Applet>> that displays and obtains information from the user. Component ***A*** is a Java <<Servlet>> which implements workflow and session management. It accepts a user input, analyses it, makes an invocation to the EJB components and issues a response to a user. In our application domain all requests must be pre-processed, which requires extensive coding within component ***A***. Hence using a servlet, as the common entry point.

The EJB containers host the application components $\boldsymbol{Tr_i}$ and $\boldsymbol{D_i}$' that use DBs, or possibly the $\boldsymbol{D_i}$ components, in order to service requests from the ***A*** component:

The $\boldsymbol{Tr_i}$ components have been designed as <<Stateless Session EJB>>. Each $\boldsymbol{Tr_i}$ contains a simple request and response functionality (e.g. translation from relational to the object DD statement), calls only one method per session, operates on arguments that the client passes to it (e.g. table name, attribute names and types for $\boldsymbol{Tr_1}$), can be used sequentially by many different clients, and needs no tailoring to suit a specific client.

The $\boldsymbol{D_i}$' components have been designed as <<Statefull Session EJB>>, because they contain more complex interactions and maintain a conversational state between a client and EJBs; they may call more than one method per session and manipulate one or more entity beans within a single session. The $\boldsymbol{D_i}$' session beans are typically instantiated for each client session. Our $\boldsymbol{D_2}$' component implements the two DD statements: it creates a table and a class. Such a session bean may access DBs using JDBC and/or the J2EE connector architecture and make entity beans obsolete.

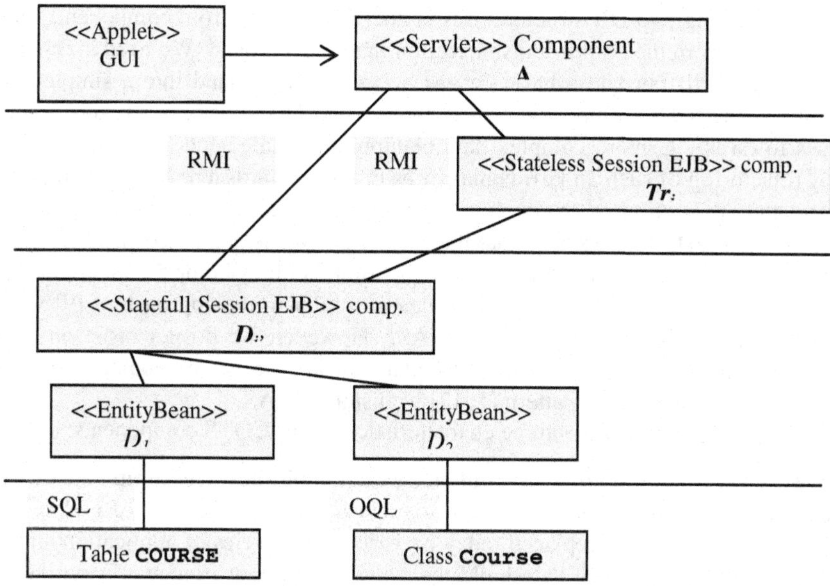

Fig. 4. The EJB application with example components

5 Characteristics of COTS Components

Constraints on AS from Section 3.3. allow the set of $\boldsymbol{D_1}' \ldots \boldsymbol{D_n}'$ and $\boldsymbol{Tr_i}$ components to be extendible (to support evolutionary changes within the system) and reusable (to serve a family of related applications). Some of them may be standardised and some may be dynamically generated and posted from individual persistent data store. Thus $\boldsymbol{D_1}' \ldots \boldsymbol{D_n}'$ and $\boldsymbol{Tr_i}$ components are ideal candidates for COTS components: they represent a certain functionality which can be reused by a family of related applications (e.g. each set of $\boldsymbol{Tr_i}$ and $\boldsymbol{D_1}' \ldots \boldsymbol{D_n}'$ components provide different implementations of the same behaviour) and accessed via an interface that is implemented by the J2EE technology, as in the motivating example.

Contextualisation of our core layer components ensures binding of component interfaces when a component plays a particular role in one or more interactions, which can be monitored by the EJB container. Hence, our COTS components from the core layer should have interfaces, which ensure their interaction in certain contexts: we may have a set of algorithms $\boldsymbol{Tr_i}$ that will translate all variations of SQL-like queries into object query languages. These algorithms can be written in advance, posted as COTS components and used by any other application in the same context. Similarly we can have a set of $\boldsymbol{D_1}' \ldots \boldsymbol{D_n}'$ algorithms that implement a required DB functionality, e.g. $\boldsymbol{D_3}'$ may be needed in the context of joining a relational table, a .jpg file and an XML document. When contextualising our components we make known which method of which component calls which method(s) of which component(s), i.e. paths through the system can be predetermined. In Fig. 4 we combine components in the context of creating two DB structure: this is not only evident from components interfaces, but also from the components' selection made beforehand. We need a Tr_1 component which will translate a basic `create table` command into a simple class declaration, and a D_2' component which creates two DB structures. If this context changes towards e.g. more complex data manipulation statements, we can either (a) deploy refactoring of such an EJB container as in [30] towards a new context that will optimise the application or (b) deploy an adequate, ready-made COTS components for the new context. Fig. 4 shows that the core of our AS is populated with EJB components, which participate in their own composition, i.e. they comprise an application according to constraints of our AS. The idea is similar to the approach of [9] where the EJB composition is based on the C2 AS. However, we do not insist on using wrappers [9] or the extension of the EJB platform [14] to accommodate composite EJB components: the façade pattern [1, 17] well suits our AS.

The discussion above raises three characteristics of our COTS components:

(i) **Our COTS components are not necessarily middleware components**: The idea of having procedural or object-oriented libraries in the core of middleware frameworks has been replaced today by various categories of application and integration servers, which then build their own component frameworks on the top of component platforms. Isolated middleware products are disappearing, leaving a space for specialised servers that combine middleware functionality and specific component frameworks. Thus, we neither wish to see our COTS being exclusively middleware components as in [15] nor do we insist that our COTS should have a role of either implementing business functionalities or delivering middleware services [3]. The EJB container configures services to match the needs of contained beans: deployed beans are contextually composed with services/resources by the EJB container [18].

(ii) **Our COTS components must conform to the AS**: We advocate generating COTS components that conform to our AS for interoperable DBs. This means that when selecting COTS components we will know automatically which functionality they must deliver: this is determined by (a) the architectural layer from Figures 1 and 2 where COTS components may reside and (b) contextualisation of components' interfaces [18]. This might eliminate the requirement from [2], that COTS evaluation is "performed in parallel with architecture design" as a prerequisite in COTS-based development. Further contrasts to our views on the role of software architecture in COTS-based systems are (a) the strategies of component integration from [32], which emphasise that the software architecture must adapt to connectors and available COTS components' functionality or (b) views that COTS-based development must constrain architectural design and in turn adapt to available COTS components [20]. We would rather see that COTS components, which conform to the our AS, contribute towards COTS identifications, selections and familiarisation as an aid in a COTS-based software development process as in [24]. Hence, we advocate an abstract software architecture to be defined first, whose components are then matched against COTS components available on the market.

(iii) **Our COTS components are EJBs:** We adhere to ideas that developing components means developing them with a dedicated component platform in mind [5], i.e. COTS should be realised according to the component platforms rules and domain specific supporting framework.

6 Conclusions

In this paper we have identified the candidates for COTS components that can populate the component-based AS in order to alleviate the DB interoperability problem in heterogeneous DBs. These potential COTS components can be placed within the core layers of our AS and used by a family of related applications. They implement a set of algorithms for translation and a set of functionalities of users' requests. We advocate that such COTS components are developed with a certain component platform in mind, interoperate within a certain context, and adhere to the constraints of our AS. Our current work analyses how component technologies address the DB interoperability problem in terms of COTS components they may have generated [19].

References

1. Alur D., Crupi J., Malks D., Core J2EE Patterns, 2nd edition, Prentice Hall, 2003.
2. Alves C., Finkelstein A., Challenges in COTS Decision Making: A Goal Driven Requirements Engineering Perspective, Proc. of SEDECS'02, Ischia, Italy, pp 789-794.
3. Bandini S., De Paoli F., Manzoni S., Mereghetti P., A Support System to COTS-based Software Development for Business Services, Proc. of the SEKE '02, Ischia, Italy, 2002, pp. 307-314.
4. Bass L., P. Clements, R. Kazman, Software Architecture in Practice, Addison Wesley, 1998, ISBN 0-201-199300.
5. Bilke A., Klischat O., Urlch Kriegel E., Rosenmuller R., Component-based Software Development, Proc. of the 5th Int. Conf. on Integrated Design and Processing Technology (IDPT 2002), Pasadena, CA, USA, 2002.
6. Brownsword L., Carney D.J., Fisher D., Lewis G., Meyers C., Morris E.J., Place P.R.H., Smith J., Wrage L. Current Perspectives on Interoperability, Technical Report, CMU/SEI-2004-TR-009.
7. Chawathe S, Garcia-Molina H, Hammer J, Ireland K, Papakonstantinou Y, Ulamn J, Widom J., The TSIMMIS project: Integration of Heterogeneous Information Sources, Proc. of the IPSJ Conf., Tokyo, Japan, 1994, pp. 7-18.
8. Chiang C.C., Development of Reusable Components through the Use of Adaptors, Proc. of the 36th Hawaii Int. Conf. on System Sciences (HICSS), IEEE, 2002.
9. Choi Y.H., Kwon O.C. Shin G.S. An Approach to Composition of EJB Components Using C2 style, Proc.of the 28th Euromicro Conf., 2002.
10. COTS-Based Systems Initiative Group website http://www.sei.cmu.edu/cbs/
11. Davis L., Gamble R.F., Payton J., The Impact of Component Architectures on Interoperability, The Journal of Systems and Software, 61(2002), pp. 31-45.
12. Dulay N., and R. Juric, On Interoperability in DB Environments: An Analysis of Past and Current Trends in the DB Field, under review for Journal of Integrated Design and Process Science

13. Elmagarmid, M., Rusinkiewicz, A., and Sheth, A., (eds.) Management of Heterogeneous and Autonomous Database Systems, Morgan Kaufman, 1999.
14. Goebel S., Nestler M. Composite Component Support for EJB, Proc. of the Winter Int. Symp. on Information and Communication Technologies, Cancun, Mexico, 2004, pp.1–6.
15. A. Gokhale, D, Schmidt, B. Natarajan, N. Wang, Applying Model-integrated Computing to Component Middleware and Enterprise Applications, Communications of the ACM, Vol 45 , Issue 10, October 2002, pp.65-70.
16. Juric, R., Kuljis, J., and Paul R., A Software Architecture to Support Interoperability in Multiple Database Systems, Proc. of the 22nd IASTED Int. Conf. on Software Engineering, Insbruck, Austria, February 2004.
17. Juric, R., Kuljis, J., Paul R., Software Architecture Style for Interoperable Databases, to appear in Proc. of the 26th Int. Conf. on Information Technology Interfaces, Croatia, 2004.
18. Juric, R., Kuljis, J., and Paul R., Contextualising Components when Addressing the DB Interoperability, to appear in Proc. of the IASTED – SEA, Boston, November 2004.
19. Juric R., Terstianszky G., Beus-Dukic Lj., Component Platforms and Data Centric Applications, paper in preparation.
20. Kalio P., Ihme, T. Evolution of the Use and Risks of Commercial Software Components, Proc. of the 28th Euromicro Conference, 2002.
21. LISI:Levels of Information Systems Interoperability, C4ISR Architectures Working Group, 30 March 1998, US DoD OSD (C31), http://www.c3i.osd/mil/
22. Lu J., Mylopoulus J., Automated EJB Client Code Generation Using Database Query Rewriting, in Proc. of the 7th Int. Database Engineering and Application Symp., 2003.
23. Medvidovic N., R. F. Gamble, and D. S. Rosenblum, Towards Software Multioperability: Bridging Heterogeneous Software Interoperability Platforms, Proc. of the 4th Int. Software Architecture Workshop (ISAW-4), Limerick, Ireland, June 2000.
24. Morisio M., Seaman C.B., Basili V.R., Parra A.T., Kraft S.E., Condon S.E. COTS-based software Development: Processes and Open Issues, in the Journal of Systems and Software, 61(2002), pp. 189-199.
25. NATO Allied Data Publication 34 (AdatP-34):"NATO C3 Technical Architecture (N3CTA), Version 4.0", March 2003, http://www.nato.int/docu/standard.htm
26. Pan A., Montoto P., Molano A., Alvarez M., Raposo J., Orjales V., Vina A., Mediator Systems in E-Commerce Applications, Proc.of the 4th Int. Workshop on Advanced Issues of E-Commerce and Web-Based Information Systems, IEEE Computer Society, 2002.
27. Sharma R., Stearns B., Ng T., J2EE Connector Architecture and Enterprise Application, Addison Wesley, 2002.
28. Singh I., Stearns B., Johnson, M., Designing Enterprise Applications with the J2EE Platform, Addison Wesley, Second Edition, 2002, ISBN 0-201-787903.
29. Soudi A, Nachouki G, Briand H., Relational DBRE A Knowledge-Based Approach, Proc. of the 3rd Int. Conf. on OO Information Systems, London, UK, 1996, pp.180-194.
30. Sczypersky C.,Component Software–Beyond Object-Oriented Programming, Second Edition, Addison Wesley, 2002, ISBN 0-201-74572-0.
31. Teknowledge Corporation http://www.teknowledge.com
32. A Trofin M., A Self-optimising Server Design for Enterprise JavaBeans Applications, Proc. of OOPSLA '03, Anaheim, CA, USA, 2003, pp. 396-397.
33. Tu S., Xu L., Abdelguerfi M., Ratcliff J.J., Achieving Interoperability for Integration of Heterogeneous COTS Geographic Information Systems, The ACM Symp. on GIS'02, Virginia, November 2002, pp. 162-167.

34. Vigder M. and Dean J., An Architetcural Approach to Building Systems from COTS Software Components, 22nd SE Workshop, NASA/Goddard Space Flight Center SEL, Greenbelt, MD, December 1997, NRC Report Number 40221, pp.99-131.
35. Wiederhold G., Mediators in the Architecture of the Future Information Systems, IEEE Computer, 25(3), 1992, pp. 38-48.

On Goal-Oriented COTS Taxonomies Construction*

Claudia P. Ayala[1], Pere Botella, and Xavier Franch

UPC-Campus Nord, c/Jordi Girona 1-3, 08034 Barcelona, Catalunya, Spain
{cayala, botella, franch}@lsi.upc.es
http://www.lsi.upc.es/~gessi

Abstract. This paper proposes the adoption of a goal-based method called GBRAM for facilitating the process of building taxonomies of COTS components. Since GBRAM was defined in a different setting, the main result of the paper is to adapt it to this new context obtaining the GBTCM method. We show how the different activities and artifacts of GBRAM change, and we apply the proposal to obtain a taxonomy for requirements engineering oriented tools.

1 Introduction

The use of Commercial Off-The-Shelf (COTS) components (hereafter, COTS) as parts of larger systems has grown steadily [1, 2]. The process of developing systems from COTS is an economic and strategic need in a wide variety of different application areas. As a result, a huge amount of COTS have become accessible in the market. This gives raise to a new problem: how to organize the knowledge about these COTS in such a way that searching the market becomes a feasible task.

In [3] we proposed to use *taxonomies* as a way to organize the COTS market (see fig. 1) and we applied the proposal to the family of business applications. At the leaves of the taxonomy there are *COTS domains*; a COTS domain encloses a significant group of functionality (e.g., the domain of anti-virus tools or mail servers systems). Domains are grouped into *categories* (e.g., the category of communication infrastructure systems or financial packages), which may be grouped at their turn. We proposed the use of *characterization attributes* [4] to discriminate among different categories or domains. We bind questions and answers to these attributes as a way for browsing the taxonomy. Dependencies among domains that belong to the taxonomy are included in the hierarchy itself (e.g., mail server systems depend on anti-virus tools to support integrity). As an additional point, we also bind *quality models* to nodes in the taxonomy, each describing the quality factors that are of interest for the particular category or domain; quality models are inherited downwards the taxonomy.

Although the main ideas of the proposal were satisfactory enough for our purposes, it turned out that the way to identify the discriminating characterization attributes

* This work is partially supported by the Spanish research program CICYT TIC2001-2165.

[1] Claudia P. Ayala's work has been supported by the Mexican Council for Science and Technology (CONACYT).

X. Franch and D. Port (Eds.): ICCBSS 2005, LNCS 3412, pp. 90 – 100, 2005.

(which capture the relevant information for discriminating categories and domains) was not properly defined. In [3], we just took an existing taxonomy as starting point and rearranged it by observation. This was clearly a weak point of our proposal, and therefore we started to look for a better suited strategy.

In this paper, we use the notion of *goal* as introduced in the context of requirements engineering [5, 6] as the rationale to identify characterization attributes and therefore COTS categories and domains. In general, goals are very stable with respect to changes, and goal refinement provides a natural mechanism for structuring and exploring many alternatives in the COTS market. Our main contribution in this paper is to present a goal-based reasoning method based on the *Goal-Based Requirements Analysis Method* (GBRAM) proposed by Annie I. Antón in the field of software requirements [7] to the context of COTS taxonomies. The resulting method, *Goal-Based Taxonomy Construction Method* (GBTCM), help us to generalize, formalize, enhance and clarify the process of building taxonomies by identifying and evaluating the most suitable characterization attributes. We apply GBTCM to a particular segment of the COTS market: systems and tools for supporting the various activities embraced by the requirements engineering phase. The resulting taxonomy can be considered as another contribution of this work.

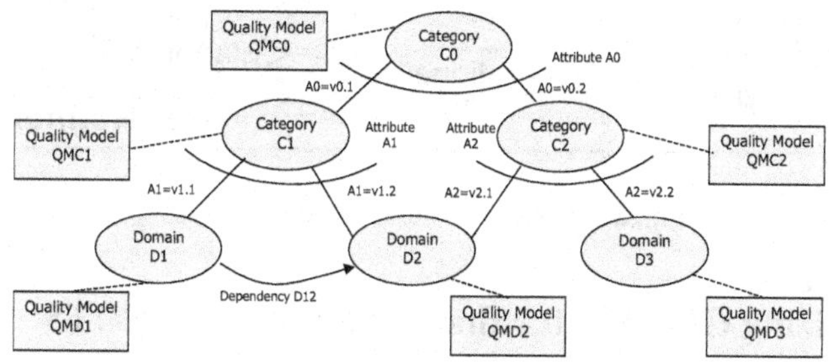

Fig. 1. The fundamental elements of COTS taxonomies

2 The Goal-Based Requirements Analysis Method (GBRAM)

GBRAM was formulated with the transformation of enterprise and system goals into requirements as primary focus, more specifically to assist analysts in gathering software and enterprise goals from many sources and to support the process of discovering, identifying, classifying, refining, and elaborating goals into operational requirements. The method's main contribution is the provision of heuristics and procedural guidance for identifying and constructing goals.

The two high level phases of GBRAM briefly explained are:

- **Goal Analysis.** Concerns the exploration of available information sources for goal identification followed by the organization and classification of goals.
- **Goal Refinement**. Concerns the evolution of goals from the moment they are first identified to the moment they are translated into operational requirements.

Fig. 2 shows the activities (ovals) and artifacts (inclined rectangles) involved in GBRAM. Its output is the Software Requirements Document (SRD) and its inputs are the diverse sources of information used in requirements elicitation. The activities are: *Explore* (entails the analysis of available information), *Identify* (aims at extracting goals applying heuristics), *Organize* (involves the classification and organization of goals according to goal dependency relationships), *Refine* (entails the actual pruning of the goal set), *Elaborate* (refers to the process of analyzing the goal set by considering possible obstacles and constructing scenarios to uncover hidden goals and requirements), and *Operationalize* (refers to translating goals into requirements for the final SRD).

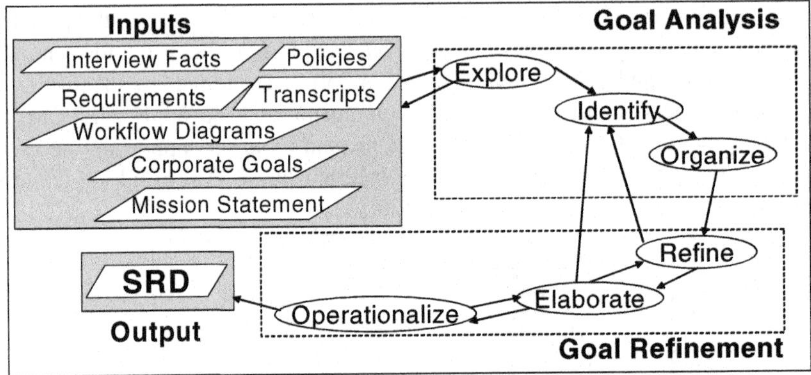

Fig. 2. Overview of the GBRAM activities

3 Customizing GBRAM for the Construction of COTS Taxonomies

We aim at applying GBRAM in a different context from which it was conceived, that is the construction of taxonomies for the COTS market using goals acquired from different information sources. The suitability of this method as a help for obtaining the characterization attributes is based on three facts:

1. It assumes the challenge of working with different sources of knowledge that are represented in different form.
2. It provides guidelines and heuristics for exploring, identifying and organizing goals (potential characterization attributes) and also allows adding new heuristics which guide us towards a high probability of success while avoiding wasted efforts.
3. It offers a guide for applying an inquiry-driven approach to goal-based analysis, that can be useful for enhancing our questions-answers mechanism linked to characterization attributes.

In the rest of the section we show how we customize GBRAM. We adjust the inputs and modify the output. We adapt and prune some activities treating the issues not as operational requirements of a system but as characterization attributes in order to obtain the statement of main goals to be considered as potential characterization attributes in the construction of COTS taxonomies in any specific area.

3.1 Adjusting the Sources of Information

We want to emphasize the importance of the information sources (the inputs), since they are the base for obtaining goals. GBRAM's inputs correspond to usual software requirements elicitation sources in order to define the SRD for developing a software system. But the inputs for GBTCM must necessarily be different.

Table 1 summarizes the most important sources of information we consider in GBTCM. The main difference is that most information is textual, available in printed form or the web, issued by different organizations or people. Sources such as domain experts and tools demos still remain, but they play a secondary role.

Table 1. Information Sources to consider in our approach

Information Source			Information type	Language	Examples
Existing Taxonomies and Ontologies			Classifications; Categories; Glossaries	Natural Language (NL); Tree-like diagrams	SWEBOK, INCOSE, Gartner, IDC
Related Standards			Descriptions; Glossaries	NL	IEEE, EIA, ISO
Vendors Information			Brochures; Evaluation forms; Benchmarks	NL; Values for attributes	Rational, Microsoft
Domain Descrip-tions	Scientific	Academic Events, Journals;Textbooks	Precise and rigorous descriptions	NL; Models; Formulas; Schemas	ICCBSS, ICSE, TSE, [MO02]
	Divulgation	Magazines, Forums and Websites	Descriptions and tips for the general public	NL; Schemas; Tables	PCWorld, IEEE Software, COCOTS website, specialized forums
	Technical	White Papers, Surveys and Comparatives	Papers, Comparative tables	NL, Tables; Figures	Gartner, INCOSE
Oral Informa-tion	Interviews		Knowledge; Tips; Practical information	NL	ICCBSS panels, SEI courses, Business luncheons
	Talks, seminars and courses				
Test of Tools and Systems			Test results; User's manuals	Visual data; NL	Outlook, Rationale Suite
Experiences on the field			Knowledge; Technical reports	Knowledge; NL	Past projects made

The use of one or another information source is determined by several qualities, among which we mention: reliability of the information, availability of the source, acquisition cost, timeliness, scope covered and time needed to process the enclosed information. These qualities depend on three factors: information source type, organization or people that creates the information, and particular item of information. A complete goal-acquisition program should take these considerations into account.

3.2 Auxiliary Models and Artifacts

Additionally to GBRAM, GBTCM considers essential the generation of some artifacts and models from the information sources cited above in order to understand, handle, formalize, and remarkably maintain the information about the domain.

As artifacts, we suggest at least to create glossaries for homogenizing terms used in the diverse information sources. As models, we suggest UML class diagrams [8] for representing a conceptual model of the domain, defining by means of classes, attributes, associations and hierarchies the underlying ontology (see [9]). As a fundamental part of our approach, we require the construction of goal-oriented models. We use *i** as notation [10] although other options are valid. Goal-oriented models align with our goal-oriented method, therefore on the one hand they aid in the process of getting goals providing a high level picture of the domain, representing and organizing its knowledge and related activities; on the other hand they are used in order to represent and record explicitly the dependencies among domains of COTS for their repeated use during different selection process, and the relationships among these domains and the actors that have an interest on them, either as users or as definers.

Of course all of these artifacts and models shall be synchronized. For instance, glossary terms and UML attributes should have the same name.

3.3 GBTCM Activities

Some activities related with goal analysis or refinement have been pruned or adapted to our approach. GBTCM finally delivers not an SRD as the original GBRAM, but a hierarchical structure of the more important goals covered in the addressed COTS market segment; the correspondence of these goals with the different sources of information (especially with existing taxonomies, standards and vendors information); the auxiliary models and artifacts; and the applicable characterization attributes.

It is worth to remark that the flow of information among activities is the same as fig 2. However, as we mentioned above, the information sources (the input of the Explore activity) in GBTCM are different, as shown in table 1. In table 2 we can realize that the output of each activity is the input of the next.

3.4 GBTCM Heuristics

One of the main contributions of GBRAM is the provision of heuristics and procedural guidance for identifying and constructing goals. Heuristics aid us by providing prescriptive guidance for managing varying levels of detail in the information available. There are four general types of heuristics used in GBRAM: identification, classification, refinement, and elaboration heuristics. Some of them are straightforward and generic, not require employing a specific inquiry technique. Others make sense only in conjunction with specific questions about the system.

Many heuristics showed in GBRAM can be mapped directly to GBTCM (section 4.2 and 4.3 show examples of applying identification heuristics –questions- that guide the obtention of specific information), but many others should be adjusted, and also some new heuristics for the specific domain can be created, which should be documented for handling the growing and evolution of the taxonomy. Applying GBTCM we can achieve a high probability of success finding the characterization attributes in a more formal way while avoiding wasted efforts.

Table 2. Activities and its inputs of GBTCM

Activity	Outputs
Explore	Information sources qualified; Some goals
Identify	Set of goals; Stakeholders and agents; Auxiliary models and artifacts
Organize	Matching of goals from different information sources Dependency relationships among goals Goal hierarchy
Refine	Refined goal set
Elaborate	Scenarios Constraints
Operationalize	Hierarchical structure of Goals Asociated information and models and artifacts Characterization attributes for constructing the taxonomy of the domain

4 Case Study: A Taxonomy in the Requirements Engineering Area

Our purpose in this section is to apply GBTCM to analyze the field of software Requirements Engineering (RE) and as a result propose a taxonomy in that area. We have chosen RE as case study because it is a critical area in the software development processes [11]. Therefore, to improve the efficiency of the activities performed in the area, COTS technology aid RE-related actors to simplify and facilitate their work. For keeping the description short, we focus on the most representative parts of the experience.

4.1 Sources of Information

As it can be expected for a topic such this, lots on information sources exist and many of them were gathered. Table 3 lists the sources of information more widely used for the construction of the taxonomy [12..23].

4.2 Identifying Goals and Objectives

Although we have many and diverse information sources, it should be considered as a good practice to base the process on the most solid and confident of them for extracting the main high level goals in order to assure the consistency of the set of goals, and then extracting subgoals from the remaining sources. Due to the standard nature of SWEBOK in the field, we started with this source for obtaining the high-level goals that guide the whole process (even considering that SWEBOK is not tool-oriented, on the contrary of other sources). For example, consider the following description in natural language from SWEBOK: "The next topics breakdowns for RE discipline are generally accepted in that they cover areas typically in texts and standards: activities such as Requirements Engineering Process, Requirements Elicitation, and Requirements Analysis, along with Requirements engineering-specific descriptions. Hence, we identify Requirements Validation and Requirements Management as separate topics". By examining the statement and asking "what goal(s) does this statement/fragment exemplify?" some goals become evident from the description. We present some of these goals in the first column of table 4. In subsection 4.4 we will use other information sources to decompose these high level goals.

Table 3. Main Sources of information used in the taxonomies for RE

Type of source	Source organization	Information enclosed	Comments
Existing taxonomies	INCOSE	Classification of Software Engineering tools	This section is available free and widely accepted
Related standards	SWEBOK	Main RE areas stakeholder types	Available free, widely accepted
	IEEE std 830-1998	Software activities related with RE	Subscription/payment needed
	IEEE/EIA 12207.1-1997		
	ISO/IEC 12207		
Vendors information	IBM-Rational	Capabilities of products and trends	Exhaustive description of products
	ComponentSource	Capabilities of products and trends focused in platforms	Available free, widely accepted
Tools	RequisitePro	Capabilities of a real RMT	Included in the IBM-Rational Suite
	IRqA		Tool used often in our projects
	EasyWinWin	Capability of a research tool for requirements negotiation	Some tutorials attended and contacts with authors
Academic sites	eCOTS	Trends	Available free, widely accepted
Scientific items	RE-related conferences	Timely state of the art	Subscription/payment needed
	RE&SE textbooks	Areas of RE	
Magazines	Requirements Engineering	Trends and timely state of the art	
WebSites	Volere	RE resources	Available Free
Technical	INCOSE	Trends and concepts in RE	Subscription/payment needed
	Gartner		
Own experiences	Academic records management	Use of RE-oriented tools in a real project	CMM-2 compliant requirements management

4.3 Identifying Stakeholders and Agents

At this stage, we aim at determining who are the stakeholders involved in the achievement of goals. Once the goals and stakeholders are specified, the goals must be assigned to their responsible agent(s). A stakeholder is any representative affected by the achievement or prevention of a particular goal. Multiple stakeholders may be associated with one goal. Agents are responsible for the completion and/or satisfaction of goals within an organization or system. Identification of stakeholders and agents is crucial to understand the domain at hand and also to identify additional sources of information, e.g. for identifying people to be interviewed.

The stakeholders for each goal are determined by asking "who or what claims a stake in this goal?" and "who or what stands to gain or lose by the completion or prevention of this goal?" For identifying which agents are ultimately responsible for the achievement of each goal, we ask the question "who or what agent [is/should be/could be] responsible for this goal?" In our case, we identified as stakeholders (see table 4): Requirements Engineer (RE), Project Manager (PM), Quality Assurance Manager (QAM), Software Configuration Manager (SCM), Testers, Final Users, Customer and Non-Technical Stakeholders (such as regulators, market analyst, system developers; NTS). The only agent is the Requirements Engineer. The relationships among these stakeholders appear in the *i** model mentioned in subsection 3.2.

Table 4. Some goals obtained from SWEBOK

Goals		Agents	Stakeholders
G1:Process of Software Requirements Defined		(RE)	RE, PM,QAM
G2:Requirements Elicitation Performed		RE	RE, Stakeholders
G3:Requirements Analysis Performed		RE	RE, Stakeholders
G4:Requirements Specification Done		RE	RE, users/customer, QAM
G5:Requirements Validation Performed		RE	RE, users/customer, Tester
G6:Requirements Management Done		RE	RE, SCM
	G6.1:Change Management in Requirements Controlled	RE	RE
	G6.2:Requirements Attributes Defined	RE	RE, SCM
	G6.3:Requirements Tracing Controlled	RE	RE, SCM

Table 5. An excerpt of organization of goals

Goals				Tools	Cathegory of INCOSE Taxonomy
G2:Requirements Elicitation Performed					
	G2.1:Requirements Sources Defined and Analized				
	G2.2:Elicitation Techniques Chosen				
		G2.2.1:Extracting Requirements		Yes	RequirementsEngineering/Requirements Management/RequirementsCapture&Identification/ ToolsForElicitationOfRequirements
			G2.2.1.1:Interviews	Yes	
			G2.2.1.2:Scenarios	Yes	Design Domain

4.4 Organization and Matching of Goals

Once we had analyzed and identified goals from all information sources, we have to organize that information firstly by means of a matching of goals from all information sources, and subsequently according to precedence relationships. We represent the process of organization of goals by means of tables. Table 5 is an excerpt of this process. We can observe the matching of the goals (collected in the mentioned *i** SD model) with the existent taxonomies and vendors information.

The level of decomposition of goals is not defined in GBRAM. In GBTCM, it clearly depends on the matching of the information sources. As an example of rule of thumb in our context, one goal should be taken into account only if it exists in the market a tool that supports it (although it could be argued that discovering of goals that are not covered by any tool is a significant issue in closing the gap between tools and processes). At the end of the process of matching we have a more complete set of goals. Next step we have to specify dependencies.

Specifying Goal Dependencies. In GBRAM, goals are organized only according to their temporal precedence relations. Adequate questions helps in the prerequisite findings and facilitate their organization, for example: "do any goal depend on the availability of this goal for achievement?" In GBTCM, we consider this aspect as twofold: we not only specify the temporal precedence relations of goals but also we define which are the dependencies among goals (both goals from the addressed COTS market segment or from other previously treated) for their completion, relying on another goal, agent, or resource; it means the explicit representation of potential dependencies among COTS domains by means i* models cited in subsection 3.2.

For example, in fig. 3 we can see that besides i* diagrams (left), we represent the precedence dependencies of goals by means of hierarchical tables (right). GBRAM refers to this last outlining mechanism as goal topography. As a result, we have a dual representation of goal models, a more technical one and a more understandable one, easy to index and read.

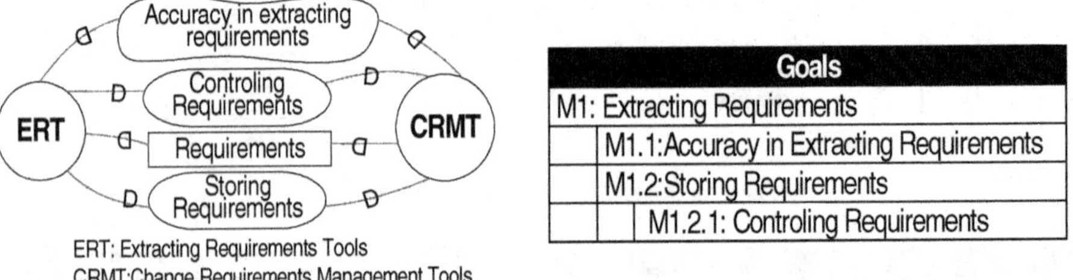

Fig. 3. An excerpt of a i* SD model (left) and a hierarchical table (right) involving the RE tools

4.5 Reducing the Size of the Goal Set and Elaborating Scenarios

The goal topography must be refined, which implies the pruning of the goal set. Three approaches were used: eliminating duplicate goals, refining goals based on system entities, and consolidating nearly synonymous goals. The use of glossaries and class diagrams supports the reconciliation of goals. For example, the terms "capturing" and "extracting" that coming from two different sources was unified and defined as "extracting" in our glossary.

In some cases it was necessary to elaborate scenarios. Scenarios facilitate the identification of special or extraordinary circumstances which occur so that goal and requirements information should be refined. Scenarios are identified considering the goals by asking "Why?" and "Why this goal could be not achieved?" Scenarios were very useful for uncovering and reconciling goals, checking for completeness and conflicts, and communicating with stakeholders.

Table 6. An excerpt of the taxonomy for Requirements Engineering Tools

Level 2	Level 3	Question	Level 4
1.2 Requirements Elicitation			
	1.2.1 Generation	Do you apply simulation for generating requirements?	1.2.1.1 Simulation Tools
	1.2.1 Extraction		
		Are you using interviews?	1.2.2.1 Interview Tools
		Are you using scenarios?	1.2.2.2 Scenario Tools
		Are you using prototypes?	1.2.2.3 Prototype Tools
		Are you using facibility meetings?	1.2.2.4 Facilitate Meetings Tools
		Are you using observation?	1.2.2.5 Observation Tools
		Are you using other techniques?	1.2.2.6 Other Extraction Techniques Tools

4.6 Operationalizing Goals

Goal information must ultimately be operationalized (related with actions). This is done by consolidating the goal information applying the Inquiry-Cycle [24] approach. The Inquiry-Cycle consists of a series of questions and answers designed to pinpoint where and when information needs arise. We apply this mechanism departing from the hierarchical set of goals in order to: get the questions-answers pair attained to each characterization attribute and appropriate organize the information resulting. Table 6 shows an excerpt.

5 Conclusions

In this paper we have described a goal-based method for the construction of COTS taxonomies called GBTCM. This approach allows the identification and elaboration of goals in a specific area and the matching and refinement of those goals into characterization attributes of the COTS field. This leads to several advantages [25]: the use of adequate information sources to obtain characterization attributes permits to browse the taxonomy in a guided way, more practical and confident; the explicit construction of i* models as artifacts of the method representing the relationships among domains, making clearer the implications of the use a particular component as it was proposed in [3]; the organization of the information and artifacts and models resulting of the method, supports not only the reusing of knowledge gained in the specific area but also the maintenance and evolution of the COTS taxonomy. The use of GBTCM can help software engineers which usually carry out COTS selection to structure better their knowledge and may aim at a better return of investment.

Our future work will concentrate on using GBTCM in other domains inside the software development processes, and in taking into account the qualities and factors of the information sources for classify them according their relevance.

References

1. Carney D., Long F.:What Do You Mean by COTS? Finally a Useful Answer. IEEE Software, 17 (2), March/April 2000
2. Craig Meyers, B., Oberndorf, P.: Managing Software Acquisition. SEI Series in Software Engineering, 2002
3. Carvallo, J.P., Franch, X., Quer, C., Torchiano, M.: Characterization of a Taxonomy for Business Applications and the Relationships Among Them. Lecture Notes in Computer Science Vol. 2959, (2004). Proceedings 3rd International Conference on COTS-Based Software Systems (ICCBSS)
4. Morisio, M., Torchiano, M.: Definition and Classification of COTS: A Proposal. In Proceedings 1st. International Conference on COTS-Based Software Systems (ICCBSS), Orlando Florida (2002)
5. Mylopoulos, J., Chung, L., Yu, E.: From Object-Oriented to Goal-Oriented Requirements Análisis. Communications ACM 42(1), January 1999
6. Van Lamsweerde, A.: Goal-Oriented Requirements Engineering: A Guided Tour. In Proceedings 5th IEEE International Symposium on Requirements Engineering (ISRE) 2001
7. Antón, A.I.: Goal-Based Requirements Analysis. In Proceedings 2nd IEEE International Conference on Requirements Engineering (ICRE) 1996
8. UML 2.0 Specifications http://www.uml.org/, last accesed July 2004
9. Carvallo, J.P., Franch, X., Quer, C.: Defining a Quality Model for Mail Servers. In Proceedings 2nd International Conference on COTS-Based Software Systems (ICCBSS). Lecture Notes in Computer Science 2580, (2003)
10. Yu, E.: Towards Modeling and Reasoning Support for Early-Phase Requirements Engineering. In Proceedings 3rd IEEE International Symposium on Requirements Engineering (ISRE) 1997
11. Standish Group Report http://www.standishgroup. CHAOS Survey 1994
12. Guide to the Software Engineering Body of Knowledge, SWEBOK, www.swebok..org
13. The Gartner Group, available on-line at http://www4.gartner.com
14. INCOSE. "Software Engineering Tools Taxonomy" http// www.incose.org
15. eCots. Software Components Open Directory Project. http://ecots.org
16. International Standard ISO/IEC 12207 Software Life Cycle Processes. 1995
17. IEEE/EIA Guide. IEEE/EIA12207.1-1997. Standard for Information Technology-Software Life Cicle Processes, April 1998
18. International Standard IEEE Std 830-1998 IEEE Recommended Practice for Software Requirements Specifications, June 1998
19. Infrastructure Software Market Definitions for Application Development. Gartner, Dataquest Guide. 4th June, 2003. http://www.gartner.com
20. Software Market Research Methodology and Definitions 2003-2004. Gartner Dataquest Guide. 16th January, 2004. http://www.gartner.com
21. CBSE Net. "Application Domain Taxonomy ". Available on-line (previous registration) at: http://www.cbsenet.org/pls/CBSEnet/ eco_ricerca_documenti.concept_search_frame
22. International Data Corporation http://www.idc.com
23. ComponenSource http://www.componentsource.com
24. Potts, C., Takahashi, K., Antón, A.:"Inquiry-Based Requirements Analysis". IEEE Software, 11(2) March 1994
25. Ayala, C.P, Botella, P., Franch, X.: Goal-Based Reasoned Construction of Taxonomies for the Selection of COTS Products. In Proceedings 8th Multi-Conference on Systemics, Cybernetics and Informatics (SCI). Orlando Florida (2004). ISBN:980-6560-13-2

Assets and Liabilities of Organizational Trust: COTS Software Adoption in Government Projects

Sally J. F. Baron

Management Consulting Services
sally@baron.biz

Abstract. Organizational theorists have long touted *trust* as a market asset for reducing transaction costs. In some cases managers have learned to depend on social relationships of firms with whom they are familiar rather than judging products on merit. The trouble arises when trust is established with a firm, and superior products from other firms are not considered. The problem is exacerbated with software, as the product itself is intangible and often difficult to judge or understand. Smaller COTS software firms with superior products have had a difficult time entering the U.S. Government market. Government managers have traditionally turned to well-known contractors with whom they have had decade-old ties, rather than seeking newer and better COTS solutions that are lesser known. This paper examines some of the barriers to trusting lesser-known software products and suggests solutions to overcome such barriers.

1 Introduction

Learning to trust people we do not know and products we cannot see. Some of the difficulties in software procurement are a product of these issues. Intuitively and practically, *trust* is thought to be an emotion that is built over time, earned and long standing. Some of these traditional concepts have been demonstrated academically. [11] [13] Newer theories present the concept of *swift trust* in which *trust* is established rapidly. [16] In economic markets, *trust* has been an essential component of efficiency as it reduces transaction costs. [25] The U.S. Government is the single largest purchaser in the world,[1] is substantial in the global market. Product procurements range from pencils to satellites, and services from janitorial to rocket science. This paper focuses on procuring high-technology COTS (commercial-off-the-shelf) software, such as that used for satellite operations.

As a framework for this paper, the government procurement process shall be simplified. In the past, the U.S. Government has primarily used largely design-and-build processes for high-tech software, and has only more recently purchased COTS software products. The COTS procurement process can be distilled to the following, as illustrated in Figure 1. This is a simplification of a process that can be considerably

[1] Proposed FY 2003 budget: $2.13T. Defense spending for FY 2002: $330.6B. Source: World Almanac, 2003.

X. Franch and D. Port (Eds.): ICCBSS 2005, LNCS 3412, pp. 101–111, 2005.

more complicated; convoluted by budget cycles, hiring freezes, complex programs and system failures. Requirements are fed to program managers who conduct a market search. Several options are analyzed, and one is selected. Testing and integration follow.[2] Technology refresh cycles are typically built into software procurements, which brings the process full-cycle.[3] The process can take years, and can be extremely complicated with prime and sub contracting a normal part of the process. Justification, budgets and politics all perturb this cycle and can make it less efficient. Networking is important as large dollar contracts are put out for companies to examine which makes the market search process less than ideal.

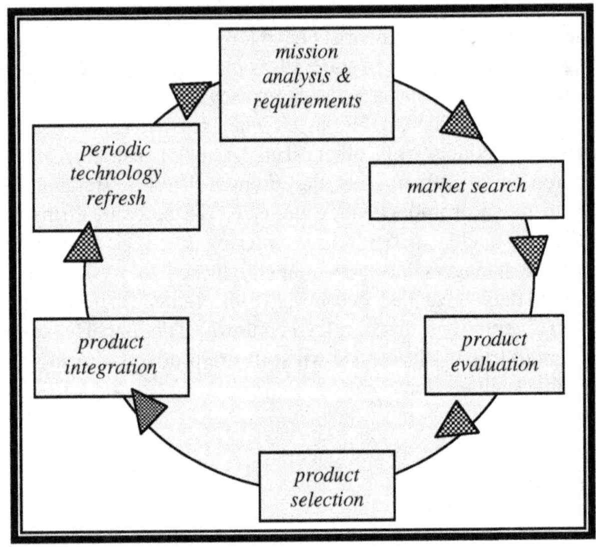

Fig. 1. COTS Software Product Government Acquisition Cycle. This process has been simplified substantially for the purpose of this paper. It is a highly complex process that can take years. DoD reform, initiated in 1994 by Dr. William J. Perry has made strides in shortening and simplifying this. [Modeled roughly after OMB circular A-109.]

Defense contractors normally have budgets to scout such opportunities. This makes them primed to jump into the bid and selection process. Bidding costs can be significant and may require funding extensive design and research stages as well as identifying subcontractors and feasible components. Meanwhile smaller commercial product companies may not even be cognizant of the RFP opportunity, let alone able to bear the cost. The lengthiness and complexity of the process make it a challenge and taking the path of least resistance can be essential to meeting deadlines and other

[2] In the new era of COTS product use; about the past ten years, if the procurement is done efficiently, the product will be tested prior to purchase.

[3] This was not the case with traditional design-and-build systems where the government assumed all risk for products.

short-term requirements. Such shortcuts can include returning to contractors with whom the government is familiar and avoiding a complete and thorough market evaluation. While this behavior is not always optimal solution, it is rational. It is easier to fall back to the perception of lower risk and high-trust than to look toward the unknown.

The market search process is often less than comprehensive. It would be impossible for the government to examine every single software firm, as an exhaustive market search to seek new bidders requires time and resources both of which are often in short supply for the government team. For companies in the *high-trust* position, however, this works well, for those who are not, the system is flawed. In one case, a small COTS software company, *Beta* (a pseudonym), bid on a project. The company's co-founder said it was a small government project that could have been done for about $250K. The government awarded the contract to company *Delta* (a pseudonym), a large, well-known government contractor. *Delta* subcontracted about 90% of the work to *Beta*. The cost to the government was $500K; prime contractor *Delta* received $250K and *Beta* received $250K. The *Beta* program manager remarked that it seemed that the lesser-known vendors needed a "big brother" to get their foot in the door to government contracts. In another case, a COTS software company, *Alpha* (a pseudonym), bid on a government contract for government agency *Rho* (a pseudonym). *Alpha* already had working software available off-the-shelf for $1M. *Rho*, however, had already allocated $100M for the contract and was anxious to design-and-build custom software. *Rho* wanted to own the source code so that system problems could be fixed without having to depend on *Alpha*. *Alpha*, however, had a good track record with the government of ensuring that upgrades and system fixes would be part of the contract and done with the greatest of integrity. Nonetheless, *Rho* pursued a custom build. After five years and $110M, the system was neither user friendly or adequate, and has since been scrapped. *Rho* ultimately turned back to *Alpha*, who sold them the system for $1M. Up and running, the agency continues to depend on *Alpha* for this well-running COTS software system. *Alpha's* CEO commented: "This is not an atypical case. We have experienced and continue to experience this type of behavior."

2 Trust Theories

In high technology such as software, the requirement to *trust* (when procuring), or to be *trustworthy* (when vending) are essential. It is not possible for every manager to understand every line of code or component of a complex system, so he or she must rely on the expertise of others. Simon's theory of *bounded rationality* states that managers are rational, but bounded by human constraints and as projects become more complex and larger, this is increasingly so. [21] [10] Earlier market theorists saw the importance of *trust* in the market as it reduces *transaction costs.* [25] [26] [27] When a firm is able to trust a supplier, there is no need to continually research the market or verify orders. These checks and double-checks can be costly. [20]

As human beings, we generally prefer to control our world, and *having* to depend on others – that is to *trust* – can create discomfort. This is especially so when the individual or organization is not well known. When we trust those who are trustworthy, it can be a comfortable feeling. Figure 2 illustrates the relative position of *trust* and *trustworthiness* from the perspective of the *trustor.* (The one in a position where he or she is required to *trust* or not *trust.*) The position of *trusting* the *trustworthy* is represented in quadrant I. Other quadrants describe other comfort levels for *trusting* and *trustworthy* behavior. We tend to trust family members, those we know, and those who are similar to ourselves over the unknown or unrelated. [9] [5] As a result, we frequently stick to well-known groups, which usually older methodologies rather than seek new, potentially better ones. We perceive those that are new as riskier, and the higher the stakes, the more risk averse we become. [23] *Prospect theory* states that we do not like losing, but we especially do not like to lose *big.* When an individual is in a position of a potentially large loss, he or she is likely to revert to his or her most primal or most comfortable behavior. This theory of *threat rigidity* is common when an individual or a group is threatened with well-being. [22] A manager responsible for the success of a large monetary program is in such a position, and therefore any loss would be *big*. He or she could be threatened with the loss of his or her job and therefore livelihood; which is understandably scary.

Thus, managers tend to stick to a known system. Since we tend to trust family and friends, social ties are important in business as well. In his studies of *embeddedness,* Granovetter emphasizes that social relations are entwined in business relations, and that these types of relationships can open a path for malfeasance. [8] He emphasizes that self-interest is a necessary part of economic life, and is to be distinguished from malfeasance. Profit-oriented companies are in business for business, and self-interest is a normal and expected part of that process. Malfeasance, however, is to be distinguished in that it is when one party knowingly takes advantage of its position to harm the other.

In his classic discussions of the market transformation, Williamson argues that in a free market, the *fundamental transformation* can occur: "Although a large numbers-exchange condition obtains at the outset, it is transformed during the contract execution in to a small numbers exchange relation…" [25] Once the *fundamental transformation* has occurred, it is an invitation for *opportunism.* Suppliers with few competitors, especially those who have developed a product over many years and have exclusive abilities and rights, are in a position to overcharge taking advantage of their market position. Thus, the relationship has been violated.

Not all *high-trust* relationships require nor allow for time to build. This phenomenon, *swift trust*, has been studied recently as it relates to small, temporary groups. [16] We use context to legitimize that which we trust. Like Simon's *bounded rationality,* if we investigated every person upon whom we had to rely, we would barely have time to eat. It is also essential for not-so-simple operations such as aircraft carrier deck teams. Weick and Roberts [24] studied these teams in the context of the collective mind. Where lives are at stake and high cooperation is required, trust is implicit and the results of failure are devastating. These temporary teams require *swift trust* in order to function in this high-stress, time-pressure environment. Though it is not the same type of thick trust that is borne of long-term, entrenched relationships, it is a practical, functional form of trust necessary for simple daily functions as well as complex operations.

Traditional *trust* is thought to be resilient. [16] Though it does not easily dissolve, once betrayed it is difficult to rebuild. *Swift trust* is more-or-less a *mindful trust*. Since the individual or organization is in the unenviable position of trusting someone of whom they have no knowledge, the actor is constantly mindful of the others' actions. Citing that sometimes we *trust* too much; or even mindlessly, Kramer used the term *prudent paranoia* to describe what he believes will keep people out of unnecessary trouble. [12] (See quadrant III of Figure 2.) Though being trusting can be important to a business relationship, Kramer suggests that it is prudent to pay attention to other parties' actions. Similarly, President Ronald Reagan liked the Russian expression and was often quoted: "Doverjai, no proverjai," meaning: "trust but verify".[4]

TRUSTWORTHINES

TRUSTFULNESS	***trustworthy***	***untrustworthy***
trusting	**I.** *Most comfortable position. Can rely on others without concern; easy to delegate responsibility.*	**II.** *Dangerous position. Usually here because the individual is not cognizant of untrustworthy behavior.*
untrusting	**III.** *The "on-your-toes; double-check" position. Though a firm may have proven to be trustworthy, it is prudent to trust and verify.*	**IV.** *A safe position, but a good one to get out of, if possible.*

Fig. 2. Trusting and Trustworthy Behavior. In this 2x2 each quadrant represents a distinct position of depending on trust. From north to south is the actor in the position of choosing to be trusting, untrusting, or anywhere in between. (As mentioned, *trust* is not a bipolar entity.) From east to west is the actor or organization in the position of having to be trusted

2.1 Market Assets of Trust

Classic theories of *trust* and the market have pointed to aspects of *trust* and *trustworthiness* that make markets and networks run efficiently. Popular management methodologies of the 1980s and 1990s frequently used trust as a cornerstone. *JIT*

---

4 Reagan liked this expression so much that Gorbachev once pressed him: "You repeat that at every meeting," to which Reagan replied: "I like it." [17]

(just- in-time) inventory control is a production methodology designed to minimize inventory and is a "pull" system. That is, little inventory is kept stocked until the manufacturer orders it. As inventory is needed it is supplied, so in order for this system to work competitively, a company must remain highly dependent on its suppliers, and must have *high-trust* in the timely delivery of functional components. JIT cannot operate without this level of trust. Similarly, *TQM* (total quality management) was based on the philosophy that responsibility should be pressed to the lowest level, and the lowest level should be competent. Another methodology dependent on *high-trust,* managers must rely on subordinates to be competent, and cannot micromanage their activities. When organizational relationships are strong, companies are *trusting* and suppliers are *trustworthy* (as in quadrant I of Figure 2), these are highly effective management philosophies.

In the U.S. Government procurement systems, and especially the DoD, *trust* has become the basis of many contractor relationships. Most large aerospace contractors began in the mid-twentieth century as small teams that were well ingrained with the customer. Over the past half-century these companies grew as did aerospace and related technologies such as computing. Companies and agencies became entrenched with one another as personnel crossed thin boundaries and thick network avenues were created from company to company to agency. Like Williamson's *fundamental transformation,* many companies existed in a highly competitive, free market at the outset, but over time, they have been slowly distilled to some five survivors. The oligopoly is a result of those that have failed, those that have merged and those that have survived on merit. [6] Their ties with the government are distinctly thick, cohesive, and *high trust.* Social ties are inevitably important in this. [8] For some government purchases, especially those not available commercially, *trust* is necessary and works well. But as theorists have noted, opportunism and malfeasance have not been absent from this network, discussed next.

2.2 Market Liabilities of Trust

Once *trust* is established between firms, such as with JIT, TQM, and organizations that that depend on one another for business and products, transaction costs are lowered as search and verification costs are nil. This works well when trust and trustworthiness are viable. But when this trust becomes blind, the doors are open for malfeasance [8] and opportunism. [25]

Here two types of sub-optimal behavior are evident: that of *omission* and that of *commission.* With *omission,* sub-optimal behavior is not necessarily intentional; the supplier may be simply getting inefficient by virtue of the environment in which it operates. With an established customer, there is little incentive to find better market products for the government. Also, depending on the program manager, there may be little understood about what software is available in the marketplace. In the DoD contracting arena, contracts are set-up to encourage contractors to spend more, and not less. [7] With *commission,* sub-optimal behavior is intentional. The supplier may well realize that there are better, cheaper software products available from other firms, but not share that information with the government for the survival of their own company. This is represented in quadrant II of Figure 2.

Favored and long-established government contractors in the enviable *high-trust* position enjoy benefits not given to other firms. The *Matthew effect* is named for a biblical passage; Matthew 13:12 that states: *"From unto everyone that hath shall be given and he shall have abundance, but from him that hath not shall be taken away even what he hath."* The concept is similar: organizations that have high status and wealth will receive wealth and customers more easily than those who do not. [15][19]

Consider company *Beta. Beta* required a "big brother," that is, a large company with a well-known name to essentially broker *Beta's* product. This is not only common in government contracting, but in the open marketplace as well. Famous clothing designers, for example, often hire lesser-known designers. The lesser-known designers, in the disadvantaged position, typically like having their name linked with a fashion icon. The icon, then receives a benefit from doing little work other than lending their good name. Like a structural hole in the system, the so-called "big brother" or "icon" is in a position to connect two players who need each other. In this case, it is as Burt suggests [2], indeed, the third party benefits. The consumer, however, in essence, ends up paying for a name.

With the exponential growth of computer technology starting in the late twentieth century, commercial software products have become sophisticated and plentiful. The commercial software market supports high-tech communications satellites, as well as high-tech operations and products. Yet, because of the precedent of design-and-build software, government managers have been slow to move to the commercial market. As Granovetter asserts, *embeddedness* can lead to many market difficulties. Social relationships become a basis for business relationships, thus skewing the manager's judgment as to the best objective solution or product. Similarly, a DoD aerospace procurement was *entrenched* in its favored networks. [7] As both a cause and result, there is lack of market knowledge and lack of market search. While *trusting* in entrenched contractors is rational behavior for government managers, it has invited opportunism and inefficiency. And so, as with the designer, the taxpayer can end up paying for a name.

3 Trust and Software

Software is one of society's closest commodities to pure *intellectual property* (IP). The software code has really no value other than what it can produce, or make hardware (such as a screen, satellite, or aircraft) do. Thus, software is completely intangible. It cannot be seen or touched. This makes it difficult to understand and its value difficult to assess. Developing software is expensive, but distributing it is not. So, once a development cost has been incurred and a software program operational, economies of scale are huge. Past aerospace software programs have been tailored to specialized programs. But today, with aerospace commonplace, the government is in a prime position to take advantage of COTS software. Since distribution costs are minimal, the perception of value is shocking to many government managers who are accustomed to paying millions. COTS software can easily be a fraction of the cost of custom. Yet, the intangibility of the product makes its value mysterious. In a *low-*

trust, high stakes position, managers are likely to lean back to a known system. The position is not necessarily *rational,* but *rationalizing*, where a manager could easily maintain that his or her path was optimal.

In the second case mentioned, lesser-known COTS software provider *Alpha* lost out to a well-known defense contractor. The program managers at *Rho* made a sub-optimal decision to develop a unique software product when a commercially available product was available at a fraction of the cost. *Alpha* had the disadvantage of being in a *low-trust* position, and *Rho* did not have the knowledge base, fortitude, nor, perhaps, incentive, to seek a better solution than a well-known, *high-trust* contractor. The loss was nearly $100M and five years. Not insignificant, and a tragic loss for the taxpayer.

The better known the component, the more likely customers will select it. [1] Bader et al. also suggest that as demand increases for these components, so will the requirement for *trust.* As software off-the-shelf products broaden their base, the requirement for government agencies to do market searches will increase accordingly. *Swift trust,* therefore, will become essential, if government agencies hope to keep pace with adversaries. Testability will be essential for a COTS product to succeed, as this will increase a program manager's knowledge of a product.

4 Moving Forward

Trust is not an absolute entity. Rather, it is a complicated emotion that exists on many levels and many scales. To say that we simply *trust* or *do not trust* would rule out the possibilities that one could trust a little, or trust a lot.

James March warns of learning from the past. Usually this type of experiential learning is flawed as the situation took place under different circumstances, in a different environment and with different technologies. It is not dependable. [14] However, March and his colleagues also describe how, when taking into account environmental factors that organizations and individuals *can* learn from relatively few; even just one experience. Suggestions how organizations can purchase COTS software from unknown providers follows.

Objectivity. Try to forget *who* and even *what* you know. A company's status and market reputation can be meaningless; especially with new, high-tech software products. Examine the product on its own merit and maintain objectivity. "The organization's memory embodied in precedents, customs of often-unknown origin, stories about how things have always been and used to be, and standard operating procedures, becomes used as a substitute for taking wise action." [18] Pfeffer and Sutton have investigated numerous organizations and found this to be a common flaw and observed that companies often act mindlessly when an organizational practice has been institutionalized. While it is difficult to kick the tires with software, it can be examined in other ways discussed next.

Fly-before-buy. Establish a fly-before-buy contract when possible. Though this seems simple enough, past government practices have assumed risk for highly technical projects. In the early days of satellites and computers, this is a practice that made sense. [3] Fledgling companies could not assume all risk for projects that were, at the time, largely experimental. The government developed contracting methods by which they assumed risk for projects even when they failed. Cost-plus contracting means that the government pays the contractor all its costs, plus the profit for the company. If the project was a failure, or in some cases a technological impossibility, the company did not go bankrupt, but rather, was able to cover its costs and stay in business. Today, satellites, computers and the software that supports them are not only critical in government operations, but well established in the commercial world as well. COTS satellite software is readily available. It is therefore reasonable to expect certain types of systems function properly before purchased. By employing a fly-before-buy system, the procurement officer is hedging, allaying unnecessary risk and building new trust based on demonstrated performance.

Ignore price. Especially with software, this can vary wildly. As discussed, once development has taken place, distribution costs are low. Social psychologists, advertisers, retailers and others have long known the association that consumers make with price and quality. That is, the perception that expensive=good. [4] Cialdini builds the case that this is an ingrained, human reaction from what we have learned throughout our lives. With little to go on, as in the theory of *bounded rationality* [21] we resort to such anecdotal evidence. In the case of COTS software, price is based on many factors such as development costs, economies of scale, and what the market will bear

Trojan Horse COTS. Sometimes things are not what they appear. The word is out in the government: politically speaking COTS solutions are preferred over custom ones. In many if not most facets of the government, custom solutions need to be justified. Companies know this, and those who do not build genuine COTS products; some well-meaning and some opportunistic, have put their software products in a COTS wrapper. Here are the warning signs. A *true* COTS software company makes about 70% of its revenue from software licenses, and about 30% from services.[5] When these numbers meander, attention should be paid to whether or not the product is really COTS.

Prudent Paranoia. Kramer used this term to describe what he asserts is a reasonable approach to trusting someone that you don't know. [12] He describes the prudently paranoid person as one who is not crazy, but who is keenly aware of his or her environment and colleagues and responds to it accordingly. They are aware observers. Individuals like this are found in successful temporary teams requiring *swift trust.* [16]

High Communication. Heedful interrelating is essential to know what others are thinking and where they are coming from. [24] When communication is high, there can be no surprises. In this day of cell phones, pagers, email, and teleconferencing, communication is available, easy and inexpensive.

---

[5] The expression "Trojan Horse COTS," and the 70/30 estimate both come from the CEO of a 250-person software company.

In a market relationship, *trust* exists on countless levels and is not bi-polar. Sensible trust, like prudent paranoia, includes taking many steps to verify and double check. It requires individuals who are keen observers and good communicators. Those companies and individuals who are trustworthy should appreciate the attention, while those who are not trustworthy will likely shy from it.

5 Epilogue

In seven years of research on this topic; countless conversations, interviews and readings, the most curious comment from program managers is: "How do we know a [new/small] COTS company will be around for the upgrade process?" In other words, how do we know to *trust* them? This begs many comments.

First, parallel with COTS procurement has come new management methodologies and philosophies. *Technology refresh* is a design technique that requires management to periodically examine the system and market as increases in computing power have driven the need for this. Appropriate technology refresh ensures that software change-out is performed based on market availability. To presuppose that the government will need the same company for the technology refresh means that there is no intention to re-evaluate the market, and the manger has missed the point. Secondly, the question supposes that concerns are about ongoing maintenance before the refresh period. Maintenance can and should be written into the contract. Third, the viability of any company, large, small, COTS, non-COTS is never guaranteed.

Given the relatively short lifespan and the availability of inexpensive software, change-outs are wise and will keep programs on the cutting-edge. It has been *favored trust* that has gotten the government entrenched, but it will be *heedful trust* in the more competitive commercial market that will keep programs running.

References

1. Bader, A., Mingins, C., and Bennett, D., and Ramakrishan, S., "Establishing Trust in COTS Components," in: *International Conference on COTS Based Software Systems 2003,* Erdogmus, H., and Weng, T. (Eds.) Springer, 2003.
2. Burt, R., *Structural Holes: The Social Structure of Competition,* Harvard University Press, 1995.
3. Carter, A., and Perry, W., *Preventive Defense,* Brookings Institution Press, Washington, D.C., 1999.
4. Cialdini, R., *Influence,* Quill, 1993.
5. Cialdini, R. and DeNicholas, M., "Self-Presentation by Association," in: *Journal of Personality and Social Psychology,* Vol. 57, 1989.
6. Dreazen, Y., Ip, G. and Kulish, N., "Big Business: Why the Sudden Rise in the Urge to Merge and Form Oligopolies? Higher Payoffs, a Lowering of Antitrust Obstacles and Some Burst Bubbles," in: *Wall Street Journal,* page 1, February 25, 2002.
7. Fellenzer, S., *Department of Defense Transformation: Organizational Barriers to the Commercial Product Use in Aerospace Projects,* Stanford Dissertation, June 2002.

8. Granovetter, M., "Economic Action and Social Structure: The Problem of Embeddedness," in: *American Journal of Sociology,* Vol. 91, No. 3, November 1985.
9. Kipnis, D., "Trust and Technology," in: *Trust in Organizations: Frontiers In Theory and Research,* Kramer, R. and Tyler, T. (Eds.) Sage 1996.
10. Krackhardt, D. and Kilduff, M., "Friendship Patterns and Culture: The Control of Organizational Diversity," in: *American Anthropologist,* Vol. 92, 1990.
11. Kramer, R., "Cooperation and Organizational Identification," in: *Social Psychology in Organizations: Advances in Theory and Research* (Murnighan, K., Ed.) Prentice Hall, 1993.
12. Kramer, R. "When Paranoia Makes Sense," in: *Harvard Business Review,* Vol. 80, No. 7, July 2002.
13. Kramer, R., and Tyler, T., *Trust in Organizations: Frontiers of Theory and Research,* Sage, California, 1996.
14. March, J., *The Pursuit of Organizational Intelligence,* Blackwell, Mass., 1999.
15. Merton, R., "Continuities in the Theory of Reference Group Behavior," in: *Social Theory and Social Structure,* New York Free Press, 1968.
16. Meyerson, D., Weick, K. E. and Kramer, R., "Swift Trust and Temporary Groups" in: *Trust in Organizations: Frontiers In Theory and Research,* Kramer, R. and Tyler, T. (Eds.) Sage, California, 1996.
17. Noonan, P., *When Character was King: A Story of Ronald Reagan,* Penguin, New York, 2001.
18. Pfeffer, J. and Sutton, R., *The Knowing-Doing Gap: How Smart Companies Turn Knowledge into Action,* Harvard Business School Press, Mass., 2000.
19. Podolny, J., "A Status Based Model of Market Competition," in: *American Journal of Sociology,* Vol. 98, No. 4, 829-872, 1993.
20. Sako, M., *Prices, Quality and Trust,* Cambridge University Press, 1992.
21. Simon, H. "A Behavioral Model of Rational Choice," in: *Quarterly Journal of Economics,* Vol. 69, 1955.
22. Staw, B., Sandelands, L., and Dutton, J., "Threat-Rigidity Effects in Organizational Behavior," in: *Administrative Science Quarterly,* Vol. 26, December 1981.
23. Tversky, A. and Kahneman, D., "Advances in Prospect Theory" in: *Journal of Risk and Uncertainty,* Vol. 5, 1992.
24. Weick, K. and Roberts, K., "Collective Mind in Organizations: Heedful Interrelating on Flight Decks," in: *Administrative Science Quarterly,* Vol. 38, 1993.
25. Williamson, O., *Markets and Hierarchies,* Free Press, 1975.
26. Williamson, O., "The Economics of Organization: The Transaction Cost Approach" in: *American Journal of Sociology,* Vol. 87, 1981.
27. Williamson, O., "Transaction Cost Economics and Organization Theory," in *Organization Theory: From Chester Barnard to the Present and Beyond,* Williamson O., (Ed.) Oxford 1995.

Filtering COTS Components Through an Improvement-Based Process*

Alejandra Cechich[1] and Mario Piattini[2]

[1] Departamento de Ciencias de la Computación,
Universidad Nacional del Comahue, Buenos Aires 1400,
Neuquén, Argentina
acechich@uncoma.edu.ar
[2] Grupo Alarcos, Escuela Superior de Informática,
Universidad de Castilla-La Mancha, Paseo de la Universidad 4,
Ciudad Real, España
Mario.Piattini@uclm.es

Abstract. Typically, COTS evaluations embody a first stage intended to determine rapidly which products are suitable in a target context. This stage – called "filtering" or "screening" – chooses a set of alternatives to be considered for more detailed evaluation. For successful filtering processes, composers increasingly focus on closing the gap between required and offered functionality, hence reducing ambiguity of information for comparison. In this paper, we introduce a filtering process, which is based on early measurement of functional suitability of COTS candidates. Measures are immersed in a Six Sigma-based process aiming at improving the filtering process itself as well as its deliverables.

1 Introduction

The adoption of COTS-based development brings with it many challenges about the identification and finding of candidate components for reuse. The search is generally driven by evaluation criteria defined at different levels or as part of an iterative process, in which the preliminary analysis of the current system is an important source for criteria definition [10].

However, the first part in the identification of suitable COTS candidates is currently carried out dealing with unstructured information on the Web, which makes the evaluation process highly costing when applying complex evaluation criteria. Currently, empirical studies indicate that the necessity of formal processes for evaluation depends on the context, but the results also confirm the necessity of accelerating the identification and filtering of candidates [14,20].

Identification of COTS candidates is a complex activity itself. It implies not only dealing with an impressive number of possible candidates but also with unstructured information that requires a careful analysis. In this context, the proposal in [12] sug-

* This work is partially supported by the CyTED project VII-J-RITOS2, by the UNComa project 04/E059, and by the MAS project (TIC 2003-02737-C02-02).

X. Franch and D. Port (Eds.): ICCBSS 2005, LNCS 3412, pp. 112–121, 2005.

gests extending the identification stage with a learning phase, which provides support to the COTS component discovery process. As a different and possibly complementary approach, other proposals use description logics to develop an ontology for matching requested and provided components [4,18]. Some other approaches try to measure the semantic distance between required and offered functionality [1,13] but these measures usually need detailed information as input to the calculations.

In addition to learning and classification issues, a filtering process is concerned with the pre-selection of candidates. It actually takes place by matching several properties of COTS components, including some inexact matching. Moreover, there are some cases where goals cannot be entirely satisfied without considerable product adaptation and other cases where these goals must be resigned to match product features [2,11].

As a possible improvement, in [19] the Six Sigma approach has been suggested selecting packaged software; however the evaluation mainly relies on the information provided by demos and additional documentation of the software. Then, the lack of measures makes this process perfectible.

Our Six-Sigma based approach focuses on fact-based decisions and teamwork, which might drive the identification and filtering process by using specific measures [6]. Particularly, we consider functional suitability as the main aspect to be measured; however, measures should be expressed in such a way that calculation is possible at early stage. Additionally, our process might be extended by classifying and standardizing information for analysis, building upon some recent works on this field.

In section 2 of the paper, we introduce our process for filtering, which is described in terms of its main activities. Specific techniques and measures are referred in that context. Then, section 3 discusses some insights of the process. Finally, section 4 addresses conclusions and topics for further research.

2 An Improvement-Based Process for Filtering

Six Sigma is typically divided into five phases, creating what is referred to as DMAIC, which is an acronym for the following phases [19]:

1. *Define* the problem and identify what is important: Identify the problem and the customers; define and prioritise the customer's requirements; and define the current process.
2. *Measure* the current process: Confirm and quantify the problem; measure the various steps in the current process; revise and clarify the problem statement, if necessary; and define desired outcome.
3. *Analyse* what is wrong and potential solutions: Determine the root cause of the problem; and propose solutions.
4. *Improve* the process by implementing solutions: Prioritise solutions; and develop and implement highest benefit solutions.
5. *Control* the improved process by ensuring that the changes are sustained: Measure the improvements; communicate and celebrate successes; and ensure that process improvements are sustained.

Filtering COTS components needs to ensure – as in any Six Sigma project – that decisions are based on facts and that customer's requirements have been considered. However, in the continuing attempt to introduce COTS-based development, organisations have problems identifying the content, location, and use of diverse components. Six Sigma might help to put all these pieces together and define a measurement-based procedure for filtering COTS components.

To clarify our approach, the next section describes the first stages of the process – Define, Measure, and Analysis – in terms of their main steps and activities.

2.1 Describing the Process

In the following diagrams, a box is a rectangle representing a function, and each box on a diagram has a number in the bottom right corner to identify it within the diagram. The layout defines information/control/mechanism flows between activities as stated by the SADT technique [15].

Figure 1 defines the external interfaces for the "Filtering" process. The *Quality thresholds/Constraints* control consists of attributes that influence or constraint system's requirements and the filtering process itself. Typically, the constraint scope will include aspects such as schedule, cost, context and domain – we consider domain constraints those in which the application domain has been the cause of changes on the system's architecture, in contrast from context constraints, which have been caused by execution environment conditions. Quality thresholds represent the acceptance thresholds associated to quality attributes of the system.

The *Scenarios* input consists of different sequences of behaviour depending on the particular requests made and conditions surrounding the requests; the *COTS candidates* input consists of a number of COTS components available from marketplace; and the *Software architecture* input consists of the architectural basic units, components, and relationships among them. At this level, a basic unit for architecture is undetermined allowing multiple instantiations – such as compound units, corresponding processes, etc.

The *Stakeholders* mechanism consists of people who are involved in the filtering process. *Component sources* represent the external resources that are explored in the search of COTS candidates to be considered for evaluation.

The *Impact on stability* output consists of an identification of functional dissatisfactions according to the stability state defined during the filtering process, which embodies quality requirements and architectural aspects among others [5]. This output might include suggestions for new requirements or requirement's updates discovered during the search for COTS candidates as well as suggestions for architectural changes.

Finally, the *Filtered components* output consists of the component or components chosen for more evaluation as a result of the filtering process.

There are three primary activities in the Filtering Process: a commitment process, a pre-filtering process, and a final filtering process, as shown in Figure 2. These processes consist of activities related to the three first phases of our Six-Sigma based process for filtering – define, measure, and analysis – implicitly referring control and improvement through reporting feedback [6].

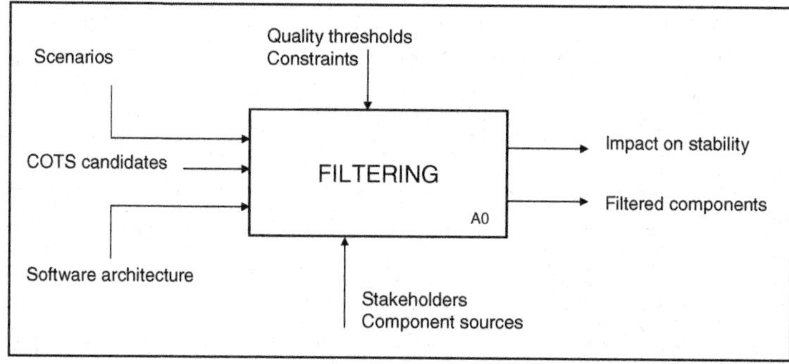

Fig. 1. Process Context

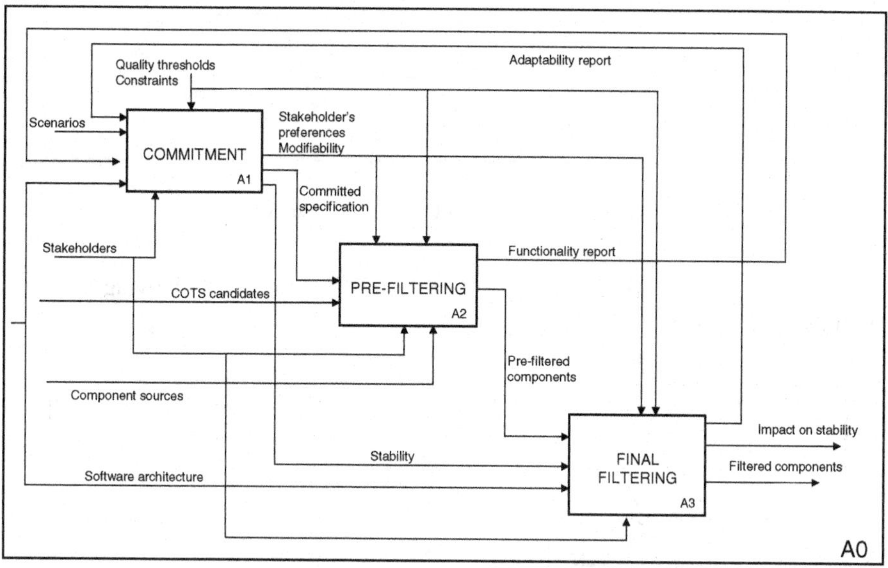

Fig. 2. Diagram 0 – Process steps

The "Commitment" process in the decomposition contains the following activities (as shown in Figure 3):

- "Derive Goals" determines the stability status of the system and provides a component specification to be committed. This activity uses information from scenario and software architecture specifications. Stakeholders use scenario authoring and goal discovering to elicit requirements at different levels of detail, and an abstract component specification is provided as input to the "Compute Preferences" process. *Desirability* is used to iteratively calibrate the abstract component specification until a *Committed specification* is produced as output. The *Goals* output consists of goals to be refined and weighted during the "Compute Preferences" process. Information about functionality and adaptability is used as refinement constraints, i.e. they drive the activities helping decide on further searching and evaluation of candidates.

- "Compute Preferences" calculates preference indicators such as desirability, modifiability and stakeholder's preferences on refined goals [7].

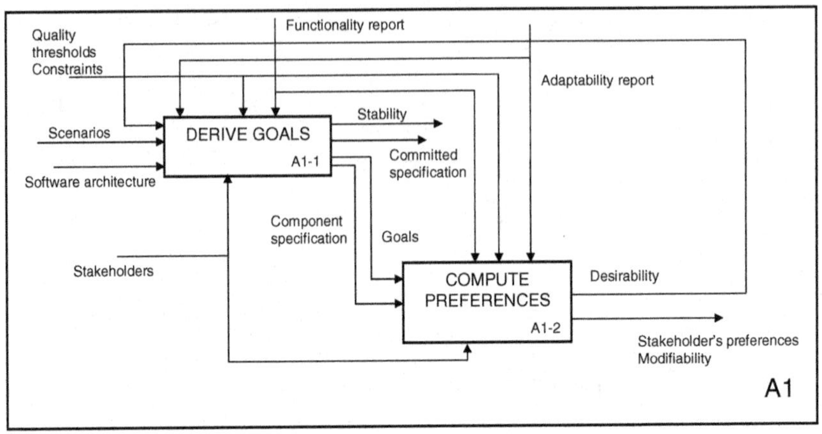

Fig. 3. Diagram 1 – Commitment steps

The "Pre-Filtering" process in the decomposition contains the following activities (as shown in Figure 4):

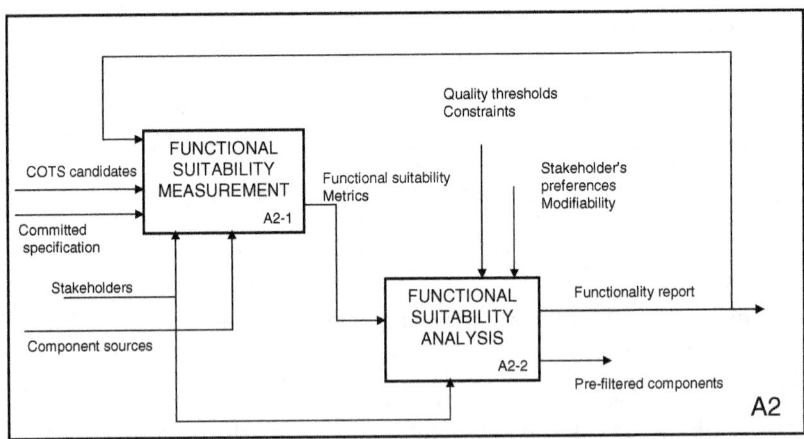

Fig. 4. Diagram 2 – Pre-filtering steps

- "Functional Suitability Measurement" computes metrics on functional suitability of COTS candidates. *Component sources* are used as a mechanism to search candidates. Then, *COTS candidates* from a marketplace are chosen and *Functional suitability metrics* [8] are produced as input to the "Functional Suitability Analysis" process. The *Committed specification* acts as a guideline to *Stakeholders*, who drive the search procedure. Information from functionality is used as refinement constraints similarly to other activities in the process.

- "Functional Suitability Analysis" analyses metrics on functional suitability measured for COTS candidates. A *Functionality report* summarises the results from the analysis and serves as an indicator to decide on how to stop the search. *Stakeholder's preferences* and *modifiability* constraint the analysis taking into account the degree in which goals can be modified. The *Pre-filtered components* output consists of the component or components that are functionally suitable, and hence candidates for further evaluation.

Finally, the "Final Filtering" process in the decomposition contains the following activities (as shown in Figure 5):

- "Architectural Adaptability Measurement" computes metrics on architectural adaptability (size and complexity of adaptation, and semantic architectural adaptability) [9] on the given *Software architecture* and considering a set of *Pre-filtered* (and functionally suitable) *components*. Then, *Architectural adaptability metrics* are produced as input to the "Architectural Adaptability Analysis" process. The *Software architecture* acts as a basement to judgments of *Stakeholders*. Information about adaptability is used as refinement constraints similarly to other activities in the process.
- "Architectural Adaptability Analysis" analyses metrics on architectural adaptability. An *Adaptability report* summarises the results from the analysis and serves as an indicator to decide on reviewing stakeholder's judgements and/or continuing the search for candidates. *Stakeholder's preferences* and *modifiability* constraints the analysis taking into account the degree in which goals can be modified – this time depending on adaptability judgments. The *Filtered components* output consists of the component or components that are finally filtered. The *Impact on stability* output reports on the degree in which initial system's stability, in terms of semantic architectural aspects, is affected by the filtered components.

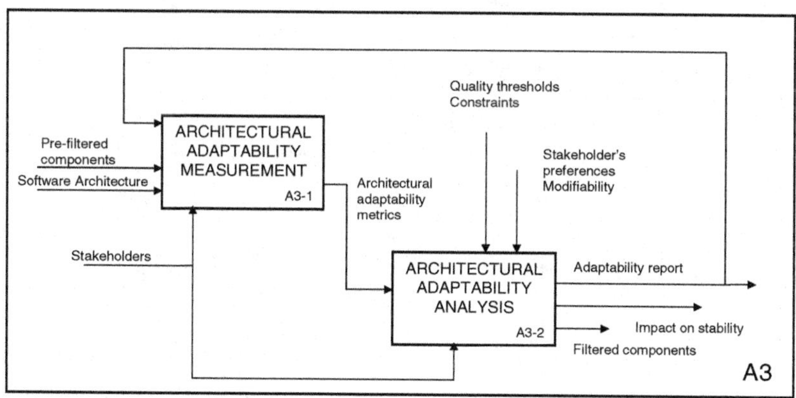

Fig. 5. Diagram 3 – Final filtering steps

3 Insights into the Process

Our proposal aims at providing a basement for improving the filtering process by a two-level improvement cycle as shown in Figure 6. The Figure additionally shows the three cycles that constitute our filtering process: (1) a "commitment" cycle, which produces a committed abstract specification S_C along with a modifiability indicator as inputs to the second cycle; (2) a "pre-filtering" cycle, in which COTS candidates are pre-selected according to their functional suitability; and (3) a "filtering" cycle, in which architectural semantic adaptability produces an indicator of stability that serves as a basis for the final candidate filtering. Note that the three cycles might also include relationships and improvements of several activities that remain internal to the process.

To define the process, we took into account how to identify suitable COTS components providing an early measure for comparison. We also considered that the evaluation of COTS candidates demands some inexact matching. The phases of our proposal were further defined by introducing some techniques and measures, which would help in establishing a basis for applying the approach. Besides, the presence of specific measures allows stakeholders to make fact-based decisions improving the analysis of COTS candidates.

But collecting effective measures is highly dependent on the amount and quality of information provided by third parties. Once requirements are categorised and weighted, a process to obtain and assess product vendor information should be carried out [3]. Closing the gap between the required and provided information also imply dealing with standard information for analysis. In this direction, recent endeavours – such as the eCots initiative [17] – might help define a web-based repository for collecting, classifying, and sharing information on software COTS products and producers.

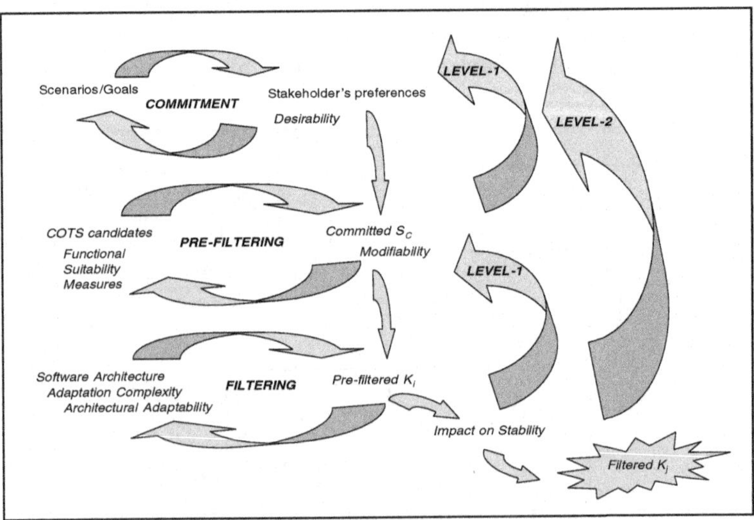

Fig. 6. Improvement in a filtering process

Metrics for COTS based systems are emerging from the academic and industrial field [15]. However, many of these definitions do not provide any guideline or context of use, which makes metric's usability dependable on subjective applications. Measures are not isolated calculations with different meanings; on the contrary, capability of measures is strongly related to the process of calculating and providing indicators based on the measures. Our approach intends to define a filtering process in which measures are included as a way of providing more specific values for comparison. At the same time, the process guides the calculation, so ambiguity is decreased.

Among other relationships, resulting measures are related to the artefact to be measured. In our approach, the artefact is expressed as functionality required by a particular application, and functionality offered by COTS candidates. Generally speaking, both cases are subject to analysing information that is modelled and weighted by people – composers or integrators on one side, and component's suppliers on the other. Different interpretations, perceptions, and judgements are then affected by the expressiveness of information. Nevertheless, our comparisons are abstract level definitions, which allow us to customise the filtering process by instantiating the calculation procedure according to different contexts of use.

As Figure 1 shows, architectural features and software requirements (scenarios) are the main inputs to drive our search of COTS candidates. From the architectural point of view, there are some additional remarks. Firstly, the impact on stability is currently based on qualitative judgements on semantic architectural adaptability, although they are combined with quantitative values of complexity and size of adaptation. We suggest here that quantitative and qualitative metrics together would help reach agreement when a decision on filtering components must be made.

Secondly, basement for decisions includes detecting architectural artefacts affected by the COTS candidate and identifying functional dissatisfactions. Causes of dissatisfaction should drive the improvement process leading to changes on the requirements definition, the host architecture, and even on the filtering process itself.

Finally, decisions on impact of stability as well as decisions made during the process might be weighted by stakeholders, in such a way that different roles and expertise are explicitly incorporated.

4 Conclusions and Future Work

We have presented a Six-Sigma based process for filtering COTS candidates. The process is based on teamwork and measurement, which allow us to provide a value for decision making. Values are calculated within a well-defined process that sets a context of use in the early stages of COTS component selection.

Of course, our process itself is subject to extension and improvement. For example, standardizing information for analysis is still an open issue that may be addressed in several ways – providing classifications and ontologies for COTS components (global and domain-oriented), defining certification issues, and so forth. Additionally, negotiation processes may be further detailed including particular features relevant to COTS development, such as negotiation on modifiability of goals.

Finally, our procedure and its particular measures are currently under validation. Among others, we are analysing the diverse ways of structuring COTS component's information to facilitate the analysis of functional matching.

References

1. R. Alexander and M. Blackburn: "Component Assessment Using Specification-Based Analysis and Testing". Technical Report SPC-98095-CMC, Software Productivity Consortium, 1999.
2. C. Alves and A. Finkelstein: "Challenges in COTS Decision-Making: A Goal-Driven Requirements Engineering Perspective". In Proceedings of the Fourteenth International Conference on Software Engineering and Knowledge Engineering, 2002.
3. B. Bertoa, J. Troya, and A. Vallecillo: "A Survey on the Quality Information Provided by Software Component Vendors". In Proceedings of the ECOOP QAOOSE Workshop, 2003.
4. R. Braga, M. Mattoso, and C. Werner: "The use of mediation and ontology technologies for software component information retrieval". In Proceedings of the 2001 symposium on Software reusability: putting software reuse in context, ACM press, pages 19–28, Ontario, Canada, 2001.
5. A. Cechich and M. Piattini: "Defining Stability for Component Integration Assessment". In Proceedings of the Fifth International Conference on Enterprise Information Systems, pages 251–256, Angers, France, April 2003.
6. A. Cechich and M. Piattini: "Managing COTS Components using a Six Sigma-based Process". In Proceedings of the Fifth International Conference on Product Focused Software Improvement, volume 3009 of LNCS, pages 556–567, Nara, Japan, April 2004. Springer-Verlag.
7. A. Cechich and M. Piattini: "Balancing Stakeholder's Preferences on Measuring COTS Component Functional Suitability". In Proceedings of the Sixth International Conference on Enterprise Information Systems, pages 115–122, Porto, Portugal, April 2004.
8. A. Cechich and M. Piattini: "On the Measurement of COTS Functional Suitability". In Proceedings of the Third International Conference on COTS-Based Software Systems, volume 2959 of LNCS, pages 31–40, Los Angeles, USA, February 2004. Springer-Verlag.
9. A. Cechich and M. Piattini: "Quantifying COTS Component Functional Adaptation". In Proceedings of the Eight International Conference on Software Reuse, volume 3107 of LNCS, 195–204, Madrid, Spain, July 2004. Springer-Verlag.
10. A. Cechich, M. Piattini, and A. Vallecillo: "Assessing Component-Based Systems". In Component-Based Software Quality: Methods and Techniques, volume 2693 of LNCS, pages 1–20, 2003. Springer-Verlag.
11. K. Cooper and L. Chung: "A COTS-Aware Requirements Engineering and Architecting Approach: Defining System Level Agents, Goals, Requirements and Architecture", Technical Report UTDCS-20-02, Department of Computer Science, The University of Texas at Dallas, October 2002.
12. L. Jaccheri and M. Torchiano: "A Software Process Model to Support Learning of COTS Products". IDI NTNU Technical Report, November 2002.
13. L. Jilani and J. Desharnais: "Defining and Applying Measures of Distance Between Specifications". *IEEE* Transactions on Software Engineering, 27(8):673–703, 2001.

14. J. Li, F. Bjørnson, R. Conradi, and V. Kampenes: "An Empirical Study on COTS Component Selection Process in Norwegian IT Companies". In Proceedings of the First International Workshop on Methods and Processes for the Evaluation of COTS Components, IEEE Press, pages 27–30, Edinburgh, Scotland, May 2004.
15. D. Marca and C. McGowan: "SADT: Structured Analysis and Design Technique", McGraw-Hill Co., 1988.
16. J. Martín-Albo, M. F. Bertoa, C. Calero, A. Vallecillo, A. Cechich, and M. Piattini: "CQM: A Software Component Metric Classification Model". In Proc. of the 7th ECOOP Workshop on Quantitative Approaches in Object-Oriented Software Engineering (QAOOSE 2003), pages 54-60, Darmstadt, Germany, July 2003.
17. J-C. Mielnik, B. Lang, S. Laurière, J-G Schlosser, and V. Bouthors: "eCots Platform : An Inter-industrial Initiative for COTS-Related Information Sharing". In Proceedings of the Second International Conference on COTS-Based Software Systems, volume 2580 of LNCS, pages 157–167, Ottawa, Canada, February 2003. Springer-Verlag.
18. C. Pahl: "An Ontology for Software Component Matching". In Proceedings of the Sixth International Conference on Fundamental Approaches to Software Engineering, volume 2621 of LNCS, pages 6–21, Warsaw, Poland, 2003. Springer-Verlag.
19. C. Tayntor: "Six Sigma Software Development". Auerbach Publications, 2002.
20. M. Torchiano and M. Morisio: "Overlooked Aspects of COTS-Based Development". IEEE Software 21(2):88–93, 2004.

Enabling the Selection of COTS Components

Sudipto Ghosh, John L. Kelly, and Roopashree P. Shankar

Department of Computer Science,
Colorado State University,
Fort Collins, Colorado 80523
{ghosh, jkelly, roopaps}@cs.colostate.edu

Abstract. Ensuring proper selection of COTS components is key to the success of component-based software development approaches. Although several approaches and criteria have been proposed for component selection, we lack techniques that can be used to systematically evaluate components against selection criteria for functionality, security, fault tolerance, and quality attributes. We propose a comprehensive approach for enabling the selection of COTS components by employing component understanding and fault injection testing techniques that aid in building an integrated comprehension model of the components. This model accumulates information regarding how each candidate component fared with respect to each criterion. This model can be used not only to aid in the final decision making process, but also serve as a guide during the component comprehension and evaluation stages.

Keywords: COTS, components, comprehension model, fault injection testing, fault tolerance, selection, security.

1 Introduction

The success of component-based software development (CBSD) approaches depends heavily on the use of systematic techniques for selecting COTS components during application integration. "Evaluation and selection of the most appropriate COTS product has a tremendous impact on the subsequent processes and products of software development and evolution [1]." The selected components affect not only the correctness, quality and dependability of the application, but also the cost and quality of the process and future maintenance activities. COTS components also increase the liability of the application developer.

Component selection involves the identification of appropriate selection criteria, assigning scores to alternative components for each criterion, and then making a decision on which component best meets the criteria [2]. However, component selection is usually difficult, mostly owing to the black-box nature of COTS components, and the often incomplete or imprecise documentation accompanying them. Not much is known about the internals of the COTS components and how they fit with original requirements and the remaining software system. Application developers who use COTS components are faced with a large

X. Franch and D. Port (Eds.): ICCBSS 2005, LNCS 3412, pp. 122–131, 2005.

number of requirements and constraints regarding the functionality, quality, security and fault tolerance requirements of the product. Since COTS component specifications do not necessarily match the exact requirements of the system, developers need to wrap the components to limit the functionality and range of inputs and outputs. Writing wrapper code and component integration requires significant effort. Moreover, components tend to evolve along with applications, thereby breaking existing versions of the assembled applications and increasing maintenance costs. Therefore, care must be taken during the selection of components to meet both short term and long term business objectives.

Although several approaches have been proposed for component selection [1], we lack techniques that can be used to systematically evaluate components against selection criteria for functionality, security, fault tolerance, and quality attributes. In this paper we present an approach for understanding the fault tolerance properties of Java components using the fault injection technique. We propose novel techniques for fault injection in Java components using: (1) aspect technologies, and (2) byte-code level manipulation.

We also propose the use of an integrated component comprehension model that accumulates all the information regarding how each component under consideration fared with respect to each selection criterion. This model can be used not only to aid in the final decision making process, but also to serve as a guide during the component comprehension and evaluation stages. We illustrate the use of the component comprehension model to understand the functionality of calendar components implemented in Java and downloaded from the world wide web. We explain the role of the component comprehension model in the overall component selection process.

2 Background

We see several important areas of existing work: (1) component selection and decision support approaches and selection criteria, and (2) testing approaches in component-based development. The first examines the overall selection process and general criteria used in selecting COTS components. The second examines strategies used in testing software components to understand their functionality and their effect on the remainder of the system.

2.1 Component Selection Approaches and Criteria

A number of approaches have been proposed to address selection of COTS components [1]. Examples are OTSO, PORE, CEP, CAP, CRE, QESTA, Storyboard, STACE, PECA, and combined selection of COTS components. Our goal is not to define a completely new approach. Instead, we describe an approach for evaluating components based on specific selection criteria related to functionality, component quality attributes, security and fault tolerance. The information obtained from the evaluation process can be used in any of the above approaches to perform an overall evaluation.

Researchers in academia and practitioners in the industry have proposed several selection criteria that may be used by application developers. Kuruganti [3] presents an initial screening process that uses "draft specifications (must have features, interface properties, performance and operational constraints), development and deployment environments, and expectations relative to vendor." Poulin et al. [4], Tracz [5], Prieto-Diaz [6], and Ramamoorthy et al. [7] have also proposed metrics for software reuse and component selection. Briand [8] categorizes criteria based on quality (reliability, maintainability, portability, efficiency, and usability), functionality, architecture, and compliance with standards. Kontio et al. [9] categorize criteria based on functional requirements, product quality characteristics, strategic concerns, and domain and architecture compatibility.

2.2 Testing Approaches in Component-Based Development

Components are tested to ensure that they meet the specifications and fulfill their functional requirements. Testing helps ensure that the interactions between the component and the rest of the system conform to the application's requirements. Non-functional properties such as security and fault tolerance are also evaluated. Since in most cases component code is unavailable, testers resort to black-box testing (e.g., see Edwards [10]). The system's operational profile is used during such testing [11].

Several approaches have been proposed for testing and understanding components. Rosenblum [12] described test adequacy criteria for testing software components and component-based applications. The use of metadata to perform component testing and regression testing is described in Orso et al. [13] and Harrold et al. [14]. Soundarajan and Tyler [15] and Bertolino and Polini [16] described the testing of components and component deployment.

Korel [17] proposed an interface probing technique to understand black-box components. The component user is required to write specifications for the required component behavior and then automatically generate *check-code* that has the required behavior. A *test case generator* generates test cases from this test-code and these tests can be used as input to the real component. The test cases can be generated using black-box or white-box techniques from the check-code. The test cases are run on the component and the user can determine whether a component has a specific property or not.

Any of these approaches can be used to obtain information that is filled in our component comprehension model. Our approach does not specify the exact technique to be used to test components. Any technique that can be used to learn the behavior and operating constraints can be used in our component comprehension approach.

3 Fault Injection Testing

Safety-critical applications have stringent fault tolerance requirements. Techniques that assess fault tolerance properties are required (e.g., fault injection testing [18, 19]). During normal testing, it is often difficult to create all the erroneous conditions that cause failures in components or the interconnections. System level fault injection tests help reveal potential problems in the application in case individual components fail. Voas developed a technique called PIE analysis [20] (for *propagation*, *infection* and *analysis*). PIE analysis is a "dynamic technique for statistically estimating three program characteristics that affect a program's computational behavior: (1) the probability that a particular section of a program is executed, (2) the probability that the particular section affects the data state, and (3) the probability that a data state produced by that section has an effect on program output." Fault injection testing combined with PIE analysis can be used to assess the fault tolerance of applications. Fault injection testing can also be used to evaluate security by perturbation of the environment of the component [21]. We use the fault injection testing technique to evaluate Java components.

Weyuker [22] emphasizes that components need to be validated, especially those that will be deployed in diverse software environments. Most of the problems that arise during the use of components stem from the fact that the components may be used in different configurations and environments than they were originally designed and tested for.

Software faults may cause the system state to be corrupted. Fault categories cause system hanging, abend, crash [23], or erroneous behavior and results. For example, the end result of deadlock may be system hang. An incorrect algorithm implementation may cause erroneous system behavior. It may not always be necessary to tolerate each fault. Instead, it may be important to tolerate the result of the fault.

We need to develop fault models and derive a set of test objectives that cover all faults in the model. We need to implement a fault injection testing technique that can be used to observe system behavior in the presence of injected faults. We also need to determine when and where faults must be injected into the system; one may use random distribution or human-specified locations of interest.

We have identified three testing categories for Java components. All three categories of testing may need to be performed for every component.

1. *State Change Injection:* This forces the state of a component to change.
2. *Forced Exception Injection:* This forces the component to throw exceptions and makes the system execute the fault-handling routines.
3. *Input Testing:* The goal is to force a component to generate a fault without using invasive testing. Component interfaces are used to receive and retrieve data. Testing may follow the contract specified by the component developer. Moreover, testers may investigate the effect of unexpected values provided to the component by the rest of the system, or unexpected values returned by the component to the system.

We propose three methods for performing fault injection. Table 1 shows the method of injection, goals and weaknesses for each category of fault injection.

Table 1. Fault Injection Types and Methods

Category	Methods	Goals	Weaknesses
Input testing	Input, Aspect, BCEL injection	Verify suitability of component with respect to rest of the system	Test is likely to create only abend states. May not be possible to force invalid states using inputs only.
Forced exception injection	Aspect, BCEL injection	Force into an abend state, No need to discover actual cause of exception raised.	Exception may be thrown even though component state is actually valid, and thus, the remainder of the system execution may be unaffected.
State injection	Aspect, BCEL injection	Creation of actual invalid states.	Invalid states may not be realistic.

1. *Input Injection:* Data is provided to the component using the component interfaces. This method of injection is used for the input testing category defined above. Input injection can be done at runtime.
2. *Aspect Injection:* The ability to weave new code into already compiled components allows the tester to inject faults. This method allows the implementation of source level (high level programming) fault injection testing. Aspects can be used to modify behavior of methods by adding new behavior that is executed *before*, *after*, or *around* a method. New code can also be *introduced* in the form of methods. Currently AspectJ (an aspect-oriented programming language associated with Java) supports compile time weaving, and thus, injection can be performed at compile time. Once AspectJ supports runtime weaving, injection can be performed at runtime.
3. *BCEL Injection:* The Byte Code Engineering Library (BCEL) is an extension to Java and allows for the dynamic creation and transformation of Java class files. BCEL offers a new way to implement the PIE technique [20], which uses program instrumentation, syntax mutation, and changed values. In this technique, likely locations of failure in code are identified based on syntax and fault injection is performed at those locations. BCEL's pattern matching capabilities make it ideal for automating the PIE technique. The locations required by PIE such as assignment statements, input statements, output statements, and conditional statements are all in the set of accessible points in BCEL, thereby making it possible to identify locations and inject code.

BCEL and AspectJ both enable pattern matching and code insertion after the component has been compiled. One difference between BCEL and AspectJ is that BCEL offers the ability to manipulate bytecode dynamically. Moreover, unlike AspectJ, BCEL is not limited to code manipulation around joinpoints. Lastly, pattern matching and code insertion is accomplished by language-based syntax in AspectJ, whereas BCEL relies on library functions.

4 Component Selection Using the Component Comprehension Model

Andrews et al. [24] proposed an integrated model for understanding software components. This model is shown in Figure 1. It has three levels: (1) Domain model, (2) Situation model, and (3) Program model. As with program comprehension models (e.g., see [25]), developers can start building a mental model at any level that appears opportune, and switch between the three levels.

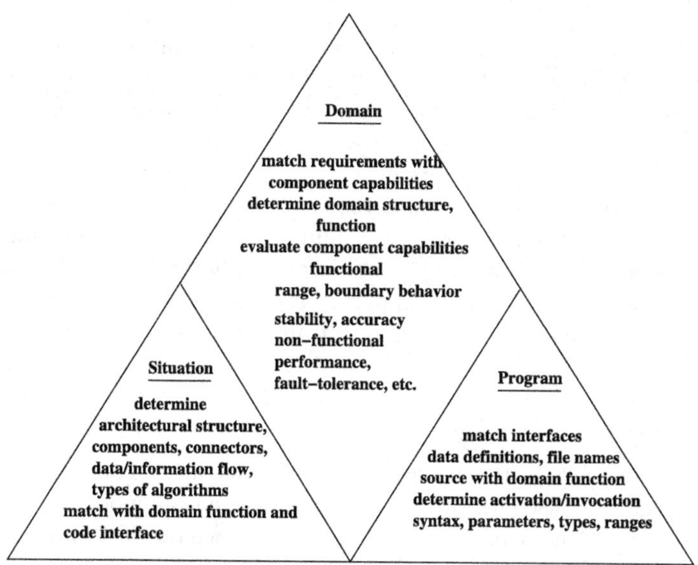

Fig. 1. Integrated Model for Understanding Software Components [24]

Since developers usually do not have access to the source code for a COTS component, the understanding process is driven mainly by domain and design knowledge. Knowledge at the program model level is limited to interface specification of the component. Knowledge about the interfaces together with domain and situation models is used to understand the structure and behavior of components.

At the domain level, the component's external structure and behavior are determined. Application requirements are matched with component capabilities. The component's domain structure, functionality, and non-functional properties (e.g., speed, fault-tolerance and performance) are understood.

At the situation level, details about the architectural design of the component, knowledge about sub-components, data and information flow are acquired. The component architecture is matched with application level entities. Situation level knowledge may be obtained from design documents (if available). Otherwise, knowledge about common design approaches and algorithms used in particular application areas helps in building the situation model.

At the program level, information about component interfaces is acquired. Program level knowledge includes details about the methods that can be invoked, their signature, parameters, type and range, API structure, and file names and package structure. Information for Java components may be obtained using Jar files, component introspection capabilities and descriptor files. All the information is matched against functional and structural requirements.

4.1 Selection Approach

The component comprehension model provides the foundation for the component selection activity. Software developers first identify the component selection criteria. This requires refining the requirements and understanding the constraints for the project. Any of the component understanding, testing, and fault injection approaches described in Sections 2 and 3 may be used to understand the component. The comprehension model for each component is filled using information obtained during the component understanding phase. The information in the comprehension model is used to determine whether or not the component satisfies the necessary criteria. An appropriate decision making approach named in Section 2 can be used to select the most appropriate component.

4.2 Example

We illustrate the use of the comprehension model using components used in a class project. We used the integrated comprehension model as a guide to understand four calendar components that were downloaded from the Internet. The goal was to select a component that provided calendar functionality along with the ability to store and retrieve appointments.

When source code was not available, we used documentation and Java reflection to obtain the information. However, in some cases the method names did not reveal the intent (e.g., method name was `a()`, or `b()` instead of something meaningful). We wrote several test applications using the downloaded components to understand their behavior. In this exercise, we did not consider fault tolerance requirements. The following paragraphs describe how the components were understood and the types of information obtained about each component.

1: This component came with two Java source files for the classes `DateChooser` and `DateButton`. Reading the source code gave us information regarding the functionality of the component. Several test cases were executed to confirm hypotheses regarding behavior. As a result, the comprehension model shown in Table 2 was created (not all details are shown for lack of space)[1].

[1] Comprehension models for other components not shown for lack of space.

Table 2. Integrated Comprehension Model for Component 1

Domain Model	**Component capabilities:** A calendar is displayed by clicking a button. A data can be chosen from the calendar. That date is displayed as the button text. There is no facility to store and retrieve appointments.
Situation Model	**Component Design and architecture:** `DateButton` and `DateChooser` are the subcomponents. `DateButton` instantiates the `DateChooser` which displays chosen date in a specified format. When the user clicks on the `DateButton` object, the control flow goes to fire the `actionPerformed()` method in the `DateButton`. This method displays the calendar and sets the text of `DateButton`.
Program Model	**Details of classes and methods:** `DateChooser` is a `JDialog` class, and `DateButton` is a `JButton`. `DateButton` implements the `actionPerformed()` operation which displays the calendar (`DateChooser`). The `DateChooser` has a `selectDate()` method that is used by the `DateButton` to set its own text. There are no methods in the class to do anything else with the dates (e.g., store and retrieve appointments).

2: There was no source code, but the vendor provided API documentation and a programmer's guide. These were used to develop the domain, situation, and program model elements.

3: This was a JavaBeans component consisting of several Java classes. We obtained method details and class hierarchy information from API documentation. A webpage that demonstrated the functionality of the component was also provided.

4: This was a JavaBeans component consisting of several other beans as subcomponents. We obtained information regarding methods and class hierarchy from the API documentation. When the downloaded component file was unzipped, two directories were created. This showed that the component came with two versions, one using Java AWT, the other using Java Swing. Code inspection showed that there were data structures and methods for manipulating appointments. However, displaying appointments was not possible. Therefore, we figured out that one would need to write another application to display the stored appointments. This was the only component that allowed us to store and retrieve appointments and was, therefore, the best candidate for the target application.

5 Conclusions and Future Work

Projections suggest that many software companies will use component-based software development approaches in their projects. The use of the integrated comprehension model to capture component information at various levels will aid in the overall component selection and decision making process.

Currently, we lack techniques that can be used to systematically evaluate components against selection criteria for functionality, security, fault tolerance, and quality attributes. The proposed fault injection testing approach will help in evaluating the fault tolerance properties of Java-based COTS components within the context of an application. The approach can be extended to components developed using other languages or middleware platforms. We will use our experience with AspectJ and BCEL-based fault injection to implement a complete fault injection tool. We will also evaluate our fault model and the effectiveness of the fault injection testing technique on Java components.

We see several interesting areas for further research. We will investigate how other extra-functional properties (e.g., security and performance) can be evaluated. As an illustration, consider components that are being selected on the basis of their adherence to security requirements. Since the reliance on pre-built components may complicate the assessment of the overall level of security provided by the system, we need to consider the security properties of individual components as well as the composite level of security provided by the component-based system. Voelter classified components as technical and logical (domain, data and user) [26]. For example, Java beans are often used to implement GUI components and domain components, and EJBs are used to implement domain, data and technical components. By identifying specific requirements for each type of component, developers can direct efforts on developing specific component security tests that test for these requirements. The use of the Common Criteria for security requirements will be explored.

We will evaluate the use of the integrated component comprehension model and its effectiveness in the selection of suitable components.

References

1. Ruhe, G.: "Intelligent Support for Selection of COTS Products". Revised Papers from the NODe 2002 Web and Database-Related Workshops on Web, Web-Services, and Database Systems, Lecture Notes In Computer Science (2002) 34–45
2. Kontio, J.: "OTSO: A Systematic Process for Reusable Software Component Selection". Technical Report CS-TR-3478, UMIACS-TR-95-63, Institute for Advanced Computer Studies and Department of Computer Science, University of Maryland, College Park (1995)
3. Kuruganti, I.: A Component Selection Methodology with Reference to the Internet Telephony Domain. URL `http://www.sei.cmu.edu/cbs/tools99/comp-select/` (1999)
4. Poulin, J.S., Caruso, J.M., Hancock, D.R.: "The Business Case for Software Reuse". IBM System's Journal **32**(4) (1993) 567–594
5. Tracz, W.: "Reusability Comes of Age". IEEE Software **4**(4) (1987) 6–8
6. Prieto-Diaz, R.: "Implementing Faceted Classification for Software Reuse". Communications of the ACM **34**(5) (1991) 89–97
7. Ramamoorthy, C.V., Garg, V., Prakash, A.: "Support for Reusability in Genesis". In: Proceedings of COMPSAC, Chicago, Illinois (1986) 299–305
8. Briand, L.C.: "COTS Evaluation and Selection". In: Proceedings of International Conference on Software Maintenance, Bethesda, Maryland (1998) 222–223

9. Kontio, J., Caldiera, G., Basili, V.R.: "Defining Factors, Goals and Criteria for Reusable Component Evaluation". In: Proceedings of CASCON, Toronto, Canada (1996)
10. Edwards, S.H.: "A Framework for Practical, Automated Black-box Testing of Component-based Software". Journal of Software Testing, Verification and Reliability **11**(2) (2001) 97–111
11. Goseva-Popstojanova, K., Mathur, A.P., Trivedi, K.S.: "Comparison of Architecture-based Software Reliability Models". In: Proceedings of the 12th IEEE International Symposium on Software Reliability Engineering (ISSRE 2001), Hong Kong (2001)
12. Roselblum, D.S.: "Adequate Testing of Component-based Software". Technical Report TR 97-34, Department of Information and Computer Science, University of California, Irvine, California (1997)
13. Orso, A., Harrold, M.J., Rosenblum, D.: "Component Metadata for Software Engineering Tasks". In: Proceedings of the 2nd International Workshop on Engineering Distributed Objects (EDO 2000), LNCS Vol. 1999, Springer Verlag, Davis, California (2000)
14. Harrold, M.J., Orso, A., Rosenblum, D., Rothemel, G., Soffa, M.L., Do, H.: "Using Component Metadata to Support Regression Testing of Component-based Software". In: Proceedings of the International Conference on Software Maintenance, Florence, Italy (2001)
15. Soundarajan, N., Tyler, B.: "Testing Components". In: Proceedings of the OOPSLA 2001 Workshop on Specification and Verification of Component-Based Systems, Tampa, Florida (2001) 4–9
16. Bertolino, A., Polini, A.: "A Framework for Component Deployment Testing". In: Proceedings of the 25th International Conference on Software Engineering, Portland, Oregon (2003) 221–231
17. Korel, B.: "Black-box Understanding of COTS Components". In: International Workshop on Program Understanding, Pittsburgh, Pennsylvania (1999) 226–233
18. Clark, J.A., Pradhan, Y.K.: Fault Injection: A Method for Validating Computer-System Reliability. IEEE Computer **28**(6) (1995) 47–56
19. Hsueh, M.C., Tsai, T.K., Iyer, R.K.: Fault Injection Techniques and Tools. IEEE Computer **30**(4) (1997) 75–82
20. Voas, J.M.: PIE: A Dynamic Failure-based Technique. IEEE Transactions on Software Engineering **18**(8) (1992) 717–727
21. Du, W., Mathur, A.P.: Testing for Software Vulnerability using Environment Perturbation. In: Proceedings of DSN, New York, NY (2000) 603–612
22. Weyuker, E.J.: "Testing Component-Based Software: A Cautionary Tale". IEEE Computer **15**(5) (1998) 54–59
23. Chung, P.E., Lee, W., Shih, J., Yajnik, S.: Fault Injection Experiments for Distributed Objects. In: Proceedings of International Symposium on Distributed Objects and Applications, 1999, Edinburgh, Scotland (1999)
24. Andrews, A., Ghosh, S., Choi, E.M.: "A Model for Understanding Software Components". In: Proceedings of the IEEE International Conference on Software Maintenance (ICSM), Montreal (2002)
25. von Mayrhauser, A., Vans, A.: "Industrial Experience With an Integrated Code Comprehension Model". IEE Software Engineering Journal (1995) 171–182
26. Voelter, M.: "A Taxonomy for Components". Journal of Object Technology **2**(4) (2003) 119–125

A Method for Compatible COTS Component Selection

Jesal Bhuta and Barry Boehm

Center for Software Engineering, University of Southern California,
Los Angeles, California 90089, USA
{jesal, boehm}@cse.usc.edu

Abstract. Software projects involving integration of multiple commercial as well as in-house components, often confront interoperability problems. This is a result of the component selection process being limited to piecewise evaluation of system capabilities while neglecting a more thorough evaluation of interoperability between candidate components. Such problems often lead to increased costs and schedule overruns. Based on empirical data gathered from five years of developing e-services applications at USC-CSE, we have developed and applied a method for component selection that focuses on piecewise evaluation, as well as the interoperability between the candidate components. In this paper we describe the method and present a real-world example showing how it operates within the spiral process model generator.

1 Introduction

Projects that require COTS, legacy, reusable and custom component integration often confront interoperability problems, where one component may not function well with the other. Such problems if detected late during the project development life cycle can result in increased costs and overrun schedules. Many development projects succumb to such issues because they do not consider the interoperability between components as a criterion when selecting components for system development. The selection instead is primarily based on piecewise evaluations of the system capabilities each component satisfies.

From our experiences in e-services projects we have observed that projects that have mitigated the risk of component interoperability earlier in the project development cycle have been more successful during the integration phases. However, those that neglected the component interoperability issues during their component selection cycle had to do a considerable amount of additional work in developing complex glueware to integrate the components, or re-work to replace certain incompatible components.

In this paper we propose a method that will help development teams reduce the risk of component incompatibilities during component assessment cycles. Section 2 of this paper describes the background and related work. Section 3 provides the definitions of the terms commonly used in this paper. Section 4 describes the method as a process element within the USC COTS process framework [14], while section 5 explains the elements that will facilitate this process. Section 6 illustrates the use of the method with a project example.

X. Franch and D. Port (Eds.): ICCBSS 2005, LNCS 3412, pp. 132 – 143, 2005.

2 Background and Related Work

In [1] and [21] researchers argue that interoperability problems amongst components occur due to multitude of reasons including functional mismatch, non-functional mismatch, architectural mismatch, component conflicts and interface conflicts [19][20][33]. For example, Garlan's Aesop [21] project found that the architectural mismatches among four COTS components caused a factor of four overrun in schedule (6 months to 2 years) and a factor of five increase in cost (1 to 5 person-years). Most contributions to reducing the problems have been product oriented [1][17][19][20][24][30][31]. Some COTS-based development papers have addressed the interoperability issue at a high level [3][4][14][15][22][26][28][29]; this paper provides a more specific method for selecting interoperable components.

In [5] researchers, based on empirical results, argue that the effort per line of glue code averages about three times the effort per line of developed applications code. Additionally they assert that the development and post deployment efforts can scale as high as the square of the number of independently developed COTS products targeted for integration. This empirical evidence is a compelling reason to provide CBA developers with better process for mitigating the integration risks, and reducing component integration effort and cost.

In [14] we have provided a recursive and re-entrant USC Composable COTS Based Application (CBA) process elements framework, which helps the developers design a life-cycle development plan using the spiral model to evaluate, tailor and integrate components in a CBA project. This paper is provides an extension to the framework, which focuses on activities for identification of a compatible set of COTS components to build the CBA.

3 Definitions

We adopt the SEI COTS-based System Initiative's definition [15] of a COTS product: A product that is:

- Sold, leased or licensed to the general public,
- Offered by a vendor trying to profit from it,
- Supported and evolved by the vendor, who retains the intellectual property rights,
- Available in multiple identical copies,
- Used without source code modification.

In [15], SEI also describes a COTS-based System (CBS) very generally as "any system, which includes one or more COTS component." The definition above for COTS-based Systems includes most current systems, including those that depend upon operating systems, or similar relatively stable frameworks. However, COTS considerations do not significantly affect the development cycle for such systems. Alternately we define a COTS Based Application (CBA) as a system for which 30% of the end-user functionality is provided by COTS components, and at least 10% of the development effort is devoted to COTS considerations. The numbers 30% for end-user functionality and 10% for development effort are approximate behavioral CBA boundaries observed in application projects. For more information on the CBA definition, and the empirical data please refer to [13][14].

In our six years of iteratively defining, developing, gathering project data for, and calibrating COCOTS cost estimation model, we identified three primary sources of project effort due to CBA considerations. These are defined in COCOTS as follows:

- COTS Assessment is the activity whereby COTS products are evaluated and selected as viable components for a user application [9].
- COTS Tailoring is the activity whereby COTS software products are configured for use in a specific context [9][25].
- COTS Glue Code development and integration is the activity whereby code is designed, developed and used to ensure that COTS components satisfactorily interoperate in support of the user application.

In this paper we will be using the terms COTS products and COTS components interchangeably. Additionally, we consider open source components, such as Apache, as COTS so long as it is being considered a black box in the user-application.

4 Compatible COTS Component Selection Method

Figure 1 below shows the method steps within the USC CBA development process framework [14] for sets of COTS components. The description of each of the activities in Figure 1 is given below:

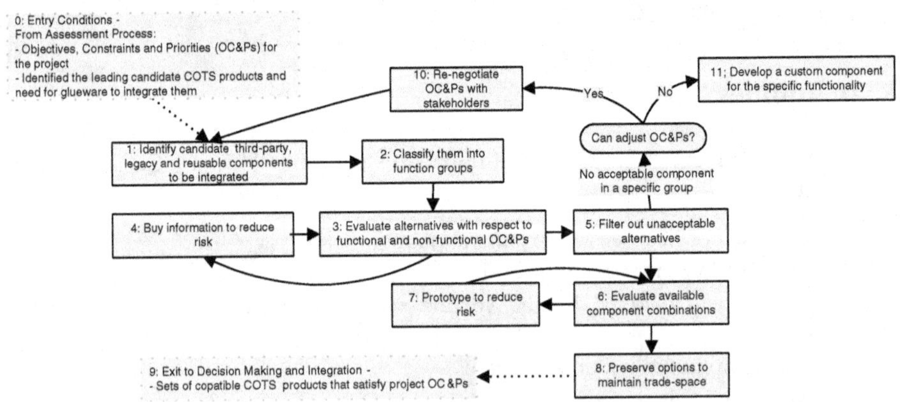

Fig 1. Compatible COTS Component Selection Method Activities

0: Entry Conditions:

We assume that the COTS assessment process has already established the Objectives, Constraints and Priorities (OC&Ps) of the CBA project. Additionally the assessment process has identified the leading candidate COTS, reusable, legacy and custom components and the need to integrate them using glueware. For more description for deriving the OC&Ps please refer to [14] and [27].

1: Identify Candidate Legacy and Third-Party Components to Be Integrated
Unlike traditional projects where the development team designs components themselves, in a CBA project the developers must design the system based on the availability of suitable components. To this end the development team must identify a set of third-party, legacy and reusable components, which when integrated in some combination and combined with custom code, meet the system OC&Ps. Third-party components can usually be found via extensive searches on the Internet and on open component directory project sites such as SourceForge, and eCOTS. For the OC&Ps that are not satisfied by any of the third party, legacy, or reusable components, the developers must plan to build custom components to satisfy those OC&Ps.

2: Classify the Components into Function Groups
Classification of components based on the function they perform in the system can help developers better understand and assess component capabilities and interoperability. Components in the same group must satisfy a similar set of system capabilities. For example, a group may consist of a set of components such as MSSQL, Oracle, or MySQL, which provide persistent data storage capability or alternately a set of frameworks such as .NET, J2EE, and Corba, which provide communication facilities for distributed systems.

In cases where multiple components are combined to provide the functionality, they should be considered as a single alternative for evaluation within the group. For example if one functional group consists of XML enabled database components, the group may include MSSQL, Oracle and an alternative where MySQL is coupled with XML Integrator, a component which converts XML to relational, and relational to XML data. Together MySQL and XML Integrator provide similar functionality that is already built into MSSQL and Oracle.

3: Evaluate Alternatives with Respect to Functional and Non-functional OC&Ps
The focus of this activity is to collect information about each COTS candidate against a set of evaluation criteria and weights obtained from the OC&Ps for the group of COTS candidates. The "evaluation criteria" is a list of functional and non-functional capabilities the component must possess in order to be considered for system. For example a functional evaluation criterion for the group of "Database Components" maybe "Storing XML documents", while a non-functional evaluation criterion for the same group maybe "a maximum response time of 5 seconds per query". Often development teams neglect non-functional OC&Ps, such as level or service capabilities, vendor support, up-front licensing costs, recurring licensing fee, vendor maintenance fee and vendor stability. These criteria, depending on the project OC&Ps may be extremely critical for the project, and must not be neglected.

The detailed process of evaluating functional and non-functional capabilities other than interoperability is outside the scope of this paper, and has been discussed in [4][14][16].

4: Buy Information to Reduce risk
Information on technologies and COTS components can be acquired by spending effort and schedule or money. This can be done by:

- Conducting market analysis to get latest COTS and technology information.
- Assess vendor supportability to address life-cycle issues.

- Develop, instrument, and evaluate prototypes, benchmarks, simulations, or analytical models to analyze key performance parameters.
- Buying technology and study reports from organizations such as Gartner to increase the market understanding of the developers.

Such information can provide the developers with a better understanding of technology alternatives, and hence reduce the project risk.

5: Filter Out Unacceptable Alternatives
Component alternatives that fail to meet the critical functional objectives are removed from consideration in this step. In the event that no single component makes it in a specific group, the developers need to re-negotiate with project stakeholders and adjust the OC&Ps (step 10) or develop a custom component for the specific functionality (step 11).

6: Evaluate Available Component Combinations
For the components still being considered, the developers must now consider the possible combinations in which they can be integrated to build the system. Figure 2 shows an example of such an evaluation. Each of the groups (developed in step 2) consists of components (COTS, reused, custom or legacy) that will provide certain capability required by the application. In most cases it is possible to develop the glueware to integrate components, if enough effort, schedule and cost resources are applied. However, the evaluation should focus on the feasibility of integrating the components under the OC&Ps of the project. If the effort required for developing glueware to integrate components A and B causes the project to exceed the maximum available effort, integrating components A and B is not feasible.

In Figure 2 below we see three functional groups of COTS products. COTS products that come from the same product family have the same names, while those that work with the same underlying platform have the same odd or even parity. If the ability of the glueware developed under the schedule, effort and cost constraints, to interoperate the components is restricted to components within the same product family, we get one set of COTS alternatives (all in the S1 family). Alternately, if the ability of the glueware developed is restricted to components with the same underlying platform we get 6 possible combinations of COTS components.

Note that the effort required to develop the glueware depends upon component interfaces available, architecture styles used by components [1][19][20][21], type of connector interfaces each component is compatible with (see [30]), component dependencies and clashes amongst them.

7: Prototype to Reduce Risk
Many developers evaluate the components interoperability simply by reading the vendor provided literature. The literature however may not be entirely reliable, or it may not provide the complete and contextual information required to evaluate the interoperability capability of the component. In such instances where the developers have little or no experience with components they are evaluating it is advisable to build prototypes, rather than depending upon the vendor provided literature. The prototypes will mostly comprise of the glueware required to integrate the components to ensure their satisfactory function upon integration. Additionally, building

prototypes will provide the developers with an estimate of the amount of effort required to integrate and test the components.

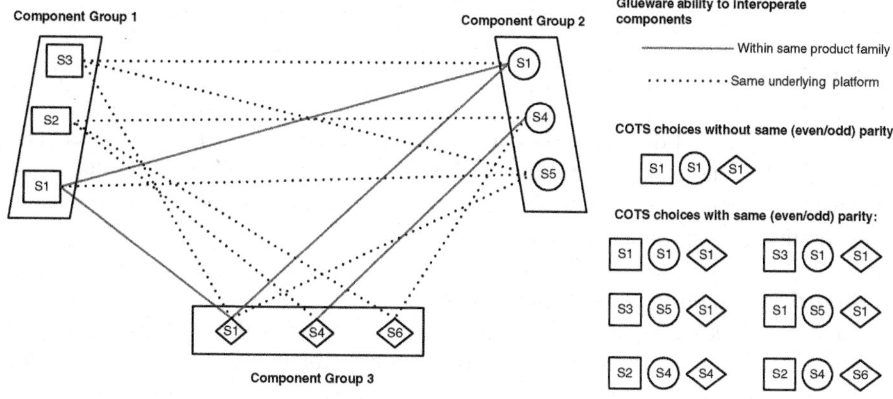

Fig. 2 Component Compatibility Evaluation Framework

8: Preserve Options to Maintain Trade-Space

Once a best-choice combination is obtained the developers often disregard all other possible satisfactory combinations. When using commercial components this can pose as a major risk, since significant changes can occur in the commercial marketplace, which may not be under the control of the developer organizations (for example: the vendor organization that created a component may go bankrupt). To mitigate such risks the developers should not disregard alternate satisfactory combinations. In the event of a market catastrophe the developers can always fall back to one of the alternate satisfactory combination, saving valuable resources in re-evaluating. Such alternate combinations, in addition to reducing the system development risks, can also be a useful tool during vendor negotiations for COTS licensing and other vendor fees.

9: Exit to Decision-Making and Integration:

At this point the developers would have a set of COTS combinations, prioritized based upon the cost, schedule and effort it would take to implement the system. The decision making process would involve careful consideration of the functional, non-functional, and component compatibility evaluation to determine the best possible set of components to chose for developing the system, based on the project OC&Ps.

10: Re-negotiate with Project Stakeholders and Adjust the OC&Ps:

In the event that no components in a particular group qualify to be selected, based on the capabilities and non-functional criteria, the developers may be required to re-negotiate the OC&Ps applicable to that group. It is possible that after re-negotiation there may be components available that can satisfy the capabilities and non-functional criteria based on the new OC&Ps.

11: Develop a Custom Component for the Specific Functionality:
If no components in a group qualify to be selected, based on the capability and non-functional criteria, and re-negotiation of OC&Ps is not possible, the developers will be required to custom make the component for the project.

5 Facilitators

In addition to the well-defined component compatibility process, CBA developers can further reduce the component integration risks using additional packages of information, which we term facilitators. Some facilitators for component compatibility analysis include:

Evaluated Taxonomy of Component Conflicts
Information of possible component conflicts can provide the developers with a medium to identify and eliminate potential incompatible component combinations. In [18][33], authors have provided a classification of component incompatibilities. CBA developers can use such classification as checklists to ensure no incompatibilities of the already-defined types exist amongst the satisfactory component combinations. Additionally in [1][19][20] authors have provided taxonomy of mismatches occurring due to the different architecture styles adopted by the components to be integrated in a system, which can be used to identify further component incompatibilities.

Evaluated taxonomy of Integration Approaches
Knowledge of various integration approaches can be an important tool for the design of component integration architectures. Connectors play a decisive role in defining the assumptions for system integration. In [25] the authors have provided taxonomy of possible connector approaches, which can be used for component integration. Middleware is another component integration approach, which is gaining increasing popularity amongst the CBA developers. In [23] the authors have identified a taxonomy that addresses the specific software mechanisms that enable compositional adaptation.

Calibrated Models of Key OC&P Satisfaction
It is extremely difficult for the developers to estimate the amount of effort required to perform component assessment and integration, especially when there are multiple components involved. Existing calibrated models for cost and effort estimation such as COCOTS [2][9] can provide the developers with an activity effort estimate. Using such estimates the CBA developers can design better project development plans, and if required perform trade-off's to meet the cost, effort and schedule constraints. Additionally models such as in [32] that help estimate the effort of integration based on the adopted architecture can provide valuable additional decision-making information for selecting one combination of components over another.

Evaluated Taxonomy of Model Approaches
An evaluated taxonomy of model approaches can help the development team identify the approach required to build the system. An example of such a taxonomy used in the MBASE guidelines [27], initially published in [8] is given below:

Table 1. Software Process Model Decision Table

Objectives, Contraints			Alternatives			
Growth Envelope	**Understanding of Requirements**	**Robust ness**	**Available Technology**	**Architecture Understanding**	**Model**	**Example**
Limited			COTS		Buy COTS	Simple Inventory Control
Limited			4GL, Transform		Transform or Evolutionary Development	Small Business - DP Application
Limited	Low	Low		Low	Evolutionary Prototype	Advanced Pattern Recognition
Limited to Large	High	High		High	Waterfall	Rebuild of old system
	Low	High			Risk Reduction followed by Waterfall	Complex Situation Assessment
		High		Low		High-performance Avionics
Limited to Medium	Low	Low-Medium		High	Evolutionary Development	Data Exploitation
Limited to Large			Large Re-usable Components	Medium to High	Capabilities-to-Requirements	Electronic Publishing
Very Large		High			Risk Reduction &Waterfall	Air Traffic Control
Medium to Large	Low	Medium	Partial COTS	Low to Medium	Spiral	Software Support Environment

6 Example Project: Caroline's Closets

One of the USC e-services COTS-based applications involved the development of an online shopping store for ladies attire. The full system capability included web-based inventory management, online shopping cart with a secure credit card payment using Bank of America eStores, online client information management, automated order processing, including generation of invoices, sending order and shipping confirmation, automatic inventory update, and access administration capabilities.

No single COTS product could satisfy all the system capabilities required by the client, under the financial constraints set by the client. However, several COTS components, when integrated together, could meet most of the system capabilities. As the Initial Operational Capability (IOC) [7] was to be developed as a student project, its scope needed to be accomplished by a five-person development team in 24 weeks. In the next section we will show how the process method described in section 4 was applied.

6.1 Applying the Compatible COTS Component Selection Method

For the sake of brevity the description provided in this section covers only the portions relevant for the description of the selection method. The project profile in Table 1 (medium size growth envelope, initially low requirements understanding, medium robustness, partial (to be determined) COTS and thereby medium architecture understanding) best fits the spiral model in the bottom row. The developers chose to follow the Model Based Architecting and Software Engineering (MBASE) [11][12] approach for design and implementation of the system [6]. The MBASE approach employs the spiral model [6][10] as the software development process for the system development. The development team applied the Win Win spiral model in six iterations:

Iteration 0 (Preliminary iteration): Analyze the existing business processes and define win conditions of the success-critical stakeholders.

Iteration 1 (Inception): Develop life-cycle objectives (Life Cycle Objective (LCO) milestone), prototypes, plans, and specifications for individual applications and verify the existence of at least one feasible architecture for the application.

Iteration 2, 3 (Elaboration I and II): Establish a specific, detailed life-cycle architecture (Life Cycle Architecture (LCA) milestone), verify its feasibility, and determine that there are no major risks in satisfying the plans and specifications.

Iteration 4 (Construction I): Achieve the system core-capabilities (Core Capability Demonstration (CCD) milestone) for the project.

Iteration 5 (Construction II): Achieve a workable initial operational capability (Initial Operational Capability (IOC) milestone) for the project including system preparation, training, use, and evolution support for users, administrators, and maintainers.

The developers implemented the selection method in the three spiral iterations - one inception, and the two elaboration cycles. During early part of the inception iteration, the team quickly determined the OC&Ps for the project and eliminated most single-solution, end-to-end COTS products, due to the cost constraint set by the client. Some initial search on the Internet resulted in a list of possible components that could be used to implement the system. The list included various databases, application servers, and commercial shopping-cart solutions. Using the information about the components available to the team they documented one feasible architecture at the LCO milestone.

Elaboration I iteration involved the detailed analysis of capabilities and non-functional criteria of the available candidate components, in various groups (databases, application servers, shopping-carts). The analysis for each group was based on evaluation criteria derived from the project OC&Ps. At the end of the elaboration I iteration the team had filtered most of the components that did not meet most of the required evaluation criteria.

During elaboration II iteration the team performed an evaluation on the possible COTS combinations that could be integrated with minimal glueware. Figure 3 shows a subset of components on which the component combination evaluation was applied. On analyzing the interoperability issues, the development team found that glueware can be made with minimal effort for components connected with a line in figure 3.

Based on this analysis the team identified the following feasible combinations, that would meet the system OC&Ps:

- MSSQL, Microsoft IIS, Cart 32
- MS-Access, Microsoft IIS, Cart 32
- MySQL, Apache-CGI, Danise Cart
- MySQL, Apache-Tomcat, X-Hub Enterprise Cart

Of the feasible combinations the development team, and the client together identified the MSSQL, Microsoft IIS, Cart 32 as the best solution since both the development team and the client had resources that were familiar with these technologies.

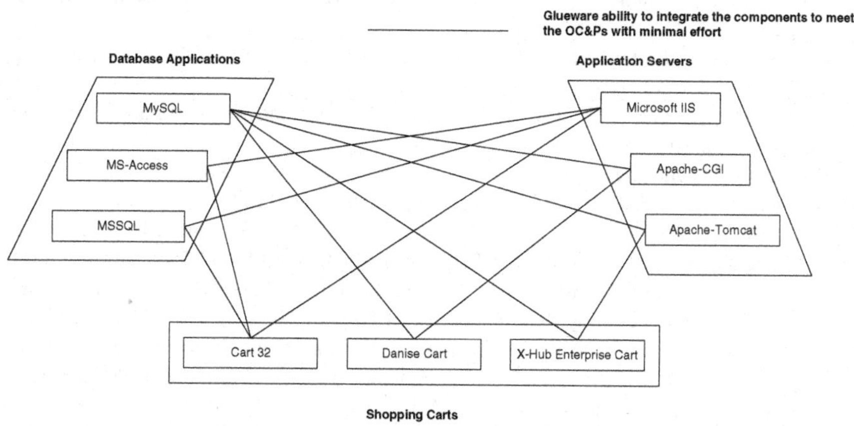

Fig. 3. Component Combination Evaluation for Caroline's Closets Project

7 Conclusions and Future Work

Many projects employ piecewise COTS capability evaluations to select COTS products and run into later problems with COTS integration. The method provided in this paper has been successful in determining satisfactorily compatible sets of COTS products on close to a dozen small-to-medium e-services projects. Its stepwise approach is compatible with the USC composable CBA process elements framework. Its component compatibility evaluation framework in Figure 2 is useful in filtering out incompatible COTS combinations and in cost-effectively analyzing remaining candidate combinations, as shown in Figure 3. Its use of process model decision table in Table 1 helps projects determine whether to use a complete spiral process or one of its special cases. Further research is needed to determine how well the method scales up to handle situations with many COTS component groups and many candidates per group.

Acknowledgements. We obtained particular valuable insights from Mr. Apurva Jain, Mr. Steven Meyers, Dr. Dan Port, and Ms. Ye Yang.

References

[1] Abd-Allah, Ph.D. Dissertation, "Composing Heterogeneous Software Architectures", USC-CSE, 1996, URL: http://sunset.usc.edu/publications/dissertations/aaadef.pdf.

[2] Abts, B. Boehm, and E. Bailey Clark, "COCOTS: A Software COTS-Based System (CBS) Cost Model," Proceedings, ESCOM 2001, April 2001, pp. 1-8.

[3] Albert and L. Brownsword, "Evolutionary Process for Integrating COTS-Based Systems (EPIC): An Overview," CMU-SEI-2002-TR-009, July 2002.

[4] K. Ballurio, B. Scalzo, L.Rose, "Risk Reduction in COTS Software Selection with BASIS," 1st International Conference on COTS–Based Software Systems, Orlando, Florida, Feb 2002, pg. 31-43.

[5] V. Basili and B. Boehm, "COTS Based System Top 10 List," Computer, May 2001, pp 91-93.

[6] B. Boehm, "A Spiral Model of Software Development and Enhancement," Computer, May 1988, pp. 61-72.

[7] B. Boehm, "Anchoring the Software Process," Software, July 1996, pp. 73-82.

[8] B. Boehm, "Software Risk Management," IEEE CS Press, 1989.

[9] B. Boehm, C. Abts, A.W. Brown, S. Chulani, B.K. Clark, E. Horowitz, R. Madachy, D. Reifer, and B. Steece, "Software Cost Estimation with COCOMO II," Prentice Hall, 2000.

[10] B. Boehm, A. Egyed, J. Kwan, D. Port, A. Shah, and R. Madachy, "Using the WinWin Spiral Model: A Case Study," Computer, July 1998, pp. 33-44.

[11] B. Boehm, D. Port, M. Abi-Antoun, and A. Egyed, "Guidelines for the Life Cycle Objectives (LCO) and the Life Cycle Architecture (LCA) deliverables for Model-Based Architecting and Software Engineering (MBASE)," USC Technical Report USC-CSE-98-519, University of Southern California, Los Angeles, CA, 90089, February 1999.

[12] Boehm, B., Port, D., Egyed, A., and Abi-Antoun, M., "The MBASE Life Cycle Architecture Milestone Package: No Architecture Is An Island," 1st Working International Conference on Software Architecture, 1999.

[13] B. Boehm, D. Port, J. Bhuta, Y. Yang, "Not All CBS Are Created Equally: COTS Intensive Project Types," Springer Verlag, 2002, Proceedings, ICCBSS 2002, Feb 2003, Ottawa, Canada pp.36-50.

[14] B. Boehm, D. Port, Y. Yang, J. Bhuta, Chris Abts, "Composable Process elements for Developing COTS-Based Applications," Proceedings of the ACM-IEEE Symposium on Empirical Software Engineering (ISESE 2003), August 2003, Rome, Italy.

[15] L. Brownsword, P. Oberndorf, and C. Sledge, "Developing New Processes for COTS-Based Systems," Software, July/August 2000, pp. 48-55.

[16] S. Comella-Dorda, J. Dean, E. Morris, and P. Oberndorf, "A Process for COTS Software Product Evaluation," 1st International Conference on COTS–Based Software Systems, Orlando, Florida, Feb 2002, pg. 86-96.

[17] L. Davis and R. Gamble, "Identifying Evolvability for Integration," COTS-Based Software Systems, J. Dean and A. Gravel (eds.) Springer Verlag, 2002, pp.65-75.

[18] L. Davis, D. Flagg, R. Gamble, and C. Karatas, "Classifying Interoperablity Conflicts," Springer Verlag, 2002, Proceedings, ICCBSS 2002, Feb 2003, Ottawa, Canada pp.36-50.

[19] Gacek, "Ph .D. Dissertation: Detecting Architectural Mismatches During Systems Composition," USC-CSE, http://sunset.usc.edu/publications/dissertations/CG_body.pdf.

[20] C. Gacek, B. Boehm, "Composing Components: How Does One Detect Potential Architectural Mismatches?" Proceedings of the OMG-DARPA-MCC Workshop on Compositional Software Architectures, January 1998.

[21] Garlan, R. Allen, and J. Ockerbloom. "Architectural mismatch: Why reuse is so hard," IEEE Software, 12(6): 17-26, 1994.

[22] N. Maiden, H.Kim, and C. Ncube, "Rethinking Process Guidance for Selecting Software Components," COTS-Based Software Systems, J. Dean and A. Gravel (eds.), Springer Verlag, 2002, pp.151-164.

[23] P. McKinley, S. Sadjadi, E. Kasten, B. Cheng, "Composing Adaptive Software," Computer Volume 37, Issue 7, July 2004, pp. 56-64.

[24] N. Medvidovic, R. Gamble, and D. Rosenblum, "Towards Software Multioperability: Bridging Heterogeneous Software Interoperability Platforms," Proceedings, Fourth International Software Architecture Workshop, 2000.

[25] N. R. Mehta, N. Medvidovic, S. Phadke. "Towards a Taxonomy of Software Connectors", In Proceedings of the 22nd International Conference on Software Engineering (ICSE 2000), pages 178-187, Limerick, Ireland, June 4-11, 2000.

[26] B. C. Meyers and P. Oberndorf, Managing Software Acquisition: Open Systems and COTS Products, Addision Wesley, 2001.

[27] Model-Based (Systems) Architecting and Software Engineering Guidelines (MBASE), URL: http://sunset.usc.edu/cse/pub/research/mbase/MBASE_Guidelines_v2.4.0.pdf

[28] M. Morisio, C. Seaman, A. Parra, V. Basili, S. Kraft, and S. Condon, "Investigating and Improving a COTS-Based Software Development Process," Proceedings, ICSE 22, June 2000, pp. 32-41.

[29] C. Ncube and J. Dean, "The Limitations of Current Decision-Making Techniques in the Procurement of COTS Software Components," COTS – Based Software Systems J. Dean and A. Gravel (eds.), Springer Verlag, 2002, RP-176-187.

[30] Mary Shaw, "Architectural Issues in Software Reuse: It's not just the Functionality, It's the Packaging", Proceedings IEEE Symposium on Software Reusability, April 1995.

[31] Mary Shaw and D. Garlan, "Software Architecture: Perspectives on an Emerging Discipline," Prentice Hall, 1996.

[32] D. Yakimovich, J. Bieman, V. Basili, "Software architecture classification for estimating the cost of COTS integration," Proceedings of the 21st international conference on Software engineering, Los Angeles, California, 1999, pp: 296 - 302.

[33] D. Yakimovich, G.H. Travassos, V. Basili, "A Classification of Software Component Incompatibilities for COTS Integration", Software Engineering Workshop, NASA/Goddard Space Flight Center, Greenbelt, MD, December 1999.

One Global COTS-Based System to Replace 20+ Local Legacy Systems

Elisabeth Hansson and Göran V. Grahn

Volvo Information Technology, Sweden

Abstract. Volvo Parts is a company within the Volvo Group handling supply chain management for the aftermarket. The company has been growing quickly through mergers and today has a diverse set of different IT systems to support similar or even identical functionalities. The business challenge is to implement one global process for material management supported by one common IT system for all the warehouses. The presentation will focus on the technical challenges and lessons learned within the project, replacing 20+ different IT systems, both in-house developed and bought packages, with one COTS-based IT system. Since the new system is expected to have a long lifetime, we need to secure that the COTS based solution is open, flexible and scalable over time. Integration to existing systems is another key part of the architecture needed in this solution.

1 Evaluation Approach

The evaluation approach was influenced by the EPIC [1] process (Evolutionary Process for Integrating COTS-Based Systems) which is an extension to IBM Rational Unified Process (RUP). The iterative approach was used and also the idea to balance the following four different areas:

- Stakeholder needs and business processes
- Product marketplace
- System architecture and design
- Programmatics (budget, schedule) and risk considerations

One challenge was to decide if we should select a good-enough solution or the best-in-class solution. We also struggled with different opinions on how long the solution should live and therefore which qualities were the most important. Strangely enough, we did not have any formal decision on weights and priorities in-between functionality, vendor reliability and technical aspects. Compared to "academical" evaluation approaches we rely more on intuition and skilled resources who knows the supporting system and how systems work within their environments than strict quantitative formal methods. In this evaluation we did hands-on evaluations with empirical tests both in the technical and functional scope. The technical evaluation on site was very useful to be able to mitigate risks on some architectural aspects like performance and capacity demands.

X. Franch and D. Port (Eds.): ICCBSS 2005, LNCS 3412, pp. 144–145, 2005.

2 Technical Challenges

We have cases at Volvo IT where surprises have occurred when deploying systems and compromises have been needed to get the COTS running in appointed environments. In other cases the original requirements on quality attributes (such as performance, capacity and security) put on a COTS system have been changed over time (before or after production launch) leading to workarounds and continuous taskforces to change the system. To be able to minimize future problems, we need to assure architectural qualities early.

The driving technical forces in the project have been

- Modifiability over time
- Scalability, flexibility and an open architecture
- Performance and availability
- Interoperability and integration

3 Key Success Factors and Lessons Learned

The major key success factors in this project are:

- The overall structure of the EPIC process with the focus on a close cooperation between business stakeholders and IT specialists
- The global project organization, to learn about the legacy systems and to get acceptance for a common solution and how to integrate it
- The hands-on technical test performed to verify the architecture

There is a difference between academic methods defined and how we usually conduct evaluations at Volvo IT. We tend to rely more on empirical tests and verifications than quantitative formal evaluations. There are more constraints on for example operational and maintenance issues. We are also guided by an "Infrastructure Architecture Framework" decided by our IT Governance committee.

Since most frameworks for COTS evaluation disregard non-measurable attributes they miss some qualities that our project handles. Those qualities are among others interoperability aspects and operability. Since our evaluation performed hands-on technical tests, we got a better understanding on both these concepts. One important attribute area is not covered at all in most generic frameworks – integration and communication. This area is very important when dealing with a COTS solution that will interface many legacy environments.

References

1. Information about the EPIC process is available at the website of Software Engineering Institute at Carnegie Mellon University, Pittsburgh, PA at http://www.sei.cmu.edu/cbs

Using Goals and Quality Models to Support the Matching Analysis During COTS Selection

Carina Alves[1], Xavier Franch[2], Juan P. Carvallo[2], and Anthony Finkelstein[1]

[1] Department of Computer Science,
University College London, London, UK
{C.Alves, A.Finkelstein}@cs.ucl.ac.uk
[2] Universitat Politècnica de Catalunya (UPC)
Barcelona, Catalunya, Spain
{carvallo, franch}@lsi.upc.es

Abstract. The selection process is a crucial activity of the development of COTS-based systems. A key step of the evaluation of COTS components carried out during selection is the matching between user requirements and COTS features. We propose a goal-based approach to guide the matching process, using quality models for leveraging goals and COTS features. The different mismatch situations that may arise are reasoned by means of exploratory scenarios. We demonstrate the approach with the mail server case study.

1 Introduction

The growing importance of COTS components (throughout the paper, we use the noun "COTS" as an abbreviation of "COTS component") requires the definition of processes, methods, models and metrics aimed at supporting COTS acquisition. One of the most important activities taking place in this context is *COTS selection* [3, 14]. For COTS selection to be successful (i.e., reliable and as less time-consuming as possible), many factors need to be taken into account, among which we mention: requirements shall play a prominent role during the process; a well-defined process shall be followed; selection usually involves multiple components; and knowledge about the COTS market shall be deep enough and shall be expressed properly. Our paper tackles these fundamental issues as follows.

Requirements. When selecting COTS, stakeholder requirements have to be assessed and matched against product features. In our approach, we employ a goal-oriented requirements engineering strategy [9].

Process. The evaluation of COTS usually reveals some mismatches that demand an extensive negotiation of requirements in order to accept products limitations [1]. In contrast with other proposed methods, our work aims at by supporting the matching process as a way to guide COTS selection.

Multiple Components. In real-world applications, selection of one component will usually require selection of others [6]. As a result, the process delivers an ensemble of components forming a configuration of the prospective system.

X. Franch and D. Port (Eds.): ICCBSS 2005, LNCS 3412, pp. 146 – 156, 2005.

Knowledge of the COTS Market. In this paper, we propose the notion of quality model [7] as a means to support the uniform description of quality features of components in the COTS market, as well as an essential aid for leveraging user requirements. This decision conforms to one of the lessons enumerated in [12], about making requirements as measurable as possible.

Summarizing, we propose a process based on goals and quality models to support the matching between COTS features and stakeholder needs. To facilitate the process we defined some matching patterns. The decision-making is based on concepts from utility theory [11] to measure to which extent COTS alternatives satisfy or not goals. We underline the importance to identify and tackle mismatches as early as possible. For that, we defined exploratory scenarios that help reasoning about mismatches and examine possible resolutions.

We use as case study some requirements for the selection of *mail servers systems*. Mail servers are a good case study not only for their strategic importance, but also because of their own nature (see [2] for details). Mail servers provide a lot of functionalities and exhibit a great deal of quality features which can be hard to analyze. In particular, features such as security control and operability shall demand additional COTS components to be selected and connected, e.g. anti-virus and backup and recovery tools. In order to demonstrate our approach in a practical fashion, we have defined a goal specification that we will use in the rest of the paper (see Table 1).

Table 1. Goal specification for the mail server case study

High level goals	Operational goals
g1 Ensure and communicate message delivery	g1.1 Configure number of delivery retries g1.2 Configure time between retries g1.3 Provide message delivery notification
g2 Ensure that messages never get lost	g2.1 Messages must never get lost if mailbox runs out of space g2.2 Messages must never get lost if a failure happens g2.3 Messages must never get lost if they cannot be delivered
g3 Ensure fast message delivering	g3.1 The average response time should not exceed 1 minute g3.2 Message throughput should be less than 5 minutes per Mb
g4 Support collaborative work	g4.1 Provide integrated document management g4.2 Provide instant messaging g4.3 Provide voice and video conferencing
g5 Ensure data security	g5.1 Provide authentication of users g5.2 Ensure data integrity
g6 Support protection against external attacks	g6.1 Provide anti-spam filters g6.2 Provide anti-virus scanning

The remainder of the paper is structured as follows. Sections 2 and 3 introduce the key concepts of goal and quality model and their relationships. Section 4 describes our proposal to guide the matching process. Section 5 introduces the notion of satisfaction function as the cornerstone of the measurement strategy. Section 6 shows the use of scenarios as a way to manage mismatches. Finally, we discuss related work and conclusions.

2 Specifying Goals to Evaluate COTS

The specification of stakeholder needs is generally the first activity of any system development. New challenges faced by COTS-based systems demand the definition of more flexible requirements statements in which stakeholder needs should be continuously negotiated and changed against the features offered by COTS. Based on that, we believe that *goal-oriented requirements engineering* is a suitable approach to specify genuine stakeholder needs without imposing unnecessary constraints. Goal-oriented requirements engineering is concerned with the formulation of requirements as goals to be achieved [9]. Goals can be specified in different levels of abstraction, ranging from high level, strategic objectives (such as "Support collaborative work") to low level operational concerns (such as "Provide voice and video conferencing").

High level goals capture the overall organizational objectives and key constraints; therefore they represent stable needs that are unlikely to change. Given that product capabilities change constantly affecting some previously defined requirements that will no longer be satisfied, requirements engineers should not spend too much time and effort to capture a complete set of goals. The initial set of goals will guide the definition of the system scope and the identification of COTS packages that might satisfy them. The specification of goals should be done in parallel with the evaluation of products. In fact, the analysis of features can help stakeholders to clarify vague goals as well as reveal desired functionalities that were not discovered with traditional elicitation techniques. Depending on the complexity of the application domain and the scope of available products, it is possible to find different COTS solutions ranging from a single, large package or several specific packages that once integrated will provide the desired capabilities. The next step of the goal specification process is the refinement of high level goals into more concrete subgoals until it is possible to objectively measure the satisfaction of subgoals that at this stage are called *operational goals*.

The prioritization of goals is particularly important when developing COTS-based systems because a number of goals might not be satisfied by any available product. Therefore, the assignment of priority helps to distinguish core goals (i.e. critical needs that should always be satisfied) from irrelevant goals (i.e. the ones that could be traded off with little trouble for stakeholders). We propose the assignment of normalized weights in order to guide the decision-making. For a detailed explanation on how to obtain goal priorities using utility theory, we refer to the systematic technique developed by Yen [13]. In particular, goal weights facilitate the identification of tradeoffs that stakeholders are willing to make. Tradeoff analysis involves the balancing of what stakeholders would like to get against what is possible to achieve with COTS products. Therefore, when performing tradeoffs, stakeholder goals should be continuously negotiated and priorities reassessed.

3 Quality Models and Goal Acquisition

In order to assess how well COTS alternatives meet operational goals, it is necessary to obtain precise metrics to quantify the satisfaction of each operational goal. We propose to use *quality models* for making goals operational. According to [8], a quality model is "the set of characteristics and the relationships between them which provide the basis for specifying quality requirements and evaluating quality". Quality models are structured in a hierarchical way by refining the *quality factors* therein. The leafs of the hierarchy represent quality factors that can be directly measured and assessed; also, other derived metrics can be bound to quality factors represented by inner nodes of the hierarchy.

Quality models shall be built selectively, as required by the particular selection process at hand [5]. This is useful not only for limiting the effort invested in building them, but also for refining some goals and subgoals, for making them measurable and even for identifying new ones. Also, some new domains to be considered in the resulting COTS configuration may be discovered. We illustrate these situations by means of some examples in the mail server case.

Subgoal Identification. The initial form of g_3 expresses a very general goal that clearly demands some clarification. An initial approach we considered was to refine this goal into a subgoal such as "*Message transmission time shall take less than 1 minute*". However, building the part of quality model corresponding to the "*Time Behaviour*" quality factor provided us with a deeper knowledge. The quality model showed that in fact there are mainly two features that influence message transmission time, message throughput and average response time. This knowledge guided us to split the original goal into two subgoals, one for each feature.

Subgoal Refinement. To provide a measurable expression of the two identified subgoals, definition of the feature units (i.e., their metrics) becomes crucial. Consider, for instance, the subgoal concerning message throughput. We analyzed the information coming from a lot of sources, including widespread benchmarks such as the Microsoft [10]. All the benchmarks that we examined provide different efficiency tables for different messages sizes (among other information). For this reason, we were able to formulate a more accurate definition of the subgoal $g_{3.2}$ taking this factor into account, as "*Message throughput should be less than 5 minutes per megabyte*".

Dependent Features. Not surprisingly, some of the subgoals depend on factors that are external to the system being developed. Subgoal $g_{3.2}$ is an example. The benchmarks showed that besides message size, some organizational aspects (e.g., number of registered users and expected concurrent access rate to the mail server) and platform components and policies (e.g., number and characteristics of hosts and protocols used) influence message throughput. Consequently, some subgoals will be said to be conditionally fulfilled, i.e. they will be attained just for particular values of these organizational aspects and particular configurations of these platform components and policies.

New Domains of Interest. Goal g_6 refers to system security. Again we built selectively the piece of the quality model related to this quality factor. In this case, one of the quality features that influences security is protection against virus attacks. In fact, we decided to define a subgoal ($g_{6.2}$) bound to just this attribute. However, market studies show that virus detection and removal is not a feature generally offered by mail server packages; instead, mail servers incorporate (mail-specific) anti-virus tools.

Consequently, goal attainment requires an anti-virus tool to be integrated in the final COTS configuration and anti-virus domain must be incorporated into the discussion.

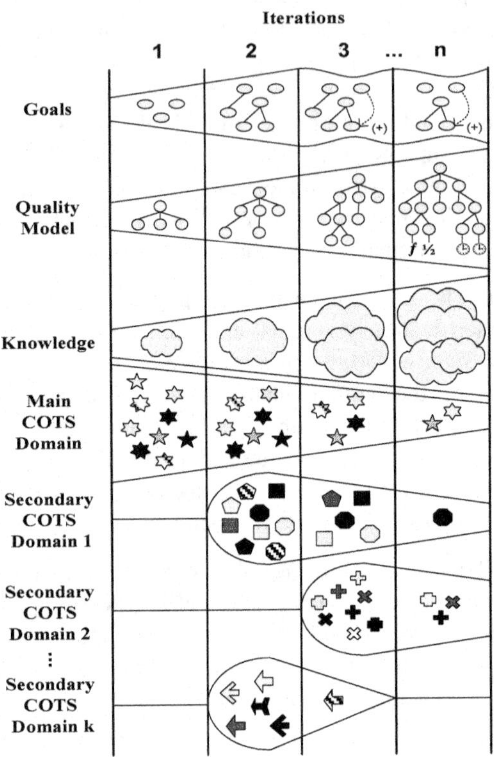

Fig. 1. Multiple COTS selection process using goals and quality models

In summary, goal specification, knowledge of the domain and quality model construction are activities closely related in our approach. Figure 1 shows in a graphical form the evolution of concepts and the solution space through time. This figure is inspired by the characterization of the PORE methodology [12], but takes multiple selection and quality models into account. In the beginning, the departing system goals and the initial set of candidate components for the domain of interest are determined; the departing quality model is also included at this initial stage. Whilst the process proceeds, goals may slightly change, some candidates are eliminated and the quality model is built selectively refining just those parts directly related to the goals; also, new domains may show up as part of the selection process. It may also happen that all the candidates for a particular domain are discarded, which means that bespoke software must be developed for covering this part of the system. At the end, some particular configurations emerge as the solutions to be proposed to the management.

4 Matching Goals and COTS Features

We have defined a set of matching patterns to help decision-makers to classify the matching between COTS functionalities and goals in a systematic way. We present below these patterns and provide examples.

Fulfill - The operational goal is fully satisfied by the product, which means that the goal is achieved at the target level. This is the usual case in operational goal $g_{5.1}$. Most mail servers available in the market provide reliable and sufficient authentication facilities and then the operational goal is fulfilled.

Differ - The operational goal is partially satisfied by the product. The *differ* pattern occurs when the satisfaction of the operational goal is within the acceptable interval but not optimal. For example, consider the feature *Delivery retries configuration* that maps the operational goal $g_{1.1}$. We have analyzed a particular mail server *Foo* that does not allow full configuration of number of delivery retries, but just allows users to configure delivery retries during the first 24 hours. Therefore we say that this particular mail server differs from the desired operational goal.

Fail - The satisfaction degree of the operational goal is below the worst level of the acceptable interval. The *fail* mismatch occurs in two situations: when the COTS product does not meet the operational goal at the requested level or when it does not exhibit the desired functionality. Some evaluated mail servers fail to satisfactorily support anti-virus facilities. In this situation, a potential alternative to satisfy $g_{6.2}$ could be acquiring a specific anti-virus tool, yielding a new candidate COTS configuration composed by mail server and anti-virus tool.

Extend - This case occurs when the COTS product provide functionalities that are not requested by the stakeholders. The *extend* pattern can give rise to the following interaction situations:

- *Hurtful* - The extra feature has a negative impact over stakeholder goals, so that it might interfere with other functions of the system (e.g. automatic data backup facility can affect the response time goal);
- *Helpful* - The extra feature is accepted, such that it might be included in the goal specification as part of the feedback mechanism;
- *Neutral* - The extra feature does not interfere with the achievement of any goal nor it is a desired functionality.

Last, we remark that in some situations, evaluators may not have sufficient information about packages features to classify the matching. Therefore, further clarification is needed in order to verify the matching. In other words, the pattern is *unknown*.

To measure the degree to which COTS candidates satisfy each operational goal, it is necessary to define the interval of acceptable values in terms of quality model elements.

5 Defining a Measurement Strategy

We use concepts from utility theory [11] to obtain the satisfaction function of operational goals. We assume that an operational goal expresses a condition over a quality factor, that we call its *underlying quality factor*. The *satisfaction function* of an operational goal g_i is defined as:

$$\text{Sat}_{gi}\text{: M} \rightarrow [0, 1] \tag{1}$$

where *M* is the set of values that the underlying quality factor q_i of g_i may take.

Each of the matching patterns defined in the last section corresponds to different degrees of goal satisfaction (see Table 2). Note that the extend pattern is not applicable since it expresses something that is not a goal, it may become a goal (helpful extend and then other pattern would be applied) or not. The unknown pattern. requires further exploration using scenarios, as explained in the next section. The acceptable interval ranges from the *target level*, i.e. the highest desirable value of the underlying quality factor q_i that fully satisfies the goal, to the *worst level*, i.e. the minimum level that a goal would be considered satisfied. These two levels are the boundaries for the application of the fulfill and fail patterns.

Table 2. Satisfaction value for each matching pattern

Matching pattern	Satisfaction function value
Fulfill	1
Differ	0.9, …, 0.1
Fail	0
Extend	Not applicable

Given the acceptable interval to satisfy each operational goal g_i, we can determine the satisfaction function of g_i. Consider that x_{target} and x_{worst} are respectively the target and worst values that q_i may take to satisfy g_i. Then, we have that $\text{Sat}_{gi}(x_{target}) = 1$ and $\forall x$: $x < x_{worst}$: $\text{Sat}_{gi}(x) = 0$. For simplicity reasons, we assume that all goals have a linear satisfaction function in the form:

$$\text{Sat}_{gi}(x_k) = a_k x_k + b_k \tag{2}$$

where a_k and b_k are constants defined as:

$$a_k = 1 / (x_{target} - x_{worst})$$

$$b_k = -x_{worst} / (x_{target} - x_{worst})$$

to make sure that the satisfaction function is continuous. Then we have:

$$\text{Sat}_{gi}(x_k) = 0, \text{ if } x_k < x_{worst}$$

$$\text{Sat}_{gi}(x_k) = a_k x_k + b_k, \text{ if } x_{worst} \leq x_k < x_{target}$$

$$\text{Sat}_{gi}(x_k) = 1, \text{ if } x_k \geq x_{target}$$

Consider, for example, that the acceptable interval for the operational goal $g_{3,2}$ ranges finally from 4 minutes/Mb to 6 minutes/Mb. These values are respectively the worst and target levels. Figure 2 shows the goal refinement tree for the high level goal *ensure fast message delivering*, the diagrammatic acceptable interval for the operational goal *message throughput*, and its satisfaction function.

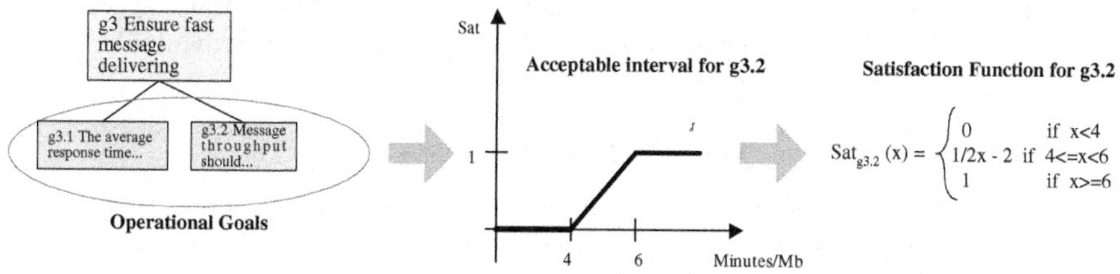

Fig. 2. Defining the acceptable interval and satisfaction functions

By solving these linear equations, we can determine the satisfaction function of each operational goal. The next step is to measure how each COTS satisfies operational goals. More formally, consider that COTS A satisfies goal g_i at level x_k, i.e. the underlying quality factor q_i of g_i has a value x_k in A, denoted by $A_{qi} = x_k$. Since we already know the satisfaction function of g_i we can easily obtain $Sat_{gi}(A_{qi})$ Then, the overall COTS satisfaction is obtained by aggregating individual preferences. We use the weighted summation to aggregate individual preferences, which is a well-known and simple aggregation operator. Then we have:

$$Sat(A) = \sum_{i=1}^{n} w_{gi} \times Sat_{gi}(A_{qi}) \tag{3}$$

where w_{gi} is the weight of goal g_i (see section 2) and $Sat_{gi}(A_{qi})$ represents the satisfaction degree that COTS A meets with operational goal g_i.

6 Scenarios to Manage Mismatches

The overall satisfaction that each COTS meet operational goals allows decision-makers to compare different COTS products. In order to perform wise decisions we still need to handle mismatches and analyse tradeoffs. Given that mismatches represent non-adherence of COTS packages to operational goals, a fundamental need to handle mismatches is the capacity to systematically structure tradeoffs.

This section describes how mismatches can be tackled using exploratory *scenarios*. The benefits of using scenarios to deal with conflicts are as follows: (*i*) to explore resolution alternatives and highlight products limitations; (*ii*) to identify associated risks with each COTS; (*iii*) to explicit evaluate the impact of decisions. Once mismatches are detected, we aim at exploring the possible conflicting situations through the combination of different scenarios. By identifying scenarios that lead to unwanted situations, evaluators can clearly reason about why a conflict has arisen and which are the consequences of the conflict. We use semi-structured textual form to represent the scenarios. Table 3 depicts an example of exploratory scenario where we investigate the involved conflicts detected on a particular COTS configuration composed by mail server and anti-virus products. The first helps to solve an unknown pattern. The second is concerned with priorisation, which affects the weighting factor in the satisfaction function. The third relates to goal decomposition. By choosing potential resolutions, more information for COTS selection becomes available.

Table 3. Exploratory scenarios

Scenario 1. Selection of COTS configuration composed by mail server and anti-virus tool.	
Conflicting situation 1	Subgoals $g_{3.1}$ $g_{3.2}$ are difficult to evaluate.
Involved issues	Efficiency benchmarks available are not trustable. Performing test cases demands great effort.
Fixed parameters	Number of users, average message size (the latter obtained from estimation)
Negotiable parameters	Communication protocol, platform
Potential resolutions	1. Increase server resources, add servers to clusters, activate load balancing in order to ensure higher system efficiency. 2. Put more human resources to obtain more trustable information.
Involved risks	High cost due to acquisition of servers or man power.
Conflicting situation 2	Conflict between $g_{2.2}$ and $g_{3.1}$.
Involved issues	Negotiate the efficiency of message delivery against the availability and recoverability capabilities.
Fixed parameters	Recovery process strategy
Negotiable parameters	Level of concurrency, maximum allowed size of messages
Potential resolutions	1. Relax g_3 since the tradeoff decision is to favor reliability with loss of efficiency.
Involved risks	1. Loose data if a failure happens 2. Sacrifice message response time
Conflicting situation 3	The definition of subgoal $g_{6,2}$ is not sufficient to choose which is the best anti-virus tool.
Involved issues	The selected anti-virus tool must be compliant to the mail server
Fixed parameters	License agreement, platform (dependent on mail server)
Negotiable parameters	Not identified
Potential resolutions	1. Refine the goal 2. Gather more information about available anti-virus tools
Involved risks	Due to the high contribution of $g_{6,2}$ the satisfaction of g_6 might be compromised if no anti-virus is selected.

7 Discussion and Related Work

In this paper we have discussed the importance to analyse how well COTS features match stakeholder needs. Our motivation has been to provide a framework for supporting the matching process and managing conflicts in COTS-based development. We have demonstrated the suitability to combine goals and quality models as both approaches represent knowledge in a hierarchical fashion. We may say that our work joins two lines of research: how to operationalize goals in a methodical way (using quality models) and how to drive quality model construction (through goal identification and refinement). Both concepts fit in a very smoothly way. The definition of matching patterns provides a qualitative and well-defined basis to assess the satisfaction of goals in terms of COTS features. Utility theory is a suitable decision-making approach to capture the notion of satisfaction degrees. Finally, exploratory scenarios provide an effective mechanism to explicitly reason about mismatches and manage risks. Most selection methods present in the literature overlooked the matching problem. One of the few works that covers these issues is provided by Wallnau et al. In [14], he proposes the use of utility techniques also in the field of COTS-based system development. They identify two situations in the matching process, fit and misfit, and for misfits they propose to quantify the costs and risks for assessing the final decision. Although the underlying ideas of their approach and ours have similarities, we emphasize the model aspects covered by quality models, matching patterns and scenarios, which are dealt with in an ad-hoc manner in their proposal. Also, the relationships among requirements and COTS feature evaluation seem not to be explicitly addressed in the matching process. In [4] Chung provides an approach called CARE that emphasizes the importance of bridging the gap between the sets of native (i.e. requirements) and foreign requirements (i.e. COTS features). As main drawback, the approach does not provide or suggest any effective solution to support the possible mismatching between both specifications.

Acknowledgement. This work is partially supported by CICYT TIC2001–2165.

References

1. C. Alves, A. Finkelstein. Investigating Conflicts in COTS Decision Making. *International Journal of Software Engineering and Knowledge Engineering*. World Scientific Publishing Company, 2003.
2. J.P. Carvallo, X. Franch, C. Quer. Defining a Quality Model for Mail Servers. In *Proceedings of the 2nd International Conference on COTS-Based Software Systems* (ICCBSS), Ottawa (Canada), LNCS 2580, 2003.
3. S. Comella-Dorda, J. Dean, E. Morris, P. Oberndorf. A Process for COTS Software Product Evaluation. In *Proceedings of the 1st International Conference on COTS Based Software Systems* (ICCBSS), Orlando (USA), LNCS 2255, 2002.
4. L. Chung and K. Cooper. A Knowledge-based COTS-aware Requirements Engineering Approach. *In Proceedings of the 14th International Conference on Software Engineering and Knowledge Engineering* (SEKE), 2003.
5. X. Franch, J.P. Carvallo. Using Quality Models in Software Package Selection. *IEEE Software*, 20(1), 2003.

6. X. Franch, N. Maiden. Modelling Component Dependencies to Inform their Selection. In *Proceedings of the 2nd International Conference on COTS-Based Software Systems* (ICCBSS), Ottawa (Canada), LNCS 2580, 2003.
7. ISO/IEC Standard 9126-1: *Software Engineering – Product Quality – Part 1: Quality Model*, 2001.
8. ISO International Standard 8402: *Quality management and quality assurance-Vocabulary*, 1986.
9. A. Lamsweerde. Goal-Oriented Requirements Engineering: A Guided Tour. *Invited mini-tutorial paper 5th IEEE International Symposium on Requirements Engineering.* 2001.
10. http://www.microsoft.com/exchange/techinfo/planning/2000/mmb2desc.asp
11. R. Keeney and H. Raiffa. Decision with Multiple Objectives: Preferences and Value Tradeoffs. Wiley, New York, 1993.
12. N. Maiden, C. Ncube. Acquiring Requirements for COTS Selection. *IEEE Software* 15(2), 1998.
13. J. Yen, W. Tiao. A Systematic Tradeoff Analysis for Conflicting Imprecise Requirements. *IEEE 4th International Conference on Requirements Engineering.* 1997.
14. K. Wallnau, S. Hissam, R. Seacord. *Building systems from commercial components.* Addison-Wesley Longman Publishing, 2002.

Addressing Malicious Code in COTS: A Protection Framework

Donald J. Reifer, Pranjali Baxi, Fabio Hirata,
Jonathan Schifman, and Ricky Tsao

Reifer Consultants, Inc.
Torrance, CA, USA
don@reifer.com
pranjali_baxi@yahoo.com
{fhirata, schifman, rtsao}@usc.edu

Abstract. The potential for problems due to malicious code increases in direct proportion with the number of COTS software used in a system. Because of this, many practitioners have used a variety of techniques to address potential attacks. Yet, little guidance has been offered as to which techniques work best, when, and under what conditions. To rectify this problem, we have created a framework that can be used to help those interested in addressing vulnerabilities with a solution. The framework matches defenses to attacks using a risk-based approach that focuses on providing cost-effective protection.

1 Introduction

The potential for malicious code within COTS (commercial-off-the-shelf) components has grown during the past few years as industry has used existing components to build their systems quicker, better and more cheaply. While many articles have been written discussing the security problems with COTS and potential solutions, little guidance has been offered in the literature as to what techniques to use, when, and under what conditions.

We launched a project early in 2004 to develop a framework to rectify this problem. The project's aim is to create a framework that practitioners could use to determine the most cost-effective defenses against potential attacks using risk management principles [1]. The framework by design addresses applications software. It seeks to protect software against the most common types of attacks using existing technology that is mature.

The purpose of this paper is to provide an overview of our proposed protection framework and discuss the rationale upon which is built. The framework is synthesized upon a combination of published approaches and also government approaches to protecting applications. Based on our trial-use experiments, this framework presents a useful and practical means for engineers to identify ways to mitigate security threats in new COTS software applications [2].

X. Franch and D. Port (Eds.): ICCBSS 2005, LNCS 3412, pp. 157 – 167, 2005.

2 Related Work

While other security frameworks have been developed in categorizing threats, few have addressed protection techniques for applications software. Most of the related work that we found seems to focus on classifying network-centric threats and approaches to mitigate them [3]. One of the few exceptions was Landwehr et al. [4] who provides a taxonomy for identifying and addressing security flaws in software applications during the system life cycle. This research focuses primarily on identifying a set of security flaws in applications by looking at how, when, and where the flaw is introduced. The research is a good start in threat identification, but it fails to focus on the security requirements of the target application. Therefore we felt that their taxonomy was not a practical tool for application protection.

We did find a hardware framework process that was developed by Battelle National Labs that seemed to provide a suitable model for what we were after [5]. Battelle's framework provides model for classifying hardware items defenses against piracy, tampering and reverse engineering. Their framework classifies the item to be protected, identifies the attacks and defenses to the item, and supports selection decision-making using risk management approaches. We followed Battelle's process to develop our framework because it seemed most applicable.

We diverged from the Battelle work when identifying vulnerabilities. Instead of using their approach, we employed an existing government standard, the Common Criteria [6], as our basis for determining vulnerabilities. The CC provides a comprehensive catalog of high level security requirements in the form of functional and assurance services that must be supported in applications. By using the CC, we were able to combine and expand on existing information instead of replicating it using uniquely determined characteristics as in the Battelle framework.

Our related work interest was to develop attack-defense mappings for security applications. The majority of the mapping research we found was in the field of network security, as in [7, 8, 9] which was not applicable to threats to applications software security. For example, Mirkovic et. al. [10] proposes a taxonomy of DDoS attack and defense mechanisms which is typical of this work.

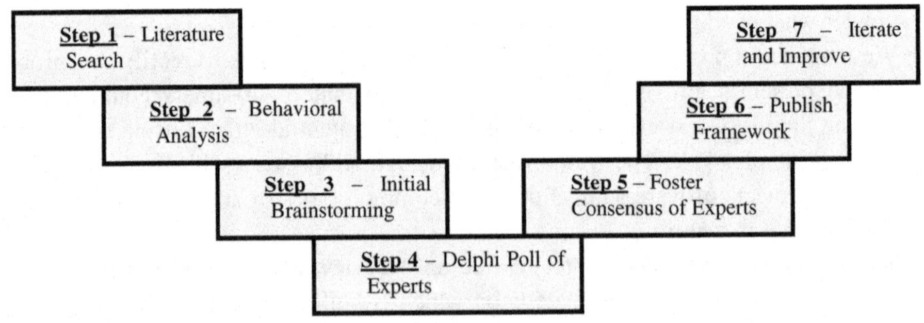

Fig. 1. Framework Development Process

3 Framework Development Process

We used the seven-step process in Fig. 1 to develop the framework over a period of six months. We started by conducting a literature search. We identified a large number of potential attacks and defenses based on the work we found that we organized into collections. We next debated what applications items we wanted to protect and how we would go about defending them against known attacks. After much debate and consultation with experts in the field, we developed the structure that revolved around a risk measure that was developed by Butler at Carnegie-Mellon University [11]. To validate the structure, we polled experts using a Delphi process and reached consensus on our findings. In parallel, we had two subcontractors experiment with the framework to validate it utility and usefulness.

As we developed the framework, we were surprised by the number of techniques that practitioners had devised to address malicious code problems in COTS. Many of these techniques are mature. Unfortunately, little of this experience had been published because firms involved in security developments felt that their work was too sensitive to put in the public domain.

4 The Protection Framework

The framework consists of the four parts shown in Fig. 2: Item Identification, Attacks Categorization, Defenses Categorization, and a Risk Assessment. Item identification is aimed at identifying the item to be protected and its vulnerabilities. Attack and defense categorization specify possible attack and defense methods. Risk assessment assesses the potential damage and computes the risk exposure associated with the defense method.

One advantage of using Battelle's was that protection techniques used for both hardware and software could be assessed from a holistic viewpoint. We felt that this was important because many techniques used to protect software used hardware and vice versa. For example, firmware guards could be used to protect hardware while hardware dongles could be employed for software.

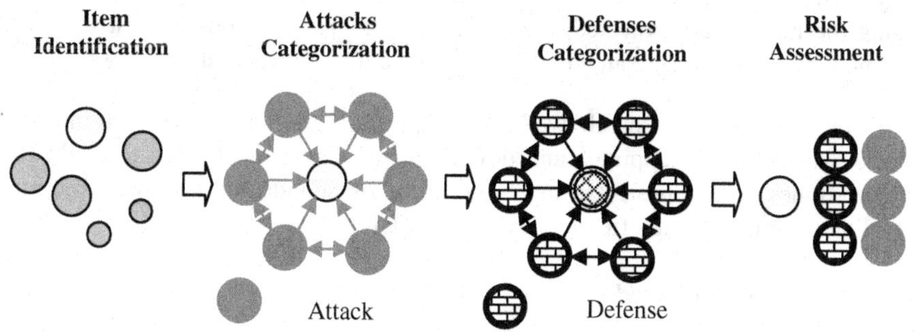

Fig. 2. Framework Elements

4.1 Overview

Item Identification. The first step in using the framework is to identify parts of the software application that hold critical information and would render an application vulnerable to an attack. For some application this may include data, a specific component, or even an algorithm. For others, it might revolve around malicious code in either patches or in COTS components.

As already mentioned, we used the Common Criteria (CC) [6] as the basis for determining vulnerabilities. The CC defines a set of implementation-independent security and assurance requirements in software applications. By using the CC to identify vulnerabilities, we can create expectations for product and process security behaviors that must be judged to be effective.

The target of evaluation (TOE) security requirement defines a set of technical, functional and assurance requirements that covers the TOE and its environment of operation. As we will see in a later section, the functional security requirement is categorized by various security classes that help engineers locate and combat threats. The assurance requirements focus on the security during the development process and ensure that security measures are implemented correctly.

Attacks Categorization. Attacks Categorization. Once item vulnerabilities are identified, the Attacks Categorization presents possible ways that exploiters might attempt to circumvent protection. As part of our research we were able to identify thirty-four unique exploits that could be mounted. Depending on the protected item, some attacks seemed more prevalent than others. Others had greater probabilities of success.

Defense Categorization. We next identified possible defenses against the attacks based on the perceived vulnerabilities. Twenty-nine defense methods were selected based on their maturity and technology limitations. All of the defenses selected provide at least one protection, detection, and recovery mechanisms against attacks. Some are more effective against an attack than others. When mapping defenses to attacks, we took such effectiveness into consideration.

Risk Assessment. The final step of the framework employs a risk model to evaluate the effectiveness of the defense selected against the attack methods. Risk is assessed taking the item to be protected, the ranking of defense methods against the attacks, and the amount of damage an attack can do to the item into account.

At this point of our research, we have completed a preliminary research of possible attacks and defense mappings, and developed risk assessment steps to evaluate the trustworthiness of the protected item. We have also conducted trial-use experiments to validate the utility and effectiveness of the approach.

4.2 Items to Be Protected

The first element of the framework identifies the item to be protected. For most projects, the four applications software items that have to be protected include:

1. Software Components
2. Databases/Files
3. Patches
4. COTS Products

Because this is a COTS conference, we will explain the framework in terms of protecting COTS Products. For brevity, the full framework will not be shown. However, we will try to provide enough detail so potential users can determine whether or not it may be applicable in their environments.

4.3 Vulnerability Analysis

The next step in our process is to characterize the vulnerabilities of the item to be protected. We use the Common Criteria (CC) [6] to do this by using functional security requirements to characterize the product vulnerabilities (no authentication, encryption of key algorithms etc.) and the assurance classes to characterize process vulnerabilities (no security audits, penetration testing, etc.). Any unsatisfied requirements represent potential security vulnerabilities. Using the CC is a realistic prerequisite as most applications that will be protected have a protection profile associated with them.

4.4 Malicious Code Attacks (on COTS)

We identified the following seven categories of attack methods as a refinement of the original attack methods proposed by Whittaker [12].

- Software Dependencies
- User Interface
- Design
- Implementation
- Reverse Engineering
- Tampering
- Malicious Code

Whittaker looked at thousands of security bugs and incidents reports in COTS software applications to understand what types of security problems were reported, the types of failure symptoms that would recognize vulnerabilities, and the types of testing techniques that would identify these failures.

We extended his methods to include attack methods that would expose intellectual property (Reverse Engineering), attacks that would render useless other components in the rest of the system (Tampering), and attacks which may be triggered remotely and automatically (Malicious Code).

The difficulty in protecting against malicious COTS software is that users do not have access to the source code and have few ways of localizing malicious code inside binaries. Based on this and other COTS software vulnerabilities, we defined the nine common types of malicious code attacks. We then conducted interviews with experts to validate that these attacks were something where protection was actually needed:

- Inserting Viruses
- Affixing Trojan Horses
- Embedding Worms
- Exploiting Backdoors
- Using User-Mode Root-Kits
- Inserting Spyware
- Examining Test Hooks
- Using Kernel-Mode Root-Kits
- Embedding Logic Bombs

4.5 Defenses

We next identified defense methods that reduce the risk associated with the attacks that we identified in the previous section. We separated the defenses into the following eight categories:

- Containerization
- Authentication/Authorization
- Obfuscation
- Encryption
- Analysis and Testing
- Integrity Checking
- Security Reviews & Audits
- Hardware

Not all of these categories provide defenses against COTS software attacks. Most address attempts to pirate, tamper with or reverse engineer binaries using methods that might not work for COTS code. The three defenses that provide practitioners with their primary protection against malicious code in COTS software are classified under the headings of containerization, analysis and testing, and security reviews and audits. Tables 1, 2 and 3 provide a detailed description of these three categories of defense.

5 Mappings

As part of our initial effort, we have mapped our twenty-nine defenses against our thirty-four attacks to see whether current technology provides adequate coverage. We circulated a questionnaire in order to reach consensus with security experts on the criteria to determine what technologies provided the most cost-effective protection possible. Based on the results of our research and feedback from the questionnaire, we have updated the decision guidelines and the final framework accordingly. The areas of sparse coverage were localized to the following seven attacks, the first column of which represent threats in COTS:

- Exploiting backdoors
- Embedding logic bombs
- Using kernel-mode rootkits
- Using user-mode rootkits
- Exploiting script loops
- Performing differential cryptoanalysis
- Conducting files differential analysis

Not surprisingly, additional defensive techniques are needed to address each of these attacks. That is one of the benefits of the framework. In addition to supporting analysis, it identifies areas where additional research in defensive measures is needed. It also pinpoints high leverage areas where defenses are thin and additional emphasis needs to be placed.

Table 1. Containerization Defenses

Defense Methods	Description
Assetions/Allegations	Mathematical proofs and checks for correctness.
Certifying Compilers	Verifying source code against a security policy at compile-time.
Wrappers	Encapsulating mechanisms imposing a security layer around sensitive components. [14]

Table 2. Analysis and Testing Defenses

Defense Methods	Description
Penetration Testing	Attempts to raise common vulnerabilities in the application [15]
Activity Monitors	Monitor the behavior of an entity and trigger alarms accurately and in a timely fashion. [16].
File Comparators	Use unique identifier for each file and compared it against saved versions to determine if a file has been altered [17].
Static Analysis	Examines the code perhaps in some abstract representation without actually executing it to understand its structure and calling behavior.
Dynamic Analysis	Observes the behavior of the program while it runs by instrumenting the code and monitoring key variables and logic usage.

Table 3. Integrity Checking Defenses

Defense Methods	Description
Checksums	A value that is computed by a function that is dependent on the contents of a data object and is stored or transmitted together with the object, for the purpose of detecting changes in the data [14].
Watermarks/ Digital Signatures	Watermark embeds a secret message into the program. Digital signature stores a unique value in each application calculated from the contents of a file [3].
Hashing	Uses an algorithm to compute a condensed representation of a message or data file to later verify data integrity. [15].
Virus Checkers Scanners	Utility that checks the hard drive for known viruses and removes them when they are found.

6 Guidance

As our final step, we developed guidelines to identify when and under what conditions to use each of the defenses. Our goal was to select important decision criteria that would help engineers decide on a particular protection technology. In the next phase of this project, we will perform experimentation to verify the reliability and performance of these defenses. Guidelines are primarily experience-based. They were developed by canvassing the community and talking with experts. An example set of guidelines is provided in Table 4 for the assertions/allegations defense category. In Table 5, we classify available defenses for the assertion/allegation category using one of the following three classifications:

1. Protection. Prevents an attack from succeeding; protection with least point of failures should be considered.
2. Detection. Identifies ongoing attacks; provides self-defense mechanism and reporting functionalities.
3. Recovery. Used to restore the system integrity.

Table 4. Security Reviews and Audits Defenses

Defense Methods	Description
Security Audit	Refer to ensuring that events triggered by security functions are reviewed on an ongoing basis for anomalies.
Security Process Assessment	Entails periodic independent reviews on the security aspects and operations of an application, during design, development, or maintenance.

Table 5. Guidelines for Assertions/Allegations Defense Category

Life cycle stage?	Requirements and Design	Implementation (including Test)	Operations and Maintenance
When?	Primary	Secondary	Secondary
Under what conditions?	▪ Critical design component	▪ Small component due to cost	▪ Small component due to cost
Maturity?	Mature	Mature	Mature
Precedence?	Orange book – A level requirement	Orange book – A level requirement	Orange book – A level requirement
Weaknesses?	▪ Costly ▪ Difficult to do with no automation ▪ Proofs could have errors in them	▪ Costly ▪ Difficult to do with no automation ▪ Proofs could have errors in them	▪ Costly ▪ Difficult to do with no automation ▪ Proofs could have errors in them
Classification?	Protection	Protection	Protection

Guidelines that we developed for use in applying defensive measures have been packaged in a similar manner in order to make them easy to understand and use. Our goal is to use these guidelines to provide protection engineers with insight into what works and what doesn't. We plan to update these guidelines continuously as we gather data from the literature and through controlled experiments.

7 Risk Assessment

The previous stopeps provide the protection engineer with the following:

- A characterization of the item to be protected along with its vulnerabilities.
- An identification of attacks aimed at taking advantage of these vulnerabilities.

- An identification of the defenses that protection engineers would mount to ward off these attacks.

Our formulas treat risk as a function of the importance of the item (in the context of the system in which it operates) and the damage potential.

7.1 Evaluation Criteria – Attack

The risk assessment approach that we use is a variation from the work in [18]. The risk assessment for an attack will be a number between 0 and 100 corresponding to an assessment of the risk associated with a possible attack on the item to be protected. For example, a file has a certain risk value, which is a combination of the importance of the file, the probability of successful attack on the file, and the amount of damage an attack could cause on the file. It is important to note that the quantification of risks and item importance are determined by security experts applying this framework.

7.2 Risk Assessment Formulas

The formula that we will use to quantify the risk associated with the attack is as follows:

$$\text{Risk} = (\text{Item Importance}) * (\text{Probability of successful attack}) * (\text{Damage Potential}) * 11.11 \quad (1)$$

The values for Item Importance and Potential Damage are determined using the following ratings:

- High (3)
- Medium (2)
- Low (1)

The scale factor used in the equation of 11.11 was used to normalize the results using a 0 to 100 range.

Defense Reliability is used to quantify the trustworthiness of a security protection. If an item contains no protections, the defense reliability value is zero. However, once a defense method is selected, the defense evaluation criteria will be rated at a value between 0 and 100. The computation of the defense evaluation is explained using the malicious code in COTS software example that follows.

7.3 Worm Attack Example

Let's assume that we were trying to protect a COTS application that manages critical personnel information, such as an HR system. If this application were compromised it could result in a significant loss of information for the employer but is backed up so the only loss is payment for time to recover the system. Therefore, the Item Importance of this application would be Medium.

Since this application is COTS, there is minimal guarantee that the software was not delivered to us embedded with malicious code, such as a worm. Here we have identified "embedding worms" as the primary attack on our COTS software. A worm could do a number of things ranging from corrupting data to secretly diverting funds to an attacker's bank account. Therefore, we rate the damage potential as High.

The next step is to look at the defense categories for COTS and compute the risk exposures associated with different defense combinations. Our expert security analysts determine that running a virus scan periodically along with implementing a secure COTS wrapper solution will mitigate the probability of a successful attack to 20% from 60% with only a virus scan.

Now we can compute our risk exposure and assess the best defense strategy:

Using Virus/Worm Scanners Only:

Item Importance (2)
* Damage Potential (3)
* 60% Prob. of successful attack * 11.11
= ~40% Risk Exposure

Using Scanners & Wrappers:

Item Importance (2)
* Damage Potential (3)
* 20% Prob. of successful attack * 11.11
= ~13.3% Risk Exposure

Table 6 shows the rating scheme we use for mapping percentages to ratings. We decided to give the High distinction a much larger range to support conservative security estimates. Our overall risk assessment for this example would be Medium using virus scanners and Low using scanners and secure wrappers. This serves as a valuable guideline for analyzing the cost/benefit tradeoff associated with COTS vulnerabilities and its associated defenses. For this situation, the costs are money, time, and performance degradation associated with each defense. The benefits are reduced risk exposure and, in turn, long term ROI.

Table 6. Risk Rating Scheme

Low	Medium	High
0 - 25%	**26 - 50%**	**51 – 100%**

8 Next Steps

We are scheduled to finish our definitional work in November 2004. As part of this effort, we have run two experiments to validate the utility of the framework. Two firms have used the framework effectively to plan defenses against common types of attacks that they are experiencing. Their feedback over the next year will provide us inputs we need to further refine the framework.

Our next step is to use our framework to develop a body of knowledge about application protection. We will start by validating our mappings between attacks and defenses using a series of controlled experiments in a laboratory environment. Using the results of these experiments, we will augment and update the guidance that we have provided with examples and quantitative results.

9 Conclusions

This paper has reported the results of a six month study that investigated how to structure defenses against malicious code attacks on COTS software. It surveyed the state-of-the-practice and identified twenty-nine defenses against thirty-four different types of attacks. It produced an initial knowledge base of wisdom associated with protecting COTS and portrayed the results as guidance.

Our hopes are that our future work will validate and add to our initial findings. We plan to continue to publish our findings especially as experimental results become available. Our goal is to stimulate as much feedback as possible so that we can extend our work into areas which have the highest payoffs.

References

1. Charette, R.: Software Engineering Risk Analysis and Management. McGraw-Hill (1989).
2. Reifer, D.: Final Report, Software Protection Framework. Reifer Consultants, Inc. (2004).
3. Charkrabarti, A. and Manimaran, G.: Internet Infrastructure Security: A Taxonomy. In: IEEE Network 16 (6) (2002) 13-21.
4. Landwehr, C., Bull, A., McDermott, J. and Choi, W.: A Taxonomy of Computer Program Security Flaws. In: ACM Computing Surveys, 26(3) (1994) 211-254.
5. House, L.: ATSIT Technical Report. Battelle National Labs (2004).
6. Hermann, D.: Using the Common Criteria for Information Technology Security Evaluation. Auerbach Publications (2003).
7. Debar, H., Dacier, M. and Wespi, A.: Towards a Taxonomy of Intrusion-Detection Systems. In: Computer Networks 31(8) (1999) 805-822.
8. Axelsson, S.: Intrusion Detection Systems: A Survey and Taxonomy. Technical Report 99-15, Department of Computer Engineering, Chalmers University (2000).
9. Houle, K. and Weaver, G.: Trends in Denial of Service Attack Technology. CERT Advisory (2001).
10. Mirkovic, M. and Reiher, P.: A Taxonomy of DDoS Attack and DDoS Defense Mechanisms. ACM SIGCOMM Computer Communications Review 34(2) (2004) 39-54.
11. Butler, S.: Security Attribute Evaluation Method: A Cost-Benefit Approach. In: Proceedings of ICSE '03, (2002).
12. Whittaker, J. and Thompson, H.: How to Break Software Security – Effective Techniques for Security Testing. Addison-Wesley (2003).
13. Stallings, W.: Network and Internetwork Security. Prentice-Hall (1995).
14. Graff, M.. and Van Wyk, K.: Secure Coding – Principles and Practices. O'Reilly & Associates, Inc. (2003).
15. Young, S. and Horwitz, S.: Protecting C Programs from Attacks via Invalid Pointer References. In: Proceedings of ESEC/FSE '03 (2003).
16. Fawcett, T. and Provost, F.: Activity Monitoring: Noticing Interesting Changes in Behavior. In: Proceedings of the 5th ACM SIGKDD International Conference on Knowledge Discovery and Data Mining, August (1999).
17. Kim, G. and Spafoord, E.: The Design and Implementation of Tripwire: A File System Integrity Checker. In: Proceedings of the 2nd ACM Conference on Computer and Communications Security (1994).
18. Hoglund, G. and McGraw, G.: Exploiting Software – How to Break Code. Addison-Wesley (2004).

Protective Wrapping of Off-the-Shelf Components

Meine van der Meulen[1], Steve Riddle[2], Lorenzo Strigini[1], and Nigel Jefferson[2]

[1] Centre for Software Reliability, City University, London, U.K.
{mjpm, strigini}@csr.city.ac.uk

[2] School of Computing Science, University of Newcastle upon Tyne, U.K.
{steve.riddle, n.p.jefferson}@ncl.ac.uk

Abstract. System designers using off-the-shelf components (OTSCs), whose internals they cannot change, often use add-on "wrappers" to adapt the OTSCs' behaviour as required. In most cases, wrappers are used to change "functional" properties of the components they wrap. In this paper we discuss instead *protective wrapping*, the use of wrappers to improve the dependability – i.e., "non-functional" properties like availability, reliability, security, and/or safety – of a component and thus of a system. Wrappers can improve dependability by adding fault tolerance, e.g. graceful degradation, or error recovery mechanisms. We discuss the rational specification of such protective wrappers in view of system dependability requirements, and highlight some of the design trade-offs and uncertainties that affect system design with OTSCs and wrappers, and that differentiate it from other forms of fault-tolerant design.

1 Introduction

As building "component-based" software systems becomes more common, it becomes more often necessary to combine existing off-the-shelf (*OTS* for brevity) components – hardware as well as software – that were not necessarily designed to work together. *Wrapping* is a popular, often cost-effective technique for integrating pre-existing components into a system. When designing a new system, ad hoc "wrappers" are developed, i.e. new, small components that will be interposed between the others, reading and sometimes altering the contents of the communications they exchange. Wrapping has the advantage of not requiring detailed knowledge of the internal structure of the components being wrapped.

In most cases, wrappers are used to adapt the functionality of a component to the requirements set for it by the system's design: they often perform simple functions like translation between the argument formats used by two communicating components. In this paper we look instead at the use of wrappers for improving dependability. We call such wrappers *protective* wrappers. Protective

This work was supported in part by the U.K. Engineering and Physical Sciences Research Council through project DOTS (Diversity with Off-The-Shelf Components), grants GR/N23912/01 and GR/N24056/01.

X. Franch and D. Port (Eds.): ICCBSS 2005, LNCS 3412, pp. 168–177, 2005.

wrapping is a way of structuring the provision of standard fault tolerance capabilities, like error detection, confinement and recovery, plus the less common capability of *preventing* component failures, in a component-based design where dependability is a concern. We wish to clarify how these wrappers can be rationally specified, the trade-offs facing system designers (simply "designers" for the rest of the paper), and the peculiarities of this form of fault-tolerant design, compared to the general case.

When designing a system with off-the-shelf components (OTSCs), it is often the case that an OTSC's functionality, and even more often its dependability, is insufficiently documented. Both these deficiencies are threats to system dependability: wrong assumptions about how an OTSC is intended to behave lead to system design faults; optimistic assumptions about an OTSC's probability of behaving as intended may lead to overestimating the dependability levels achieved by the chosen system design. Wrapping can help a designer to compensate for this lack of information.

Wrapping for dependability has been addressed by other authors. Wrappers are used to transform or filter unwanted communications that may cause failures. Fault injection may be used to identify such failure-causing values [7, 3, 5]. Wrappers are proposed to protect OTS applications that do not deal properly with kernel-raised exceptions, by transforming these into other exceptions or error return codes [7]; or to protect OTS kernels against inappropriate requests ([3]; here, an extended notion of wrappers is proposed that can access the kernel's internal data). In [5], the goal is automatic protection of library components against failure-causing parameter values, submitted by accident or malice. In [4], wrappers protect name servers from receiving unverifiable requests. A somewhat general approach to wrappers for common security concerns is described in [6].

Most of this previous work assumes that a good knowledge can be gained about which communications will cause OTSC failure. We have argued for a more general view of protective wrapping [9], to take into account the fact that this knowledge is usually deficient, the specification of the OTSC may be incomplete, and designers need to be concerned with failures of both the OTSC and the rest of the system. Here, we discuss issues of design, verification and quantitative dependability trade-offs that arise in protective wrapping.

In the rest of this paper, Section 2 introduces terminology and an illustrative example. Section 3 introduces the specifications of components in relation to system-level requirements, including those concerning fault tolerance. Sections 4 and 5 discuss the options for the actual semantics of wrappers, i.e. the cues that can trigger their intervention and the forms of these interventions. Section 6 sets the previous discussion of wrapper specifications in the context of probabilistic system dependability requirements and discusses the important design trade-offs that arise. Our conclusions follow.

2 System Model and Example

Throughout this paper, we will use a simple example to clarify the concepts introduced. The example system (Fig. 1) is a water boiler. We focus on a single

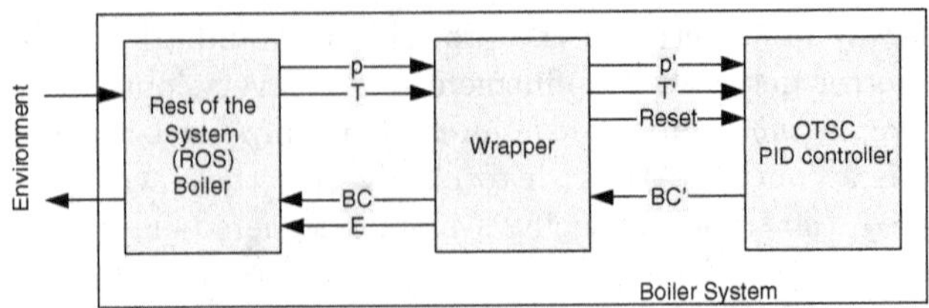

Fig. 1. The boiler control system used as an example

OTSC, in this case a PID (Proportional-Integral-Derivative) controller which provides feed-back control for the burner of the boiler, and on its communications with the rest of the system ("ROS"), seen as a single black box; the ROS may contain other OTSCs. This example omits some of the possible complications of a real system (an OTSC may have direct communication links with the environment around the system, or communications with the ROS that cannot be intercepted by a wrapper) but will suffice for this brief discussion. The OTSC, ROS and wrapper may be hardware or software or any combination of the two.

The ROS outputs readings (p, T) of pressure and temperature in the boiler, and accepts a burner control input, BC, and an exception signal, E, which causes an alarm signal to a human operator. The OTSC accepts as inputs two real numbers (p', T') and a *reset* signal, and outputs a (real-valued) control signal for the burner, BC'.

The designer is concerned with the dependability of this system: how frequently the components will behave abnormally (will fail), whether these component failures will cause system failure, and whether the frequency and severity of these failures will be acceptably low. Because of this concern, instead of connecting the ROS outputs directly to the OTSC's inputs and vice versa, the designer introduces a protective wrapper between the ROS and the OTSC, as depicted, which transforms p into p', etc.

The wrapper monitors communications between the ROS and OTSC, and possibly changes the values transmitted to the ROS or the OTSC. The ROS sees the combination of the OTSC and wrapper as one component, which we call the "wrapped OTSC" (WOTSC); likewise, the OTSC sees a "wrapped ROS" (WROS).

For the sake of simplicity, we assume here that the OTS and ROS, if connected without the protective wrapper, would, in the absence of failures, produce the combined behaviour required from the system. So, the OTSC in Fig. 1 does not need "functional" wrapping, limiting our discussion to protective wrapping.

3 Roles of Components and Protective Wrappers

3.1 System Requirements, Components and Interfaces

The designer's problem is how to ensure the required behaviour of the whole system, using a given OTSC. When considering dependability, a designer usually deals with multiple sets of requirements on system behaviour. First, there is a specified *nominal* behaviour: what the system ought to do, at least if none of its components fail. The designer usually has an understanding of a nominal behaviour for each component, and makes sure that if all components exhibit their nominal behaviours, then so will the system. Making the system fault-tolerant means ensuring that even if components violate their nominal behaviours (they fail), the system will still exhibit nominal behaviour (failure masking) or some degraded but acceptable behaviour (graceful degradation), or at least will remain within an envelope of safe behaviours; the choice being determined by the system dependability requirements and by the costs of these various options.

The complete dependability requirements will inevitably be probabilistic: in addition to defining a nominal behaviour and zero or more degraded behaviours (or *modes* of operation) it will include required upper bounds on the probabilities of the system operating in the degraded modes [1]. A similar hierarchy of a nominal behaviour and more or less acceptable failure behaviours applies to dependability requirements for any component or subsystem.

In this and the next two sections, we will discuss the deterministic part of these dependability properties. In a proper design, the specified system-level properties need to be *verifiable*, in the sense that, given clear descriptions of how the various components will behave (in their nominal and degraded modes) and of their connections, one can deduce that the requirements for the whole system (for a nominal or degraded mode, as specified) are satisfied. The expected or required behaviours (*models* and *specifications* in what follows) of the components and of the system need to be described in some unambiguous language, e.g., preconditions and postconditions characterising the relation between sequences of their inputs and outputs [8].

These descriptions need not specify all details of behaviour of a component, i.e. they may be partial specifications. We might for instance describe a component in a numerical library as computing a certain floating-point result with a relative error of less than 1%, although in reality the relative error is smaller, and variable; or, rather than trying to describe in detail what a component would do if it failed, we would rather describe an envelope of plausible behaviours it may exhibit, and prove that some system-level requirement will be satisfied provided the component remains within that envelope.

The behaviour that the designer expects the OTSC, as procured, to exhibit can be described abstractly as pairs of pre and post-conditions [8]. The looser the postconditions (the fewer the restrictions assumed on the behaviour of the OTSC), the more arbitrary behaviours of the OTSC one will need to require the wrapper and ROS to cope with in order to guarantee any given system-level

[1] It is true that such a formal way of specifying dependability requirements is only in common use for a few categories of systems. For many everyday systems, probabilities may not be mentioned at all. Yet, we think that any rational definition of requirements will include some idea of what probabilities would be unacceptably high for each given failure (i.e., degraded behaviour) mode, and a partial ordering between more and less acceptable modes.

requirement. This may make the system more robust, but at a cost, which will be the more acceptable, the more likely the extra erroneous behaviours allowed by the less restrictive model of the OTSC are in reality. Symmetrical considerations apply to the designer's expectations about the behaviour of the ROS.

3.2 The Models of the OTSC and ROS

We assume that the designer has chosen a particular OTSC, either procured on the market or already available within the same company. For an OTSC from the commercial market, the documentation will often be of lower quality and procuring extra information is often cumbersome and expensive; on the other hand, if the component is in frequent use, the supplier may have reliable data on its dependability. Any publicly available, dependability-relevant data can also be valuable, e.g., collections of bug reports for software packages, or information about maintenance requirements, failure modes and their failure rates.

The documentation of the OTSC may not specify its behaviour in certain circumstances, and the designer's most prudent approach would then be to assume that it is completely undetermined. At the opposite extreme, designers may choose to guess the OTSC's behaviour, based on previous experience, expert knowledge or other information.

By contrast, the designer may have a more precise model of the ROS, if custom-designed or if it also uses wrapping to ensure predictable behaviour.

Boiler Example. A specific PID controller has been chosen as the OTSC. Suppose that its documentation is unclear about what happens when either p or T is negative. The designer's model of the OTSC may then prudently assume its behaviour as undefined when these preconditions are violated. There may be other preconditions, documented or suspected, for the PID controller to behave properly, e.g., upper bounds on the values and rates of change of p' and T'.

As for the model of the ROS, to prove that the system has correct (nominal) behaviour if no component fails, the designer will use a model that includes the sensors and actuators, the physical properties of the burner, the fluid in the boiler, etc. This alone may not guarantee the above preconditions for nominal behaviour of the OTSC. It will then be the wrapper's task to guarantee them.

3.3 Requirements on the Wrapped OTSC and ROS

The designer's specification for the WOTSC may differ from the model of the OTSC even in its nominal behaviour, e.g. by hiding some of the functions offered by the OTSC. In addition, it has to describe dependability requirements, which determine the fault tolerance provisions needed in the wrapper.

Boiler Example. The boiler needs from the PID controller a control signal, BC, derived from the pressure and the temperature of the boiler according to a PID control law. A degraded, safe behaviour from the system viewpoint is to switch off the boiler ($BC = 0$). Knowing that the OTSC's behaviour is undefined for negative p' or T', the designer may then specify that the WOTSC must behave like the OTSC, if $p \geq 0$ and $T \geq 0$, but if not, it must set BC to 0.

In addition, since the precondition for nominal behaviour of the OTSC requires $p' \geq 0$ and $T' \geq 0$, the designer might specify that the WROS must guarantee these properties (e.g. if $p < 0$, p' will be 0), All these specifications together define the specifications of the wrapper. Since the wrapper alters the interface behaviour of the ROS and OTSC, the designer needs to verify that these modified behaviours imply the required system behaviour. For instance, at the interface of the ROS with the wrapper, the ROS sees a WOTSC that behaves (nominally) as a PID controller but with the important change that, if p or T is negative, its inputs and output are clamped to zero.

4 Specifying the Protective Wrapper: Cues for Intervention

Usually, designers of fault-tolerant systems use the detection of errors to trigger defensive actions. This relies on a fairly accurate knowledge of the behaviour of all components when failure-free. In designing with OTSCs, though, this knowledge cannot be assumed. Furthermore, the design of an OTSC often makes it difficult to monitor it closely for early error detection. So, designers may want their wrappers to react to a pattern of component behaviour that merely suggests a failure, although it may be correct, especially if the type and circumstances of the suspected failure would cause severe consequences to the system.

So, designers may take an attitude similar to that frequently taken in designing for safety: aiming more at keeping the behaviour of components within an envelope of behaviours that prevent unacceptable damage at system level, than at guaranteeing their correct (nominal) behaviour. They also face the same kind of trade-offs: the interventions of the wrapper will usually prevent some requested operation of the OTSC, possibly providing in its place a safe failure, or an alternative, degraded or less efficient service. Designers thus know that the more cues they decide to react to, the less likely the system will be to fail in unpredictable ways, but also the more likely for wrapper interventions to be the result of false alarms, and the more degradation in performance or availability.

The wrapper, as depicted in Fig. 1, monitors the outputs of the ROS and of the OTSC for cues, and can manipulate their values before forwarding them to the corresponding inputs of the OTSC and of the ROS, respectively. It can also insert communications not initiated by the ROS or OTS, for instance exception signals in response to cues it has detected.

In the wrapper's specifications, preconditions about the possible cues will be matched with postconditions about actions for the wrapper to take in response.

5 Examples of Specifications for Wrapper Actions

For any given cue, the designer may choose among various possible reactions by the wrapper, depending on the system's architecture and dependability requirements. A few possible reactions were described in Sect. 3. We now discuss other possibilities for providing fault tolerance via the wrapper. Some of these have been applied in our project in a case study in a simulated environment [1].

For instance, let us consider the case in which the ROS fails and issues a suspicious p value, e.g. a negative value, violating a precondition for the PID controller, whose behaviour is then unspecified. As in Sect. 3, the wrapper could mitigate the consequences of such a failure by *substituting this erroneous, dangerous or suspicious signal value with other values*. This keeps the PID controller in a region of operation for which its behaviour is predictable. This may not ensure correct *system* behaviour, but it may be sufficient protection e.g. against noise spikes on sensor readings, given the robustness of the PID control law. With a slight complication, the wrapper could be specified to set p to its last previous value, rather than 0, to reduce the step change in the input to the OTSC.

If correcting a suspicious input value (to the ROS or the OTSC) is not a solution, harm can still be prevented by checking and if necessary correcting their subsequent outputs. If, e.g., a failure causes suspicious values of p., the designer can specify that the wrapper will then perform additional plausibility checks on the output of the PID controller. If the checks fail, the wrapper could ensure *graceful degradation* by providing a simpler version of the OTSC's (or ROS's) function. The designer might specify this kind of switch if the degraded control were proven to keep the boiler in an acceptable degraded mode of operation for as long as the OTSC cannot be trusted to perform correctly.

All these palliative measures may only be acceptable for a short time. If they persist, a reaction can be for the wrapper to enforce at least safe system-level behaviour, by switching the burner off ($BC = 0$): an extreme form of graceful degradation suitable for all undesired situations.

Another possibility is *error recovery*. In many OTSCs, after most failures a reset is sufficient to restore an internal state such that the OTSC will subsequently exhibit correct (nominal) behaviour. In our example, the wrapper could reset the PID controller (OTSC) if its output is clearly out of bounds. Reset erases the OTSC's memory of previous history: it does not generally guarantee that its future behaviour will be appropriate *from a system viewpoint*, but it may in a control system like our example, if the designer can demonstrate that the internal state of the OTSC will then return to a correct state (through the OTSC reading and processing its inputs) quickly enough.

More complex recovery actions can be specified. If, for instance, an OTSC has an "undo" operation, the wrapper could use it for *backward recovery and retry*; a wrapper could store sequences of input messages to an OTSC and replay them after recovery, possibly even with slight variations to reduce the risk of repeated failure ("retry blocks" architecture [2]). The possibilities here are bounded by the risk implicit in increasing the complexity of the wrapper, and thus the risk of specification or implementation errors. For instance, designers may often limit themselves to stateless wrappers.

The case of reset is an example of a wrapper generating *exception* signals rather than just manipulating the normal ROS-OTSC communications. As another example, the wrapper can generate an exception signal to the ROS, E, when e.g. the OTSC's BC' output, or the T reading, exceeds specified bounds.

Last, many of the actions described so far may not be effective, e.g. if the cue to which they react is caused by a permanent or recurrent fault. If this is considered too likely, wrappers may be designed to escalate to more drastic and safer actions (multi-level recovery). E.g., once it has entered a "graceful degradation" state, a wrapper could become sensitive to cues that it would otherwise ignore, and trigger a more drastic action if any of these cues occurs. After the wrapper has reset the PID controller, it may set a time-out after which it will shut down the boiler if normal control has not resumed. Again, designers need to judge at which point the added complexity becomes counterproductive.

6 Probabilistic Dependability Properties

Up to this point, we have approached wrapper design mostly from a deterministic viewpoint: the designer considers the possibility of certain unplanned-for sequences of actions of the OTSC or ROS, and specifies the wrapper so that it will mask or alter those behaviours in ways that appear desirable, to achieve one of the specified nominal or degraded modes of operation. This desirability must be determined in view of the system-level dependability requirements, which are inevitably, in their general form, probabilistic, as outlined in Sect. 3.

A wrapper's role may be to avoid or mask certain component failures, or to mitigate them; it may improve system dependability by avoiding certain system failures (increasing the probability of nominal behaviour), or by mitigating them (shifting probability from more severely to less severely degraded behaviours).

As always with fault tolerance, wrapping faces two kinds of trade-offs, i.e. between, on the plus side, the improvement in dependability that it produces by avoiding or mitigating some failures, and, on the minus side, (i) its direct costs (in terms of development effort and of run-time resources); and (ii) the dependability loss due to wrappers *causing* failures or making them more severe.

Direct costs are generally the easiest factor to estimate. Estimating dependability improvements may be difficult. In some cases, specific failure modes of OTSCs cause frequent enough system failures that it is easy to predict the effect of avoiding them (and to determine how to). But if a system is already reasonably dependable without wrapping, the dependability gain will be uncertain. Even so, designers will think it reasonable to provide abilities at least to deal with predictable component failures that have a clear potential for severe effects and can be avoided or tolerated at low cost. This appears to be the approach, for instance, of the HEALERS project [5]. However, this common sense approach, when extended to less obvious failures, is not guaranteed to improve dependability, due to difficulties with the second trade-off.

Interventions by wrappers generally substitute a controlled degraded system behaviour (a more acceptable failure) for a potentially uncontrolled failure (*cf* Sect. 4). The designers decide to which cues the wrapper reacts. Including more cues avoids more uncontrolled failures, but also causes more wrapper interventions on "false alarms", *causing* degraded behaviour when nominal behaviour would otherwise occur. Designers cannot *a priori* judge which occurrences of a given cue are false alarms, and thus whether, statistically, wrapper intervention on that cue improves dependability. Besides, in many systems the effects of wrapper interventions on the behaviour of the whole system will be more complex to trace than in our boiler example.

A wrapper may also cause system failures in the obvious way, because of bugs or physical faults, and deliver, for instance, a wrong input for the ROS despite having received a correct OTSC output; or, for the same reason, not react to a cue as specified. For many systems this risk will be negligible, however, because the wrappers will be simple and easy to verify, compared to the risk of either false alarms or failures to intervene that are directly due to the designers' choices. That is, most wrapper failures will be due to the inherent limits of the algorithms that a designer can feasibly apply. Error detection, for example, often depends on reasonableness checks, which cannot flag values that are erroneous but "reasonable". They can be made more stringent at the cost of using cues that are not sure indications of errors. Designers thus know how to shift the balance between false alarms and uncontrolled failures, and can even choose which component failure modes the wrappers will not detect or tolerate, and in which circumstances they may produce false alarms. Unfortunately, they still do not usually know the frequency of these events, so that the uncertainty on the actual dependability improvement achieved by wrapping is not resolved.

Design faults in wrappers remain a potential problem in the case of more complex wrappers. Designers must decide how sophisticated a wrapper they can specify before this very sophistication becomes counterproductive. This transition may be made less sharp if a designer finds wrapper design techniques that bias wrappers towards benign failures, whose consequences can be assessed, rather than uncontrolled ones, like injecting arbitrary values into a communication stream.

7 Conclusion

We have tried to clarify some issues concerning *protective* wrapping. Protective wrappers are components that monitor and ensure the non-functional properties at interfaces between components. We have described the role that protective wrapping may play as a special case of fault-tolerant design, from both the viewpoints of deterministic and of probabilistic dependability properties.

These considerations should help designers in specifying wrappers, using the spectrum of fault-tolerance techniques within the special constraints of wrapping as a design structuring scheme. These peculiarities are not always acknowledged in previous literature. Our main considerations are: wrappers can be rigorously specified on the basis of the designers' specification of the OTSC's behaviours in its possibly multiple modes of operation: from nominal, correct behaviour to manageable, non catastrophic failure modes; due to poor documentation and poor ability to detect run-time errors inside OTSCs, protective wrappers may have to act on cues of potentially erroneous and/or error-causing communications between components; all of this increases the importance of design trade-offs between reducing the probabilities of the more dangerous system failure modes and avoiding too frequent false alarms leading to degraded service or "safe" system failures.

Research developments that appear desirable concern formal proof, probabilistic modelling and experimental evaluation. Formal proof methods, tailored to the restricted sets of structures defined by wrapping and the kinds of properties it involves, are desirable to support the verification steps described in Sect. 3. Probabilistic modelling should support designers in choosing trade-offs as discussed here; it must cover both the structural aspects of how component failures cause system failure, aspects that are well developed in modelling of fault tolerance, and the uncertainty on the reliability of the individual components and their probabilities of failing together, as studied in software reliability research and the assessment of software diversity. Last, experimental evaluation of systems using protective wrapping is required, to document the ranges of error coverage levels, "false alarm" rates and system dependability achieved with various classes of wrapper designs and of OTSC components, and thus give some basis for informing probabilistically based decisions.

References

1. T. Anderson, M. Feng, S. Riddle, A. Romanovsky, *Protective Wrapper Development*, Proc. 2nd Int. Conf. on COTS-Based Software Systems, Ottawa, Canada, 2003.
2. P. E. Ammann, J. C. Knight, *Data Diversity: An Approach to Software Fault Tolerance*, IEEE Transactions on Computers, C-37, pp. 418-25, 1988.
3. J. Arlat, J.-C. Fabre, M. Rodriguez, F. Salles, *Dependability of COTS Microkernel-Based Systems*, IEEE Transactions on Computers, C-51, pp. 138-63, 2002.
4. S. Cheung, K. N. Levitt, *A Formal-Specification Based Approach for Protecting the Domain Name System*, Proc. DSN 2000, International Conference on Dependable Systems and Networks, New York, USA, 2000.
5. C. Fetzer, Z. Xiao, *HEALERS: A Toolkit for Enhancing the Robustness and Security of Existing Applications*, Proc. DSN 2003, International Conference on Dependable Systems and Networks, San Francisco, U.S.A., 2003.
6. T. Fraser, L. Badger, M. Feldman, *Hardening COTS Software with Generic Software Wrappers*, Proc. 1999 IEEE Symp. on Security and Privacy, Oakland, CA, USA, 1999.
7. A. K. Ghosh, M. Schmid, F. Hill, *Wrapping Windows NT Software for Robustness*, Proc. 29th IEEE International Symp. on Fault-Tolerant Computing (FTCS-29), Madison, USA, 1999.
8. B. Meyer, *Applying "Design by Contract"*, IEEE Computer, 25, pp. 40-51, 1992.
9. P. Popov, L. Strigini, S. Riddle, A. Romanovsky, *Protective Wrapping of OTS Components*, Proc. 4th ICSE Workshop on Component-Based Software Engineering: Component Certification and System Prediction, Toronto, 2001.

An Automated Dependability Analysis Method for COTS-Based Systems

Lars Grunske[1] and Bernhard Kaiser[2]

[1] School of Information Technology and Electrical Engineering ITEE,
University of Queensland, Brisbane, QLD 4072
grunske@itee.uq.edu.au
[2] Department of Software Engineering and Quality Management,
Hasso-Plattner-Institute for Software Systems Engineering,
University of Potsdam, Prof.-Dr.-Helmert-Straße 2-3,
D-14482 Potsdam, Germany
bernhard.kaiser@hpi.uni-potsdam.de

Abstract. The increasing application of COTS-components and component-based software engineering has entailed the development of appropriate component specifications. In the embedded systems domain it would be desirable to benefit from these component specifications to integrate and automate safety and reliability analysis. For this reason, we propose in this paper a component-based dependability analysis technique that annotates components with failure mode assumptions. The probabilities and dependencies of these failure modes are specified by Component Fault Trees (CFT's). Based on these CFT's and the architectural model the propagation of failures throughout the system can be automatically determined and a quantitative analysis is possible.

1 Introduction

Constructing software systems with reusable or COTS-components has become a popular approach for several reasons, including cost reduction, quality improvement and shorter time to market. Moreover, humans are incapable of handling highly complex systems without decomposing them.

Another predominant paradigm in modern software development is model-based development, because it facilitates the development of complex systems and supports their decomposition: modeling techniques such as ROOM [16] or some UML 2.0 models reflect the component structure and depict communication mechanisms between the components. Models have been unified and integrated to cover all development phases from requirements analysis to code generation and testing. Safety and reliability analysis however have not yet been integrated with the other phases, mainly due to their different modeling approaches. Safety or reliability cases must be built from scratch, causing additional workload and compromises the consistency of the analyses with the actual system. Reusable component dependability models and their automatic integration according to the system structure would facilitate an integrated development process.

X. Franch and D. Port (Eds.): ICCBSS 2005, LNCS 3412, pp. 178 – 190, 2005.

As a solution to this issue, we present a method that annotates component models with Component Fault Trees (CFTs). These CFTs describe how failure modes of the incoming messages together with internal faults of the components propagate to failure modes of the outgoing messages. Since the interconnection of the components of a system by their ports is described in the structure diagram, we can compose these CFTs automatically and perform the quantitative analysis on the system-level Fault Tree.

The rest of the paper is organized as follows: In Section 2, the basics of the component-based models and of CFTs are introduced. In Section 3, we explain the proceeding of a component-based dependability analysis in detail. The case study of a protection system in Section 4 demonstrates the application in practice and in Section 5 we present the safety analysis tools BALANCE and UWG3 that support the method. We conclude with a survey of related work in Section 6 and a summary in Section 7.

2 Preliminaries

2.1 Component Based Software Engineering

Building a software system with self-contained and exchangeable components is a precondition for efficient modeling and reuse, which are both key elements of mature engineering disciplines. Thus, many current design approaches divide systems recursively into components (sometimes called capsules), which are instances of component-classes. Each component-class is described by an appropriate set of models, i.e. structure and behavioral models. A component-class can either be flat, i.e. not supposed to be refined any further, or contain subcomponents. In the latter case, the component is called a hierarchical component of which the entire system is a special case.

Components are encapsulated entities that hide their internal details and communication with their environment is only possible via ports. The selected model implicitly determines the kind of information that is transferred via ports; examples are discrete event signals, continuous data streams, or any kind of service requests and the corresponding responses. In many models it is allowed that different messages or services are transmitted across the same port. Ports or their associated services can have a direction (in or out). In this case, they must be connected as complementary pairs (input to output, service provider to service consumer etc.). The associated semantics is that information flows from a source component to a target component or that a service is required by a client component and provided by a server component.

The architecture of the system, graphically depicted by the structure diagram, specifies how a higher-level component is built of lower-level components and how these can interact during the runtime of the system. Therefore it must be described which ports of the components must be connected. Two basic connection mechanisms can be distinguished, connection and binding [6]. The difference is that a connection interconnects two ports on the same hierarchical level, whereas a binding interconnects two ports in different hierarchical levels, i.e. a port of a subcomponent with a port of its enclosing component [6]. As an example Figure 1 depicts the structure specification of a component class C with two ports. This component contains two subcomponents Sub1 of class C1 and Sub2 of class C2, both of them possessing two ports. The edges between the ports represent the communication links. Thereby the edge between the portsSub1.p1 and the port Sub2.p1 is a connection and the edges between the other ports are bindings, because they link different hierarchy levels.

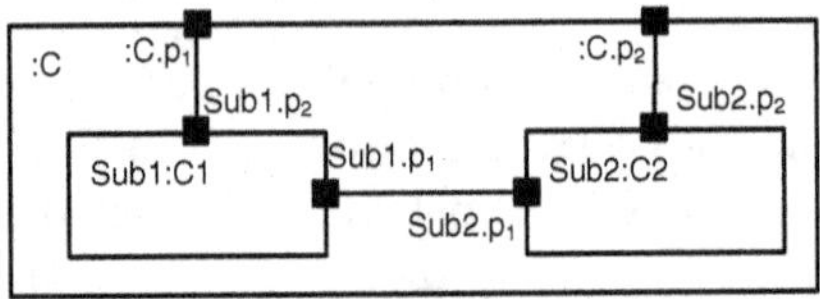

Fig. 1. Structure Specification Example

2.2 Attribution of Failure Modes to Components and Ports

The structure diagram describes the static architecture of a system. During design phase, models for the behavior are attached to it, for example state machine models that describe the reaction of components to messages received via its ports. During the construction phase, only the intended behavior is of relevance. Safety or reliability analysis in contrast focuses on possible derivations from the intended behavior. So instead of behavioral models, models for the emergence of incorrect behavior and its propagation between components could be attached to the architecture model.

As by assumption the ports are the only interfaces that allow any kind of interaction, they are also the spots where failures propagate. Thus, the available architecture diagram can be exploited for the automatic construction of safety cases. Components can generate failures and they can propagate, mitigate or transform failures from other components whose services they rely on. When incorrect behavior propagates to the ports of the top-level component, i.e. the system under examination, this is perceived from outside as a failure or hazard of the system as a whole.

An arising question is how failures should be classified, i.e. in which way the provided service can derive from what is expected. For dependable systems, there is an accepted categorization for failure modes [5]:

- value failure (wrong data or service result)
- early timing failure (event or service is delivered before it was expected)
- late timing failure (expected event or service is delivered after the defined deadline has expired)
- omission (no event or service is delivered when it is expected)
- commission (unexpected event or service)

This schema helps the analyst to identify and classify all relevant failure modes that can occur at the output ports of each component. It is good engineering practice to keep as small as possible the number of ports and different services per port. Additionally, out of the 5 potential failure categories at most one or two will practically apply to any service. In consequence the failure modes to be considered in total are not too numerous and it is possible to generate a description for each of them by standard analysis models.

When modeling the failure pathology, three basic ways of failure propagation have to be considered:

1. Incorrect service can be evoked by an outside component via an incoming message through a port and propagate to an outgoing message. This includes the case that the failure mode is transformed into another failure mode
2. Incorrect service can be generated within the component itself
3. Incorrect service delivered to the component at a port can be mitigated in some way by the component so that no failure is propagated to any port.

We suggest Fault Trees (FTs) to describe the failure propagation within a component. FTs [7,18] are a widely accepted model that graphically shows how influence factors (faults or failures) contribute to some given hazard, accident, or failure mode. They provide logical connectives (called gates) that allow decomposing the system-level hazard recursively (mainly AND-, OR-, NOT-gate). The AND gate indicates that all influence factors must apply together to cause the hazard and the OR gate indicates that any of the influences causes the hazard alone. The logical structure is depicted as an upside-down tree with the hazard to be examined (called top-event) at its root and the basic influence factors as the leaves.

2.3 Component Fault Trees (CFTs)

To be compatible to the architecture model that shall serve for automatic construction of the safety case, the models for the failure behavior must be attachable to the components and account for the assignment of failures to the ports. They must take into account that the components are in general not independent from each other because the ports are access points for possible influences from other components.

Unfortunately, standard FTs are only compositional in the sense that independent subtrees (called *modules*) can be cut off and handled separately. As mentioned above, components are typically influenced by other components via their ports, so that the assumption of independent subtrees fails. To allow for a modularization that corresponds to the component and port concept, we recently proposed a more advanced component concept [8] that we call Component Fault Trees (CFTs). It allows deliberately defining partial Fault Trees that reflect the actual technical components. These CFTs can be modeled and archived independently from each other. In correspondence to the port concept of design models, we introduced input and output failure ports to put these parts together. The outstanding difference lies in the treatment of subtrees. Traditionally a module was treated like a "compound event"[18] with a corresponding probability. We regard a CFT as a set of propositional formulas describing the truth-values of each output failure port as a function of the input failure ports and the internal events. CFTs need not be trees but can be directed acyclic graphs. An output failure port in CFTs replaces the top-event of traditional FTA and there may be more than one output failure port in each CFT. Each component constitutes a namespace and internal events are hidden to other component instances. Once defined, CFTs may be instantiated several times. The model is integrated and flattened during analysis. Apart from the component and port concepts, CFTs are ordinary FTs and provide the same expressive power and analysis techniques. Figure 2 gives an example of a CFT. The left CFT describes the failure behavior of the system, i.e. an instance of the top-level component-class C1. The system incorporates two instances Sub1 and Sub2 of another component type C2 as its subcomponents. On the higher hierarchy level subcomponents are represented as black boxes that show only the ports, representing the external interface of the embedded CFT. As in UML we use the colon to separate instances from classes, e.g. Sub1:C2 denotes that Sub1 is a component (instance) of component-class C2. Note that the invisible internal events Sub1.E1 and Sub2.E1 are two distinct instances of: C2.E1 and thus independent events, while System.E1 is another distinct event and a common failure cause to both subcomponents.

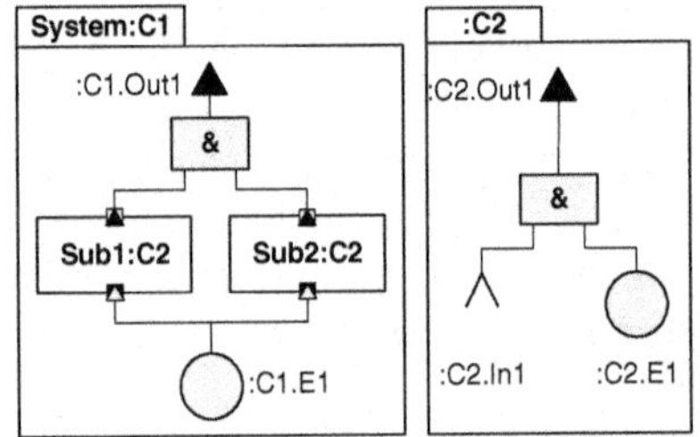

Fig. 2. Example of a Component Fault Tree

In summary, CFTs are an appropriate means to annotate components with a description of their failure mechanisms. The new technique saves effort and is less error-prone than traditional Fault Trees or most other models used in safety analysis. It pays of especially in contexts where redundancy and reuse of formerly developed components are issues. However, as CFTs are a variant of standard Fault Trees, enough trained safety and reliability experts can immediately start working with this technique.

3 Component-Based Dependability Analysis

In this section, we propose a component-based dependability analysis technique that exploits the given preliminaries. It can be structured into three phases. In the first phase, the component suppliers must construct a CFT for each component-class instantiated in the project. This CFT describes the failure behavior of the component with respect to all working environments for which the component-class is specified. In the second phase based on the CFT of the used component-classes, a CFT is constructed for the entire system. All necessary information for this algorithm is contained in the architectural model and the CFTs of the subcomponents. In the third phase, the resulting CFT is analyzed quantitatively to determine the probability of the relevant system failures. If these failure probabilities are lower than the tolerable failure probabilities defined in the requirements specification, the system fulfils its reliability or safety requirements. In the following, we present in detail the activities that are performed in each phase.

3.1 Construction of Component Fault Trees for Flat Components

For each used component-class, a CFT must be provided to enable the component-based dependability analysis. This CFT describes the causal dependencies between the failures of the provided services from the internal faults and failures of the requested services. A recommendable way to identify these dependencies is the Interface Focused Failure Mode and Effect Analysis (IF-FMEA) [13]. This IF-FMEA investigates in a structured process the provided and required services of a component for possible failures. The causes for each possible failure of a provided service are represented as logical combinations of internal malfunctions and failures of required service. This investigation is complemented by a forward search that finds the consequences of each possible failure of a required service. By alternating application of these two search directions the emergence, propagation, mitigation and detection of failures in the component can be identified. These causal chains are then represented by CFTs, which are actually directed acyclic graphs.

For the analysis of the CFTs, the probability of each internal failure must be specified with an appropriate probability function or measure. For hardware components, there are mature models to do so, whereas for software components the determination of the failure probabilities is a complex task. There is a growing research body regarding failure probability estimation for software [1]. In industrial projects, this estimation is often based on expert knowledge. Estimation can also refer to the process model and the used quality assurance techniques [4]. Another method is to use empirical reliability growth models and testing results to forecast the probability of internal failures [11].

3.2 Construction of Component Fault Trees for Hierarchical Components

In this subsection we introduce the algorithm that recursively constructs CFTs for hierarchical components or the complete system from the structure specification and the CFTs of all component-classes.

To construct these CFTs for a hierarchical component, in the first step a new CFT is created. By iterating over all subcomponents in the structure diagram, the CFTs of all subcomponents are embedded into this new CFT. As for flat components, these CFTs have been specified manually, this is a simple step if the component contains only flat subcomponents. If the component contains hierarchical subcomponents, the CFT of these hierarchical components must be constructed first before they can be embedded into the new CFT. This is the reason for the recursive nature of the algorithm. In the second step the input and output failure ports of the embedded CFTs must be connected according to the structure diagram that defines all possible paths of failure propagation. For this, all connections and the involved components are investigated. Each time one component uses a service from another, it is checked whether the provider CFT contains an output failure port and the user CFT contains an input failure port with matching failure modes. In this case, both failure ports are connected by an edge in the system level CFT.

In the third step, the failure propagation between subcomponents and the environment of the enclosing component must be identified. Such kind of failure propagation can only occur via the bindings that relay subcomponent ports directly to ports of the enclosing component. Thus, each binding and the involved components are investigated. If a subcomponent requires a service from the environment and its CFT contains an input failure port with the name of the service, then an input failure port concerning the same service and failure mode is added to the new CFT and both input failure ports are connected. In a similar way, a new output failure port is added and connected in the CFT under construction, if a component provides a service to the environment via a binding. In summary, we present the following algorithm to construct CFTs for hierarchical components:

Algorithm CFT ConstructCFT (ComponentClass c)
Input: the component for with the CFT should be constructed
Output: the CFT of the component-class c

1. If *c* is a flat component-class then return the CFT of *c* and terminate the algorithm, else generate a new CFT *cft* for the component-class *c*, if it has not been generated before.
2. Iterate over all subcomponents *ec* instantiated in the structure diagram of *c*
   a. Construct a CFT *ef* for the component-class of subcomponent *ec* by a recursive call of the algorithm *ef* =ConstructCFT(*ec.getClass()*)
   b. Add an instance of the CFT *ef* to *cft*.
3. Iterate over all connections *v* in *c*
   a. Identify the CFT instances *scft1* and *scft2* of the attached components to the connection *v* in *cft*.
   b. Iterate over all services *a* that are requested via the connection *v*
      - If *scft1* contains an output failure port and *scft2* contains an input failure port with the name of the service *a* and an identical failure mode then connect both failure ports in *cft* by a CFT edge.
      - If *scft1* contains an input failure port and *scft2* contains an output failure port with the name of the service *a* and an identical failure mode then connect both failure ports in *cft* by a CFT edge.
4. Iterate over all bindings *b* in *c*
   a. Identify the CFT instance *scft1* of the attached component to the binding *b* in *cft*.
   b. Iterate over all services *a* that are requested via the binding *b*
      - If *scft1* contains an output failure port with the name of the service *a*, then add an output failure port with an identical failure mode to *cft* and connect both failure ports by a CFT edge.
      - If *scft1* contains an input failure port with the name of the service *a*, then add an input failure port with an identical failure mode to *cft* and connect both failure ports by a CFT edge.
5. return *cft*

3.3 Analysis of the Component Fault Trees of the System

As the result of the first two phases, a component fault tree has been generated for the complete system. This fault tree can be used to analyze the dependability of the system with respect to given failure modes of the system. To specify the relevant failure modes and the services of concern, the user deliberately marks output failure ports of the system. In case of a safety analysis, these output failure ports represent failures or hazards of the system of which the probability is to be determined. In case of reliability, analysis the focus is on failure modes that inhibit the intended function of the system or the quality of service. If a failure is caused by a logical combination of failure modes at any of the failure output ports, the analyst can join these ports by logical gates since the model to be analyzed is still a Component Fault Tree. After flattening of the hierarchical CFT, the quantitative analysis can be performed in the same way as in traditional FTA, since all probabilities and relations between failures are fully specified. The analysis algorithm does some optimization and additional checks for preconditions, in particular that the integrated CFT is actually acyclic.

4 Example

To explain how an automated analysis works in practice, we present a steam boiler system as small case study. It incorporates a triple-redundant pressure sensor and a double-redundant safety valve, which exemplifies multiple instantiation of component classes. Furthermore, the system contains a software controller that implements a two-out-of-three voter for the sensors and gives command to open both valves if a pressure higher than the allowable level is detected. Each of the valves is sufficient as a pressure relief, so if one fails, the system is still safe.

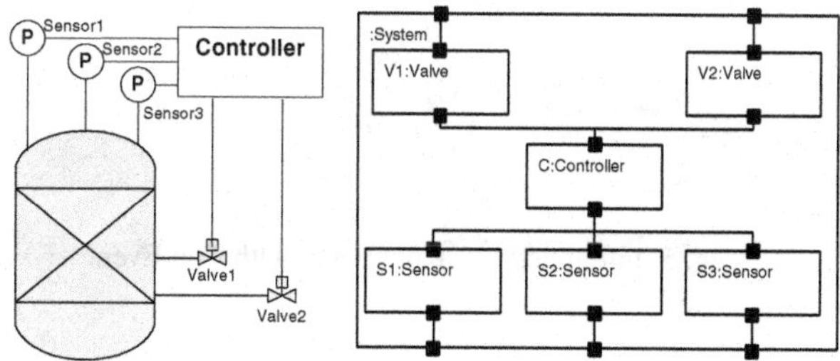

Fig. 3. Steam Boiler Schematic and Structure Diagram

The interconnection of the components is shown in the structure diagram in Fig 3. In principle, it shows the normal flow of information and does not refer to any kind of failures. However, the connections between the components are at the same time the spots where faulty behavior can be propagated from one system component to another. To model potential failures, CFTs for each component-class are generated. Each CFT has input failure ports and output failure ports that must be associated to failure categories with respect to messages or services at the ports of the corresponding component-classes. Between input failure ports and output failure ports the failure propagation or transformation and the internal failure generation of the component-classes are modeled (Fig 4).

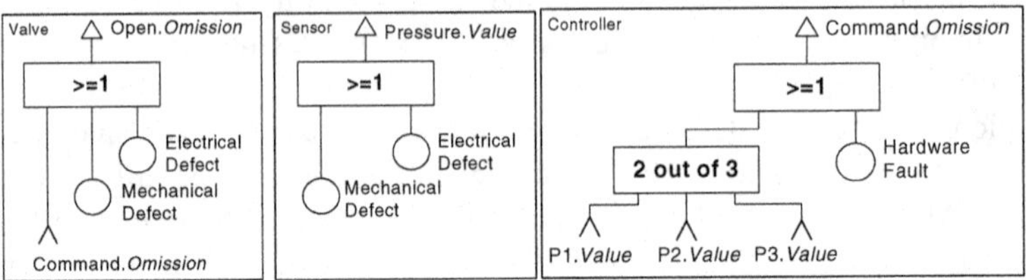

Fig. 4. Valve, Sensor and Controller CFTs

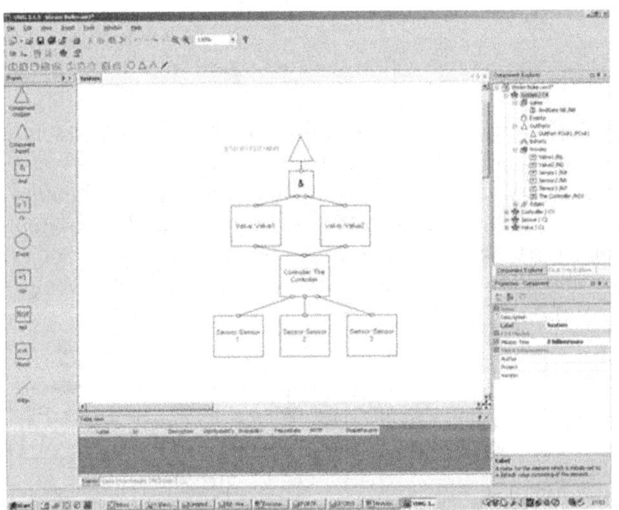

Fig. 5. Integrated FT, Completed with Top Event

To keep the example simple, we assume only a few failure modes: A sensor fails with a value failure (wrong pressure indicated) if a mechanical or an electrical failure occurs. A valve can fail to open (omission) for electrical or mechanical reasons, but also because of a missing command (omission at the input failure port *Command*). The controller, which is a piece of software running on a microprocessor, fails to give the open commands (omission at the output failure port *Open*) either if at least two of the connected sensors give wrong signals (value failure at the corresponding ports *P1*, *P2* or *P3*) or if there is a hardware defect.

The CFTs given so far allow in conjunction with the structure diagram to integrate the system level CFT. However, before starting the analysis, another manual step is necessary: The user must complete the system-level Fault Tree by specifying which system hazard is to be examined. This can be performed directly in the graphical editor of the CFT analyzer. The resulting Fault Tree is shown in Fig 5, which is a screenshot taken from our analysis tool UWG3 that will be introduced in the following section. The lower part of the structure has been generated automatically, the top-event and the AND gate have been added manually by the user. The AND gate attached to the failure output ports V1open.omission and V2open.omission specifies that if both valves fail to open when expected, the hazard to be examined is present.

Assuming all events to have constant failure probability of 0.1 we calculated the hazard probability to 0.10 using the tool UWG3.

5 Implementation in a Tool Chain

For practical application of the component-based dependability analysis tools are necessary that allow for an intuitive modeling of both the architecture diagram and the CFTs. The tools must perform the automated integration of the models and the subsequent analysis. A further requirement is the possibility to build and manage a component repository so that component-classes that have been defined once can later be reused in other projects. Based on these goals and the previously described work we have developed two tools called UWG3 and Balance.

The first tool, UWG3, is a Windows-based tool for modeling and analyzing CFTs. It has been developed in cooperation at the HPI, with support from the companies Siemens and DaimlerChrysler. It incorporates all previously mentioned features of the Component Fault Tree concept and has been used in several industrial projects where it proved its intuitive handling. It uses an XML format to store models, projects and component repositories that also serves as an exchange format to other tools. UWG3 provides an efficient analysis algorithm that makes use of Binary Decision Diagrams [3] to handle efficiently even large CFTs. The component concept is efficiently exploited to speed up the analysis. Besides the calculation of the top-event probability or equivalent rate, UWG3 offers qualitative analysis by listing all Minimal Cut Sets, even across component boundaries. In our example project, UWG3 is used both for editing of the Fault Trees that describe the individual component classes and for analysis of the system level Fault Tree in the end.

The second tool, BALANCE, was developed to analyze the dependability of complex technical systems based on the software and system architecture. This tool enables the user to specify an architecture specification or to import it from a CASE tool. The component-classes of this architecture specification can then be annotated with CFTs. To facilitate this process, CFT-stubs can be generated automatically that contain five output failure ports for each provided service, corresponding to the five specified failure modes (omission, commission, too early, too late and value). In a similar way, five input failure ports are generated for each requested service. In the next step, the user can manually complete these CFT-stubs with the specification of the failure behavior of the component, for instance by applying the proposed IF-FMEA. An unconnected output failure port means that the probability of this failure is zero and an unconnected input failure port means that this failure does not affect the proper operation of this component. Based on the specified information of the CFTs and the architectural model Balance generates a CFT for the complete systems according to the algorithm specified in section 3.2. For the analysis of this system level CFT the tool Balance interfaces directly to UWG3, which analyses the CFT and determines the probabilities of the output failure ports.

6 Related Work

This section reviews existing approaches that deal with the dependability analysis for component-based systems and compares them to the work described in this paper.

An important source that influenced our work is the Failure Propagation and Transformation Notation (FPTN) described in [5]. This approach first introduced the basic concepts for a modular specification of the failure behavior of components. In the FPTN a mixture of graphical and textual representations is used to describe the mitigation, transformation, propagation and detection of failures in a system. The assumed failure modes are the same as in our method. Our approach enhances the ideas behind FPTN by seamlessly integrating suitable analysis techniques to determine the probability of a failure of the system. FPTN modules and CFTs are similar in expressive power, so FPTN modules could be transformed to CFTs in order to benefit from the analytic power and tool support available for CFTs.

A very closely related approach to ours is the HiP-HOPS method described in [12,13]. This method also identifies the failure behavior of a component with an IF-FMEA. For the identification of the relevant system level failure the Functional Failure Analysis (FFA) is used. Based on the classified failure description on component and system level an automatic fault tree synthesis is possible. As in our approach, the integration is derived from the hierarchical structure of the system. The missing piece in comparison our approach is the CFT concept. HiP-HOPs uses traditional flat fault trees, leading to very complex fault trees that cannot be checked manually any more. We argue that for the integration of component-based techniques all analysis techniques must support the component concept and that thus CFTs are a significant contribution to component-based automated safety analysis.

The previously mentioned approaches focus especially on the analysis of safety properties. In contrast, the approach described in [15] describes a component-based reliability analysis. For the specification of the reliability information of a component the concept of parameterized contracts is used. These parameterized contracts are a generalization of the design-by-contract principle [10]. For the analysis of the contracts Markov-Chains are used. Therefore, the dependence matrix between the reliability of the required and the provided services is constructed.

7 Conclusion and Future Work

In this paper we proposed a technique for the component-based dependability analysis. This technique annotates component-class specifications with Component Fault Trees. Based on the CFTs of the basic component-classes and the structure and dataflow specification of the system an algorithm to construct the CFT for the complete system is proposed. This CFT allows for the evaluation of the hazard or failure probabilities.

The method is subject of current research and has some potential for new research directions. A fundamental improvement potential is the research for better models to estimate the probabilities of internal failures, in particular for software components. Up to now, predictions depend strongly on expert knowledge and premature models. A potential application domain of our method is to help software architects to select appropriate components so that the final system fulfills the safety requirements. Our aim is to create a component library that contains CFTs for recurring component classes and readily connected models for recurring patterns in safety critical systems.

With respect to the analysis performance we tend to further exploit the component structure to reduce the analysis workload, especially if components are reused very often. This can be achieved by caching pre-simplified BDD versions of the Boolean structure of CFTs and by storing them in the repository along with the original model. Another suitable extension to our approach is to add more powerful failure modes to the existing set, in particular protocol failures that occur if the correct ordering of events at interfaces is violated. This requires appropriate interface specifications that specify the correct order of events. A third current research project aims at adding a state / event distinction into standard FTA. This extension, called State-Event-Fault-Trees, would enable more accurate modeling of typical failure scenarios in software-controlled systems and would facilitate the integration of state-based models.

References

1. Birolini, A.: Reliability engineering: theory and practice, New York, Springer, (1999)
2. Bondavalli A., Simoncini, L.: Failure Classification with Respect to Detection, in: Predictably Dependable Computing Systems, Task B, Vol. 2, May (1990)
3. Bryant, R.E.: Graph-based algorithms for boolean function manipulation. IEEE Transactions on Com-puters, C-35(8), Aug. (1986) 677--691
4. CENELEC:, Railway applications The specification and demonstration of dependability, reliability, availability, maintainability and safety (RAMS), European Committee for Electrotechnical Standardisation, Brussels, Standard EN 50126, 128, 129, (2000-2002)
5. Fenelon, P., McDermid, J.A., Nicholson, M., Pumfrey, D. J.: Towards Integrated Safety Analysis and Design, ACM Applied Computing Review, (1994).
6. Grunske, L.:A Visual Architecture Description Language for Embedded Systems with Hierarchical Typed Hypergraphs, in Proceedings 3rd Workshop on Domain-Specific Modeling at the 18th ACM SIGPLAN Conference on Object-Oriented Programming, Systems, Languages and Applications (OOPSLA), Anaheim, (2003) pp 1-8
7. IEC 61025: International Standard IEC 61025 Fault Tree Analysis. International Electrotechnical Commission. Geneva(1990)

8. Kaiser, B., Liggesmeyer, P., Mäckel, O.: A New Component Concept for Fault Trees. in Proceedings of the 8th Australian Workshop on Safety Critical Systems and Software (SCS'03), Adelaide, (2003)
9. Laprie, J.C.(ed.): Dependability: Basic Concepts and Associated Terminology. Vol.5, Dependable Computing and Fault-Tolerant Systems Series,Vienna: Springer (1992)
10. Meyer, B.: Applying design by contract. IEEE Computer 25, 10, (1992) 40-51
11. Musa, J.D.; Iannino, A.; Okumoto, K.: Software Reliability - Measurement, Prediction, Application, McGraw-Hill International Editions, (1987)
12. Papadopoulos, Y., McDermid, J.A., Sasse, R., Heiner, G.: Analysis and Synthesis of the Behavior of Complex Programmable Electronic Systems in Conditions of Failure, Reliability Engineering and System Safety, 71(3), Elsevier Science, (2001) 229-247.
13. Papadopoulos, Y., McDermid, J. A.: Hierarchically Performed Hazard Origin and Propagation Studies, SAFECOMP '99, 18th Int. Conf. on Computer Safety, Reliability and Security, Toulouse, LNCS, 1698 (1999) 139-152
14. Pumfrey, D. J.: The Principled Design of Computer System Safety Analyses, Dissertation, University of York, (1999).
15. Reussner, R., Schmidt, H., Poernomo, I.:. Reliability Prediction for Component-Based Software Architectures, Journal of Systems and Software, 66(3), Elsevier, The Netherlands, (2003) 241--252
16. Selic B., Gullekson G., Ward P. T.: Real-Time Object-Oriented Modeling. Wiley, (1994)
17. Szyperski, C.: Component Software. Beyond Object-Oriented Programming. ACM Press/ Addison Wesley, (1998)
18. Vesely, W. E., Goldberg, F. F., Roberts, N. H.,. Haasl, D. F.: Fault Tree Handbook. U. S. Nuclear Regulatory Commission, NUREG-0492, Washington DC, (1981)

Loose Integration of COTS Tools for the Development of Real Time Distributed Control Systems

Javier Portillo, Oskar Casquero, and Marga Marcos

Escuela de Ingenieros de Bilbao (University of the Basque Country)
Alameda Urkijo s/n, 48013 Bilbao, Spain
jtppobej@bi.ehu.es, cvzcaoio@lg.ehu.es, jtpmamum@bi.ehu.es

Abstract. The development of Real Time Distributed Control Systems (RTDCS) is a very complex and multi-part issue where different specific tools are to be used. As these specialized tools are not designed to work together, it would be desirable to have a flexible tool framework where all the information were managed and stored following a predefined Model Driven Architecture. XML technologies and Web Applications (implemented as a component-based multi-tier application design defined by J2EE) have been selected to put into practice such a framework. It is proposed a model-based approach to develop software systems that require the collaboration of specific tools. This collaboration is achieved thanks to a Tool Collaboration Engine based on XML and Web Applications. A prototype of the framework was built for RTDCS, yet these concepts can easily be applied to any area of knowledge. The paper presents some conclusions on the integration of COTS.

1 Introduction

The development of Real Time Distributed Control Systems (RTDCS) is a very *complex and multi-part* issue implied in the generation of *heterogeneous applications* with *changing needs*. It is a *complex* topic because several phases are involved: requirements gathering, specification, design, simulation, analysis and code-generation. It is a *multi-part* matter because several knowledge areas are implied. The suitability of different concepts such as control algorithms, network communications and real-time constraints must be considered as a whole. Very *heterogeneous applications* are produced because Real Time or embedded applications vary in size and scope; from microwave ovens to factory automation, aerospace industry or railway control. Finally, the development of RTDCS must progress with these *changing needs* and one cannot ignore the support of new control algorithms, HW devices, network protocols, programming languages, operating systems, temporal constraints, etc.

Therefore, different specialists (control engineers, real time experts, software engineers) should work together and understand each other's needs. Each expert is assisted by domain specific tools (mainly COTS, Commercial Off The Shelf tools), but there is a gap in connecting specific tools from different domains and, therefore connecting different (but inter-related) knowledge areas.

X. Franch and D. Port (Eds.): ICCBSS 2005, LNCS 3412, pp. 191 – 200, 2005.

As new features and tools are constantly added, software vendors adopt a tool integration approach. The current market offers well-known software packages for system analysis and simulation that allow some exchange of information between the tools that cover the design phase. For instance, the two packages Xmath and Statemate [4] can be linked together at the code level and an interface allows the joint simulation within the Statemate environment. The Matlab / Simulink / StateFlow environment [11] offers graphical tools that allow cooperative simulation of models edited in Simulink and Stateflow. Some of these COTS tools allow code generation but they only consider a single design domain and further code is necessary to support network communication, signal conditioning, input/output data checking, fault detection, isolation and accommodation, etc.

Previous work of the authors [13] proposed a Matlab-based Framework for the integration of all the phases involved in the design of Real-Time Distributed Control Systems (RTDCS). Nevertheless, this framework was based in Matlab programming environment. A more general open framework is required to integrate COTS tools from different fields of expertise so they can work together in the generation of the RTDCS application.

Portillo [14] presented a Model Driven Framework aimed at the integration of COTS tool used in the development of Real Time Distributed Control Systems. This approach is based on Domain Specific Models; they must be understood as formal descriptions (of the system to develop) from the point of view of different knowledge areas. The key element of this approach is the *Model Collaboration Engine* (MCE) that stores, manages and coordinates the information of different models. A *Tool Collaboration Engine* (TCE) links COTS tools to those models handled by the MCE. Integration is achieved by means of data sharing because particular tools read/write information automatically from/to the Domain Specific Models. The major advantage here is specialists still use their own tools but the framework feeds them with results obtained from other domain specific tools (see Fig. 1). The TCE offers an open and standard interface to COTS thanks to XML and Web Services. The initial findings in tool and model integration of some open source projects (like Eclipse [2]) are very promising efforts and support the results presented here.

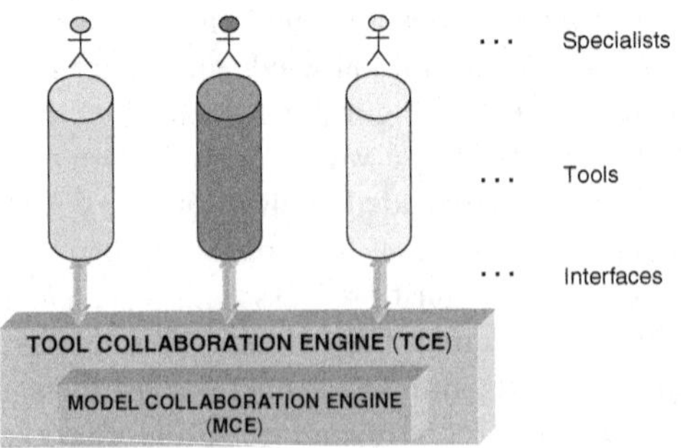

Fig. 1. TCE (Tool Collaboration Engine) embodies the MCE (Model Collaboration Engine)

In summary, it is proposed the integration of domain specific COTS tools, in the sense of automatic interchange of formally expressed information through standard and free software middleware. This kind of integration has been applied here to build a prototype, which integrates several COTS tools aimed to develop RTDCS.

The paper is presented as follows: section 2 considers XML and Web Services for the interface between the TCE and any COTS tool; section 3 and 4 discuss the architecture of the framework and identify appropriated integration paradigms; section 5 summarizes some technologies applied as 'glue code'; finally, some concluding remarks.

2 Framework Interface to COTS: XML and Web Applications

In [7] the architecture of software-intensive systems is described using multiple concurrent views, defining the so-called '4+1' View Model Approach. These views are: *logical, process, physical* and *development*. The fifth view is made up by *scenarios*, which illustrate relationships between the other views.

The Model Collaboration Engine (MCE) follows a similar architecture. Each of the *Domain-Specific Models* shows only the information about the system relevant to a specialist (or tool). Four models or views (more can be added) are identified as Domain-Specific: *Control System* (architecture independent system functionality), *Distribution System* (network topology and services), *Real Time System* (software architecture and temporal issues) and *Software Engineering* (code and documentation generation). The use of specialized formal languages, to detail the features of the system under development according to each view, results in formal descriptions of the RTDCS. While these can be grammar-based specialized languages, some kind of Rule-Based Language is needed to formally express the relationships between domain-specific views. XML meta-language meets all these requirements.

XML (eXtensible Markup Language) [19] can describe hierarchically structured information; it is extensible to suit user-defined requirements; documents are formally validated (against a user-defined model or *XML schema*) using a standard *parser* and documents are transformed (following user-defined rules) using a standard processor (*XSL*). All these features make XML an excellent language for inter-application communication and for achieving the *formal description*, *validation* and *translation* of the MCE Domain Specific Models:

- *XML schema* for *formal description*. The lexicon, syntax and semantics of Domain-Specific Languages are specified in four different XML schemas that define the Markup Languages to be used in the views: ControlML, DistributionML, RealTimeML and SWEngineeringML.
- *XML standard parser* for *validation*. The parser compares an XML document (domain specific description of the RTDCS) with its corresponding XML Schema (language definition) to perform the validation.
- *XSLT* for *translation*. Standard XSLT processors apply a set of patterns (XSLT stylesheet) and perform automatic translation of data between instances of models.
- *SCHEMATRON [6]* for *semantics and crossed domain relations*. This rule-based language complements schemas including those semantics that cannot be expressed in an schema. Besides, it allows the formal description of relations among different views.

The Tool Collaboration Engine (TCE), which is built on top of the MCE, provides access-points for COTS tools to the models being handled by the MCE. Web Services offer great flexibility for XML data interchange between external tools and the TCE. Fig. 2 shows the basics of Web Applications [20]. An *agent* identifies the computing resource devoted to obtaining or offering a web service automatically (without human interaction) through HTTP protocol. Prior to the connection between machines, humans must first agree on the way of describing the interface to the service (WSD, Web Service Description) and then on the semantics of the information to be interchanged. This agreement means the agents can be configured (roles of *service requester agent* and *service provider agent*) to interact automatically.

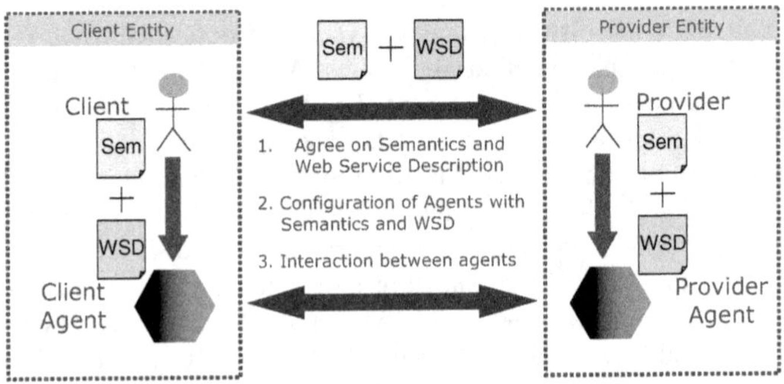

Fig. 2. Roles in Web Service architecture

The TCE can be built as a set of *service provider agents* and any COTS tool can thus interact through a *service requester agent*. There should be a provider agent per domain in the TCE and the semantics of each provider agent are formally expressed in the Domain-Specific XML Schemas. Only the WSD (ports, IP directions, protocols, etc) remains to be defined and WSDL [18] is the widely adopted standard to describe the loosely coupled services exposed by participants to each other. The main advantages of this Service Oriented Architecture based on XML and Web Services are:

- Data interchanged based on XML using standard protocols (HTTP) and locators (URLs).
- The analogy between linguistics and COTS-Based Systems Engineering [17] can be developed thanks to the Domain-Specific Languages.
- The previous agreement on particular domain (XML Schema) and type of service (WSD) constitutes a service-based contract that allows controlling security issues.
- Component, models and data storage and traceability services can be centralized in the MCE and make them independent of any COTS tool. This enforces reuse.
- Any new tool can be connected to the framework and different sets of tools can be used each time because interactions (between agents) are formalized independently of other tools.
- COTS tools running on heterogeneous (different Operating Systems) and distributed platforms can be connected.

3 Service Oriented Architecture of the Framework

The real collaboration between COTS tools is not resolved simply by the use of web services. The Framework has to manage all the information following an inner logic towards a concrete purpose. In this sense, the aim of our framework is the development of the software for a RTDCS and a specific kind of software process is implicit. The SW process that rules the operation of this framework is divided in:

- *Formal Specification Phase*. Fig. 3 shows how the work done by specialists in particular tools is reflected in the Domain-Specific Models: Control System (CS), Distributed System (DS) and Real Time System (RTS). Continuous interaction among these models (expressed in domain specific languages) results in a global specification that satisfies every requirement from each view and every constraint related to more than one view (expressed in the Rule Based Language).

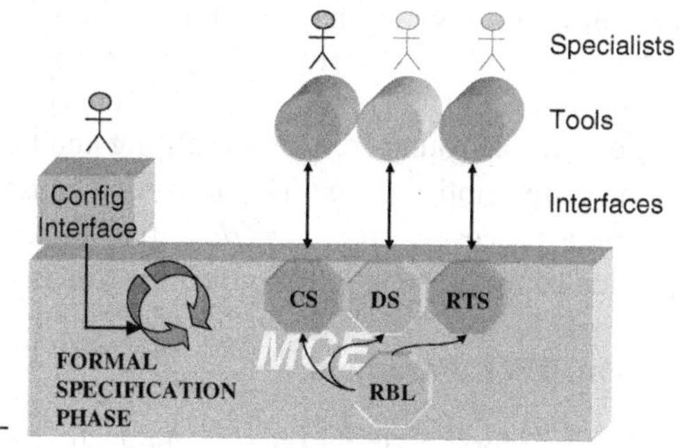

Fig. 3. Formal Specification Phase in the MCE

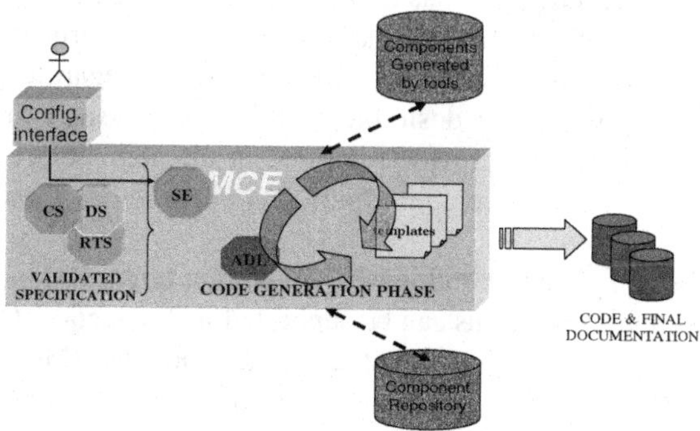

Fig. 4. Code Generation Phase in the MCE

- *Code and Documentation Generation Phase*. (Fig. 4). The project coordinator configures this second phase according to the SW Engineering (SE) model. This information, together with the validated 3-view specification, leads the code and documentation generation phase. Some code is automatically generated, some code is obtained from external tools, and some components are recovered from a repository. A specific kind of Architecture Description Language and the use of templates would facilitate modular implementation.

In short, the Service Oriented Architecture of the framework divides different services offered to COTS into these different phases. So, the integration methodology is guided by different paradigms for the Formal Specification service and the Code Generation Service.

4 Paradigms for the Integration

Putting in practice the two phases of the SW development Process involves very different skills, so separate concepts must be handled by the implementation:

- The Formal Specification Phase implies *interactive features* (TCE reacts to events as they occur, responds to tools when they ask for something). The *Model-View-Controller* (MVC) paradigm is particularly well suited for interactive Web Applications, where a requester agent (tool) interacts with a provider agent (TCE), with multiple iterations and multiple round-trips of requesting and transferring data.
- The Code Generation Phase implies *proactive features* (it causes things to happen; it is an actively initiated process). The *Workflow* paradigm (a group of tasks performed in sequence to reach a common goal) fits this phase.

4.1 Formal Specification: MVC Paradigm

When a server application supports a single type of client, it is sometimes useful to focus on the client's specific needs in order to develop the whole logic of the server. However, such an approach is poor when multiple types of clients must be supported because client-server interface code has to be rewritten for each application.

This is exactly the problem the TCE has to solve. It must provide the same core functionality (proper access to the MCE) for every tool, regardless how different they are. Therefore, it would be desirable to think of a design that achieves the complete *Separation of Concerns* (SoC) implied in the architecture of the TCE. In this sense, four concerns can be identified: *Business Logic*, *Control Logic*, and *Presentation Logic*.

As a result of the complete separation of *Presentation Logic* within the server, multiple types of views and interactions can be supported for each client (COTS tools), irrespective of the components that provide the core functionality (MCE).

The isolation of the *Control Logic* enables the flow control of the application to be encapsulated in some particular and independent components. The RTDCS must be developed using a predefined methodology, where each step is respected. These can be encoded in those components, which operate altogether like a finite state machine.

The key point in the architecture is the *Business Logic*, where the core functionality of the TCE relies on, or the management of tool-specific models. The Business Logic publishes a set of services for its clients and makes all the information, which it is managed and stored by the MCE, accessible via those services.

This kind of Separation of Concerns (SoC) can be accomplished for the TCE by applying the Model-View-Controller (MVC) architecture. Following the MVC architecture [3], each of the detailed concerns can be placed in one of the following layers:

- *Model.* It represents the *business logic* that governs the Tool-Specific Model management.
- *View.* It handles *presentation logic* for the client. The view renders the contents of a tool-model instance (tool-specific description of the RTDCS). It retrieves data through the Model and specifies how that data should be presented. It is the view's responsibility to maintain consistency in its presentation when the Model changes.
- *Control.* It organizes the *control logic* (flow or interaction system) of the application. The controller translates interactions with the View into actions to be performed by the Model. In a Web Application, those interactions appear as HTTP requests produced by button clicks or menu selections by the client (COTS tool). Based on the user interactions and the outcome of the Model actions, the controller responds by selecting an appropriate view.

4.2 Code Generation: Workflow Paradigm

A workflow system is a proactive system that supports the development, execution, and analysis of multi-step, multi-user business processes. The steps to be followed in the code generation phase are described in a configuration file. The flow is a compound of work units or steps (with their own descriptions) or additionally other nested flows. The modular way in which steps are designed allows them to be combined by dependence between modules. The workflow system can develop into a superstructure gluing together disparate systems whose business purposes are interconnected.

5 Technologies for the Integration

The 'glue code' used for programming the framework makes use of suitable technologies selected according to: coherency with integration paradigms, low cost, adoption of open standards, use of open software and *Declarative Programming* whenever possible.

The use of declarative programming rather than traditional hard-coded programming approach must be emphasized. This feature increases the modularity of the design, but enforces the reuse of existing components instead of building them from scratch. Declarative Programming also improves the flexibility (configuration and management of the framework) and extensibility (addition of new features).

Here we provide a brief description of some of the technologies that were used in a first prototype of the framework. The *Model View Control* concepts were implemented through Web Applications in J2EE architecture, while Apache Ant tool [1] played an important role implementing the *Workflow* services needed for code generation.

5.1 Formal Specification: *J2EE*

The interactive services used during the formal specification phase were designed following the J2EE standard described by [16] for a component-based multi-tier web application. The following technologies were used in each of the layers of the MVC architecture:

- *Cocoon* [8]: it is a servlet specialized in XML data processing. It is particularly powered to perform XSL transformations and this makes it suitable to carry out the translations of data between models instances (Domain-Specific descriptions) and tool instances at the presentation logic.
- *Struts* [5]: it is another servlet, but focuses on handling navigational flow at the control logic. It can be viewed as a collection of "invisible underpinnings" that help developers turn raw materials like databases, java classes (for example, EJBs) and web pages into a coherent application.
- *EJBs*: Enterprise Java Beans are a group of classes responsible for achieving the tasks implied in the *business logic* (the implementation of the services offered over RTDCS data).

The selected design approach leads the architecture to a three-tier enterprise application. Next, and equally as important, the connectors between these tiers must be identified:

- *Cocoon plug-in for Struts* (between Struts and Cocoon). This plug-in allows tool instances to be carried from the module where they are created (data formatting in Struts) to where they are translated into tool specific data format (presentation logic in Cocoon).
- *Business logic delegate* (between EJBs and Struts). This "delegate" is formed out of a set of classes which are responsible for announcing the available services.

5.2 Code Generation: *Apache Ant*

Apache Ant is a Java-based build tool designed to improve the functionality of old Make files. The configuration file ('build.xml') describes a target tree of various tasks. The Ant engine executes these tasks as a workflow. Ant can be extended using Java classes that will be invoked with new tags in the configuration file. Apache Ant satisfies the requirements of the code and documentation generation phase (proactive features and workflow paradigm). The specific language used for 'build.xml' can be extended to obtain the Domain-Specific Language SEML (Software Engineering Markup Language).

6 Conclusions

Several tools (Matlab by Mathworks [11]; BERTA and RTF [10]; EdROOM [15] and MAST [12]) devoted to the development of Real Time Distributed Control Systems were integrated following the architecture described in this paper. Integration was resolved in several layers:

- *Integration of data format and location*. Heterogeneous data from diverse COTS are expressed in XML and stored in a single server, the *Tool Collaboration Engine* (TCE). Any plug-in COTS tool (offering specific services within the application domain) can be easily connected to this environment. This approach proves to be more flexible than customizing pairs of tools to work together.
- *Integration of communication protocols*. The communication between the TCE and each COTS tool is performed using flexible Web Services (HTTP protocol), which avoid a tight integration. It is a Service Oriented Architecture where the TCE offers service descriptions written in WSDL to any external tool (not previously known) that should try to connect.
- *Integration of semantics*. As all the COTS tool within a knowledge-area share similar semantics, the definition of a Domain-Specific XML language (XML Schema) establishes a kind of standardization. This is the basis for plugging new tools into the TCE in a safe and predictable way and it also permits to have formal descriptions of the relations among Domain-Specific Models.
- *Integration of service types*. The Model-View-Control and the Workflow programming paradigms have been identified as appropriated in order to implement interactive and proactive services, respectively, within the TCE.

XML technologies (XSLT, Schematron), open standards (J2EE), open source software (Cocoon, Struts) and declarative programming (rule-based instead of hard-coded) turned out to be very useful for developing the above integration issues.

Many of the concepts within the designed framework are applicable to very general COTS integration and allow achieving an inexpensive and flexible solution, always open to new COTS. While most of the integration issues can be resolved in a standard way, the integration of semantics is the most critical one because it must be resolved according to the specificities of one concrete area of knowledge.

Web Services and XML promise to change the target of application developers; many applications will no longer be designed to work stand-alone, they will obtain services from other remote applications (COTS) running in heterogeneous platforms. In fact, very different ranges of applications are moving towards this kind of solutions. For instance, Business Process Management systems are migrating from expensive legacy EAI systems designed for batch operating environments to service oriented architectures where applications talk to each other according to rules embedded in the model.

Acknowledgements

Authors want to thank the support of the Spanish Ministry of Science and Technology through project DPI2003-02399.

References

1. Apache Software Foundation: Ant (2003) http://ant.apache.org/
2. Eclipse Foundation: Eclipse (2001). http://www.eclipse.org
3. Gamma, E., Helm, R., Johnson, R., Vlissides, J.: Design Patterns Elements of Reusable Object-Orientated Software. Addison-Wesley (1995)

4. Harel X., D., Lachover, H., Naamad, A., Pnueli, A., Politi, M., Sherman, R., Shtull-Trauring, A., Trakhtenbrot, M.: STATEMATE: A Working Environment for the Development of Complex Reactive Systems. IEEE T on SW Eng. Vol.16 (1990) 403-414
5. Husted, T., Dumoulin, C., Franciscus, G., Winterfeldt, D.: Struts in Action. Building web applications with the leading Java framework. Manning Publications Co (2003)
6. Jellife, R.: Schematron (2000). http://www.ascc.net/xml/resource/schematron
7. Kruchten, P.: The 4+1 View Model of Architecture. IEEE Software 12(6) (1995) 42-50
8. Langham, M., Ziegeler, C.: Cocoon: Building XML Applications. New Riders (2003)
9. Marcos, M., Portillo, J., Bass, J.M.: Matlab-based real-time framework for distributed control systems. Proceeding of the Workshop on Algorithms and Architectures for Real-Time Control. Palma de Mallorca - Spain (2000)
10. Marcos, M., Portillo, J.: Basic Environment for Real Time Systems Analysis using CAN bus, Proceeding of the Workshop on Real Time Programming. Palma de Mallorca - Spain (2000).
11. Mathworks: Using Matlab version 6.0 (2001). http://www.mathworks.com.
12. Medina, J.L., González, M.,Drake, J.M.: MAST Real-Time View: A Graphic UML Tool for Modelling Object-Oriented Real-Time Systems. Proceedings of the 22nd IEEE Real-Time Systems Symposium. IEEE Computer Society Press. London UK (2001) 245-256
13. Portillo J., Marcos, M.: Contributions to the Design of Real Time Distributed Control Systems, Proceedings of European Control Conference. Porto Portugal (2001)
14. Portillo, J.: Entorno multidisciplinar de herramientas para desarrollo de Sistemas de Control Distribuido de Tiempo Real. PhD Thesis. Univ. of the Basque Country. (2004)
15. Rodríguez, O.: EdROOM, una herramienta abierta para el desarrollo de sistemas SW de tiempo real basados en componentes. PhD Thesis. Univ. Complutense de Madrid. (2003)
16. Sun Microsystems: Designing Enterprise Applications with the J2EE Platform 2nd Edition (2003) http://java.sun.com/blueprints/patterns/MVC-detailed.html
17. Thanh, N., Comyn-Wattiau, I.: COTS-Based System Engineering: The Linguistics Approach. Lecture Notes in Computer Science Volume 2255 / 2002 (2003) 188
18. WDSL. Web Services Description Language (WSDL) Version 2.0 Part 1: Core Language. http://www.w3.org/TR/2004/WD-wsdl20-20040803/
19. World Wide Web Consortium: Extensible Markup Language (XML) 1.0; Schema W3C Recommendation; Extensible Sylesheet Language (XSL). (2003) http://www.w3.org
20. World Wide Web Consortium: *Web Services Architecture*. W3C Working Draft (2003) http://www.w3.org/TR/2003/WD-ws-arch-20030808

Managing Dependencies Between Software Products

Mark Northcott[1] and Mark Vigder[2]

[1] School of Computer Science, Carleton University,
1125 Colonel By Drive, Ottawa, Ontario, K1S 5B6, Canada
mnorthcott@rogers.com
[2] National Research Council of Canada,
1200 Montreal Rd., Ottawa, Ontario, K1A 0R6, Canada
Mark.Vigder@nrc-cnrc.gc.ca

Abstract. Systems constructed from diverse software products are often difficult to assemble and deploy correctly, particularly as the products evolve and the underlying platform changes over time. Many of these problems arise because of the many assumptions and dependencies, often implicit, that software products make about the context in which they are deployed. This paper describes an approach to managing the dependencies between the software elements of a system during assembly and deployment. A formal model of dependencies is developed, and it is shown how the model can be applied during the deployment process to verify the correct assembly of a system. The approach is designed to allow system developers, assemblers, and deployers to be part of the user group that collectively manages the dependencies that exist within an assembly.

1 Introduction

Assembling an application from software products is a non-trivial process. Software products may originate from different sources and evolve independently. The dependencies between products involve many types of constraints, and deploying the application to a particular platform introduces additional constraints. As the products and platform evolve, so too do the constraints, and the maintenance of constraints becomes increasingly difficult [6,7,8].

In current practice, developers of software products are directly responsible for defining the dependencies and constraints of the product. However, developers may not know a priori all of the contexts in which the software product will be used. Therefore, it is impossible to know all possible constraints of the product. Users of the software product, whether they be developers integrating the product into an application or end users deploying the product to a particular platform, are likely to encounter undocumented dependencies and constraints [7].

Currently, these newly discovered constraints may be documented through user groups, mailing lists or bug reports. However, it is often a tedious process investigating solutions to problems using any of these methods, especially for new users that may feel intimidated by the expertise of more experienced users. An approach for managing constraints that is accessible by both developers and users

X. Franch and D. Port (Eds.): ICCBSS 2005, LNCS 3412, pp. 201 – 211, 2005.

would aid in alleviating this problem. This will allow for newly discovered constraints to be properly documented by either developers or users, and it will provide a method for automatically verifying a particular deployment of an application or system.

This paper introduces such an approach for managing dependencies between software products that are assembled into a system. It does so by first presenting a formal model to describe system assemblies and the dependencies and constraints that exist between the elements of the assembly. Using this formal model, the activities associated with developing and deploying systems can be augmented by allowing constraints to be specified by any actor involved in the development and deployment process. Moreover, it is possible to specify the constraints in a fashion that can be automatically verified during the deployment process.

Section 2 describes a model for defining dependencies between software products. Section 3 explains how the model is used in practice in order to model a software system and specify constraints that may be automatically verified. An example application of the model is given in Section 4, which demonstrates how the open source xPetstore application is deployed to two different environments. Finally, Section 5 provides a discussion as to how the proposed model compares with current systems for managing dependencies between software products.

2 Modeling Dependencies Within Software Systems

In order to provide a tool for managing constraints, a suitable method for modeling dependencies between software products must be developed. This method should provide the following capabilities:

- Systems are developed in a hierarchical manner.
- Systems can be specified with *virtual components* that allow integrators to provide specific implementations of the component at deployment time.

In this context, a software product is viewed as a component that is a replaceable piece of a system that provides a clear function within the context of the system. Components could be COTS products, open source software, internally developed software, or any other large scale reusable piece of software.

Our model defines three types of components: concrete, virtual and composite.

- A ***concrete component*** implements services without being divisible into subcomponents. It is the most primitive type of component.
- A ***virtual component*** defines the services offered, but does not provide an implementation. It serves as an abstraction layer that allows for any component that provides the required services to be substituted into the system. This is similar to the concept of a virtual component as found in package managers such as in reference [1].
- A ***composite component*** is an assembly of subcomponents. The subcomponents of a composite component are not visible outside the composite component within which they are contained.

A ***component dependency*** is a requirement that exists between two components of the system. Component **A** *depends on* component **B** if **A** requires something from **B** in order to function properly. A ***constraint*** is a condition that is added to a dependency that must evaluate to true in order for the dependency to be satisfied. A dependency can have any number of constraints associated with it.

The model does not restrict in any way what the constraints of a dependency may be. A constraint could state that a particular interface must be provided by component **B**, the existence of an object, a particular file system structure, the existence of a configuration file, or any other condition for the correct functioning of the system. The dependency indicates that there exist constraints between two components; the set of constraints associated with the dependency define the exact nature of the dependency.

An ***assembly*** is defined as a collection of components and all the dependencies between the components. Figure 1 shows an example of an assembly containing four components and three dependencies. In the graphical notation, ovals represent virtual components, rectangles represent concrete components, and bold rectangles represent composite components. Dependencies are represented as solid arrows between components.

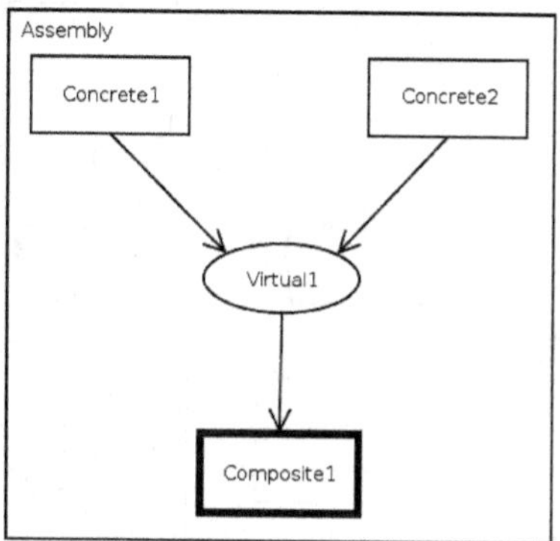

Fig. 1. Components and Dependencies Forming an Assembly

A composite component is hierarchically decomposed into an assembly. The embedded assembly represents the composite component decomposed into subcomponents and dependencies.

A configuration is defined as a set of assemblies, with each composite component being mapped to at most one assembly. A configuration is used to represent the hierarchical decomposition of a system through all the components and subcomponents. It can be represented as a directed graph where each node is an assembly, and **Assembly1** is a parent of **Assembly2** if and only if one of the composite components of **Assembly1** is decomposed into **Assembly2**. In order for a configuration to be valid it must satisfy the following properties:

- Every composite component is mapped to exactly one assembly.
- No two composite components are mapped to the same assembly.
- The directed graph representing the assembly does not contain any cycles.

The above restrictions mean that every configuration can be represented as a tree (or perhaps a set of trees) with the top level assembly being the root node, the non-leaf nodes being assemblies containing at least one composite component, and the leaf nodes being assemblies containing only virtual and concrete components. This is illustrated in Figure 2, with a configuration consisting of four assemblies, with two of the assemblies containing composite components. In the graphical notation, the mapping from a composite component to its corresponding assembly is represented by a dashed arrow.

Configurations with assemblies containing virtual components may be specialized by replacing a virtual component with either a concrete or composite component. The component being substituted in place of the virtual component may be a new component or it may be a component that currently exists elsewhere in the same assembly. All that is required is that it provides the services specified by the virtual component.

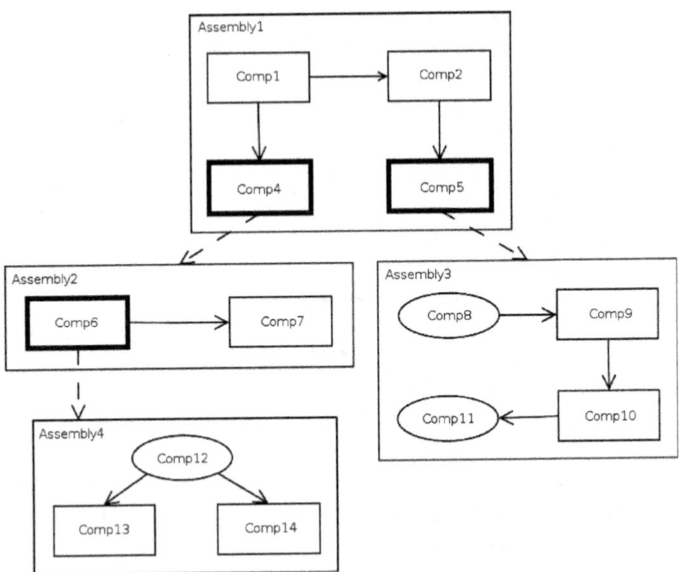

Fig. 2. Connecting Assemblies to Form a Valid Configuration

Since virtual components do not have an implementation, in order for a configuration to be deployed all virtual components must be replaced with concrete or composite components. A ***deployable configuration*** is defined as a configuration that does not contain any virtual components.

3 System Assembly and Verification

As part of the development and deployment process, assemblies are created and specialized into deployable systems. Creating deployable assemblies involves three main activities of interest to this research:

- Creating and specializing configurations
- Specifying constraints
- Verifying configurations

These three activities are described in the following sections.

3.1 Creating and Specializing Configurations

System development involves beginning with a *base configuration* and going through a process of *specialization* until a deployable configuration has been created. The base configuration specifies all the components and dependencies of the system, but leaves the components as virtual components wherever possible.

From the base configuration, deployers can go through a process of *specialization* by replacing the virtual components with concrete or composite components. This replacement of virtual components represents decisions being made as to how the system will be deployed within a particular environment. For example, the base configuration may specify, as virtual components, the existence of a file system, a database, and a mail system, as well as some concrete components developed as part of the application. Once a deployer has selected particular implementations for these virtual components, the virtual components in the base configuration can be replaced by the concrete or composite components selected.

The specialization process continues until all virtual components have been replaced. At this point, a deployable configuration exists and can be installed.

During the specialization process, a deployer must maintain the structure of the system in terms of its components and dependencies. That is, components cannot be added or removed from the base configuration; it is only possible to replace the virtual components with components that are concrete or composite. Moreover, all the dependencies between components are specified initially in the base configuration and do not change during the specialization process. An example of the specialization process is illustrated in Figure 3. Note that even though the dependencies do not change during the specialization process, the constraints associated with a dependency will change, as described in the next section.

3.2 Specifying Constraints

Constraints are the mechanism by which deployers manage the consistency of a configuration. The base configuration defines whether there exists a dependency between components. However it is the constraints associated with a dependency that provide the detailed description of what the dependency implies and how it can be verified.

As configurations are created and specialized constraints are specified and added to dependencies. These constraints can be added by any number of actors, including developers, deployers, and even end users. It is assumed that many of the constraints will not be known initially and will be discovered during the operation and evolution of the system. For example, as new versions of components are released, new constraints regarding version compatibility may be discovered. These constraints can be entered by anyone who discovers them along the development and deployment chain.

The concept of a constraint is kept as general as possible in order that there are no restrictions on the kinds of things that can be specified by a constraint. For example, a constraint may be specified to ensure that a particular file system structure is present, a necessary environment variable is set, or a particular version of a component is present.

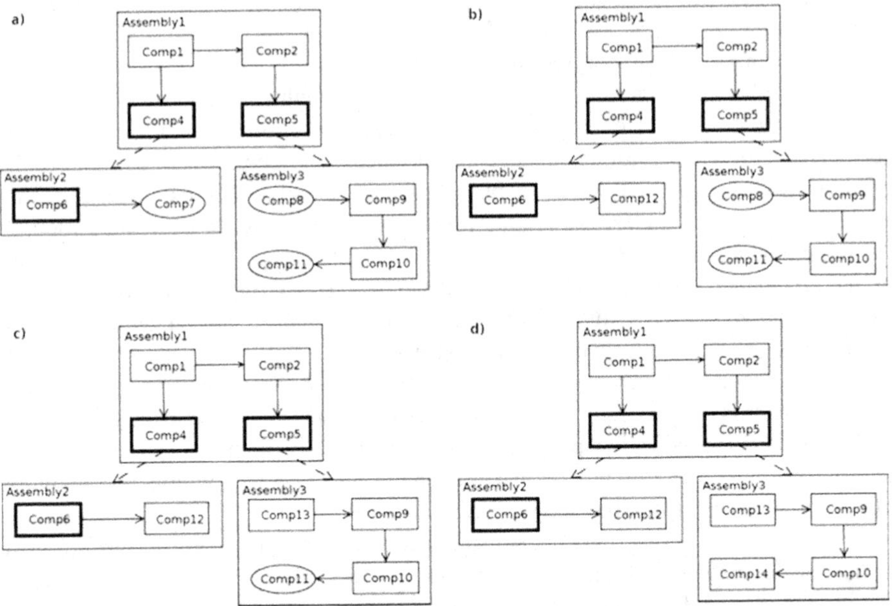

Fig. 3. Specialization process. a) Base configuration; b) virtual component Comp7 replaced by concrete component Comp12; c) virtual component Comp8 replaced by concrete component Comp13; d) virtual component Comp11 replaced by concrete component Comp14

A constraint consists of three parts. First there is an *identifier* that gives the constraint a unique identity within the namespace of the system. Second there is a textual *description* of the constraint. And third there is the *rule set* that defines how the constraint is to be verified.

Every constraint must contain the identifier and description. A constraint should have a rule set only if it is associated with a dependency between concrete or composite components. This is required because it is generally not possible to specify the details of a constraint between components that are virtual. For example, it is possible to say that a concrete application depends on a virtual database. However until a specific database is chosen it is not possible to give the details of the dependency. Once the concrete database is selected, constraints can be attached to the dependency to describe the necessary data type mappings, performance configurations, etc., that are unique to the selected database within the context of its interaction with the application.

If configuration A_1 is converted to configuration A_2 through specialization, then all constraints of A_1 must be carried forward to A_2. Thus once a constraint is added to the system during development or deployment, it is carried through to the creation of the deployable configuration. However, A_2 may have more constraints than are specified in A_1. Since A_2 has more concrete components, more constraints may be discovered related to these components.

3.3 Verifying Configurations

At any time during the process of development and deployment, a configuration can be verified. This involves verifying that the rule set for each constraint is satisfied. Although verifying a rule set can be done manually, ideally the rule set is specified in a way that allows for a tool to automatically verify the constraint.

For a deployable configuration, if the verification process completes without encountering any problems, the deployment is believed to be complete and working. A deployer should be able to immediately deploy it.

However if a deployable configuration is verified and does not deploy correctly, it is likely that a new constraint has been discovered. When a deployer discovers a previously unidentified constraint it should be added into the configuration and made available to other system deployers. The constraint should be specified in the least specialized configuration possible in order for it to be propagated to all affected deployable configurations. This allows other users to directly benefit from the work done by a single user, and it avoids people from having to reinvent the wheel.

4 Example: xPetstore Application

In order to demonstrate how a system is modeled and dependencies are defined, the Enterprise JavaBeans (EJB) version of the xPetstore application was used as a proof of concept. The xPetstore application is a port of the J2EE™ Blueprint Petstore application that uses xDoclet to generate EJB interfaces, deployment descriptors and platform specific configuration files.

This example deploys the xPetstore application on two different platforms. The platforms being tested are the JBoss application server with the Hypersonic database, and the Orion application server with the PostgreSQL database. First the base configuration, including components and dependencies, is created and the constraints associated with each dependency are identified. Then, the base configuration is specialized to represent the two deployable configurations containing the different application servers and databases. Once the two deployable configurations are created, the rule sets for the constraints are constructed and used to verify the deployments.

The creation of the base configuration requires that all components and dependencies be specified using virtual components whenever possible. As illustrated in Figure 4, the only concrete component is the X*petstore.* It is dependent on a deployment environment represented by the composite component *DeployEnv*. This dependency has five associated constraints:

1. **J2EE**: *DeployEnv* provides a full J2EE implementation at the appropriate version level.
2. **OrderProcessingQueue:** There exists a properly configured JMS queue for processing orders.
3. **PurchaseInfoQueue:** There exists a properly configured JMS queue for sending purchase information via email.
4. **DataSource**: A datasource is configured for storing/retrieving persistent data.
5. **JavaMail**: JavaMail support is installed and configured.

The composite component *DeployEnv* is hierarchically decomposed into the assembly *DeployEnvAssembly* consisting of two virtual components: the application server represented as component *J2EEAppServer*; and the relational database represented as component *Database*. The *J2EEAppServer* is dependent on the *Database*, with a single constraint associated with this dependency:

1. **JDBCDriver**: A JDBC driver is installed on the server.

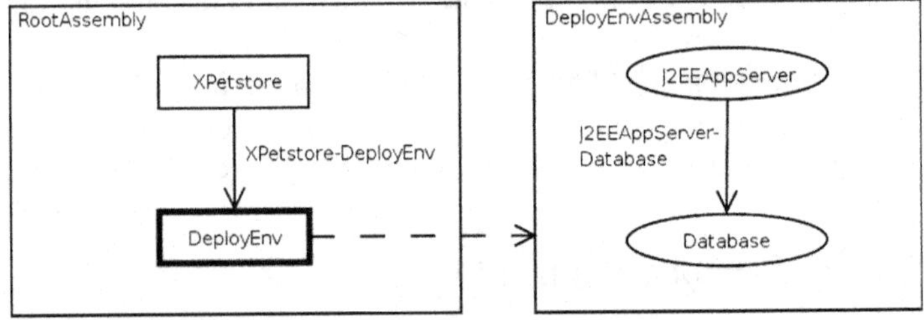

Fig. 4. Base Configuration of the xPetstore Application

The base configuration is then specialized by replacing the virtual application server and database components with concrete components. The two deployable configurations created are:

1. JBoss as the application server and Hypersonic as the database.
2. Orion as the application server and PostgreSQL as the database.

These two deployable configurations are shown in Figure 5 and Figure 6, respectively.

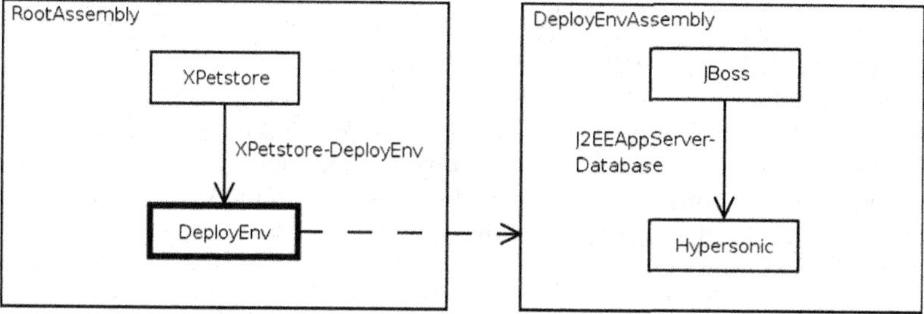

Fig. 5. JBoss-Hypersonic Deployable Configuration

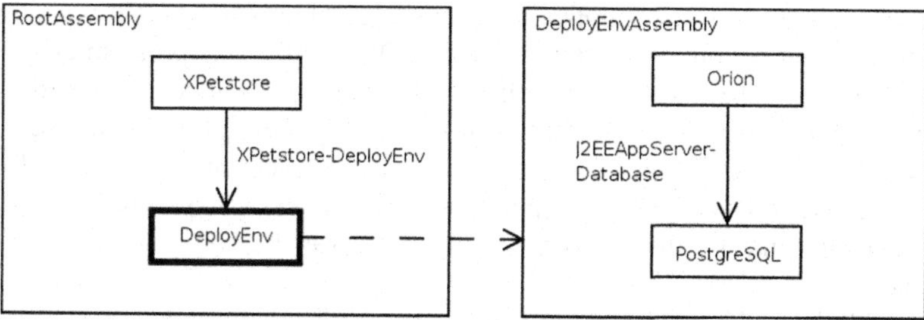

Fig. 6. Orion-PostgreSQL Deployable Configuration

For each deployable configuration, the rule sets for the constraints are defined. At this stage, we do not have a formal method for specifying rule sets. Although it is desirable to eventually have a formal method, currently our approach is to describe the rule set in a way that can be manually verified, or to describe the rule set as an executable script for automatic verification. As an example, the rule sets for verifying the **OrderProcessingQueue** constraint under both deployable configurations are summarized below.

For the JBoss-Hypersonic deployable configuration, verifying the **OrderProcessingQueue** constraint involves the following rule set:

1. Set the variable $JBOSS_HOME to the installation directory of JBoss
2. Set the variable $SERVER_NAME to the name of the server on which the xPetstore application is installed
3. Open the file $JBOSS_HOME/server/$SERVER_NAME/deploy/jms/jbossmq-destinations-service.xml
4. Check for the proper configuration of the order queue within the xml file

For the Orion-PostgreSQL deployable configuration, the corresponding verification rule set is:

1. Set the variable $ORION_HOME to the installation directory of Orion
2. Open $ORION_HOME/config/jms.xml
3. Check that the Order queue is configured with the location jms/queue/order

This example has been completed in practice with the xPetstore application successfully deployed to both deployable configurations and functioning properly. All parts of the example were done manually including the drawing of diagrams and the definition of constraints. Support for the automatic verification of constraints was not tested. The example may be extended to support other deployable configurations by substituting various application servers and databases into the base configuration and following the process outlined in the example.

5 Discussion

The problem of maintaining dependencies between components is not new. Many developers and users of applications available for Microsoft™ Windows™ experienced what is commonly referred to as "DLL hell". This problem arose when products were bundled with a particular version of a dynamically linked library (DLL), and when the product was installed it would overwrite the existing version of the library without informing the user. If any changes were made to the API of the library, this would cause previous applications that depended upon the DLL to stop working. Unfortunately, there was no mechanism available that helped prevent this situation.

Microsoft has addressed this issue with its .NET platform by introducing the Global Assembly Cache (GAC) [5]. The GAC allows for multiple versions of the same library (assembly in .NET terminology) to co-exist on a single machine. Developers are able to reference and use the appropriate version of a library without worrying about it being overwritten by another application. Thus, the problem of DLL hell no longer exists with libraries installed into the GAC.

Several package management systems have been developed for various Linux distributions. Most notable are the Debian package management system [1] and the RPM Package Manager (RPM) system [2]. Each of these allows package maintainers to specify the other packages that are required along with basic constraints, such as required and incompatible versions. This permits users to install a package and all other packages that it is dependent upon quickly and effectively while maintaining a stable working system.

Unfortunately, there are several major problems that exist with each of these solutions. First, these solutions are platform dependent. The .NET platform is specific to Microsoft Windows operating systems. Although work on the Mono project [4] has provided an implementation of the .NET platform for other operating systems, it is still in its infancy. Also, both the Debian package management and RPM systems are limited to specific Linux distributions.

Second, each of these solutions is targeted specifically towards developers. Deployers and users have little, or no, input into the constraints that exist between software products. As a result, when problems occur because a constraint has been incorrectly defined by a developer, deployers are required to wait for an update or patch to be released. It also implies that deployers cannot enter constraints that are unique to the environment into which they are deploying.

Third, all three solutions are restrictive in the types of constraints that may be defined. This restriction on the types of constraints prevents certain constraints from being defined. These constraints must be documented outside of the system. The lack of a central location for defining constraints causes problems for users when they encounter problems deploying the system.

In an attempt to overcome the limitations of existing solutions, our model defines a platform independent approach for modeling dependencies within a software system. The Deployment and Configuration of Component-based Distributed Applications Specification [3], adopted by the Object Management Group (OMG), outlines many of the concepts expressed in our model. The formal model presented in the specification was not used for this work, but ideas from the specification were used and extended. This led to a model that is geared towards both developers and deployers without placing restrictions on the types of constraints that may be defined. The next step is to develop a tool that implements the model to allow developers and users to manage constraints in a system made up of independently evolving software products.

References

1. Aoki, O.: The Debian Package Management System. In: Debian Reference (2001)
2. Bailey, E. C.: Maximum RPM. Red Hat, Inc. (2000)
3. Deployment and Configuration of Component-based Distributed Applications Specification. Object Management Group, Inc. (2003)
4. Mono. Available At: http://www.mono-project.com
5. Pratschner, S.: Simplifying Deployment and Solving DLL Hell with the .NET Framework. Microsoft Corporation, November (2001)
6. Van der Hoek, A. and Wolf, A. L.: Software Release Management for Component-Based Systems. In: Software – Practice and Experience 33, January (2003)
7. Vieira, M. and Richardson, D.: Analyzing Dependencies in Large Component-Based Systems. In: 17th IEEE International Conference on Automated Software Engineering, Edinburgh, UK, September (2002)
8. Vieira, M. and Richardson, D.: The Role of Dependencies in Component-Based Systems Evolution. In: 24th International Conference on Software Engineering, Orlando, Florida, May (2002)

Analysing the Impact of Change in COTS-Based Systems

Gerald Kotonya and John Hutchinson

Computing Department, Lancaster University, Lancaster, LA1 4YR, UK
{gerald, hutchinj}@comp.lancs.ac.uk

Abstract. Commercial off-the-shelf (COTS) software components promise benefits in terms of greater productivity, reduced time to market and reliability. However, their blackbox nature poses significant challenges assessing and managing the impact of change. We propose an approach to help developers to understand the impact of change. It relies on the use of a COTS component-oriented development process and an architecture description language (ADL) for documenting component system architectures; both elements contributing to create a combined approach to impact analysis in COTS-based system.

1 Introduction

Component-based software engineering (CBSE) promises to revolutionize the way software is developed with the re-use of stable software components giving more functionality for less effort along with benefits in terms of time to market and reliability. Components-based development (CBD) should make it possible for developers to buy in "expertise" from the market place in a form that is tested and reliable, pluggable and cost effective. Pluggable in this case means in a form that can be incorporated in the intended system with minor or no modification. This view is consistent with both the application software market for PCs and the prevailing situation in other engineering disciplines where it would be inconceivable to think about developing each and every component from scratch.

Unfortunately, the potential benefits of COTS components come at a price. Their blackbox nature presents novel maintenance challenges while their commercial nature leaves their users the dilemma of choosing between enforced upgrade and obsolescence; change is imposed for what are essentially arbitrary reasons [12, 14].

2 Code as Documentation

The fundamental problem associated with blackbox components is that they can never be fully documented. In a traditionally developed system, the final level of documentation that can be used to resolve all questions about the system is the code. This is not to suggest that program code forms a straightforward and easy to understand documentation of the system, but ultimately, the question "what will happen if I change X?" can be answered by an experienced engineer examining the code to assess the consequences of the proposed change. If a software component is

X. Franch and D. Port (Eds.): ICCBSS 2005, LNCS 3412, pp. 212–222, 2005.

provided as a blackbox component, then its code is not available for inspection, and thus an engineer can assess the consequences of a change only by examining the component documentation, or by carrying out blackbox tests.

The documentation supplied with a component can only ever be prepared to satisfy the foreseen needs of users. Where unforeseen needs coincide with a component's undocumented design assumptions, the user will have a system that is potentially almost impossible to maintain. Underpinning the task of impact analysis (IA) in COTS component-based system is the notion of "process". It is necessary to document the process by which a system is developed, *as it is developed*, if it is going to be possible to analyse the potential impacts of future changes.

3 A Component-Based Development Process

We have developed a method called COMPOSE – COMPonent-Oriented Software Engineering [7] – for CBD. A significant element of the method, with respect to later IA, is COREx – Component-Oriented Requirements Expression [6]. The process by which requirements are elicited and manipulated is vitally important in CBD [1].

There has been little work on the problem of how to derive requirements for component-based systems. Vigder [10] rightly points out that flexibility is vital and proposes that system requirements should be defined according to what is available in the marketplace. However, some requirements are specific in nature and flexibility is not always an option. Another approach integrates the requirements process with COTS product selection (the Procurement-Oriented Requirements Engineering method - PORE [8]). Whilst this sheds light on the product evaluation process, it reduces the scope for requirements negotiation.

The COMPOSE method, illustrated in Fig. 1, embodies a cyclical development process that integrates verification into every part of the process to ensure that there is an acceptable match between components and the system being built. It also includes "negotiation" in each cycle as an explicit recognition of the need to trade-off and accept compromise in the successful development of component-based systems. This ensures that even the earliest stages of system development are carried out in a context of COTS component availability, system requirements and critical architectural concerns.

We use an intermediate modelling layer, comprising services and constraints, to map from requirements to components [6, 11]. Services represent expressions of functionality expressed in a way which shows how available components satisfy requirements. Constraints may represent non-functional requirements such as a component cost, certification, memory and platform restrictions, or dependability requirements such as security, performance and availability [13]. They may also represent elements of interdependence that are introduced to allow services to meet certain architectural considerations (e.g. Service X and Service Y may not reside in the same COTS component).

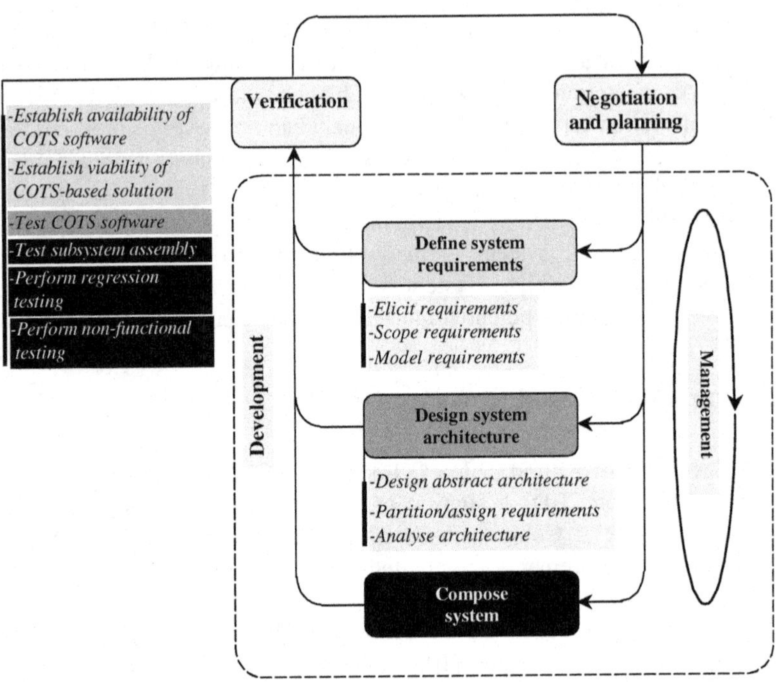

Fig. 1. The COMPOSE process for component-based development

A significant aspect of our process is its architecture-centric nature. We support this by using a dedicated constraint-driven Component Architecture Description Language, CADL [5], to model components and system architectures. CADL is supported by an extensive toolset that facilitates system design and composition [15].

CADL architectures typically consist of components, component interfaces (ports, signatures and roles), and connectors that model channels of interaction between components. Furthermore, assemblies of components can be modelled at different levels of abstraction. An important aspect of CADL is its integral constraint language that is used to describe the interaction between components, their elements, and the mapping between design-time and compose-time components. CADL architectures are directly linked to the system being developed, which allows structural aspects of architectures to be formally validated.

Our requirements approach is based on the notion of *viewpoints* (VPs). VPs correspond to requirements sources that map onto system operators, existing components and other system stakeholders. In short, the proposed system (or required component) delivers services (functional requirements) to viewpoints, which may impose constraints on them [11]. Requirements can be negotiated according to available functionality and, where appropriate, traded to achieve an optimal configuration. If a COTS component to deliver critical functionality cannot be found, custom development may be required. Whilst our approach is not intended to support custom development directly, a required component will generate architectural service descriptions, which together form an initial specification of the component that must be developed. Ultimately, the functional and non-functional requirements are modelled as services and constraints. These services and constraints represent the mapping between "ideal" requirements and what is available from identified components. Thus a service description may not be identical to an elicited requirement (because such functionality was not readily available and an alternative was considered acceptable), and a service may only obliquely represent the functionality of a given component (because what a component has the potential to do and what it is used to do in a specific context may differ significantly).

3.1 Documenting the Development Process

We believe the mapping from requirements to available COTS components is the key intellectual effort in COTS-oriented CBSE. In a traditionally developed system, it equates to parts of the design and coding stages and therefore results in the primary documentation of the system design decisions. Documenting the activities in our process poses certain difficulties. We do not wish to prescribe a particular way of modelling services, because the modelling represents both an expression of required functionality and also a result of verifying the suitability of the component used. This model will be entirely different in different situations (see Fig. 2).

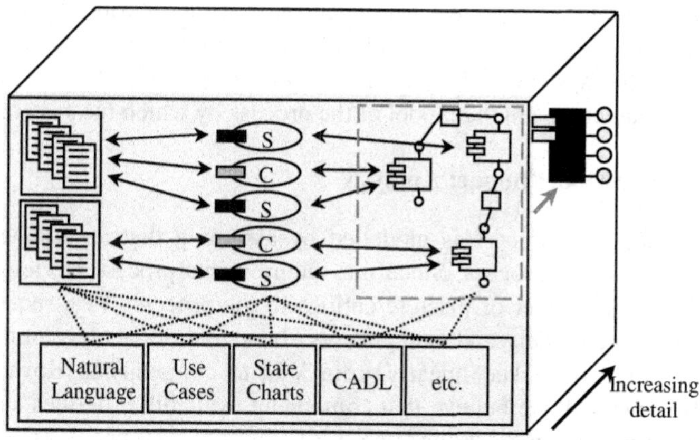

Fig. 2. Requirements on the left are mapped to components on the right (using CADL components and connectors) using services and constraints in the middle

We overcome this problem by noting that it is the links between the entities illustrated in Fig. 2 that hold the important information about the system, from which an engineer can determine the dependencies between those entities. If natural language is an appropriate modelling mechanism, the model should suffice to explain the decision. Similarly, if formal modelling is required then that model should explain the decision. A single approach will not be suitable for all occasions.

This pragmatic solution has important consequences for what we can achieve in terms of change IA. The degree to which we can analyse the impact of a proposed change to the system is linked to the detail in which we model the system itself and the design decisions made. Since we do not require the developer to document his/her design decisions explicitly, we can expect to achieve only an identification of the parts of the system that may be *dependent* on the entity to be changed.

As Fig. 2 illustrates, the means of modelling services available to the developer are many and varied. CADL is used to represent abstract components that represent services (with appropriate description). Many of the means of modelling services (e.g. natural language) are not amenable to automatic analysis. Formal methods find limited applicability in general software development because they represent a significant overhead for the developer. For a method to be more generally applicable, it should not inconvenience the developer more than is necessary. Our approach requires only that the links between design artefacts be documented in addition to the artefacts themselves, which can be done automatically with tool support.

4 Analysing the Impact of Change in Component-Based Systems

The approach to impact analysis that we propose is concerned with identifying the parts of the system that may require attention to ensure that they are still consistent and will operate as expected. The analysis is made possible by having appropriate models of that system. If a system has been developed according to our process, two models of the system will be available for analysis: the CADL description of the system architecture and the model of the process by which the system was developed.

4.1 Process Model Impact Analysis

The development process is modelled by assuming that an artefact is produced at every stage of the process. Since our requirements process is viewpoint driven, we can identify a number of discrete entities in the process: VPs, requirements, service and constraint models and components. In a traditional development cycle, these entities would be linked linearly from VPs to components. However, as we have already explained, we believe that component availability defines a context in which the requirements engineering phase of the process proceeds, and service and constraints are the means by which requirements map onto components, and vice versa. Furthermore, we are concerned with COTS components and so COTS developers and COTS vendors, not the system developers, will determine the form and availability of COTS components. Therefore, we must be able to support the analysis of change that is imposed on the components used in the system regardless of the requirements of the system.

The result is that our process model must view services and constraints as being as dependent on components as they are on requirements. Fig. 3 illustrates a simple graph of the process model. The mostly undirected nature of the graph is a result of the two-way dependency of services and constraints. (We expect that in most cases, the arc from VPs to requirements can be directed, as illustrated.)

The nodes representing VPs, requirements and components can all be considered as the targets of possible change. The items potentially impacted by a change will be all those represented by nodes that are reachable from the node representing the item to be changed. This highlights the desirability of achieving a minimum of coupling between requirements and services and constraints and similarly between services and constraints and components. The best example shown in Fig. 3 is the crosscutting constraint, c1, which affects most of the components of the system. Any change that adversely affects c1 is likely to have a significant impact on the system.

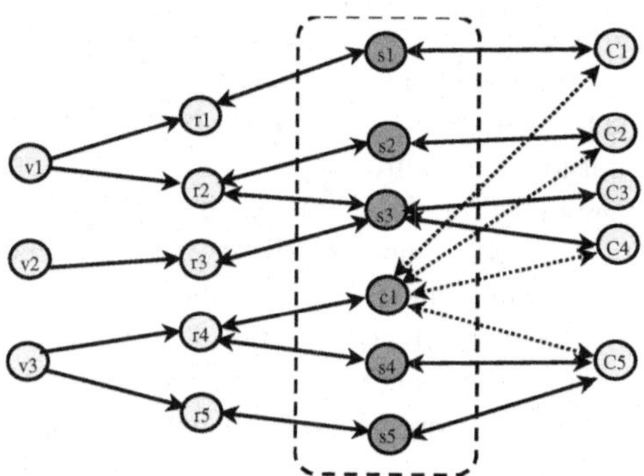

Fig. 3. A process model represented as a mostly undirected graph. Viewpoints (v) give rise to requirements (r) which are mapped onto components (C) using services (s) and constraints (c)

4.2 CADL Impact Analysis

CADL is central to the description of system designs in our process. CADL "provides a formal mechanism for defining component architectures ... [and] ... provides a systematic framework for integrating design-time activities and compose-time activities" [5]. Stafford and Wolf [9] suggest that change IA (in their sense: the need for rerunning test cases following a change, which of course amounts to identifying the parts of the system which *may* have been impacted by the change) is an "implementation" activity, although it can benefit from architectural analysis. They warn that the drift between the design described in the architectural description and the design implemented limits the contribution that architectural analysis can make. However, the direct correspondence between CADL descriptions and composed systems means that architecture based IA has more potential in our process.

As an ADL, CADL architectures are validated to ensure that they are consistent and syntactically correct. For IA purposes, along with the syntactic checking, which will identify impacts resulting from violation of syntactic dependencies, we propose a level of analysis which attempts to identify the consequences of a particular change.

Although components provide and use services, CADL does not support the explicit representation of behaviour and so we require another model to capture the "semantic" dependencies between components that may have consistent interfaces but may impact on each other when their behaviour changes. We developed a changeability model based on Chaumun *et al*'s [2] work on C++ for OO development. We identified the elements of the CADL language, determined the types of change that they could be subjected to and then determined the likely impact that such changes might have on collocated elements. An example from Chaumun *et al* is:

$$Impact(cl_j, C_{ch}) = \mathbf{SH'} + \mathbf{G}$$

This denotes that classes which are in association (**S**) with, and not derived (**H'**) from the changed class cl_j, or classes which are in aggregation (**G**) with cl_j are impacted by change C_{ch}. In our model, the CADL elements are used in the changeability model. However, we are not able to attain the degree of expression achieved by Chaumun *et al* because CADL is inherently extendable and therefore the set of possible element and possible changes can never be considered complete.

Our changeability model identifies three types of impact. A "primary" impact is one that affects a changeability model element that is linked to the changed element (e.g. it is an impacted connector if it is connected to a changed component, or an impacted component if that is connected to changed connector). A "secondary" impact is one that affects a CADL component connected to the changed component by a CADL connector. This distinction is useful because "functionality" is conveyed by components. However, because connectors can overcome many mismatches between components, a potential impact may be handled in the connector itself. Finally, a peripheral impact is one which may affect any changeability model component but which does not fall into either the primary or secondary impact categories (e.g. when a component providing no services is removed).

We are then able to associate a type of impact with each combination of CADL element, connected element and change type. As an example, Table 1 lists the specific CADL impacts that we can identify for "components".

NB Components* are those connected to the changed component by a connector.

Table 1. Changeability model components, links, changes and impacts

Element	Change	Link	Impacted element	Impact
Component	*Addition*	Required	-	-
		Provided	-	-
	Deletion	Required	Connectors	Peripheral
			Components*	Peripheral
		Provided	Connectors	Primary
			Components*	Secondary
	Property change	Required	Connectors	Primary
			Components*	Secondary
		Provided	Connectors	Primary
			Components*	Secondary
	Constraint change	Required	Connectors	Primary
			Components*	Secondary
		Provided	Connectors	Primary
			Components*	Secondary

4.3 Combining the Two Approaches

The true contribution made by the CADL IA can be seen when it is combined with the process model IA. If we examine Fig. 3 closely, we will see that it does not show any dependencies directly between components (implicit dependencies via interconnections with service and constraints are shown); this is clearly nonsense. Nevertheless, such dependencies may not be part of the developmental process.

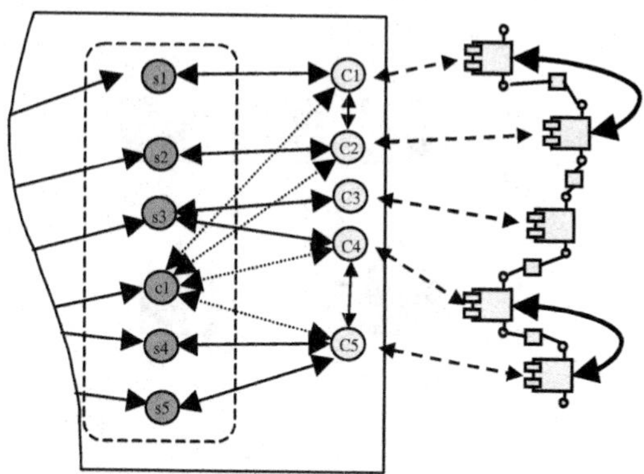

Fig. 4. The process model includes nodes that represent components in the system, which are also represented in CADL architectures

The nodes representing components in the process model graph represent real components in the system. These components are also represented as components in a CADL architecture, as illustrated in Fig. 4. Using CADL IA, we can now uncover dependencies between components that otherwise remain hidden.

The result is that we have a snapshot of the system being developed. Combined with the expertise of the developer, the snapshot contains a view of the system that indicates both the way the requirements of the system have been met (including any trade-offs that have been deemed necessary) and the rationale for the inclusion of the components that make up the system. Using simple graph operations (i.e., reachability), the model can provide an indication of what other parts of the system may suffer some form of impact if a part of the system is subjected to a change.

5 Example

We illustrate our approach with an example that illustrates the efficacy of the approach when tool support is provided. Fig. 5 shows the architecture for a remote back-up application which was developed in a software development company. User access services (on the left) are allocated to a UI component in the architecture (on the right), which is a composite component comprising a small number of components including a UI_Toolbar component. If this toolbar is upgraded, how do we assess the possible impact in our application? In this instance, we select the IA view and then select the item of interest. This carries out a pruning of the dependency tree to highlight elements in the process model that are linked in some way to the UI_Toolbar. The result of this is illustrated in Fig. 6.

Carrying out IA for a potential change to the UI_Toolbar shows that it is linked to many parts of the system. For the developer to be certain that an upgrade will not adversely affect system performance, s/he must examine the nature of these dependencies to check whether the upgrade can be made without causing problems.

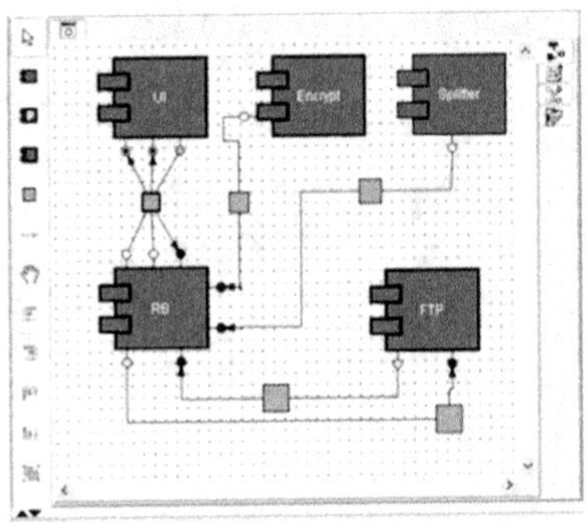

Fig. 5. The architecture of a back-up application in the ECO-ADM tools

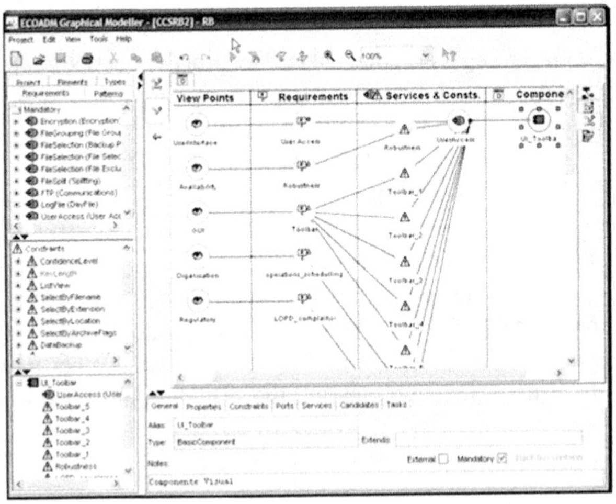

Fig. 6. IA assessment for the UI_Toolbar

6 Conclusion

Components represent the latest attempt to exploit the advantages of genuinely reusable software. COTS components promise potentially greater rewards because packaged expertise can be purchased in an open market place. Unfortunately, the commercial concerns of component developers, eager to protect both their intellectual and financial investments, mean that the components provided to application developers will have to be treated as blackboxes. We believe there are significant problems in attempting to apply traditional approaches to change IA to systems made up of blackbox components. However, we have recognized that the problems posed by managing change in such systems are inherently linked to the problems of successfully employing COTS components to create systems in the first place. We have exploited this link to propose a method for change IA that is integrated with our component-oriented development.

We are currently exploring ways: (1) to allow the developer to qualify the nature of the link between entities (e.g., assign properties to the arcs in the graph) in order to limit the propagation of impacts resulting from certain sorts of change – we currently implement a simple heuristic which limits to chain of dependency to a local vicinity and this markedly improves usability; and (2) to assign certain properties to the nodes in the graph as metrics to provide indications of the overall degree of impact (e.g., a "severity" or "criticality" property to indicate how central the represented entity is to the system; summing the property for all reachable nodes would provide an indication of how significant the impact of the proposed change might be).

References

1. B. Boehm and C. Abts., COTS Integration: Plug and Pray, IEEE Computer 32(1): 135-138, Jan. 1999.
2. M.A. Chaumun, H. Kabaili, R.K. Keller and F.A. Lustman, Change Impact Model for Changeability Assessment in Object-Oriented Software Systems, in: Proc. Third Euromicro Working Conference on Software Maintenance and Reengineering, pp.130-138, Amsterdam, The Netherlands, March 1999.
3. J. Hutchinson, G. Kotonya, W. Onyino and P. Sawyer, Managing Change in Component-Based Systems: A State-Based Approach, in: Proc. Informatik 2001, Vienna, pp.829-833, September 2001.
4. J. Hutchinson, G. Kotonya, B. Bloin and P. Sawyer, Understanding the Impact of Change in COTS-Based Systems, in: Proc. 2003 International Conference on Software Engineering Research and Practice (SERP'03), Las Vegas, USA, 23-26 June 2003.
5. G. Kotonya, W. Onyino, J. Hutchinson, and P. Sawyer, Component Architecture Description Language (CADL), Technical Report, CSEG/57/2001, Lancaster University, 2001.
6. G. Kotonya and J. Hutchinson, Viewpoints for Specifying Component-based Systems, in: Proc. of 7th International Symposium on Component-based Software Engineering, Edinburgh (LNCS 3054, Springer) pp.114-121, May 2003.
7. G. Kotonya, J. Hutchinson and B. Bloin, COMPOSE: A Method for Formulating and Architecting Service-based Systems, in: Z. Stojanovic, and A. Dahanayake, eds., Service-Oriented Software System Engineering: Challenges And Practices, Idea Group Inc., (forthcoming/December 2004).
8. C. Ncube and N. Maiden., PORE: Procurement-oriented requirements engineering method for the component-based systems engineering development paradigm, in: Proc. 2nd IEEE International Workshop on Component-Based Software Engineering, Los Angeles, USA, pp.1-12, 1999.

9. J.A. Stafford, and A.L. Wolf, Architecture-Level Dependence Analysis for Software Systems, Journal of Software Engineering and Knowledge Engineering, Vol. 11, No. 4, pp.431-453, August 2001.
10. M. Vigder, M. Gentleman and J. Dean, "COTS Software Integration: State of the Art", Institute for Information Technology, National Research Council, Canada, 1996.
11. J. Hutchinson and G. Kotonya, A Service Model for Component-Based Development, in: Proc. of the 30th Euromicro Conference (forthcoming/2004).
12. J.M. Voas, The Challenges Of Using COTS Software In Component-Based Development, Computer, 31(6), 44, 1998.
13. J.M. Voas, Composing Software Component "ilities". IEEE Software 18(4): 16-17, 2001
14. S.D. Kim, Lessons Learned From A Nationwide CBD Promotion Project. Communications of the ACM, Vol. 45(10), pp.83-87, 2002.
15. ECOADM website: http://ecoadm.ccs.biz.

Considering Variability in a System Family's Architecture During COTS Evaluation[1]

Nelufar Ulfat-Bunyadi, Erik Kamsties, and Klaus Pohl

Software Systems Engineering, ICB, University of Duisburg-Essen,
Schützenbahn 70, 45117 Essen, Germany
{ulfat-bunyadi, kamsties, pohl}@sse.uni-essen.de

Abstract. COTS (commercial off-the-shelf) component designers and developers often envision different usage contexts for their component and, therefore, provide it with adaptation possibilities. These adaptation possibilities are especially important when considering system families. System family engineering is currently an emerging discipline. Variability is a core property of system families which allows deriving different customer-specific applications from a core artifact base. A system family's core artifact base may also be populated with COTS components. These COTS components then need to support the system family's variability, i.e. they have to offer the possibility to adapt them to different customer-specific applications. Through their adaptation possibilities COTS components are able to meet this requirement. During COTS evaluation, a system family's requirements and architecture need to be taken into account. Variability is inherent in both. That is, the question is how to evaluate COTS with regard to variable features. In this paper, we describe variability in architecture in more detail and point out how this variability needs to be reflected in COTS evaluation criteria. The contribution is an extension of 'traditional' COTS evaluation criteria in order to consider a system family's variability.

1 Introduction

The idea of reuse is fundamental to emerging disciplines such as component-based software engineering and system family engineering. During system family engineering, not only executable components are reused, but also development artifacts such as requirements and test cases. COTS components may also be considered for reuse in the context of system families either during domain engineering or during application engineering. Domain engineering is concerned with the development of artifacts that are shared among the applications of the system family. Application engineering, on

[1] This work has been funded by the BMBF Verbundprojekt CAFÉ „From Concept to Application in System Family Engineering" (Förderkennzeichen 01 IS 002 C), the European ITEA Project ip02009 FAMILIES „FAct-based Maturity through Institutionalisation Lessons learned and Involved Exploration of System-family engineering" Eureka Σ! 2023 Programme, and the DFG-Project PO607/1-1 PRIME "Prozessintegration von Modellierungsarbeitsplätzen".

X. Franch and D. Port (Eds.): ICCBSS 2005, LNCS 3412, pp. 223 – 235, 2005.

the other hand, is concerned with the development of system family applications through selection and configuration of shared artifacts (developed during domain engineering) and addition of application-specific extensions. If COTS components are used during application engineering, they are considered for use in a single application which resembles traditional software engineering using COTS components. In this case, the component has to be adaptable to the needs of the application. If COTS components are used during domain engineering, they are considered for use as core artifacts. Such a component must be adaptable to needs of several customer-specific applications. In this case, greater emphasis is placed on the component's ability to support the system family's variability. In this paper, we concentrate on this case.

During COTS evaluation for a system family, a COTS candidate component has to come up to three kinds of expectations: (a) it has to fulfill system family requirements, (b) it has to be integratable into the system family architecture, and (c) it has to support the variability inherent in system family requirements and architecture (cf. [16]).

Variability is defined as the ability to change and customize a system (cf. [18]). For this purpose, variation points are provided on different abstraction levels during system family development (i.e., for example, in the requirements specification, in the architecture description, in the source code). Each variation point offers the possibility to select a variant or to choose between variants. The point in time when this decision has to be made is referred to as the binding time of the variation point. Examples of binding times are compilation, linking, and installation time.

In an earlier publication, we have surveyed current approaches for COTS evaluation, for example, [1, 7, 10, 12, 13, 14, 15, 17, 19, 21] and did not find any support for variability (cf. [16]). Therefore, we have developed a new approach: the CoVAR process (Component Selection considering Variability, Architectural concerns, and Requirements). In this paper, we only present one part of the process that helps answering the question how a system family's variability (especially in the architecture) should be considered during COTS evaluation. Thereby, the focus lies on pointing out which kind of variability may be expected from a COTS component. The contribution of this paper is an extension of 'traditional' COTS evaluation criteria in order to consider a system family's variability. For more details on the CoVAR process, refer to the paper of Pohl and Reuys [16] and Chapter 8 in [14].

In the following, we firstly describe variability in a system family architecture, different ways to realize this variability, and its impact on COTS evaluation (Section 2). Afterwards, we shortly describe variability in requirements (Section 3). Note, that we focus on functional and quality requirements and do not consider other (strategic) aspects (e.g. stability / reputation of COTS vendors). Finally, we conclude with a summary in Section 4.

2 Variability in the System Family Architecture

Architectural design represents the first activity towards realizing requirements. This is true for single system development as well as system family engineering. As a first step, quality attribute requirements are prioritized in order to identify the most important attributes that the final architecture shall exhibit. These quality attributes must already be considered during architectural design, since they impact the whole architecture or a larger part of it. Thus, they will mainly drive the architectural design process (i.e. they are architectural drivers; see Fig. 1). In this way, software architecture allows design for quality attributes (cf. [2, 5, 9, 20]) and even constrains the quality attributes of a system. Examples of architectural drivers are functionality, performance, security, and, variability (cf. [3, 8]).

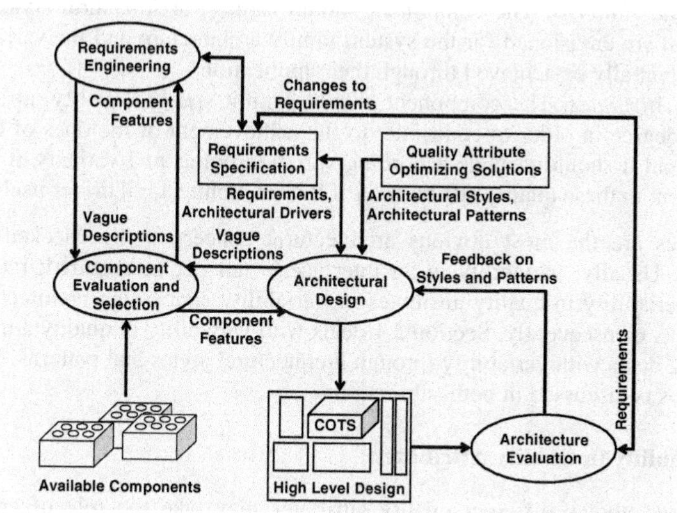

Fig. 1. Component Selection, Requirements Engineering, and Architectural Design

Note that variability is a special kind of attribute. On the one hand, it may be an architectural driver itself. On the other hand, it may only be inherent in an architectural driver such as performance. If variability is inherent in quality attributes of a system family architecture, the qualities of the system family architecture are not relevant in themselves, but rather the way these qualities translate to the architectures of the system family applications (cf. [6]). Thus, the system family architecture should enable each application in the system family to fulfill its quality requirements.

In order to design the system family architecture for specific quality attributes, architecture transformations such as architectural styles and patterns may be imposed on the architecture (refer to [6] for a definition of architectural styles and patterns). An architectural style often improves the possibilities for certain quality attributes and is less supportive for others. A well known style is, for example, the layered architecture style. As soon as a first draft of the system family architecture exists, it may be evaluated with regard to the achievement of important quality attributes (see Fig. 1). If necessary, decisions made regarding architectural styles and patterns are revised to achieve the required quality attributes or quality attributes are even changed.

As illustrated in Fig. 1, the component evaluation and selection process is conducted in parallel to requirements engineering and architectural design, since all three may influence each other.

From this view of how architectural design is conducted, the following architectural concerns should be considered for a component that shall be integrated into a system family's architecture.

1. *Interfaces*. The component should collaborate with other components in the system family architecture (may it be optional or alternative ones), i.e. its interfaces should match with the ones provided and required by the other architectural components.
2. *Styles and Patterns*. The component should support architectural styles and patterns that are envisioned for the system family architecture and the variability that shall potentially be achieved through their application.
3. *Quality Attributes*. The component should exhibit specific quality attributes to a certain degree in order to contribute to the achievement of the ones of the system family and it should provide according variation points and variants, if variability is inherent in these quality attributes or if it is an architectural driver itself.

Interfaces are the most obvious architectural concern to be checked in COTS evaluation. Usually, variability in an interface is not per se required; rather it is a result of variability in quality attributes or variability concerning architectural styles and patterns. Consequently, Section 2.1 deals with variability in quality attributes and Section 2.2 deals with variability through architectural styles and patterns. Variability in interfaces is discussed in both subsections.

2.1 Variability in Quality Attributes

As described above, different quality attributes may take the role of architectural drivers (e.g. functionality, performance). In this section, we provide some more detail on two cases: (1) the impact on a COTS component, if variability is inherent in an architectural driver of the system family and (2) the impact on a COTS component, if variability is an architectural driver itself. Thereby, we use the following template: first, we describe ways to realize the kind of variability considered, then, we explain how it should be considered during COTS evaluation.

Variability Inherent in an Architectural Driver. In literature, different quality attribute definitions are given as well as different categorizations of them. We adopt the ones of Bass, Clements, and Kazmann in [3]. They distinguish between system quality attributes discernable at runtime (e.g., performance, security, availability, functionality, usability) and system quality attributes not discernable at runtime (e.g., modifiability, portability, reusability, integrability, testability). Furthermore, a distinction is made between quality attributes having architectural and nonarchitectural dependencies. Performance, for example, has both types of dependencies (cf. [3]): "Performance depends partially on how much communication is necessary among components (architectural), partially on what functionality has been allocated to each component (architectural), partially on the choice of algorithms to implement selected functionality (nonarchitectural), and partially on how these algorithms are coded (nonarchitectural)." In the following, we will consider performance as example for an architectural driver. We will explain what it means, if variability is inherent in performance and how this possibly impacts COTS evaluation.

Variability inherent in performance means that different performances are expected from different system family applications. This could, for example, be realized by (1) the system family architecture providing alternative and/or optional components exhibiting different performances or (2) a component that offers possibilities to adjust its performance. We will explain these two cases in the following in more detail.

Variability Realization – Alternative/Optional Components: The absence of an optional architecture component may, for example, lead to an application architecture that exhibits a higher performance than the same application architecture with the integrated component. In this way, the two application architectures would exhibit different performances. Another way to achieve variability in performance would be to provide the system family architecture with several alternative components that exhibit different performances but perform the same functionality. An application engineer could then select the component that fits best the needs of the application at hand.

COTS Evaluation: If variability in performance is realized by alternative and/or optional architecture components and a COTS component is supposed to be this optional or one of the alternative components, then this makes no difference to the COTS evaluation. From the viewpoint of evaluation, there is no difference between evaluating a component that shall become a mandatory, optional, or alternative architecture component. In any case, the component has to come up to its expectations.

Variability Realization – Adjustable Component: A component's performance could, for example, be adjusted by changing the hardware platform it is deployed on. On the other hand, it may also be adjusted as a consequence of adjusting it regarding its functionality, i.e. binding functional variants to variation points. In this way, an algorithm could, for example, be excluded from the resulting configuration of the component that decreased its performance.

COTS Evaluation: Although components today are usually not developed with the goal in mind that they become part of a system family, COTS developers often envision different usage situations and prepare the component for them. That is, COTS components are often adaptable in many respects. One example is functionality that can be optionally included or excluded from a COTS component. But COTS components are not only adaptable with regard to the functionality they provide, but also with regard to quality attributes they exhibit. Performance of a COTS component may, for example, vary, if it is possible to make the component run on one server/CPU or on multiple servers/ CPUs to share the workload. Sometimes required adaptations with regard to quality attributes depend on the possibility to adapt the component with regard to its functionality. For example, an encryption component may be expected to be adaptable to support either 128-bit key or 256-bit key AES (Advanced Encryption Standard) encryption. From each of these variants a different response time is expected. This second statement regarding variability in performance only makes sense, if the first variation point regarding the encryption strength is provided. Admittedly, this example describes a special kind of quality requirement that is bound to a functional requirement and has only local impact. Nevertheless, we can say that performance of a COTS component may vary as a consequence of varying functionality or if the resources, the COTS component is provided with, vary. If a COTS component provides the first kind of variability, its performance has to be measured during COTS evaluation depending on the variants bound for the according variation points. If it provides the second kind of variability, its performance has to be measured depending on the resources it is provided with.

Variability as Architectural Driver. To realize variability in a system family, several realization mechanisms exist that can be used. Depending on the mechanism chosen, different requirements result that a COTS component would have to fulfil, if it was integrated into the system family architecture. In the following, we consider the realization mechanisms described by Svahnberg, Gurp, and Bosch in [18] (mainly because it is a comprehensive list) and explain their possible impact on a COTS component and the COTS evaluation. The mechanisms are:

- Architecture Reorganization;
- Variant Architecture Component;
- Optional Architecture Component;
- Infrastructure-Centered Architecture;
- Variant Component Specialization;
- Multiple Component Implementations;
- Optional Component Specializations;
- Multiple Component Specializations;
- Code Fragment Superimposition;
- Binary Replacement – Linker Directives;
- Binary Replacement – Physical;
- Condition on Constant;
- Condition on Variable.

Variability Realization – Architecture Reorganization: A system family architecture may provide variability by allowing its reorganization. That is, the architectural components may be reorganized in order to derive application architectures. On the one hand, this results in variability in control flow, since it is possible to change the order in which components are connected to each other. On the other hand, this may result in changes in how particular components are connected to each other, i.e. provided and required interfaces of the components may differ from one application to another.

COTS Evaluation: If the order in which components are connected to each other may be changed and the COTS component is one of these components, then this means that the COTS component has to collaborate with different component sets. A component set denotes all components with which the COTS component would have to collaborate when considering one control flow. Thus, different component sets have to be taken into account during COTS evaluation when variability in control flow is possible in the way described above. Especially, an architectural mismatch analysis [11] would have to be conducted for each component set in order to identify all potential mismatches.

If provided and required interfaces of the components may vary from application to application, this could mean for a COTS component that it has to provide varying provided and required interfaces or that is has to cope with varying provided and required interfaces of other components. From the viewpoint of evaluation this means the COTS component has to be checked for several required and several provided interfaces.

Variability Realization – Variant Architecture Component: As described by Svahnberg, Gurp, and Bosch in [18], it makes sometimes sense to provide the system family architecture with the possibility to replace an architectural component with another one, maybe with a differing interface and even representing a different domain.

COTS Evaluation: If the COTS component shall become one of these variant architectural components, this makes no difference to the COTS evaluation. From the viewpoint of evaluation there is no difference between a COTS component that is a mandatory architectural component and one that is a variant architectural component. In both cases, there are the same expectations to the COTS component that it has to come up to.

Variability Realization – Optional Architecture Component: An optional architectural component may be present in some application architectures and absent in others. The system family architecture has to provide support for both cases. If the component is present, other components interact with it. If it is absent, the same components do not interact with it.

COTS Evaluation: This problem of presence and absence of the component can be solved in two ways. If the solution is implemented on the calling side, i.e. on the side of the component calling an optional component, this means it is delegated downwards to other mechanisms such as optional component specialization, condition on constant, condition on variable (described later in this section). If it is implemented on the called side, a "null" component would have to be created that would reply with dummy values. If the COTS component is supposed to be an optional architecture component, this, again, makes no difference to the evaluation of a mandatory architectural component. This is especially true, if the solution is implemented on the calling side. If it is implemented on the called side, then the existence of a "null" component in the system family architecture besides the COTS component is indifferent to the COTS evaluation.

Variability Realization – Infrastructure-Centered Architecture: Using this mechanism, connections between components are made a first class entity, i.e. components are no longer connected to each other, but are rather connected to the infrastructure, i.e. the connectors. This infrastructure then matches required interfaces of components with provided interfaces of other components (see, for example, COM or CORBA).
COTS Evaluation: If this mechanism is used, variability in interfaces is handled on the side of the infrastructure. Thus, no peculiarities result that have to be considered during COTS evaluation.

Note that we exclude variability in a required or provided interface itself (which is also possible) from further consideration. An example would be a parameterized interface (cf. [3]). It is quite seldom that a component is selected just because it provides a special kind of interface. Rather, provided functionality and quality are the main reasons for the selection of a COTS component. Thus, we do not assume that variability in an interface can be expected from a COTS component, but it is nice to have such a feature. In consequence, variability in interfaces will not be considered as input for the COTS evaluation process, but it may be assessed during evaluation.

Variability Realization – Variant Component Specializations: The use of some realization mechanisms on the architecture design level requires support in later stages, too. When variant architectural components are provided in a system family architecture, it may be required that parts of the implementation of other components that have to collaborate with these components are replaceable as well. In this case, those parts of a component that are concerned with interfacing a varying component, need to be replaceable, too.

COTS evaluation: The case where the COTS component is one of the varying components has already been considered above. On the other hand, if the COTS component has to collaborate with varying components, it may be necessary that parts of its implementation are replaceable as described above.

Variability Realization – Remaining Mechanisms: The other realization mechanisms described by Svahnberg, Gurp, and Bosch in [18] are: Multiple Component Implementations; Optional Component Specializations; Multiple Component Specializations; Code Fragment Superimposition; Binary Replacement – Linker Directives; Binary Replacement – Physical; Condition on Constant; Condition on Variable.

They are not further explained here because an analysis of them in the way done in the previous sections results in the same requirements for the COTS component. Thus, we will just explain the result which is important from the viewpoint of COTS evaluation and refer the reader to [18] for more information on these mechanisms.

COTS evaluation: All these mechanisms result in the need for variability internal to the COTS component. We mainly consider variability required in functional and quality features of the COTS component. The reason for omitting variability in data, behaviour, etc. is that we consider functional and quality features as the most important features that are taken into account during COTS evaluation. In Section 3, we explain in more detail how variability required in functional and quality features of the COTS component impacts COTS evaluation.

2.2 Variability Through Architectural Styles and Patterns

In order to design the system family architecture for specific quality attributes, i.e. the architectural drivers, architecture transformations such as architectural styles and patterns may be imposed on the architecture. We distinguish between architectural styles and architectural patterns, just as [6] do, and adopt their definitions of these architecture transformations respectively. The distinction results from differentiating between the scope of impact of each transformation and the transformation type (see Fig. 2).

Imposing an architectural style affects the software architecture as a whole and results in a complete reorganization of the architecture. Imposing an architectural pattern affects the complete architecture too (or at least a larger part of it) but it differs from an architectural style in its transformation type: an architectural pattern imposes a rule on the architecture that specifies how the system will deal with one aspect of its functionality, e.g. concurrency or persistence.

Architectural styles and patterns may also be imposed on a system family architecture. The selection of the most appropriate styles and patterns depends primarily on the quality requirements of the system family, mainly on the architectural drivers. Since variability is often inherent in these quality requirements, styles and patterns can be variable to a certain degree, too.

An architectural style chosen for a system family architecture may vary in its variants. If, for example, the layered architectural style has been chosen for a system family's architecture, then variants of this style may be the strict layered style (where each layer is only allowed to call its immediate subordinate layer) and the relaxed layered style (where each layer can invoke all lower-level layers, rather than just the layer immediately below it). Using the strict layered style increases flexibility, but generally decreases performance of a system. Using the relaxed layered style improves performance, but influences maintainability negatively.

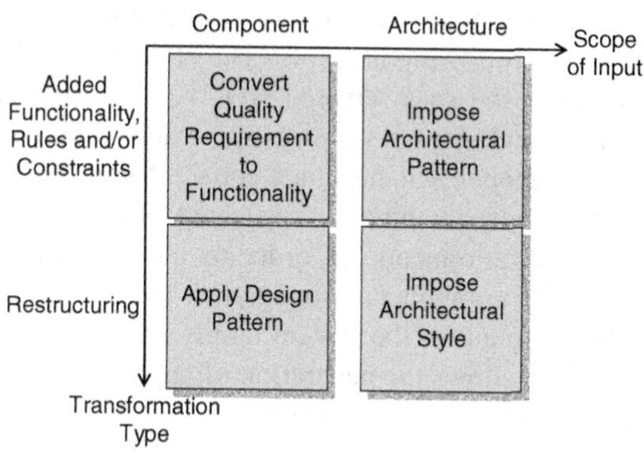

Fig. 2. Taxonomy of Transformation Categories (cf. [6])

Generally, the decision for the imposition of a specific architectural pattern on a software architecture may lead to requirements for architectural entities, for example, regarding interfaces that have to be supported by them or limitations in their execution time. If, for example, an application-level scheduler is used to implement concurrency, each architectural entity needs to support a particular interface. In a system family architecture, several architectural patterns may be envisioned. To this end, components may be provided in the system family architecture that support different architectural patterns. These components may offer the variability that is needed for this purpose on component level, i.e. they may be optional or alternative components, or on subcomponent level, i.e. they may be adaptable to the specific needs of the architectural patterns that are envisioned. In this way, different architectural patterns may be imposed on different application architectures.

In the following two sections, we will describe how architectural styles and patterns may impact the COTS evaluation process and vice versa.

Architectural Styles During COTS Evaluation. The architectural style designated for a system family architecture may influence the COTS evaluation process indirectly. More precisely, the quality requirements that lead to the decision in favour of the designated style (i.e. the architectural drivers) influence the COTS evaluation process: a COTS component has to contribute to their achievement. Quality requirements exist in the context of specific goals (cf. [8]). A system is, for example, modifiable (or not) with respect to a specific kind of change. It is secure (or not) with respect to a specific kind of threat. It is important to state system family quality requirements in this way, even if variability is inherent, because it facilitates refining them to the level of components. When quality requirements (probably including variability) have been stated for each component of the system family architecture, the COTS evaluation process may start. During COTS evaluation, the quality requirements for the COTS component are then checked.

On the other hand, the COTS evaluation process may require allowing more variants of the architectural style that was supposed to be imposed on the system family architecture. Consider the following example. The style that is designated for a system family architecture is the strict layered style because it enables the reuse and exchangeability of layers and increases portability, extensibility, and flexibility. After evaluating candidate components it becomes apparent that the performance of this component, regardless of which candidate is selected finally, will not be sufficient to satisfy the performance requirements. In order to increase the performance of the applications into which the component is integrated, the relaxed layered style is considered as an additional variant for the system family architecture. In other words, the system family architecture allows the generation of applications using either the strict layered style or the relaxed one. For applications, where the COTS component is integrated, the relaxed layered style is then favourable. In this way, the COTS evaluation process may influence the architectural style of a system family.

Architectural Patterns During COTS Evaluation. As described above, the decision for the imposition of a specific architectural pattern may lead to requirements for architectural entities/components, for example, regarding interfaces that have to be supported by them or limitations in their execution time. Thus, a COTS component has to come up to such expectations, too.

In order to support variability in architectural patterns used for different application architectures, optional or alternative components may be provided in the system family architecture or components that are adaptable in this regard. The COTS component has to collaborate with these components in a correct way, i.e. architectural mismatch between components should be avoided. To this end, the assessment guidelines for detecting architectural mismatches that are described in [11] should be used. The COTS component has to be checked for architectural mismatch in different combinations with the components it has to collaborate with. The goal is to make sure that there will be no architectural mismatch between the finally chosen COTS component and its adjacent, maybe optional or alternative, components.

On the other hand, the COTS component may enforce the use of particular architectural patterns. Since we deal with components that shall provide a large fraction of the functionality of the applications into which they are integrated, the evaluation of such a component may lead to the insight that a particular architectural pattern (the one the component comes with) is more adequate for the system family than the one envisioned before. Thus, there is some kind of interference between architectural patterns of a component and the system family architecture.

3 Variability in System Family Requirements

Expecting variability in functional and quality features of a COTS component means that a candidate component has to be checked in two ways. First, it has to be checked for the existence of required variation points and variants. Then, configurations of the component have to be checked for the degree of functionality provided depending on bound variants. In a configuration of a component, all variation points are bound whose binding times are before runtime (i.e., for example, compile time or linking time). Thus, a particular configuration may still contain runtime variability.

While evaluating COTS components in this regard, the following problems occur that have to be solved. Firstly, provided variation points and variants are often not specified explicitly in component documentations. This situation requires a deeper look at the component itself. But for investigation purposes conventional information sources, such as documentations and evaluation copies, are not sufficient. An evaluation copy is executable and, thus, contains bound variants. Consequently, depending on the binding time of variation points, more artifacts of a component must be investigated such as source code and compiling and linking instructions. Because of the variability provided by a component, not all features exist in parallel in one executable version of the component. That is, a component's provided functionality may vary from one configuration to another. This third problem requires an evaluation of component configurations with respect to the provided functionality.

4 Summary and Future Work

In this paper, we described the different kinds of variability and how it should be considered during COTS evaluation:

- *variability in component sets*: the COTS component's collaboration with different component sets has to be ensured and architectural mismatch analyses have to be conducted;
- *variability in provided/required interfaces*: the COTS component has to be checked for several required and several provided interfaces during evaluation;
- *variability in component specialization*: the COTS component has to checked for replaceable parts of its implementation, i.e. its evaluation copy and other development artifacts have to be investigated for according variation points and variants;
- *variability in architectural styles*: the COTS component may suggest the use of another variant of an architectural style (– the one the COTS component comes with), since this results in advantages such as better performance;
- *variability support through architectural patterns*: the COTS component has to be adaptable to the specific needs of the architectural patterns and, thus, needs to be checked for according variation points;
- *variability in functional or quality attributes*: (1) the COTS component has to be checked for the existence of variation points and variants and (2) component configurations have to be checked for the functionality and quality provided.

These considerations help COTS evaluation teams in extending their COTS evaluation criteria when considering variability of a system family.

As stated before, this work represents one part of the CoVAR process we developed. CoVAR has been partially validated in a case study focusing on variability in system family requirements. Another case study is planned to validate our results regarding variability in system family architecture.

References

1. Alves, C.; Castro, J.: CRE: A Systematic Method for COTS Component Selection. XV Brazilian Symposium on Software Engineering, Rio de Janeiro, Brazil, October 2001.
2. Bachmann, F.; Bass, Len: Managing Variability in Software Architectures. Symposium on Software Reusability, Toronto, 2001.
3. Bass, L.; Clements, P.; Kazman, R.: Software Architecture in Practice. Addison-Wesley, 1998.
4. Böckle, G.; Knauber, P.; Pohl, K.; Schmid, K. (Eds.): Software-Produktlinien – Methoden, Einführung und Praxis. dpunkt.verlag, 2004.
5. Bosch, J.; Florijn, G.; Greefhorst, D.; Kuusela, J.; Obbink, H.; Pohl, K.: Variability Issues in Software Product Lines. 4th International Workshop on Product Family Engineering, Bilbao, October 2001.
6. Bosch, J.: Design & Use of Software Architectures – Adopting and evolving a product-line approach. Addison-Wesley, 2000.
7. Chung, L.; Cooper, K.: A COTS-Aware Requirements Engineering (CARE) Process: Defining System Level Agents, Goals, and Requirements. TR UTDCS-23-01, Department of Computer Science, The University of Texas at Dallas, 2001.
8. Clements, P.; Kazman, R.; Klein, M.: Evaluating Software Architectures. Addison-Wesley, 2002.
9. Clements, P.; Northrop, L.: Software Product Lines: Practices and Patterns. Addison-Wesley, 2002.
10. Fox, G.; Lantner, K.; Marcom, S.: A Software Development Process for COTS-based Information System Infrastructure. Proceedings of the 5th International Symposium on Assessment of Software Tools (SAST'97), 1997, pp. 133-142.
11. Gacek, C.: Assessment Guidelines for Detecting Architectural Mismatches. IESE Report No. 021.00/E, Fraunhofer IESE, January, 2000.
12. Kontio, J.: A Systematic Process for Reusable Software Component Selection. Technical Report CS-TR-3478, University of Maryland, 1995.
13. Kunda, D.; Brooks, L.: Applying Social-Technical Approach for COTS Selection. Proceedings of the 4th UKAIS Conference, University of York, McGraw Hill, April 1999.
14. Ncube, C.: A Requirements Engineering Method for COTS-Based Systems Development. PhD Thesis, City University London, May 2000.
15. Ochs, M.; Pfahl, D.: COTS Acquisition Process (CAP) Instrumentation. Fraunhofer IESE-Report No. 049.99/E, Version 0.5, October 1999.
16. Pohl, K.; Reuys, A.: Considering Variabilities during Component Selection in Product Family Development. 4th International Workshop on Product Family Engineering, Bilbao, October 2001.
17. Polen, S.M.; Rose, L.C.; Phillips, B.C.: Component Evaluation Process. Software Productivity Consortium, SPC-98091-CMC, Version 01.00.02, May 1999.
18. Svahnberg, M.; Gurp, J. van; Bosch, J.: On the Notion of Variability in Software Product Lines. Proceedings of Working IEEE/ IFIP Conference on Software Architecture, 2001.

19. Tran, V.; Liu, D.B.: A Procurement-centric Model for Engineering Component-based Software Systems. Proceedings of the 5th International Symposium on Assessment of Software Tools (SAST'97), 1997, pp.70-79.
20. Wallnau, K.C.; Hissam, S.A., Seacord, R.C.: Building Systems from Commercial Components. Addison-Wesley, 2002.
21. Yakimovich, D.: A Comprehensive Reuse Model for COTS Software Products. Dissertation, University of Maryland, 2001.

An Approach to Analysis and Design for COTS-Based Systems

Grace A. Lewis

Carnegie Mellon® Software Engineering Institute, Pittsburgh, PA, USA
glewis@sei.cmu.edu

Abstract. From an analysis and design perspective, developers of COTS-based systems face many challenges driven by built-in product paradigms as well as the volatility of the marketplace. One way to deal with these challenges is to adopt a spiral development process that allows for concurrent discovery and negotiation of user needs and business processes, applicable technology and components, the target architecture, and organizational constraints. This paper outlines a workflow for Analysis and Design that can be used within spiral-based development processes for building systems from commercial components.

1 Introduction

From an analysis and design perspective, developers of COTS-based systems face many challenges, especially in COTS-aggregate systems[1]:

- Product selections have dependencies on other products that need to be considered in the design.
- Product selections have built-in models of use and architectural paradigms that make integration difficult if this information is not available to the developers.
- The volatility of the marketplace and the frequency and content of product releases cause disruptions in the design process.
- Design decisions may have to be made with incomplete information because the products are treated as black boxes.
- Integration becomes a primary source of risk.

One way to deal with these challenges is to adopt a spiral development process that allows for concurrent discovery and negotiation of user needs and business processes, applicable technology and components, the target architecture, and organizational constraints. The Software Engineering Institute has defined a process framework called Assembly Process for COTS-Based Systems (APCS) and an instantiation of APCS called the Evolutionary Process for Implementing COTS-based systems (EPIC) [1] [3]. These are both spiral approaches to COTS-based systems (CBS) development.

[1] A COTS-aggregate system is a system composed of multiple COTS products from multiple vendors, integrated to collectively provide system functionality [4].

X. Franch and D. Port (Eds.): ICCBSS 2005, LNCS 3412, pp. 236–247, 2005.

This paper outlines a workflow for Analysis and Design that can be used within CBS development processes such as EPIC. The workflow uses several techniques for building systems from commercial components to deal with the challenges outlined above [7].

2 The Analysis and Design Workflow

EPIC is a risk-based, disciplined, spiral-engineering approach to COTS-based systems development which leverages the Rational Unified Process (RUP). The element of interest for this paper is the Analysis and Design workflow. Workflows are sequences of activities that produce a result of observable value [5]. The goal of the Analysis and Design workflow in RUP is to produce an architecture and design that is refined and analyzed over the system's lifecycle. The main elements of the Analysis and Design workflow in RUP are system architecture, component design, and database design. These elements, although important in custom development, do not accurately represent the analysis and design process for COTS-based systems. Figure 1 presents a variation of this workflow that takes into consideration the nature of COTS-based systems[2].

In spiral development, all iterations have objectives and address certain risks. An objective of an early iteration, once the problem is better understood, should be the initial version of the system architecture and design. In subsequent iterations an objective might be a better understanding of technologies, evaluation of alternatives, or the selection of an alternative as the system architecture[3].

The development of the architecture of any software system usually starts with a box-and-line diagram where boxes represent system components and lines represent the interaction between components. The difference with CBS is that depending on what stage the project is in, these components can be technologies, products or versions. As the project advances and decisions are made, certain components will go from technology, to product, to version. On the other hand, if the use of certain products is an organizational mandate, components can start as versions. An example of a box-and-line diagram for a typical web application is shown in Figure 2.

When you put together a box-and-line diagram, you have an idea of what types of components you want to use and how they should be connected, but there are many unknowns about the components and the way these components interact. For example:

- What servlet engines and application servers are good choices for this web application?
- What application servers interact well with Oracle DB (organizational mandate)?
- What browsers have to be supported?
- Will all servlet engines work well with all browsers?
- What combinations work better?

---

[2] For readers not familiar with RUP, the Analysis and Design workflow is executed in every iteration that has a goal related to system architecture and design.

[3] The terms architecture and design will be used indistinctively throughout the paper. In CBS the line between the two is very blurry because components are treated as black boxes for which the detailed design is unknown; therefore a single artifact usually represents the architecture and design of a system.

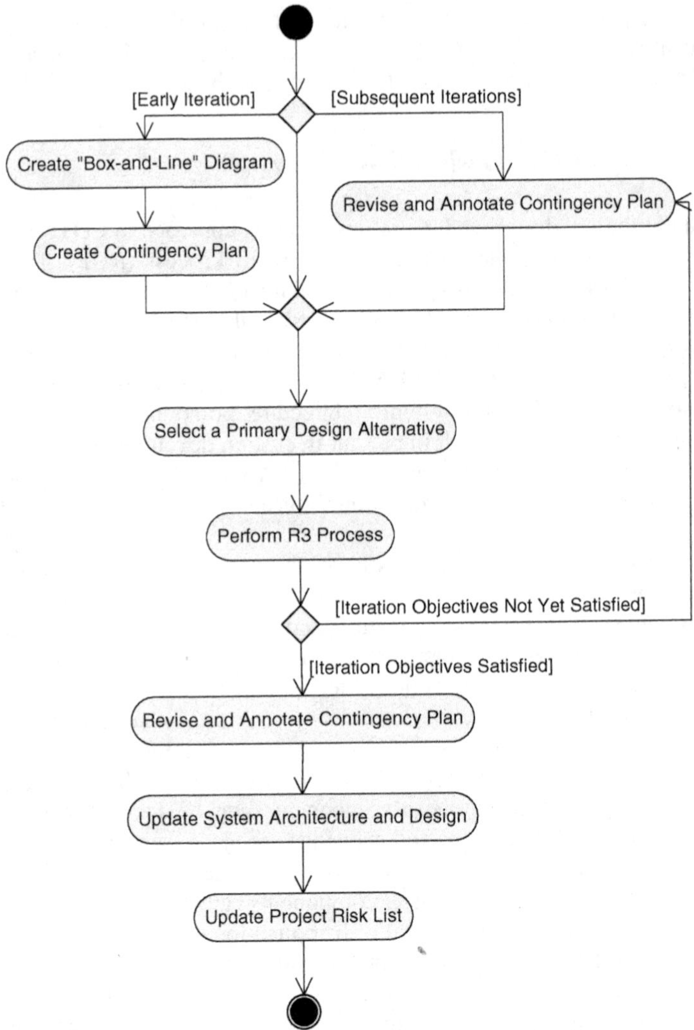

Fig. 1. Analysis and Design Workflow for COTS-Based System Development

A technique that is useful for recording these unknowns and eventually the answers to these unknowns is an *ensemble*. An ensemble is a formalism for recording design alternatives, including what has been accomplished and what still needs to be done [7]. Figure 3 shows an example of an ensemble. Two main elements are used to annotate ensembles:

- Credentials: Credentials are used to specify properties of components. The value of a property is known with the level of confidence associated with the verification technique. In the example in Figure 3, there is a credential for a component property called *Supported Browsers* with value *Navigator 4, 6, 7; IE 4, 5, 6; AOL 7* that has been verified through looking at *Documentation*.

- Constraints: Constraints specify conditions on an interaction. They document the required component properties supporting the interaction. In the example in Figure 3, there is a constraint for an interaction property called *Driver* whose value is *Oracle JDBC Driver* that has been verified through *Experimentation*.

Credentials and constraints can also be in postulate form. In this case, *verify* is a plan to obtain knowledge rather than a statement of how it was obtained. Visually, the only difference is the question mark after the word Credential or Constraint, but in practice it is what differentiates what is known from what is unknown.

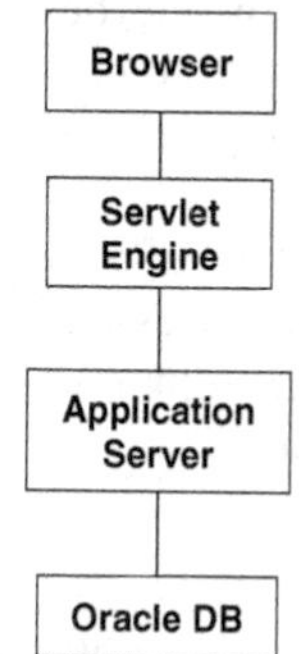

Fig. 2. Box-and-Line Diagram for a Typical Web Application

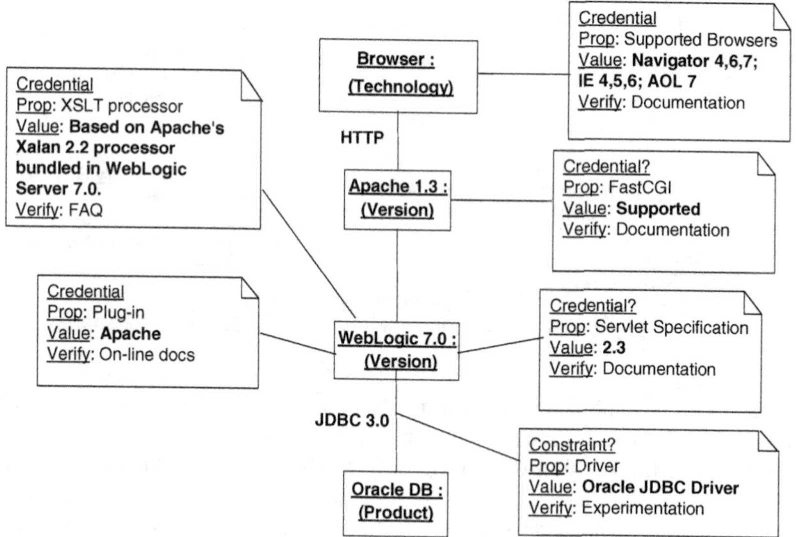

Fig. 3. Ensemble for a Web Application

In CBS development, there will usually be several options for building the system. In fact, one of the differences between EPIC and RUP is that the Lifecycle Objectives (LCO) anchor point is redefined to allow multiple candidate solutions to proceed to the Elaboration Phase [1]. A technique to keep track of the design alternatives that are being considered for the system and their status is *contingency planning*. Figure 4 shows a contingency plan for a web application. The boxes represent ensembles and the arrows represent refinements. Leaf ensembles are current designs and non-leaf ensembles are historic designs. The status of an ensemble can be:

- Feasible: Ensemble that has acceptable risk (meets project objectives and can be executed within project constraints)
- Conditionally Feasible: Ensemble that would be feasible if repairs are executed. Product repairs are fixes made by the development team, e.g. additional code, additional product, modification of other components. Context repairs require negotiation with other actors, e.g. requirements negotiation, negotiation with vendor for additional features.
- Unknown Feasibility: Ensemble that contains unknowns that represent unacceptable risk and need further investigation.
- Infeasible: Ensemble that contains unknowns that represent unacceptable risk for which there is no acceptable repair.

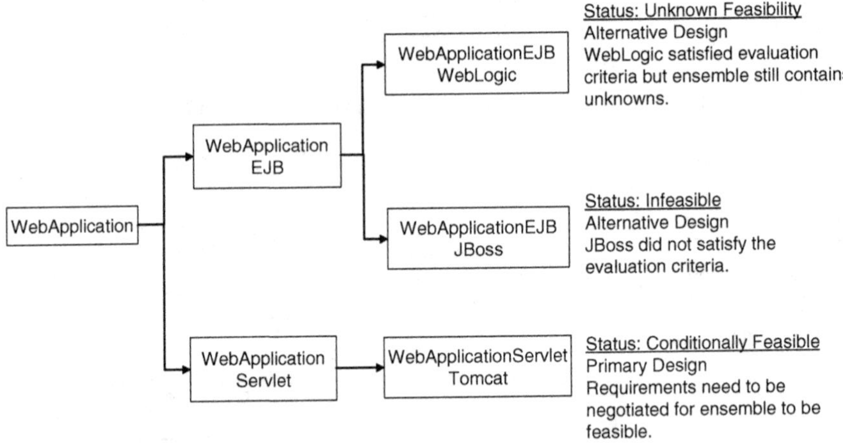

Fig. 4. Contingency Plan for a Web Application

A change to an ensemble represents a refinement and therefore a new box in the contingency plan. Although Figure 4 only shows the status and some rationale for the current designs, all information of historic designs should be maintained because an alternative determined infeasible might start looking very attractive if one of the major vendors for the primary design goes bankrupt! The recording of the rationale is important knowledge for future developers and maintainers.

To continue through the workflow, an ensemble has to be selected as the primary design alternative. How to select which is the primary design can be as informal as instinct or guessing, or as formal as risk quantification where the ensemble that poses the least risk is selected as the primary design.

The *R3 Process* is performed on the primary design alternative. The goal of the R3 Process is to determine the feasibility of an ensemble, identify critical unknowns, and acquire technology competence [7]. The details of this process are given in the next section.

If the objective of the iteration from the analysis and design perspective has not been satisfied, the contingency plan is updated with the results of the R3 Process and the process is repeated. If the objective of the iteration has been satisfied, the contingency plan is updated with the results of the R3 Process and the formal architecture and design document is updated. It is important to note that the artifacts generated in this process do not replace a formal architecture and design document, but can provide much of the information and rationale to support it. A recommendation is to keep the ensembles, blackboards[4] and contingency plans either as appendices to the architecture and design documentation or as part of the project repository. Having all the information handy saves a lot of work if a design alternative needs to be revisited during the system life cycle.

Finally, the project risk list is updated. Some of the unknowns can become major risks for the project, especially if a finding makes all alternatives infeasible. Elevating this risk increases the possibility that it will be addressed in a future iteration.

3 The R3 Process

As explained previously, the goal of the R3 Process is to determine the feasibility of an ensemble, identify critical unknowns, and acquire technology competence. R3 stands for:

- R1 = **R**isk Analysis
- R2 = **R**ealize Model Problems
- R3 = **R**epair Analysis

A workflow for the R3 Process is presented in Figure 5. The process ends when the ensemble is declared infeasible, the remaining risk in the ensemble is acceptable and is declared feasible, or there are identified repairs that make the ensemble conditionally feasible.

3.1 R1: Risk Analysis

In this step of the R3 process, the risk represented by the unknowns in the ensemble is analyzed through scenarios. The execution of the scenario through the ensemble is depicted using a *blackboard*. Blackboards represent usage scenarios that exercise one or more of the unknowns that pose a risk to the system [7]. They are similar to UML collaboration diagrams and contain only those components and interactions required to execute the scenario. Figure 6 shows a blackboard for the scenario "System can support 200 HTTP requests/second during peak loads" that exercises the unknown

[4] Blackboards are a part of the R3 Process. The term will be explained in the next section.

represented by the postulated credential referring to handling of peak loads. For example, in analyzing the scenario it is discovered that the particular version of Tomcat does not support load balancing (Value=None)[5].

At this point a decision needs to be made. Either the ensemble is infeasible because there is belief or evidence that the ensemble cannot handle the requirement, feasible because the risk imposed by the unknown is accepted, or of unknown feasibility and therefore requires further investigation through the use of model problems.

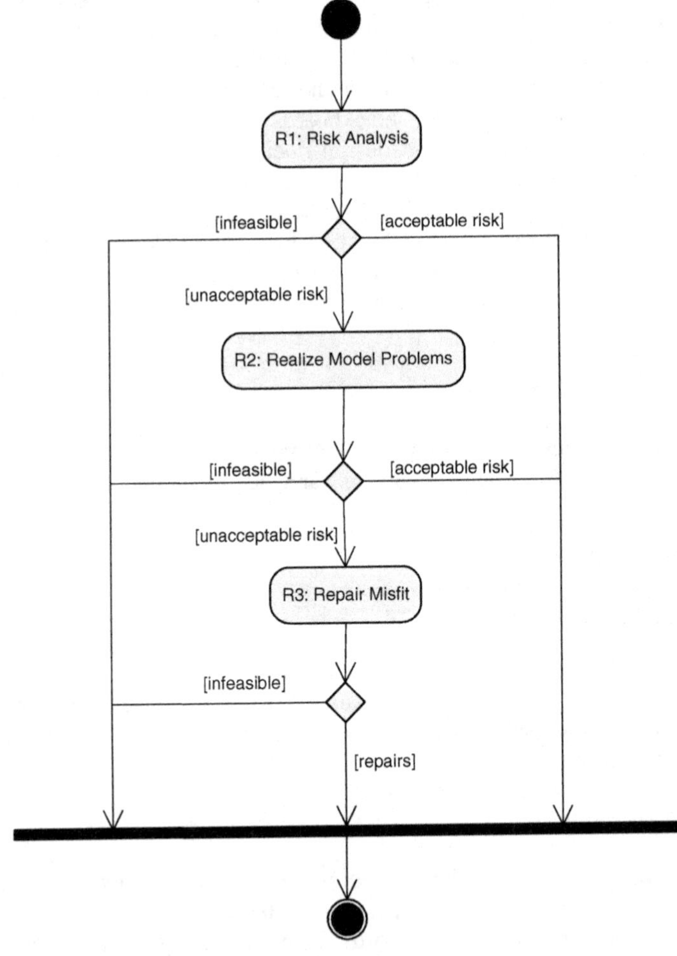

Fig. 5. The R3 Process

[5] This is only an example and not representative of the actual products.

3.2 R2: Realize Model Problem

Model problems are prototypes, situated in a specific design context, where the consumer is the architect/designer. Model problems help generate component expertise, focus on evaluating a specific set of unknowns, and help establish ensemble feasibility [7]. A summary of the model problem process is:

1. Express the unknown as a hypothesis; e.g. The Tomcat Servlet ensemble can manage peak loads of 200 requests/second.
2. Define evaluation criteria to determine if the solution to the model problem sustains or falsifies the hypothesis; e.g. Loads of 200 requests/second can be sustained for 30 seconds without system crashes or lost requests.
3. Define minimum relevant constraints (if any) to ensure the model solution is realistic; e.g. Model problem environment must not exceed the capabilities of deployed hardware.
4. Setup the model solution (Figure 7 contains a potential setup for the previous blackboard). Some recommendations in this step are to imagine the simplest experiment possible, install the components yourself, and save all your notes. Keep in mind that the idea is simply to validate the hypothesis while gaining component expertise.
5. Evaluate the model solution against initial criteria, plus any criteria that were discovered as a by-product of implementing the solution.
6. Create a statement of "hypothesis sustained" or "hypothesis refuted" with supporting notes.
7. Analyze the remaining risk.

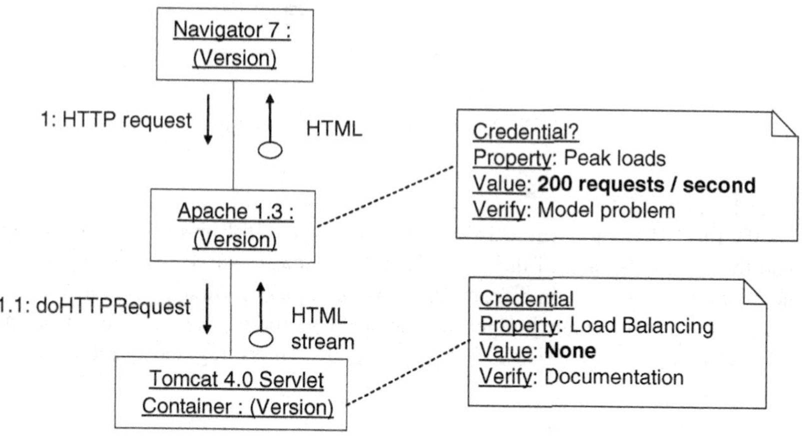

Fig. 6. Blackboard

Once again, a decision needs to be made. Either the ensemble is infeasible because there is now proof that it cannot handle the requirement and the risk is considered unacceptable, feasible because the hypothesis was sustained and any remaining risk is considered acceptable, or of unknown feasibility and therefore the architect/designers wish to analyze potential repairs.

3.3 R3: Repair Analysis

There can be many potential repairs for a model problem: negotiate with the vendor, modify other system components, add custom code, negotiate requirements, change user processes, buy new products, enhance training material, etc. The method for selecting which is the best repair, as is the case with how to select which is the primary design, can be as informal as instinct or a guess, or as formal as risk quantification. It will depend on the environment in which you are applying the process. What follows is an example of a risk quantification method.

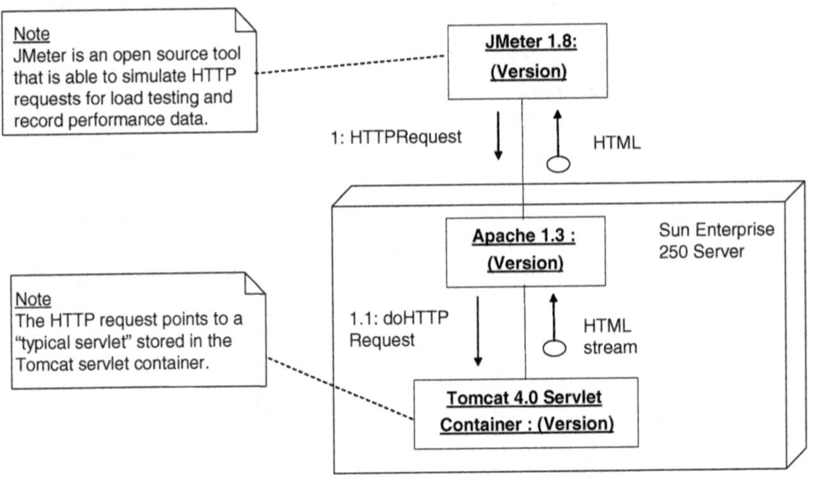

Fig. 7. Potential Model Solution Setup

1. Quantify the risk

Qualify the risk with a value from the table shown in Figure 8 [2]. Then, apply a formula that converts each of these values into a numeric value. An example of a very simple formula is shown in Figure 9. Next, the project manager determines what portion of the development budget can be used to reduce the risk to an acceptable level. Finally, the cost per risk unit is calculated as the budgeted amount divided by the risk value.

Impact \ Probability	Very Likely	Probable	Improbable
Catastrophic	High	Major	Significant
Critical	Major	Significant	Moderate
Marginal	Significant	Moderate	Minor
Negligible	Moderate	Minor	Low

Fig. 8. Risk Exposure Table

For the previous example, the architect (s), designers, project manager, and relevant project stakeholders determined that the risk of not supporting peak loads is *High* and warrants a value of *58*. The project manager determines that he or she is willing to spend *$180,000* to reduce this risk to an acceptable level. Therefore, the cost per risk unit is $180,000 divided by 58, for a value of approximately *$3,103* per risk unit.

$$f(impact, probability) \rightarrow \begin{bmatrix} 1 \leq low \leq 10 \\ 11 \leq minor \leq 20 \\ 21 \leq moderate \leq 30 \\ 31 \leq significant \leq 40 \\ 41 \leq major \leq 50 \\ 51 \leq high \leq 60 \end{bmatrix}$$

Fig. 9. Risk Conversion Formula

2. Identify repair options.
   Repairs are identified for the ensemble. This method requires accepting the existing risk as an option. A list of repair options is shown in column 3 of Table 1.

3. Quantify residual risk.
   For each repair option, residual risk is qualitatively assessed using the same scale as before. It is important to keep in mind that there has to be an "aggregate" sense of risk. For example, asking the vendor to provide an enhancement for the product can take the risk down to almost zero, but there is new risk that arises from the vendor not meeting the set deadline or providing a feature that does not work exactly as expected. The residual risk for each of the options in the example is shown in column 4 of Table 1. Given the selected function, the qualitative risk judgments for each repair are quantified. Values for the example are calculated using the formula in Figure 9 and are shown in column 5 of Table 1. Accepting the degraded performance is accepting the risk and therefore, its value is the number calculated in step 1.

4. Estimate repair cost.
   Repair cost can be estimated as any other software engineering effort. Values for the example are shown in column 6 of Table 1.

Table 1. Repair Options

Risk (1)	Risk Value (2)	Repair (3)	Residual Risk (RR) (4)	Quantified RR (5)	Cost ($) (6)
System response time degrades at peak loads	58	1: Custom wrapper	Minor	12	$95,000
		2: Vendor enhancement	Minor	18	$50,000
		3: Vendor plug-in interface	Minor	15	$55,000
		4: Accept degraded performance	High	58	$0
		5: Improve existing infrastructure (i.e. faster CPU, more memory, higher bandwidth networks)	Significant	35	$175,000

5. Perform domination analysis.

Domination analysis simplifies aggregation by removing false options. Repair A dominates Repair B if and only if Repair A is as least as good as Repair B with respect to all criteria, and Repair A is better than Repair B in at least one criterion. In the example Repair 1 dominates Repair 5 because it reduces the risk to 12 for $95,000 as compared to reducing the risk to 35 for $175,000 (better in both criteria). If domination analysis has been done correctly, the remaining options have the property that lower repair cost implies higher risk. At this point, it is helpful to eliminate the dominated options and order the remaining options from lowest to highest cost to make the next steps easier.

6. Calculate cost-to-risk ratio for each repair.

The cost-to risk ratio for each repair is calculated by dividing the difference in cost with respect to the option of accepting the risk by the difference in residual risk with respect to the option of accepting the risk, as shown in the formula in Figure 10. R_1 is the option not to repair, which for the example is repair 4 in column 3 of Table 2. The cost-to-risk ratio for the example is shown in column 6 of Table 2.

$$\left(\frac{\Delta Cost}{\Delta RRisk}\right)_N = \frac{Cost(R_N) - Cost(R_1)}{RRisk(R_1) - RRisk(R_N)}$$

Fig. 10. Formula for Cost-to-Risk Ratio

Table 2. Repair Options After Domination Analysis

Risk (1)	Risk Value (2)	Repair (3)	Residual Risk (4)	Cost ($) (5)	Cost-to-Risk Ratio (6)
System response time degrades at peak loads	58	4: Accept degraded performance	58	$0	$0/risk
		2: Vendor enhancement	18	$50,000	$1250/risk
		3: Vendor plug-in interface	15	$55,000	$1279/risk
		1: Custom wrapper	12	$95,000	$2065/risk

7. Select repair.

The optimal repair strategy is selected by comparing the cost per risk unit (CPRU) calculated in Step 1 with the cost-to-risk ratio for each option. For the example in Table 2

If CPRU < $1,250, then select Repair 4.
If $1,250 ≤ CPRU < $1279, then select Repair 2.
If $1279 ≤ CPRU < $2065, then select Repair 3.
If CPRU > $2065, then select Repair 1.

In this example, because CPRU is equal to $3,103 the optimal repair strategy would be Repair 1, that is, to build a custom wrapper.

The above risk quantification method has known limitations that have to be addressed. First of all, we recognize it can be very difficult for a project manager to determine upfront the budget he or she can allocate to mitigate a risk. Nonetheless, this value is an approximation of how much resources are available to spend on this task, which should be in control of the project manager. Another comment we have received is that the proposed process treats all units of risk as equal and does not take into consideration that, for example, if the residual risk of one repair option is 40 and the other is 30, those 10 units of risk that differentiate one repair option from another may be harder to reduce.

At this point of the R3 process, the ensemble could be declared infeasible because none of the repair options reduce the risk to an acceptable level, or a repair has been selected that has to be addressed in the current or a subsequent iteration.

4 Conclusions

COTS-based systems require a spiral-based development process that allows for concurrent discovery and negotiation of user needs and business processes, applicable technology and components, the target architecture, and organizational constraints. This paper proposes an approach to the analysis and design of COTS-based system that

- Uses contingency planning to track design alternatives represented as ensembles
- Evaluates the feasibility of ensembles using the R3 process
- Provides input for the formal architecture and design of the system
- Elevates technical risks to the project-level risk list and hopefully addressed in future iterations
- Generates component expertise early in the life cycle

References

1. Albert, C. & Brownsword, L. Evolutionary Process for Integrating COTS-Based Systems (EPIC): Building, Fielding, and Supporting Commercial-off-the-Shelf (COTS) Based Solutions. Pittsburgh, PA: Software Engineering Institute, Carnegie Mellon University, 2002.
2. Alberts, C; Dorofee, A; Higuera, R.; Murphy, R; Walker, J; & Williams, R. Continuous Risk Management Guidebook. Pittsburgh, PA: Software Engineering Institute, Carnegie Mellon University, 1996.
3. Carney, D.; Place, P; & Oberndorf, P. Basics for Assembly Process for COTS-Based Systems (APCS). Pittsburgh, PA: Software Engineering Institute, Carnegie Mellon University, 2003.
4. Comella-Dorda, S.; Dean, J; Lewis, G.; Morris, E.; Oberndorf, P; & Harper, E. A Process for COTS Software Product Evaluation. Pittsburgh, PA: Software Engineering Institute, Carnegie Mellon University, 2004.
5. IBM. Rational Unified Process Documentation. 2003.
6. Kruchten, Phillippe. The Rational Unified Process: An Introduction, 2nd ed. New York, NY: Addison-Wesley Object Technology Series, March 2000.
7. Wallnau, Kurt; Hissam, Scott; & Seacord, Robert. Building Systems from Commercial Components. New York, NY: Addison-Wesley, 2001.

Resolving Architectural Mismatches of COTS Through Architectural Reconciliation

Paris Avgeriou and Nicolas Guelfi

Software Engineering Competence Center (SE2C), University of Luxembourg,
6, rue Richard Coudenhove-Kalergi L-1359 Luxembourg-Kirchberg, Luxembourg
{paris.avgeriou, nicolas.guelfi}@uni.lu

Abstract. The integration of COTS components into a system under development entails architectural mismatches. These have been tackled, so far, at the component level, through component adaptation techniques, but they also must be tackled at an architectural level of abstraction. In this paper we propose an approach for resolving architectural mismatches, with the aid of architectural reconciliation. The approach consists of designing and subsequently reconciling two architectural models, one that is forward-engineered from the requirements and another that is reverse-engineered from the COTS-based implementation. The final reconciled model is optimally adapted both to the requirements and to the actual COTS-based implementation. The contribution of this paper lies in the application of architectural reconciliation in the context of COTS-based software development. Architectural modeling is based upon the UML 2.0 standard, while the reconciliation is performed by transforming the two models, with the help of architectural design decisions.

1 Introduction

The inevitable problem with reusing COTS components is that they simply don't correspond perfectly to the requirements specification and consequently to the envisioned architecture of the system [1]. Even when COTS-based systems are designed by taking into consideration pre-existing components from the market that roughly correspond to the requirements, eventually there will still be disparities when the COTS are integrated. One of the major causes of this problem is **architectural mismatches**: differences between a COTS component and the software system, where it will be integrated, which occur when the former makes the wrong assumptions about the latter [1, 8]. For example, a commercial component can falsely assume that it is in charge of controlling the sequence of interactions between itself and other components, or that other components should comply with specific protocols of interactions. To make matters worse, such assumptions are implicit and are usually in conflict with each other. The consequences are that system-wide properties are diverged from the requirements, both functional and quality ones. Especially quality requirements such as performance, reliability, and flexibility that depend profoundly on the architecture [4, 5, 24] may be to a large extent distressed by the use of COTS components.

X. Franch and D. Port (Eds.): ICCBSS 2005, LNCS 3412, pp. 248 – 257, 2005.

The research community has attempted to tackle the problem of architectural mismatches, focusing on the component level, by means of **component adaptation** techniques, which attempt to incorporate unintended changes in a component for use in a particular application [3]. These techniques are distinguished into **white-box** (e.g. inheritance) and **black-box** (e.g. wrapping), depending on whether the component itself is adapted or whether its interface is adapted [4]. In the case of COTS components, black-box techniques are usually applied since the component's source code is usually prohibited from being inspected or modified [1]. There are several techniques proposed so far [3, 12, 15, 16, 29], and they can be applied according to the context of use and the possible benefits and liabilities they entail [12].

However architectural mismatches cannot only be resolved at the component level since they do not concern an isolated component but they affect a greater part of the system, which collectively includes a number of components and connectors [8, 25]. Architectural mismatches caused by a single component may influence not only the components that communicate with it but may also be propagated further on to other components. Therefore such mismatches may require not only the adaptation of the COTS component but also the modification, addition or removal of other architectural elements. In order to perform these changes we need to examine a greater part of the system's architecture, identify those elements that are affected and subsequently decide on how exactly the architecture should be modified. We thus need to tackle the problem of architectural mismatches from an architectural perspective [8].

This paper proposes an approach to resolve architectural mismatches, caused by integrating COTS, using the technique of **architectural reconciliation**. In specific, it suggests the design and subsequently the reconciliation of two architectural models: one that is forward engineered from the requirements specification and a second that is reverse-engineered from the COTS-based system implementation. The former expresses the architectural decisions in an *ideal* system, which conforms to the requirements. The latter not only grasps the implementation constraints, but also explicitly specifies the architectural impact of COTS that were incorporated in the implementation, making their design assumptions explicit, with respect to the rest of the application. These two models are reconciled into a third model that will combine the two perspectives in the best possible tradeoff, by taking under consideration the design assumptions of the COTS components, but also addressing the requirements, to the best possible extent. The reconciliation is performed by transforming the two models, based on architectural design decisions, depending on which side, requirements or implementation should be more supported. The reconciled model can eventually be used to re-engineer the COTS-based system and also update the requirements. Architectural modeling is based upon the UML 2.0 standard.

The rest of the paper is organized as follows: section 2 provides the details of the proposed approach for resolving architectural mismatches through architectural reconciliation. Section 3 illustrates the implementation of the approach through a case study while Section 4 presents some related research work with respect to architectural reconciliation. Finally Section 5 wraps up with conclusions and future work.

2 Architectural Reconciliation

2.1 The Reconciliation Process

The process of reconciliation is graphically illustrated in Fig. 1., and is comprised of six consecutive phases.

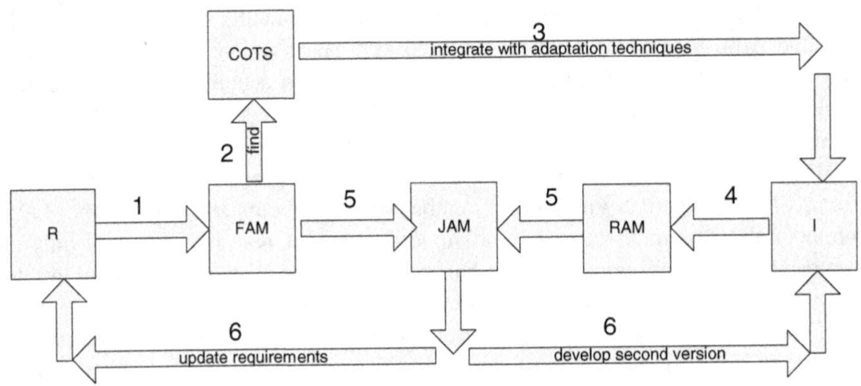

Fig. 1. Process of Architectural Reconciliation

The first three phases follow a simplistic forward engineering style. The process commences by using the requirements specification (R) to design the *ideal* architecture of the system, which we name the **Forward Architectural Model** or **FAM.** This model should, if possible, take into account pre-existing COTS from the market that correspond more or less to the requirements. This forward-engineering design of the architecture can be performed by following any architecture-driven software development process. We thus do not impose or even suggest a specific process to be followed, since we consider that our approach is independent of specific processes. In sequence, commercial components are located in the market, that is, if they haven't already been found. Eventually the implementation (I) is developed according to the FAM, by building new components from scratch and by including the COTS found. At the best-case scenario, the COTS components will be adapted at a component level according to one of the aforementioned component adaptation techniques.

The fourth phase is to reverse-architect the COTS-based implementation in order to *recover* its architecture, which we name the **Reverse Architectural Model** or **RAM.** It is obvious that reverse-architecting is a special case of reverse-engineering, which concerns only architectural design. Here, similarly as before, we do not prescribe a specific reverse-architecting approach, though there are a few such techniques and tools proposed, such as those in [11, 20, 22, 23, 25, 27, 28].

The fifth and most crucial phase is to bridge the RAM and the FAM into the **Joint Architectural Model** or **JAM**, which must compromise between the COTS-based implementation and the set of ideal requirements. This is achieved by performing a transformation, which accepts the RAM and the FAM as inputs and produces the JAM as the output. A necessary tradeoff must of course be made since it is highly impossible to perfectly satisfy the requirements, especially the non-functional or quality requirements. The transformation enforces a set of design decisions that resolve the incompatibilities between the RAM and the FAM. In specific, the architect must go through the following steps:

- **Identify the architectural mismatches between the RAM and the FAM.** The architect must start by looking for the four different kinds of false assumptions that integration of COTS components may entail, as explained in [8]. These assumptions may lead to architectural mismatches, or more simply differences between the FAM and the RAM, that must be explicitly specified. The architectural mismatches can be detected by comparing the RAM and the FAM, either informally (e.g. UML diagrams) or more formally (e.g. formal models with precise semantics).
- **Resolve the architectural mismatches.** By resolving the architectural mismatches, the architect needs to decide between one of the following:
  - Keep the part of the FAM and delete the part of the RAM that causes the mismatch, if enforcing the requirements is more significant.
  - Keep the part of the RAM and delete the part of the FAM that causes the mismatch, if requirements can be compromised in favor of the COTS components.
  - Come up with a tradeoff solution that mixes both parts. In this case some of the elements from both models may be deleted, others may be retained and possibly modified, while more elements may be added. Component adaptation techniques can be again enforced here, if it is necessary to adapt the behavior of COTS components.
- **Complete the JAM.** The resolution of the architectural mismatches will probably have consequences to other architectural elements that were not themselves part of the problem. Therefore, the architect needs to take some last decisions with respect to keeping, deleting or modifying architectural elements that were affected by the reconciliation actions.

The final phase in this process is to re-engineer the system according to the JAM, and update the requirements document to reflect the changes that occurred during the reconciliation. How exactly the JAM is implemented into code is again out of the scope of this paper. We emphasize that our goal in this process was not to invent yet another forward or reverse-architecting process, but to focus on the reconciliation of architectural models.

2.2 The Architectural Description

An architectural description is comprised of multiple views [6, 13, 14, 17], for example the component-connector view, the logical view, the implementation view, the data view and the deployment view. In order to reduce the complexity of bridging two complex multiple-view architectural models, we have focused on the *component-and-connector* view [6] for two reasons: it is considered to contain the most significant architectural information, and it is the most appropriate view to describe COTS components. This view deals with the system run-time by showing the *components*, which are units of run-time computation or data-storage, and the *connectors*, which are the interaction mechanisms between components.

As far as the language for describing the architecture, we have selected the widely accepted Unified Modeling Language. We have been working on the emergent UML 2.0 standard, to describe the component and connector view, and especially chose modeling elements from the Composite Structures and Components packages, namely: components, connectors, interfaces, ports, and classes that belong to the internal structures of components. In UML 2.0 components are associated with provided and required interfaces and may own ports that formalize their interactions points. A special case of connectors, that are called *assembly connectors* connect the required interface of one component to the provided interface of a second. For more information, in [2] we have elaborated on the UML 2.0 elements for describing the component and connector view.

3 A Case Study

The system that was used as a case study for the approach, is a popular open-source Learning Management System, named Ganesha [7], which supports e-learning in higher education and training institutes. This system was chosen for two reasons: a) being an open-source project, its code can be inspected and thus re-engineered without the copyright issues of commercial systems; b) its simple PHP-based and medium-sized code makes it manageable and suitable for this kind of experiment. We have experimented with integrating various COTS components in this system, in order to check the validity of the method. For illustrative purposes, this section focuses on the integration of a particular commercial chat component. Ganesha already had a simple chat component, which allowed for basic chat functionality, but we attempted to replace it with a COTS component, which offered more advanced functionality.

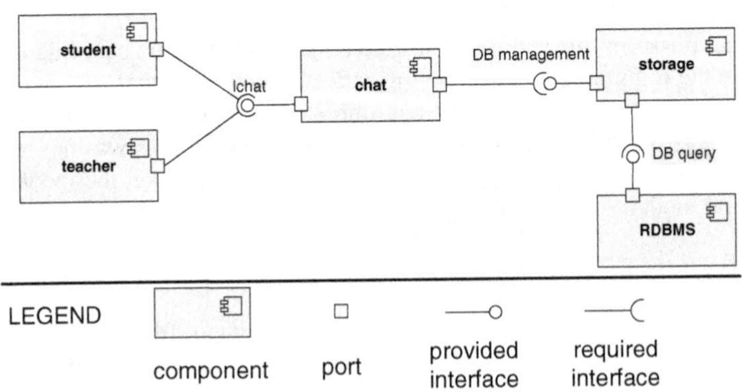

Fig. 2. Part of the Forward Architectural Model concerning the Chat Component

Fig. 2 depicts the *chat* component as well as the rest of the components, which it interacts with, in the Forward Architectural Model, designed to conform to the requirements. The *chat* component provides its functionalities through the *Ichat* interface, which is used by the *student* and *teacher* components that implement the application logic for students and teachers. The *Ichat* interface mandates that the *student* and *teacher* components call the *chat* component, by passing a unique identifier as a parameter, that proves they are authorized to use it. The *chat* component needs to query and update the database in order to store the currently-connected users, and maintain a log file of conversations. It accesses the database by using the interface *database management*, offered by the *storage* component, which in sequence handles direct *database queries* to the *RDBMS*.

We then integrated the new commercial chat component into Ganesha, which we had located in the component market. This specific component was provided as a fully functional evaluation version, implemented as a Java servlet, which can be parameterized through a text configuration file. The integration of the COTS component into the system, yielded the reverse architectural model, as shown on Fig. 3. The new *chat2* component provides a slightly different interface, called *Ichat2*, since there is a new way of calling the servlet and passing parameters. For the same reason the *student* and *teacher* components are also slightly modified (*student2* and *teacher2*) in order for them to require this new interface. Also the new chat component offers an interface for *WML access*, so that mobile clients can connect and access the chat functionality. Other than that, the COTS component makes two false assumptions that lead to architectural mismatches:

- The component assumes that it can have direct access to the database and thus requires an interface from the *RDBMS* to connect and perform queries. In this sense, it overrides Ganesha's database access mechanism through the *storage* component.
- The component assumes that it should not take care of access control, but can allow any potential web client to call the servlet and participate to the chat. This assumption is again wrong in the context of a Learning Management System, which mandates a strict access control to students and teachers registered for a particular course.

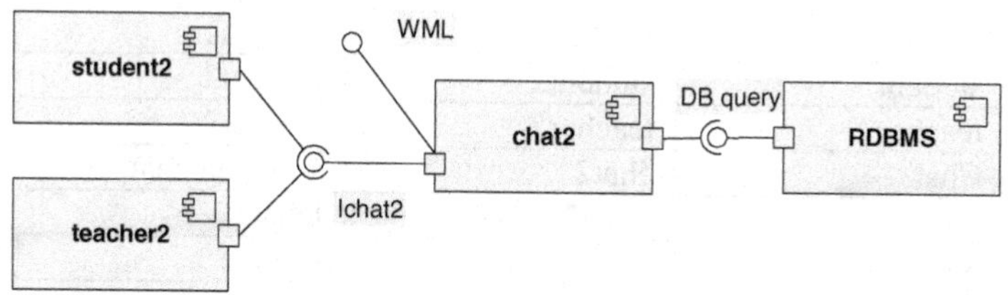

Fig. 3. Part of the Reverse Architectural Model concerning the Chat Component

In the first step of the reconciliation process, the architectural mismatches, which are caused by the above false assumptions, are identified:

- database access should be performed indirectly, as the *chat* component does through the *database management* interface in the FAM; however it is performed directly by the *chat2* component through the *database query* interface in the RAM.

- access control is managed by the *Ichat* interface of the *chat* component, but it is not managed by the *Ichat2* interface of the *chat2* component.

In the second step, that is the resolution of the mismatches, it is obvious that the *chat* component in the FAM and the *chat2* component in the RAM cause both mismatches. We cannot keep either component as it is, so the design decision is to use the wrapping adaptation technique [3], in order to adapt the *chat2* component to the functionality of the *chat* component. In specific, the wrapping technique involved a new component, the *wrapped chat*, which encapsulates the *chat2* component and delegates requests from other components to it and vice versa. The two assumptions were resolved as follows:

- The assumption about the direct database access is resolved by having the *wrapped chat* forwarding SQL queries that were previously meant to go directly to the *RDBMS*, to the *storage* component through its *DB management* interface.

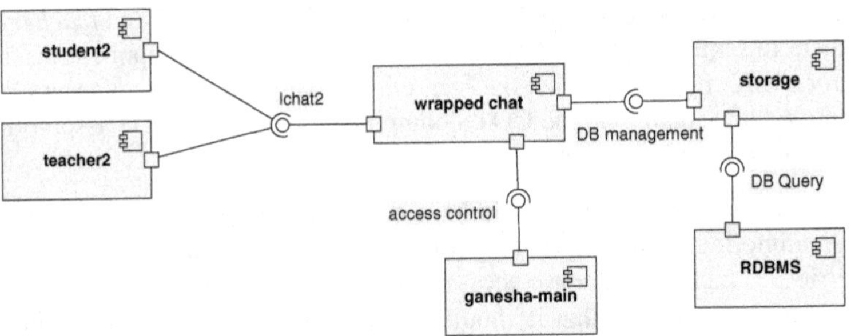

Fig. 4. Part of the Joint Architectural Model concerning the Chat Component

Table 1. Correspondence of architectural elements in the three models

FAM	RAM	JAM
student	student2	student2
teacher	teacher2	teacher2
Chat	chat2	wrapped chat
Ichat	Ichat2	Ichat2
Storage	-	storage
DB management	-	DB management
RDBMS	RDBMS	RDBMS
DB query	DB query	DB Query
-	WML	-
-	-	ganesha-main
-	-	access control

- The assumption concerning the lack of access control is resolved by having the *wrapped chat* check if each client that requests to connect to the *chat2* component is authorized through the *access control* interface that the *ganesha-main* component provides. If the client indeed has access rights, the chat invocation is forwarded to the *chat2* component.

Completing the JAM in the third step involved the following decisions:

- The *storage* component of the FAM is required by the *wrapped chat* so it is retained in the JAM.
- The *ganesha-main* component comes neither from the FAM or the RAM, but it is a central component of Ganesha that provides an *access control* interface, and thus it is added to the JAM.
- Since the *Ichat2* interface is provided by the *wrapped chat* component, the *student2* and *teacher2* components were retained from the RAM.
- The *WML access* interface of the COTS component is not needed in the FAM, which expresses the requirements, and was thus removed in the joint architectural model.

The reconciliation process resulted in the JAM, which is illustrated in Fig. 4, while the correspondence between the elements of all three models is shown in Table 1.

4 Related Work

The approach described in this paper has been based on research work with respect to bridging the gap between the system implementation and its requirements. Perry and Wolf in [21] first introduced the architectural problems of *erosion* and *drift*, which express the phenomenon of having the implementation architecture driven away from the ideal architecture, either on purpose or due to indifference. In [25, 26], Tran et al. introduced an architecture 'repair' technique for fixing this gap, by discovering and further eliminating the differences between the ideal architecture and the implementation architecture. They distinguish between *forward repair* where the implementation architecture is altered to match the conceptual, and *reverse repair* for the opposite. Architectural repair is then performed by combining both forward and reverse repair. They have also defined a number of repair techniques for removing unexpected dependencies from the architectural models [25]. They do not propose an approach for performing the design of the conceptual architecture but they do suggest tools such as those in [22, 23] for reverse-architecting.

Roughly, the same problem has been dealt with in [19], where Medvidovic et al. propose the introduction of two intermediate steps: a) designing the 'discovered' architecture from the requirements and b) designing the 'recovered' architecture from the implementation. These two architectural models are then much easier bridged into the actual Architecture of the system. The 'discovery' of the architecture is performed using the CBSP method [9] that transforms the requirements into a handful of simple architectural elements that represent something between requirements and architecture. The 'recovery' of the architecture is performed using a blend of techniques that reverse-engineer the code and package the derived classes into architectural elements. The final bridging is performed manually by applying architectural styles to one of the two models and then mapping the second model to the outcome, or by first integrating the two models and then applying architectural styles.

Our own approach has been influenced by both the aforementioned approaches. However we propose specific actions on how to perform the reconciliation, by transforming the two models based on design decisions. We also do not use repair techniques for removing dependencies in the models, but decisions for modifying, removing or retaining the elements of both models. Finally we extend these approaches by working on providing formalisms for the definition of the architectural models and subsequently their transformations, as will be explained in the next section.

5 Conclusions and Future Work

In this paper we have argued that COTS-based software development entails architectural mismatches that must be dealt with, not only at a component level through component adaptation techniques, but also at the architectural level. By doing so, we can examine a number of components and their connectors in a group, and thus make modifications to a considerable part of the system's architecture. We have thus proposed to design two architectural models, the first based on the requirements and the second based on the existing implementation, and then reconciling these two models through a tradeoff decision process. The added value of our approach concerns the adoption of architectural reconciliation in the context of COTS-based software development in order to resolve architectural mismatches at an architectural level.

We are currently working on formalizing the specification of the architectural models as well as their transformation, based on our previous work on model transformation [2, 10]. Our approach is established on defining the reconciliation as a mathematical relationship between a subset of our UML 2.0 architectural models (FAM, RAM and JAM). We specify this relationship by employing a logical formula that in turn uses a pre-defined formal metamodel defined for the architectural models. This formalization of the architectural models and their transformations will provide further added value to our work by allowing an explicit and simple specification of the reconciliation and offering support for semi-automatic reconciliation.

References

1. Albert, C., Brownsword, L. "Evolutionary Process for Integrating COTS-Based Systems (EPIC)". SEI Technical Report CMU/SEI-2002-TR-005. Software Engineering Institute, Carnegie Mellon University, 2002.
2. Avgeriou, P., Guelfi, N. Perrouin, G., Evolution Through Architectural Reconciliation, workshop on Software Evolution Through Transformations (SETra) 2004, Rome, Italy, Electronic Notes in Theoretical Computer Science, Elsevier, 2004.
3. Bosch, J., Superimposition: A component adaptation technique, *Information and Software Technology*, No. 41, pp. 257-73, April 1999.
4. Bosch, J., Design and Use of Software Architectures. Addison-Wesley, 2000.
5. Clements, P., Kazman, R., Clein, M., Evaluating Software Architecture, Addison-Wesley, 2002.
6. Clements, P., Bachmann, F., Bass, L., Garlan, D., Ivers, J., Little, R., Nord, R., Stafford, J., Documenting Software Architectures: Views and Beyond, Addison-Wesley, 2002.
7. Ganesha web site. http://www.anemalab.org/ganesha/.

8. Garlan, D., Allen, R. and Ockerbloom, J., "Architectural Mismatch: or Why It's Hard to Build Systems Out of Existing Parts," Proceedings of the International Conference on Software Engineering, Seattle, 1995.
9. Grunbacher, P., Egyed, A. and Medvidovic, N., Reconciling Software Requirements and Architectures with Intermediate Models, Journal of Software and Systems Modeling (SoSyM), to appear.
10. Guelfi, N., Ries, B., Sterges, P., *MEDAL: A CASE Tool Extension for Model-driven Software Engineering*, SwSTE'03 IEEE International Conference on Software - Science, Technology & Engineering, Hertzeliyah, Israel, 2003
11. Guo, G. Y., Atlee, J. M. and Kazman, R., A Software Architecture Reconstruction Method. *WICSA-1*, San Antonio, Feb. 1999.
12. Heineman, G., A model for designing adaptable software components, Twenty-second International Conference on Computer Software and Applications Conference (COMPSAC), pp. 121-127, Vienna, Austria, August, 1998.
13. Hofmeister, C., Nord, R. and Soni, D., Applied Software Architecture, Addison-Wesley, 1999.
14. IEEE, Recommended Practice for Architectural Description of Software-Intensive Systems, IEEE std. 1471-2000, 2000.
15. Keller, R. and Hölze, U., Binary component adaptation, Technical report TRCS97-20, University of California, Santa Barbara, December 1997.
16. Kiczales, G., Lamping, J., Lopes, C., Maeda, C., Mendhekar, A., Murphy, G., Open implementation design guidelines, Proceedings of the 19th international conference on Software engineering, p.481-490, May 17-23, 1997, Boston, Massachusetts, United States
17. Kruchten, P., "The 4+1 view model of architecture", IEEE Software, November 1995.
18. Medvidovic, N., Taylor, R.N., "A classification and comparison framework for software architecture description languages". *IEEE Transactions on Software Engineering*, vol.26, (no.1), p.70-93, Jan. 2000.
19. Medvidovic, N., Egyed, A., Gruenbacher, P., Stemming Architectural Erosion by Coupling Architectural Discovery and Recovery, Proceedings of the Second International Requirements to Architecture Workshop (STRAW 03), Portland, Oregon, May 3-11, 2003.
20. Mikic-Rakic, M., Mehta, N. R. and Medvidovic, N., Architectural Style Requirements for Self-Healing Systems. 1st Workshop on Self-Healing Systems, Charleston, Nov. 2002.
21. Perry, D.E. and Wolf, A.L. Foundations for the Study of Software Architectures. *Software Engineering Notes*, Oct. 1992.
22. Portable Bookshelf website, http://www.swag.uwaterloo.ca/pbs/
23. SHriMP web site, http://shrimp.cs.uvic.ca/
24. Szyperski, C., "Component Software – Beyond Object-Oriented Programming", ACM Press, 1999.
25. Tran, J. and Holt., R., Forward and Reverse Architecture Repair. Proc. of CASCON '99, Toronto, pages 15–24, November 1999.
26. Tran, J., Godfrey, M., Lee, E. and Holt, R., Architecture repair of open source software, *Proc. of 2000 Intl. Workshop on Program Comprehension* (IWPC-00), Limerick, Ireland.
27. Tzerpos, V. and Holt, R. C., A Hybrid Process for Recovering Software Architecture. In CASCON'96, Toronto, Nov. 1996.
28. Tu, Q. and Godfrey, M., An Integrated Approach for Studying Software Architectural Evolution, *Proc. of 2002 Intl. Workshop on Program Comprehension* (IWPC-02), Paris, June 2002.
29. Welch, I. and Stroud, R., Adaptation of connectors in software architectures, Third International Workshop on Component-Oriented Programming, Brussels, Belgium, July 1998.

Reuse of Existing Software in Space Projects — Proposed Approach and Extensions to Product Assurance and Software Engineering Standards

Manuel Rodríguez[1], João Gabriel Silva[1,*], Patricia Rodríguez-Dapena[2], Han van Loon[3], and Fernando Aldea-Montero[4]

[1] Critical Software S.A., Parque Industrial de Taveiro Lote 48, 3045-504 Coimbra, Portugal
{mrodriguez, jgabriel}@criticalsoftware.com
[2] SoftWcare S.L., C/ Serafín Avendaño 18 Int., 36201 Vigo, Spain
rodriguezdapena@softwcare.com
[3] SynSpace AG, Hardstrasse 11
CH - 4052 Basel, Switzerland
hvl@synspace.com
[4] ESA/ESTEC, Noordwijk, Netherlands
Fernando.Aldea.Montero@esa.int

Abstract. Reuse has the potential to substantially decrease the skyrocketing costs of space missions. The European Space Agency sponsored a study on the product assurance aspects of reuse of previously developed software on space projects, called PA-PDS. Several recommendations emerged from this study, along with change proposals to the main standards of software engineering and software product assurance followed by the European space industry. This paper describes those recommendations, the scope of reuse in the existing standards, and provides a justification for the proposed changes to them. A working group has been formed to develop a standard specifically addressing product assurance aspects of reuse.

1 Introduction

Developing large space software systems with demanding dependability and safety requirements entails significant costs. This is the reason why many organizations have begun to consider implementing such systems using existing software components. The European Space Agency (ESA), like other government and system developers acquiring software-intensive space systems, faces quite often the problem of assessing whether these components proposed for reuse are 'good enough' for the intended usage. This creates a need to specify what can be considered as 'sufficient evidence' of the adequacy of a given software component, from a product assurance viewpoint. This was the main motivation for the PA-PDS study that is at the origin of this paper.

* João Gabriel Silva is a professor at the University of Coimbra, Portugal, acting in this study as a senior consultant to Critical Software.

X. Franch and D. Port (Eds.): ICCBSS 2005, LNCS 3412, pp. 258–267, 2005.

PA-PDS is an ESA sponsored study aimed at defining the product assurance aspects required to ensure that development with reuse of existing components is a success.

There is a fundamental change required in the approach to system development for component-based systems. In the traditional custom-development approach, requirements (or system context) are first identified, then the software architecture is defined, and finally a (custom) implementation is undertaken. However, this approach needs to be adapted when some existing components are proposed for reuse, since it is unlikely that the marketplace will yield any products that fit the a priori requirements and architecture. Instead, it is necessary to consider the tradeoffs between the system context, architecture and potential candidates for reuse in the marketplace simultaneously. Any of these three parameters may have an impact on the other two, so none can be set without knowledge and accommodation of the others. This substantial change necessitates the adaptation of several industrial processes used to develop systems. The move to reuse-based systems development is not just an engineering or technical change, it is also a business, organizational and cultural change.

The so-called Commercial Off-The-Shelf (COTS) software is a subset of the overall domain of input assets for reuse in the space domain. With this terminology one means the reuse of general-purpose software available on the market usually with no access to the source code. The space industry, due to its small size compared to other software markets, is not known as a primary source of COTS software products. A few exceptions to this exist however, mostly at the ground segment level. Notably in the US, where there is a considerably technology overlap between the space and defense markets, some significant space COTS software products are available (e.g. EPOCH mission control system [1]). In the European space industry, the usage of COTS software products for dependability-critical systems has mostly taken the form of reusing real-time operating system kernels (e.g., Virtuoso [2]).

In the framework of the PA-PDS study, Pre-Developed Software (PDS) is defined as existing software components developed outside the framework of a space project or in previous space projects and used either 'as is' or with adaptations. This is a quite general definition not implying any contractual, structure, location or usage restriction. In particular, this definition encompasses not only COTS software but also in-house (or custom) developed software, shareware, freeware, public-domain (or open source) software, and 'copyleft' software (e.g., GNU software). As described later, the PA-PDS study has shown that careful reuse of PDS has the potential to significantly reduce development costs and to lead to space systems requiring less time to specify, design, develop, test and maintain, yet satisfying the stringent reliability and quality requirements. To achieve this, new requirements and processes must be defined within the European space standards.

The structure of the paper is as follows. Section 0 provides an overview of the state of the practice on PDS reuse in different domains. The PA-PDS study is described in Section 0, where the motivations, purpose, and main results are presented. Section 0 focuses on the extensions that have been proposed for inclusion into the main European space standards on product assurance and software engineering. It also introduces the main activities carried out by a recently formed ESA working group, whose purpose is to develop a standard specifically addressing product assurance aspects of reuse. Finally, Section 0 concludes the paper.

2 State of the Practice on PDS Reuse in Different Domains

Software reuse appears in various forms depending on the considered domain. Different nomenclature is used in standards and in the literature to name the so-called predeveloped software. An overview is provided hereafter.

In the military domain, standard MIL-STD-498 [3] –the U.S military standard for software development and documentation– defines a 'reusable software product' as a software product developed either for a specific use, or for being usable in multiple projects or in the same project with different roles. Examples include COTS software, acquirer-furnished software, pre-existing developer software, and reuse libraries. Each use may include all or part of the software product and may involve its modification. This definition is not just limited to software code, but extends to any software-related product (e.g., requirements, architectures, etc.).

In the avionics domain, ED12B [4] introduces the term 'Previously Developed Software'. It encompasses COTS software as defined by DO178B-PDS [5], namely 'commercially available applications sold by vendors through public catalogue listings'. According to this standard, COTS software is not intended to be customized or enhanced, which means that contract negotiated software developed or adapted for a specific application cannot be considered as a COTS software. In ARP4754 [6], which addresses certification of complex aircraft systems, software reuse is not considered as a separate issue.

In the railway domain, EN50128 [7] introduces the term 'standard software' to refer to software commercially available to implement general functions within a computer system but which has not necessarily been developed according to any standard.

In the nuclear domain, IEC60880-2 [8] addresses software aspects of defense against common cause failures, use of software tools and of pre-developed software. In UCRL-ID-122526 [9], an overview of safety categories is provided, and a COST acceptance process is proposed.

In the space domain, software reuse is addressed by ECSS-Q-80 [10] and ECSS-E-40 [11], which can be considered as the two main European standards for product assurance and software engineering of space software applications. These standards use the terms Pre-Developed Software (PDS), COTS, OTS and MOTS (Modifiable-Off-The-Shelf). Reuse of PDS includes software from previous (internal or external) projects or supplied by the customer that are to be used as is or with adaptation.

In a space system, software reuse has to be performed differently depending on the specific system level that is targeted. A space system can be divided into *space segment software*, that corresponds to the software executed on-board of the spacecraft and also software for launchers; *ground segment software*, that corresponds to the software performing on ground the various mission support functions required by space projects; *EGSE* (Electrical Ground Support Equipment) software and real-time simulators, to check the spacecraft status and provides system and software test and training and test facilities; and *support software*, that corresponds to all other software not belonging to the previous categories.

Along with proprietary systems like EPOCH and Virtuoso, Open Source Software (OSS) is yet another compelling issue when addressing reuse of PDS, especially regarding maintenance aspects and documentation availability. The space industry, and ESA in particular, have been looking at OSS for quite a long time. SCOS 2000 [12] for instance, a reusable platform for ground segment systems, is one successful case of a space OSS product. However, it is commonly accepted that there is still a huge set of benefits to be taken if reuse of ground segment software is leveraged by also reusing e.g. test plans and test infrastructures, or even in-service history. A remarkable case of reuse of OSS in the space segment is the RTEMS [13] adoption as the basic real-time kernel for the on-board data handling of the Herschel-Planck missions. Suitability of RTEMS to this operational environment regarding its robustness, maintainability, documentation, etc., are matters that have also been tackled by the PA-PDS study.

A major conclusion drawn from the PA-PDS study regarding the existing practice within space projects was that reuse is performed occasionally (or informally) rather than systematically, independently of the space system level considered. Indeed, the reuse that occurs to date in space projects is quite often performed through the 'reuse' of key personnel from other (earlier) projects, who informally select and reuse items such as plans, documents or code. This is partly due to the fact that most companies in the space business do not implement reuse at an organizational level. There exists an important lack of processes and infrastructures effectively supporting reuse, for example a process to identify potentially reusable items, or a common repository of reusable software components. This informal practice of performing reuse in the space business today does not allow for a systematic reduction of time-to-market and development costs.

3 The ESA Study on Product Assurance Aspects of Reuse

PA-PDS is a European Space Agency study about the reuse of Pre-Developed Software (PDS) in space projects. The main contribution of this study consists of the definition of a set of requirements that support the acquisition, evaluation, integration and maintenance of PDS to be reused in a new development of a space system. From these requirements, a method for achieving systematic software reuse in an organization has been proposed, which accounts for both technical and organizational issues.

The problem of PDS reuse was primarily approached from a product assurance perspective. Software product assurance aims at providing adequate confidence to both the customer and the suppliers that the software satisfies the applicable requirements throughout the whole project lifecycle. The software product assurance areas targeted during the study were the following: development lifecycle phases, quality models, product evaluation and certification, risk management, safety and dependability methods and techniques, and process assessment.

Based on an extensive survey and analysis of both industry and research literature and software standards, an extensive set of product assurance requirements covering the mentioned areas and some associated processes were defined taking into account software reuse. The scope of these requirements naturally depends on the circumstances of reuse. Indeed, it is not the same to reuse a commercial real-time operating system that runs on a satellite, or a mathematical routine that processes off-line data received from that satellite. These different reuse scenarios are called PDS types, and are used to characterize (or tailor) each individual requirement.

A set of top-level requirements was also identified that would facilitate an organization to move from occasional reuse to systematic reuse. This transition would be necessary to achieve significant benefits from the application of software reuse. The proposed requirements take into account technical and organizational aspects, and target different groups within industry and ESA, such as product assurance personnel, project managers and software engineers.

The reuse related requirements may be summarized as follows:

1. "The same product assurance activities that are applied to custom developed software shall be applied to PDS". This includes verification and validation activities, risk assessment or quality/certification metrics measurement. Indeed, the reuse scenario is never exactly the same as the one where the reused asset was originally developed, and even tiny differences can lead to catastrophic events, as the accident in the maiden flight of Ariane 5 has clearly shown. This might look like jeopardizing the potential benefit of reuse, but this is not necessarily the case, since also the support documentation required to apply those quality assurance methods can largely be reused.
2. "Black-box PDS[1] shall be avoided for the highest criticality level functions". As far as practicable, only the simplest functions of the black-box PDS shall be used.
3. "Deactivated[2] and dead[3] code of a reused PDS shall be controlled or removed". Deactivated and dead code should only be allowed to remain in the final application where it can be shown that the risks of leaving it are less than the risks of removing it.
4. "Reused software shall be supported by all the elements based on which the decision for reusing was taken". The reused PDS should consist of a package containing not only code, but also specifications, design documentation, test suites, safety and dependability analyses, quality metrics as appropriate, in order to provide the evidence that the candidate PDS is "fit for purpose" for its intended use in the new environment. Otherwise, the cost savings may be significantly lower than initially expected, or not relevant enough to justify reuse. Note that the customer will be contrary to the idea of accepting intensive reuse of software in highly critical systems unless it is provided with enough safety and dependability evidence.
5. "In-service history shall be used to provide the evidence that the candidate PDS will meet the project requirements when it is not possible to satisfy them directly". This may be the situation when source code or design documentation are not available, for example, but also when significant costs can be saved through the use of in-service history. However, in-service history always requires negotiation between the developers and the customer/certification authority/system safety responsible. In particular, it should be determined whether the previous usage profile of the candidate PDS is relevant enough to the reuse scenario.

---

[1] *Black-box PDS*: Assets for which the source code is not available to the reusers.

[2] *Deactivated code*: It is executable object code (or data) which by design is either (a) not intended to be executed (code) or used (data), or (b) only executed (code) or used (data) in certain configurations of the target computer environment.

[3] *Dead code*: It is executable object code (or data) which, as a result of a design error, cannot be executed (code) or used (data) in a operational configuration of the target computer environment and is not traceable to a system or software requirement.

Most of the above is covered in ECSS-Q-80, subclauses 6.2.3, 6.2.6 and 6.2.7. In addition, the following considerations should be taken into account in order to achieve profitable reuse:

6. Reuse should be considered when time and budget savings are envisaged. Also the benefit of using a 'proven/mature' product might motivate reuse". To benefit from reuse, there needs to be a systematic consideration of reuse aspects during the requirements specification phases of a project lifecycle. Flexibility for waivers might be necessary. The customer should be ready to accept non-compliances to accommodate a reuse offer involving aspects like functional requirements and non-functional requirements (e.g., design/programming languages, V&V tools). During this negotiation, the supplier should demonstrate that the acceptance of non-compliances is also profitable for the customer (e.g., because of a reduction of effort and development costs).
7. In order to introduce systematic reuse in an organization, the following new processes would need to be established: reuse program management process, asset management process, and domain engineering process. These are the fundamental processes necessary to achieve a systematic application of software reuse in an organization: (i) reuse program management process (to plan, establish, manage, control, and monitor an organization's reuse program), (ii) asset management process (to apply administrative and technical procedures throughout the lifetime of the reusable assets), and (iii) domain engineering process (to identify, develop and maintain models and architectures for a particular engineering domain).

These recommendations are the core of the whole set of product assurance requirements proposed to support the acquisition, evaluation, integration and maintenance of Pre-Developed Software to be reused in a new space system development. Many other requirements and guidelines were produced under the study, and they are available at [14].

4 Proposed Extensions to the Space Standards

This section summarizes the list of extensions (or change requests) about software reuse that have been proposed under the PA-PDS study for inclusion into the ECSS standards.

The European Cooperation for Space Standardization (ECSS) [18] is an initiative established to develop a single and coherent set of user-friendly standards for use in all European space activities and particularly projects. The European space industry has been fully associated with ECSS from the outset. The main two ECSS standards for software product assurance and software engineering are respectively ECSS-Q-80 [10] and ECSS-E-40 [11]. These two standards are then further developed into dedicated lower level standards (the so-called "Level 3 standards"), which are aimed at describing methods, procedures and recommended tools to satisfy the requirements of the higher-level standards on specific aspects (e.g. software dependability, software process assessment, software quality models and metrication, software life cycles, etc). The Level 3 standards constitute supporting guidelines and are allowed to be adapted to the project needs, but they do not introduce new requirements in any case.

Due to the detailed nature of the recommendations and guidelines derived from the PA-PDS study, most of these will fit better in the corresponding Level 3 standards addressing software reuse (not yet available) than in the main ECSS-Q-80 and ECSS-E-40 standards.

Both standards already cover most of the requirements for software reuse at a high level. The proposed changes and extensions aim at elaborating the existing requirements so as to provide a more precise and structured coverage of software reuse that the European space industry can readily apply. The proposed changes relate to product assurance aspects and include guidelines for (i) PDS acquisition and problem resolution processes, (ii) development with reuse, (iii) PDS quality assurance and (iv) PDS safety assessment. As far as software engineering aspects is concerned, the extensions cover (i) reuse domain engineering, (ii) generic reuse engineering activities, (iii) planning and management activities involving PDS, (iv) PDS architectural design and maintenance, (v) common lifecycle reuse activities and (vi) PDS verification and validation activities.

A full description of these extensions can be found in [14]. The most significant extensions proposed to the product assurance standards are summarized hereafter:

- *PDS quality assurance*. The quality assurance requirements for PDS reuse are aimed at guaranteeing that changes to the software lifecycle processes due to PDS reuse, including assessment activities, are foreseen in the software plans. Also, space quality models for software products integrating PDS should define metrics aimed at characterizing and quantifying (i) static properties (*internal metrics*), (ii) dynamic properties (*external metrics*), and (iii) the extent to which the needs of different kinds of users are met (*quality in use metrics*).
- *PDS dependability and safety assessment.* Dependability and safety critical PDS software whether modified or not, shall be subject to the same software dependability and safety analysis and testing requirements as the software that was specifically developed under the project. At the acquisition stage, PDS shall be analyzed for dependability and safety related concerns following the steps presented in Fig. 1.

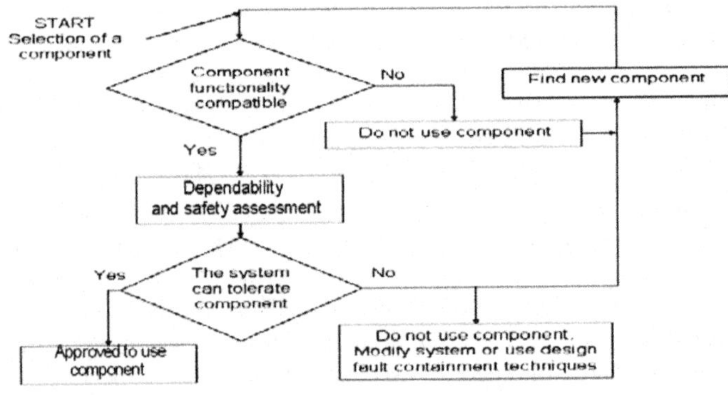

Fig. 1. PDS usage assessment for dependability and safety related systems

The policy for the use of PDS in dependability critical applications should also define the criteria for acceptability (e.g., provision of in-service data of the PDS).

The following are the most significant extensions proposed to the software engineering standards:

- *Generic reuse engineering activities.* Any re-user shall perform the generic reuse engineering activities at all development lifecycle phases for the potential reuse of any asset (requirements, documents, templates, code, etc.). These activities are the following: (i) asset search and selection (from reuse repositories, other on-going internal projects, or outside suppliers), (ii) asset assessment (of non-functional requirements such as safety and dependability), (iii) asset integration (into each lifecycle phase), and (iv) feedback of asset impact (regarding the reusability or usability of the reused assets).
- *Common lifecycle reuse activities.* An analysis of the potential reusability of assets shall be performed for any project at any stage of the development lifecycle. The following assets should specially be considered for reuse: templates, proposals, system and software requirements, software architectures, software designs, test requirements, test cases, test procedures, test data, internal/external interfaces, databases and user documentation.
- *PDS verification and validation activities.* The verification and validation requirements for PDS reuse shall be the same as for software developed without reuse. The difference is that some already existing verification and validation plans and results may be available with the reused products. However, the full verification and validation requirements apply to reused software as for any other part of the software development.

These proposed extensions to the ECSS standards, together with the top-level requirements described in Section 0, constitute two of the main results of the PA-PDS study. However, many other interesting results (available at [14]) were produced under the study, in particular: (i) the proposed extension of SPICE for Space (S4S) with two new reuse-related processes [15][16], (ii) the definition of PDS types for reuse in space projects, (iii) a technical specification of tools supporting reusable component repositories, (iv) two pilot projects based on the reuse of SCOS 2000 [12] and OBOSS-II [17] in the Herschel-Plank satellite missions, and (v) tutorial materials for managers and technical personnel.

In order to allow the European space industry to effectively benefit from this study, the main results will be proposed for inclusion into the ECSS standards. All proposed extensions will be critically assessed for their suitability to be incorporated into a Level 3 product assurance standard about software reuse or into a Level 3 software engineering standard on reuse. At the time of writing this paper, a recently created working group (ECSS-Q-80-01, "Re-use of existing software", initiated on May 2004) is already addressing the first point. A working group that will address the second point (ECSS-E-40-06, "Guidelines for reuse engineering") is still in the proposal phase.

5 Conclusions and Future Work

The PA-PDS study suggests that careful reuse of software has the potential to lower development costs and shorten development cycles, while fulfilling the stringent dependability and safety requirements of space projects. A set of requirements was defined to support the reuse of Pre-Developed Software (PDS) of different types (e.g., open source software, tools with no visibility of the source code, etc.). From these requirements, a method for systematic software reuse was proposed, which is intended to help the European space industry achieve full benefits from the application of software reuse. These new requirements and the industrial processes they describe, are proposed for inclusion into the main European space standards on product assurance and software engineering (i.e., ECSS-Q-80 and ECSS-E-40). A working group composed of people coming from well-known companies and institutions in the European space business today (e.g., EADS Astrium, Alcatel Space, Alenia Spazio, CNES, DLR, ESA, etc.), is currently producing a new standard specifically addressing product assurance aspects of reuse. Some new aspects derived from the PA-PDS study will be proposed for inclusion in this standard. This new standard will be available for public review by mid 2005.

From a subcontractor viewpoint, although reuse can improve productivity and quality, there might be some resistance to implement reuse for several reasons: (i) reuse currently entails an extra effort to 'prove' the product meets the project requirements (both domain and product assurance aspects), (ii) reuse means any customer has an expectation to pay less for the work, (iii) investment is restricted due to project-by-project funding and schedule pressures, and (iv) significant productivity and quality gains are generally only achieved when items are used several times for space project software (at least 3 or 4 times when systematic reuse is occurring). Indeed, the implementation of systematic reuse, which is necessary for companies to obtain significant benefits from reuse in the long term, is not an easy task to put into practice. That is the reason why customers should promote systematic reuse with the main aim of helping industry to move from occasional (or informal) reuse to systematic reuse. This matter of implementation of reuse can be divided into three steps: (i) further study of current reuse practices in industry, (ii) collection of available reusable information (e.g., quality metrics, candidate PDS, etc.), and (iii) establishment of a precise roadmap on how to progress from occasional reuse to systematic reuse. These ideas set the basis for future projects and studies.

References

[1] http://www.integ.com/EPOCHV4.htm
[2] http://www.windriver.com/news/press/20010402a.html
[3] MIL-STD-498, Military Standard, Software Development And Documentation, December 1994
[4] ED12B, Software Considerations in Airborne Systems and Equipment Certification, EUROCAE, December 1992 (identical to RTCA/DO-178B http://www.rtca.org)
[5] Guidelines for applying the RTCA/DO-178B level D criteria to Previously Developed Software (PDS) US Department of Transportation. FAA, 26/3/99

[6] SAE ARP 4754, Certification considerations for highly-integrated or complex aircraft systems

[7] EN 50128 Railway applications - Software for Railway control and protection systems (http://www.cenorm.be)

[8] Software for computers in the safety systems on nuclear power stations. Part 2: Software Aspects of defence against common cause failures, use of software tools and of pre-developed software, CEI IEC 60880-2

[9] UCRL-ID-122526, A Proposed Acceptance Process for Commercial Off-the-Shelf (COTS) Software in Reactor Application, U.S Nuclear Regulatory Commission, September 1995

[10] ECSS-Q-80B, ECSS Space Product Assurance, Software Product Assurance, 10 October 2003

[11] ECSS-E-40B, Part 1B ECSS Space Engineering, Software, 19 June 2003

[12] SCOS 2000, http://esapub.esrin.esa.it/bulletin/bullet108/kaufeler.pdf

[13] http://www.rtems.org/

[14] ftp://ftp.estec.esa.nl/pub/tos-qq/qqs/PDS/

[15] J.G. Silva, M. Rodríguez, D. Costa, H.v. Loon, P. Rodríguez-Dapena, K. Pederson, F. Aldea-Montero, "Product Assurance of Software Reuse in the SPICE for Space Framework", Proc. of the 4th Intl SPICE Conference on Process Assessment and Improvement (SPICE 2004), Lisbon, Portugal, April 28-29, 2004.

[16] Han Van Loon, Robert Dietze, Fernando Aldea-Montero, "Software Reuse and SPICE for Space", Proc. of SPICE 2003 - Joint ESA - 3rd International SPICE Conference on Process Assessment and Improvement, ESTEC, Noordwijk, The Netherlands, March 17-21, 2003.

[17] http://spd-web.terma.com/Projects/OBOSS/Home_Page/

[18] http://www.ecss.nl/

Ten Signs of a Good Reuse Management Plan

Edwin Morris, Wm B. Anderson, Mary Catherine Ward,
and Dennis Smith

SEI/CMU
Pittsburgh, PA
www.sei.cmu.edu

Abstract. A Reuse Management Plan defines the strategy for selecting, approving and upgrading common reusable software components The SEI, in conjunction with the U.S. Army, the Boeing Company, and the Fraunhofer USA Center for Experimental Software Engineering, is developing a Reuse Management Plan for a large Army program. Ten critical features of quality Reuse Management Plans have been identified and are presented..

1 Introduction

Commercial, military, and other government organizations continue to increase their reliance on reused software to provide major capabilities in new systems. This reused software goes by many different labels, including: commercial off the shelf (COTS), government off the shelf (GOTS), shareware, freeware, open source, and non-developmental items. While the sources of these types of software vary, they have two key characteristics in common from the perspective of an organization attempting to use them: imprecise knowledge of the internals (e.g., architecture, design, assumptions, and dependencies) and limited control over the evolution of the component.

Too frequently, organizations are disappointed in their experience using such reused software components. This is particularly the case when components are being used for large scale "systems of systems" where components can have unforeseen affect on other parts of the system. Often, the problems experienced can be directly traced to imprecise knowledge and limited control that result in faulty selection processes, conflicts between components, inappropriate integration strategies and inability to sustain the component across the system life cycle.

Acknowledgements. We wish to thank Sue Hermanson and Sam Montgomery of Boeing Company and Michele Shaw of the Fraunhofer USA Center for Experimental Software Engineering, University of Maryland for their collaboration in developing the Reuse Management Plan from which this paper was abstracted. We believe this collaboration of industry and academic experts has led to a good, and still improving, approach for managing the incorporation and sustainment of reused components.

X. Franch and D. Port (Eds.): ICCBSS 2005, LNCS 3412, pp. 268–277, 2005.

2 The Ten Critical Features

Careful planning for appropriate processes, techniques and artifacts can help organizations avoid or overcome common problems associated with reuse. Boeing Company, supported by the Fraunhofer USA Center for Experimental Software Engineering and the Software Engineering Institute, is defining such a plan to manage commercial and other reused software on a large government program. While the details of the plan are beyond the scope of this paper, ten critical characteristics of the plan are presented here. We believe that the following characteristics are fundamental to plans addressing long term use of complex "reusable" software:

- A product line strategy
- An iterative process
- A component manager
- Risk-based management of components
- Full lifecycle coverage
- Aggressive evaluation and selection of components
- Careful configuration and change management
- A complete historical record
- A component health checkup
- Metrics that lead to improvement

These essential characteristics are discussed in sections 2.1-2.10.

2.1 A Product Line Strategy

In standard reuse approaches, a reusable asset is discovered, modified as appropriate[1], and installed in the product. While this saves some development time, this "clone-and-own" method makes each system unique, with maintenance and evolution no longer shared with other members of the family. Where several similar systems will be developed within a market segment or performing a specific mission, organizations should strive to create a software product line.

A software product line is a set of software-intensive systems sharing a common, managed set of features that satisfy the specific needs of a particular market segment or mission and that are developed from a common set of core assets in a prescribed way. Reusable core assets include software components, but also the associated documentation, architecture, software design, Application Programming Interface (API), user interface design, test plans, test cases, schedules and budgets, development processes, and more. Building a set of software systems as a software product line has been shown [1] to dramatically shorten development time, increase productivity, increase quality, and reduce cost, as compared to developing the systems one at a time in isolation from each other. In effect, where several similar systems will ultimately be developed, a product line strategy presents an opportunity to maximize reuse.

[1] The phrase "as appropriate" is critical. We do not advocate the modification of some sorts of reusable components, conspicuously including COTS.

To effectively implement a software product line, the Reuse Management Plan should define processes for:

- determining when a product line is appropriate
- developing a flexible product line architecture
- identifying the key (core) components within the product line
- building a production plan that describes how the core components will be reused
- developing and following construction management process to control maintenance and evolution of the product line.

Information about creating and using software product lines can be found in Software Product Lines, Practices & Patterns [1].

2.2 An Iterative Process

Use of existing components like COTS products does not lend itself to waterfall type development, since neither reuseable components nor our understanding of them is static. Managing the dynamic nature of components and their interactions with each other and the rest of the system is a key to effective reuse. The processes identified within a reuse management plan must support mechanisms for reconsideration and re-execution of steps as more is known about components through better understanding and risk reduction activities.

Several iterative processes have been developed and are appropriate for systems employing reusable components. Traditional approaches require early and complete knowledge of a system's requirements and architecture, often a very difficult task to accomplish. The Win-Win Spiral [2] simplifies this requirement development through a series of risk reduction cycles. The Rational Unified Process [3] focuses on iterations that lead to increasing understanding of the developing system through successive refinements. The Evolutionary Process for Integrating COTS based systems [4] adapts RUP to use for systems that make significant use of commercial components. Each of these processes incorporates strategies that support:

- Iterative refinement of system requirements, architectures, and reuse component commitments to balance the tension between operational needs and implementation expedience enabling efficient reuse of components.
- Early identification of risks and application of risk mitigation strategies.

By employing an iterative process, an organization not only improves a system under construction, but positions itself to leverage advances in reuse component technology that become available during system development and sustainment.

2.3 A Reuse Component Manager

Another key to successful reuse of components is the consolidation of management activities involving that component under a central authority. This authority serves as the clearing house for information, the organizer of reviews and other tasks, and the "belly button" to push for the component. To support this effort, each component considered for reuse should be assigned a *Reuse Component Manager*. The Reuse Component Manager's responsibilities include:

- Notifying affected organizations of plans or changes to plans for use of a component
- Organizing and stewarding lifecycle activities such as component (re)evaluations, version upgrades, analysis of patches, reviews health checks (see section 2.10)
- Monitoring existing and communicating new risks associated with use of the component
- Coordinating and consolidating impact statements for/from users affected by use of, changes to, or problems with a component
- Identifying and planning for major component upgrades and end of life
- Ensuring that information about the component is up-to-date and complete
- Directing market watch activities for the component
- Developing and implementing a strategy to create and manage vendor/provider relationships
- Establishing liaisons with other customers (or potential customers) of the vendor/provider

The Reuse Component Manager can delegate responsibility for certain activities to other parties, but retains oversight authority and responsibility.

2.4 Risk-Based Management of Components

Components differ along dimensions such as size, complexity and cost. More complex and expensive components commonly represent higher risk to a program. However, there are many other component characteristics – and characteristics of how a component is used in the system – that suggest greater attention be paid to component management.

For example, the degree to which a reused component is isolated (or alternately, loosely or tightly coupled) to the system should influence the rigor of the processes for component evaluation, integration, testing, upgrade, and many other activities. However, a reused component can be coupled to a system in many ways. Some ways are obvious (e.g., exposed interfaces and/or data provided to or received from other parts of the system) while others are not (e.g., expectations about timing, sequencing, quality of service, testing and maintenance constraints, and configuration dependencies).

In general, virtually any characteristic of a component or component provider may increase the risk to a specific system. Each system owner must determine the characteristics of reuse components that present significant risk and develop processes that mitigate component risk by encouraging:

- Increased rigor of evaluation activities
- Enhanced engineering focus on the component and its interactions with the rest of the system
- Problem and risk reporting that quickly elevates problems with high risk components
- Detailed processes for validating and approving patches and upgrades
- Increased frequency and depth of review

In short, not all components are alike. A process that does not distinguish between types of components based on the risk they present is likely to give short shrift to the most critical components – and may also increase the expense of managing less critical components.

2.5 Full Lifecycle Coverage

Obviously, selecting and carefully integrating reuse components is a key to successful use. However, our experience suggests that, like for developed software, long term costs of maintaining reused code often exceed initial procurement costs. Reuse components create unique lifecycle challenges, since the evolution of the component and lifecycle milestones are typically outside the control of the program. The challenges that should be addressed in the Reuse Management Plan include[2]:

- Impact of reuse components on requirements elicitation and management processes
- Market survey, evaluation, and selection of reuse components
- Guidance on architecting, designing, integrating, and testing with reuse components
- Risk identification and management for reuse components
- Problem reporting and management
- Analysis of the impact on the reused component due to changes in system requirements, architecture, design, and other components
- Analysis of the impact on the system from changes in the component (e.g., new versions, how the component is used) as well as for problems and potential patches
- License management
- Management of minor and major upgrades
- Configuration management of versions, tailoring and integration code, tests, etc.
- Component tracking and market watch
- Deployment planning, training and support
- Managing relationships with component providers
- Metrics for reuse components
- Periodic reviews of component health (health check)

The Reuse Management Plan is not intended to stand on its own. Many of the activities addressed in the Reuse Management Plan will be closely tied to activities in other (e.g., Software Development, Risk Management, CM) plans. Overall, plans should present a consistent and holistic approach to development and sustainment of all types of components – reused or custom built.

The lifecycle direction provided by the Reuse Management Plan should be available early in the software lifecycle – typically long before handover of the system to a maintenance organization.

2.6 Aggressive Evaluation and Selection of Components

The potential cost associated with faulty selection of a reuse component can be large. These costs include not only licensing and other acquisition fees, but also additional cost associated with incorporating, testing, or applying patches to upgrade the faulty

---

2 Several of these lifecycle topics (configuration management, metrics, health check) are addressed in separate sections. They are included here for completeness.

component. Even worse, there is often a "design cost" associated with poor component selection. In some cases, this is the cost of rework that must be done to incorporate a new component. In other cases, this cost is evident in engineering compromises that lead to poor capability and performance, increased sustainment effort, and unhappy users.

The best (and only) defense against selection of an inappropriate reuse component is a good offense in the form of a wide ranging and aggressive evaluation and selection process for components that are documented as part of the Reuse Management Plan. The components of this process include:

- A make-reuse decision that is based on analysis of the expectations for the component within the system and of the marketplace (commercial or otherwise) of components that can be reused. This analysis should address characteristics of the marketplace, components and vendors within the marketplace, and other users of the components.
- Organized (rather than ad hoc) planning for evaluation and selection of components.
- Wide ranging evaluation criteria that address many aspects of the component, including:
  - Functional suitability
  - Architectural compatibility
  - Standards
  - Component development process suitability
  - Dependencies on other software and hardware
  - Interoperability with other components (reused and custom coded)
  - Human-Machine interface
  - Performance, reliability, safety, security, and other quality attributes
  - Provider suitability, including trust, processes, reputation, etc.
  - Patches, version upgrade and support
  - Licensing
  - Required tailoring and adaptation to the system
- Defined processes for evaluation and selection of components. [5] and [6] provide guidance on evaluation and selection of large scale assets (like subsystems) and COTS components, respectively. These processes can be modified to fit other types of reuse components.
- Mechanisms for capturing not only information about components, but also suggested impact of components on requirements, architecture, design, implementation, testing, and deployment of the system

Regardless of the care taken in evaluation and selection, changes in components and in the system can lead to additional evaluations to determine whether a component remains viable, or to replace a component. As expressed by one expert[3], you need to employ a sound selection process, then "pick a horse and ride it until the legs fall off".

---

[3] Anonymity preserved at the speaker's request

2.7 Careful Configuration and Change Management

We are all familiar with situations where a necessary upgrade of one system component (reused or custom) cascades into upgrades of other system components due to dependencies among components. We are also familiar with the frequent releases of software incorporating critical fixes for security holes and flaws. Such forced upgrades often have a major affect on system development activities, and can become the major factor in long term sustainment of the system. Managing software evolution is a critical problem for any program.

Managing the evolution of reused components is particularly difficult due to the rapid rate and uncertain direction (at least for us) of component evolution. A good Reuse Management Plan must provide the foundation for orderly evolution of reuse components through sound configuration and change management processes that include:

- Processes for building and maintaining a matrix of dependencies between reuse components and other system components[4]
- Configuration management processes that maintain a wide range of information related to reuse components and component versions, including:
  - executables, versions, and patches
  - documentation of other reused assets such as architecture and design,
  - source code (when applicable), integration code, tailoring, parameters
  - initial data loads
  - installation scripts
  - unit, system, and integration tests, test data, and results
  - training materials and documentation
  - licenses and other information for various installation sites
  - site-related variations in reuse components
  - incompatibilities with other components (hardware and software)
  - limitations/restrictions for use
- Reporting and change management processes that:
  - support the identification of problems and other system changes related to reuse components
  - determine the scope of the impact
  - involve affected parties in determining solutions
  - manage the rate of release and upgrade to affected parties

The configuration management approach must do more than identify configurations. It must support the management, engineering, and sustainment of systems with reused components.

2.8 A Complete Historical Record

Central to any good reuse management plan is complete documentation about reuse components considered, selected and used within the system. While some of this

---

[4] Note that dependencies are not limited to the API, and often include data provided (or received) directly and through intermediaries, expectations regarding memory, timing, or other qualities, and constraints regarding development, testing and other strategies.

information is maintained by good configuration and change management practices (Section 2.7), additional historical information should be maintained that is normally outside of the scope of the configuration or change management. This is particular important for situations where the system is developed by one or more organizations under contract to another organization. (e.g., the system owner). In this scenario, the system owner normally maintains oversight authority, as is typical of many government sponsored development efforts.

The data gathered should reflect the many engineering activities, management decisions, and history of component use. Data should include:

- Information and analysis of market segments
- Make-reuse decision rationale
- History of evaluation/selection of reuse components, including criteria, rationale for criteria, data/results of evaluation and rationale for selection
- History of communications with component supplier, including documentation of all commitments and decisions.
- Pointers to risks and risk mitigation strategies associated with reuse components
- History and lessons learned regarding version releases
- Metric data and analysis
- Links to relevant information in other software artifact plans, documents, and repositories (e.g., management, engineering, problem reporting, configuration management, installation, training).
- Results of periodic reviews and component health checks

Even the best historical data is of little value if it is not useful for making decisions about components. Organizations should review the strategy for maintaining history with the intent of improving the quality and value of the data gathered.

2.9 A Component Health Checkup

The status of reuse components should be reviewed on a frequent (e.g., bi-annual) basis to determine whether existing strategies toward use of the component remain valid. We call this review a component health checkup, because we like the analogy to a periodic procedure performed by expert personnel who look both for symptoms of common problems and listen carefully for hints about developing problems[5].

The Health Checkup is commonly organized and chaired by the component manager. Attendance is open to representatives of all affected users as well as suppliers of components, as appropriate.

The health checkup normally considers four primary sources of information:

- Information gathered by the component manager while performing his/her activities (e.g, vendor/provider relationships, user interactions and problems, changes to plans and strategies).
- Information summarized from tracking the reuse component (e.g., problems, risks, patches, versions, vendor plans)

[5] We first became familiar with the phrase "health check" as applied to periodic review of COTS products through documentation provided to us by the Air Force's Global Broadcast System Program.

- Information gathered during market watch activities that track intermediate and long term direction of the market in which the component is placed (e.g., new technologies, shifting or failing market positioning)
- Information from users about evolving expectations for the component

The results of the health checkup are used to build or modify plans for component use, initiate risk reduction and iterative development cycles, initiate new make/buy/reuse decisions and component evaluations, and for other purposes identified by the checkup team.

2.10 Metrics That Lead to Improvement

The typical metric associated with reuse components is an equivalent SLOC count that is intended to represent the effective savings of procuring rather than building the component. Often this count includes measures of the integration effort associated with the component. This information is rightly used as one important consideration during the evaluation and selection process.

Later in the development process, actual performance in incorporating the reuse component against earlier estimates is often tracked. While this information is useful, other readily available (if less formal) data can provide good insight into progress and success in using a reuse component. This data includes:

- Instability of requirements related to reuse components can serve as an early indicator of changing expectations that can potentially complicate or even preclude component reuse.
- A summary and (more importantly) analysis of defects in reuse components can indicate many problems, some characteristic of the component, such as poor component engineering and technological immaturity, and some characteristic of the system engineering activity incorporating the component (e.g., inadequate evaluation and selection practices, overly optimistic expectations, use of a component outside its intended environment)
- Changing contacts and inconsistent information from contacts may indicate emerging problems, issues, and risks related to component suppliers
- Slipping or overly frequent release schedules may hint at engineering and quality problems
- Increasing quantity or complexity of adaptation code and data (e.g., tailoring, wrapping, data loads) developed for incorporating the component into the system may hint at insufficiently detailed evaluation criteria or poor engineering practices and decisions
- Periodic survey/analysis of the Reuse Management Plan processes, are they sufficient, too complicated, being used?

As with any good metric its utility is evidenced by its contribution to improving the processes that are being measured. Don't collect data for the sake of data; use it to reveal what process changes are leading to process improvements.

3 Conclusions

The lifecycle management of reusable software components is a complex task that requires preparation equal to that required for custom developed code. A large Army program has provided the ideal venue to explore these complexities and document solutions in a Reuse Management Plan.

Key features of that plan are abstracted and presented in this paper. While no plan can guarantee success in reusing software components, careful planning *and project follow-through* that addresses these features can mitigate many risks.

Our next step will be to produce a detailed template of a Reuse Management Plan that organizations can draw from when creating their own plans. In the mean time, the information in this paper can help organizations get started.

References

1. Clements, P. & Northrop, L.M. *Software Product Lines: Practices and Patterns.* Addison-Wesley Professional, SEI Series in Software Engineering, New York, August, 2001.
2. Boehm, B. "A Spiral Model of Software Development and Enhancement." *IEEE Computer*, 21, 2 (February 1998): 61-72.
3. Kruchten, P. *The Rational Unified Process: An Introduction,* 2nd ed. New York, NY: Addison-Wesley Object Technology Series, March 2000.
4. Albert, C. and Brownsword, Lisa. Evolutionary Process for Integrating COTS-Based Systems (EPIC). SEI Technical Report CMU/SEI-2002-TR-005. Carnegie Mellon University, Software Engineering Institute, November, 2002.
5. Bergey, J.; O'Brien, L.; Smith, D.. Options Analysis for Reengineering (OAR): A Method for Mining Legacy Assets. SEI Technical Note CMU/SEI-2001-TN-013. Carnegie Mellon University, Software Engineering Institute
6. Comella-Dorda, S., Dean, J., Lewis, G., Morris, E., Oberndorf, p., and Harper, E. ; A Process for COTS Software Product Evaluation. SEI Technical Report CMU/SEI-2003-TR-017. Carnegie Mellon University, Software Engineering Institute, July, 2004

Preliminary Results from a State-of-the-Practice Survey on Risk Management in Off-the-Shelf Component-Based Development

Jingyue Li[1], Reidar Conradi[1,2], Odd Petter N. Slyngstad[1], Marco Torchiano[3], Maurizio Morisio[3], and Christian Bunse[4]

[1] Department of Computer and Information Science,
Norwegian University of Science and Technology (NTNU),
NO-7491 Trondheim, Norway
{jingyue, conradi, oslyngst}@idi.ntnu.no
[2] Simula Research Laboratory, P.O.BOX 134, NO-1325 Lysaker, Norway
[3] Dip.Automatica e Informatica, Politecnico di Torino,
Corso Duca degli Abruzzi, 24, I-10129 Torino, Italy
{morisio, marco.torchiano}@polito.it
[4] Fraunhofer IESE, Sauerwiesen 6,
D-67661 Kaiserslautern, Germany
Christian.Bunse@iese.fraunhofer.de

Abstract. Software components, both Commercial-Off-The-Shelf and Open Source, are being increasingly used in software development. Previous studies have identified typical risks and related risk management strategies for what we will call OTS-based (Off-the-Shelf) development. However, there are few effective and well-proven guidelines to help project managers to identify and manage these risks. We are performing an international state-of-the-practice survey in three countries - Norway, Italy, and Germany - to investigate the relative frequency of typical risks, and the effect of the corresponding risk management methods. Preliminary results show that risks concerning changing requirements and effort estimation are the most frequent risks. Risks concerning traditional quality attributes such as reliability and security of OTS component seem less frequent. Incremental testing and strict quality evaluation have been used to manage the possible negative impact of poor component quality. Realistic effort estimation on OTS quality evaluation helped to mitigate the possible effort estimation biases in OTS component selection and integration.

1 Introduction

OTS components (Off-The-Shelf) includes COTS (Commercial-Off-The-Shelf) and OSS (Open Source Software) components. More and more software projects start to use OTS components. However, using such external components introduces many risks [1, 3, 4, 5]. Before project managers decide to acquire an external component, instead of building it in-house, they must identify possible risks. Although several risks and risk management strategies in OTS-based development have been identified [1-7, 10, 11, 14] from case studies, few empirical studies have been done to verify

X. Franch and D. Port (Eds.): ICCBSS 2005, LNCS 3412, pp. 278–288, 2005.

their conclusions. As a result, software project managers have few effective and well-proven guidelines to identify the relative effects of the various risks, and to manage them properly.

We designed a questionnaire to perform a state-of-the-practice study on risk management in OTS component-based development. The survey is being performed in three European countries (Norway, Italy, and Germany). We currently have gathered 42 filled-in questionnaires.

The findings of this study show that some risks are more frequent than others, such as the ability of OTS components to follow requirement changes, and estimating effort in component selection and integration. Results also show that some risk management methods, such as serious consideration of quality of the component in the selection process, helped to mitigate effort estimation risks in the selection and integration phases.

The rest of this paper is organized as follows: Section 2 introduces some related work. Section 3 describes our research design. Section 4 presents the preliminary results, and Section 5 discusses them. Conclusions and future work are presented in section 6.

2 Background

Risks are factors that may adversely affect a project, unless project managers take appropriate countermeasures. Risk management in software development has been studied for many years [8, 9, 15, 18]. These studies have proposed classical risks and risk management in software development. In addition to the classical risks associated with developing large systems, OTS components requires managers to modify their typical mitigation strategies for some of the classic risks and to develop new mitigation strategies for risks that are particular to the use of OTS component in a system.

2.1 Risks in OTS Component-Based Development

Different stakeholders, such as component providers, component integrators, and customers, may face different kinds of risks [12]. Risks relevant to the component integrators in OTS components-based development are a subset of risks in component-based development [12], COTS-based development [1,3, 14], and Open Source based development [11]. Typical risks in OTS components-based cover different phases of a project as showed in Table 1.

2.2 Risk Management in OTS Component-Based Development

To manage possible risks in OTS component-based development, some previous studies have proposed risk management strategies based on case studies and lessons learned [1, 3, 14, 18]. The most typical ones are summarized in Table 2.

Table 1. Typical risks in OTS-component based development

Phase	ID	Possible risks
Project plan phase	R1	The project was delivered long after schedule [1].
	R2	Effort to select OTS components was not satisfactorily estimated [3].
	R3	Effort to integrate OTS components was not satisfactorily estimated [1].
Requirement phase	R4	Requirement were changed a lot [3].
	R5	OTS components could not be sufficiently adapted to changing requirements [3].
	R6	It is not possible to (re) negotiate requirements with the customer, if OTS components could not satisfy all requirements [14].
Component integration phase	R7	OTS components negatively affected system reliability [12,13].
	R8	OTS components negatively affected system security [11, 12, 13]
	R9	OTS components negatively affected system performance [11,12, 13]
	R10	OTS components were not satisfactorily compatible with the production environment when the system was deployed [12]
System maintenance and evolution	R11	It was difficult to identify whether defects were inside or outside the OTS components [3].
	R12	It was difficult to plan system maintenance, e.g. because different OTS components had asynchronous release cycles [1].
	R13	It was difficult to update the system with the last OTS component version [1].
Provider relationship management	R14	Provider did not provide enough technical support/ training [1, 10].
	R15	Information on the reputation and technical support ability of provider were inadequate [1, 10].

3 Research Design

3.1 Research Questions

Our study was designed to address two basic research questions:

- **RQ1**: What are the risks that software project managers met most frequently in OTS component-base development?
- **RQ2**: Can performed risk mitigation actions help to mitigate the corresponding risks?

Table 2. Typical risk management strategies in OTS-component based development

ID	Risk management strategies
M1	Customer had been actively involved in the "acquire" vs. "build" decision of OTS components [7, 14].
M2	Customer had been actively involved in OTS component selection [7].
M3	OTS components were selected mainly based on architecture and standards compliance, instead of expected functionality [18]
M4	OTS components qualities (reliability, security etc.) were seriously considered in the selection process [3, 14]
M5	Effort in learning OTS component was seriously considered in effort estimation [3]
M6	Effort in black-box testing of OTS components was seriously considered in effort estimation [3, 14]
M7	Unfamiliar OTS components were integrated first [1]
M8	Did integration testing incrementally (after each OTS component was integrated [14]
M9	Local OTS-experts actively followed updates of OTS components and possible consequences [14].
M10	Maintained a continual watch on the market and looked for possible substitute components [14].
M11	Maintained a continual watch on provider support ability and reputation [1].

3.2 Questionnaire Design

The questionnaire includes three main sections:

- Background questions to collect information of the company, project, and respondents.
- Main questions about risk and risk management. The risks and risk management strategies selected in the questionnaire are the most typical ones as showed in Table 1 and Table 2. Respondents are asked to give their opinions on these risks and risk management actions as "don't agree at all", "hardly agree", "agree somewhat", "agree mostly", "strongly agree", or "don't know". We assign an ordinal number from 1 to 5 to the above alternatives (5 meaning strongly agree).
- Questions to collect information about OTS components actually used in their project.

3.3 Concepts Used in This Study

Concepts used in the questionnaire are listed in the start of the questionnaire.

Component: Software components are program units of independent production, acquisition, and deployment and which can be composed into a functioning system. We limit ourselves to components that have been explicitly decided either to be built from scratch or to be acquired externally as an OTS-component. That is, to components that are not shipped with the operating system, not provided by the development environment, and not included in any pre-existing platform.

An OTS Component is a component provided (by a so-called provider) from a commercial vendor or the Open Source community. An OTS component may come with certain obligations, e.g. payment or licensing terms. An OTS component is not controllable, in terms of provided features and their evolution. An OTS component is mainly used as closed source, i.e. no source code is usually modified, and even it may be available.

3.4 Data Collection

3.4.1 Sample Definition

The unit of this study is a completed software development project, and its OTS-relevant properties. The projects were selected based on two criteria:

- The project should use one or more OTS components
- The project should be a finished project, possibly with maintenance, and possibly with several releases.

3.4.2 Sample Selection and Data Collection

We used random selection to gather a representative sample.

- In Norway, we gathered a company list from the Norwegian "Census Bureau" (SSB) [17]. We included mostly companies which were registered as IT companies. Based on the number of employees, we selected the 115 largest IT companies (100 IT companies and 15 IT departments in the largest 3 companies in 5 other sectors), 150 medium-sized software companies (20-99 employees), and 100 small-sized companies (5-19 employees) as the original contacting list.
- In Italy, we first got 43580 software companies from "yellow pages". We then randomly selected companies from them. For these randomly selected companies, we read their web-site to ensure they are software companies or not. 196 companies were finally clarified as software companies, and were used as the original contacting list.
- In Germany, we selected name list from a company list from an organization similar to the Norwegian "*Census Bureau*". We then used the existing IESE customer database to get contact information.

In the end, we aim for more than 150 filled-in questionnaires to have statistically valid results.

The final questionnaire was first designed and pre-tested in English (internal and external previews). It was then translated into the native languages and published on the SESE web survey tool [19] at Simula Research Lab in OSLO. Possible respondents were contacted first by telephone. If they have suitable OTS-based projects and would like to join our study, a username and password was sent to them, so that they could use the SESE web tool to fill in the questionnaire (they could also use a paper version or electronic word version). The respondents who didn't want to answer the questionnaire were also registered. We logged the main reasons of non-response, such as no software development, no OTS-based projects, and busy.

4 Results

Although the data collection process is still on-going, we have already gathered results from 42 projects (33 from Norway, 9 from Italy).

4.1 Companies and Projects

The filled-in questionnaires come from 18 small, 11 medium-sized and 8 large companies. 19 are software vendors, 15 are IT consulting companies one is in Telecom, and two are IT branches of the traditional industry.

We selected one project in 35 companies. We also selected more than one different project from two large companies. Most projects used more than 10 person-months in the development phases. The developed software systems also cover different application domains as showed in Table 3.

Table 3. The distribution of the application domains of the systems

Application domains	Percentage
Bank/Finance/Insurance	19%
Other private services (consulting, wholesale, retail, etc.)	19%
Public sector	29%
ICT sector	16%
Traditional industry/engineering/construction	17%

4.2 Respondents

Most respondents have a solid IT background. Four respondents are IT managers, 17 are project managers, 18 are software architects, and three are senior software developers. 90% of them have more than three years of software development experience, and 86% of them have more than two years working experience with OTS-based development.

4.3 Answers to Research Questions

4.3.1 Frequency of Risk Occurrence

For the relative importance of the risks we listed 15 in the questionnaire, the distribution of their relative frequencies are showed in the following Fig 1.

Based on distribution of these risks, we can classify the relative frequency of these risks into four categories from the most frequent to the least frequent:

- Risk R4 is the most frequent risk.
- Risks R2, R3, R6, R12, and R14 are classified as the second most frequent risks because they have an up-skewed distribution.
- Risk R1, R5, R9, R10, R11 and R13 are the third most frequent risks.
- Risk R7, R8, and R15 are the least frequent risks. These risks have either a lower median or a down-skewed distribution.

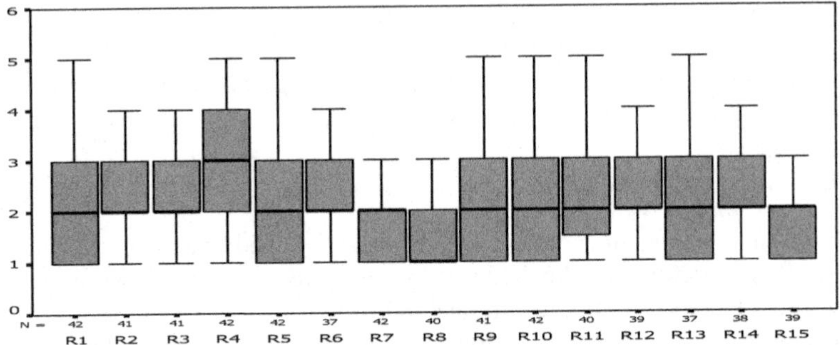

Fig. 1. Frequency of the risk occurrence

The results show that some risks were more frequent than others, such as requirement relevant risks (R4 and R6), cost-estimation risks (R2 and R3), maintenance plan risk (R12), and provider support risks (R14). Some risks relevant to OTS components reliability (R7) and security (R8) were less frequent.

4.3.2 Frequency of Risks Management Actions

For the risk management actions, their relative frequencies are showed in Fig. 2.

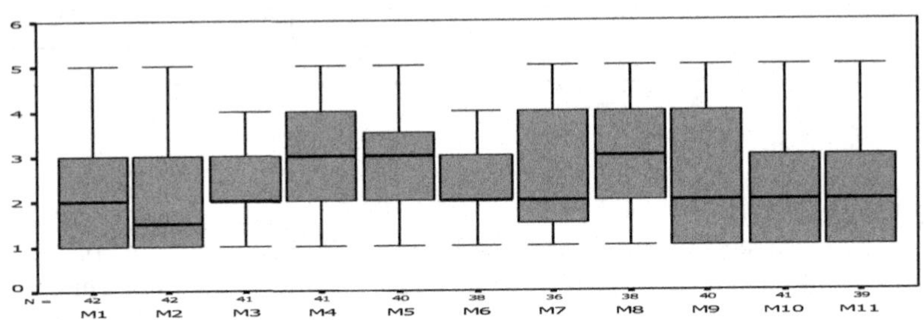

Fig. 2. Frequency of the performed risk management actions

Based on distribution of these performed risk management actions, we can classify them into three categories from the most frequent to the least frequent:

- Risk management action M4, M5, and M8 are the most frequently used methods.
- Risk management action M3 and M6 are the second most frequent methods.
- Other risk management actions as M1, M2, M7, M9, M10, and M11 are the least frequent.

The results show that quality control methods, such as quality evaluation in selection (M4) and incremental testing (M8) were used much in practice. Results also show that possible effort in learning OTS components was seriously considered (M5). However, risk management methods relevant to customers (M1, M2) and providers (M9, M10, and M11) were seldom used.

4.3.3 Relationships Between Risks and Risk Management Actions

Although many risk management actions were proposed to mitigate possible risks, we investigated only the most frequent ones, i.e. M4, M5, and M8. The reason is that it is not reliable to verify the effect of risk management methods if they have rarely been used.

We calculated the correlation between risk mitigation actions performed and their corresponding risks using *Somers's d* analysis method (in SPSS version 11.0). We regarded the frequency of risks as a dependent variable and risk management actions as an independent variable. A negative correlation between them means that the more the risk management action performed, the less frequent is the risk. Only M4 showed significant effect on corresponding risks as in Table 4.

Table 4. Correlation between M4 and corresponding risks

Risks	Risk management actions	Correlation	P-value
R2	M4	-.307	.018
R3	M4	-.327	.013

The results show that if an integrator has taken seriously consideration on the quality of the OTS component, they will plan the effort on OTS selection more completely. In addition, the effort on OTS component integration can easily be estimated. This is possibly because the actual OTS component did not cause much quality problems in the whole system after its integration.

5 Discussions

5.1 Comparison with Related Work

In OTS component-based development, many typical risks and risk management methods have been proposed. Our study contributed to show their relative frequency in practice. Our study also studied the effect of some risk mitigation actions to corresponding risks.

- Our findings show that the **requirement** relevant risks are the most frequent risks. The customer requirements were changed a lot. It was difficult for OTS components to follow these changes, and it is difficult to (re) negotiate the requirements because of OTS components' inability to satisfy all requirements.
- Our findings also show that **estimation of selection and integration costs** in OTS-based projects is perceived as a challenge. These results make sense intuitively, as saving time and effort is the main perceived advantage of using OTS components [4]. Most proposed risk mitigation methods focus on solving this problem by having experienced project manager or a formal cost-estimation model [2]. Our results show that giving complete estimation on the possible effort in OTS component quality evaluation helped to mitigate these risks.
- Most previous studies regard OTS components' negative effect on the **reliability and security** of the system is very challenging in OTS-based development [1, 4, 5,

6, 7, 10]. Our results show that they are not as frequent as assumed. The possible reason is that project managers used careful selection and incremental testing to help to mitigate OTS components' negative impact on the quality of the system.

5.2 Threats to Validity

5.2.1 Construct Validity

In this study, most risks and risk management strategies variables are taken directly, or with little modification, from existing literature. The questionnaire was pre-tested using a paper version by 10 internal experts and 8 industrial respondents. About 15% questions have been revised based on pre-test results.

5.2.2 Internal Validity

We proposed to offer respondents participated in this study a final report and a seminar to share experience. The respondents were persons who want to share their experience and want to learn from others. In general, we think that the respondents have answered truthfully.

5.2.3 Conclusion Validity

This study is still on-going. A larger sample will be gathered to give more significant statistical support on conclusion of this study.

5.2.4 External Validity

We used different random selection strategies to select samples in different countries. It is because the limited availability of the necessary information. In Italy, there is no official organization as a national "Census Bureau" in Norway and Germany. The samples have to be selected from "yellow pages". The methods problems by performing such a survey in three countries will be elaborated in a future paper. Another possible limitation is that our study focused on fine-grained OTS components. Conclusions may be different in projects using complex and large OTS product, such as ERP, Content management system.

6 Conclusions and Future Work

More and more IT companies start to use OTS components in their software development projects. In addition to the classical risks for developing large systems, using OTS components brings additional risks. It therefore requires new mitigation strategies to manage these risks. In this study, we investigated the frequency of risks and risk management actions in 42 finished OTS component-based projects. The contribution of this study can be summarized into three categories:

- Risks relevant to **requirement changes and cost-estimation** happened more frequent than reliability and security risks regarding OTS components.
- Some risk mitigation methods, such as **incremental testing and strict OTS component quality evaluation** have been used more frequent than others.
- If the integrator **seriously considered the possible effort on the quality evaluation** of OTS components, it helped to solve the effort estimation risks in the OTS selection and integration.

The data collection is still on-going. More data will be gathered to give further support to conclusions in this paper. Based on the results of this survey, we will do more qualitative studies to investigate the underlying cause-effect of risk management strategies. Some typical projects in this survey will be selected as targets for the next steps.

Acknowledgements

This study was partially funded by the INCO (INcremental COmponent based development) project [15]. We thank the colleagues in these projects, and all the participants in the survey

References

1. Louis C. Rose: Risk Management of COTS based System development. Component-Based Software Quality - Methods and Techniques, LNCS Vol. 2693, Springer (2003) 352-373.
2. Chris Abts, Barry W. Boehm, and Elisabeth B. Clark: COCOTS: A COTS Software Integration Lifecycle Cost Model - Model Overview and Preliminary Data Collection Findings. Technical report USC-CSE-2000-501, USC Center for Software Engineering, 8 March 2000, Available at: http://sunset.usc.edu/publications/TECHRPTS/2000/usccse2000-501/usccse2000-501.pdf.
3. Barry W. Boehm, Dan Port, Ye Yang, and Jesal Bhuta: Not All CBS Are Created Equally COTS-intensive Project Types. Proceedings of the 2nd International Conference on COTS-Based Software Systems (ICCBSS'03), Ottawa, Canada, February (2003), LNCS Vol. 2580, Springer (2003) 36-50.
4. J. Voas: COTS Software – the Economical Choice?. IEEE Software, March/April (1998), 15(2):16-19.
5. J. Voas: The challenges of Using COTS Software in Component-Based Development. IEEE Computer, June (1998), 31(6):44-45.
6. Gerald Kotonya and Awais Rashid: A Strategy for Managing Risk in Component-based Software Development. Proceedings of the 27th EUROMICRO Conference 2001, Warsaw, Poland, September (2001) 12-21.
7. COTS risk factor. Available at: http://www.faa.gov/aua/resources/cots/Guide/CRMG.htm
8. Tony Moynihan: How Experienced Project Managers Assess Risk. IEEE Software, May/June (1997), 14 (3): 35-41.
9. Janne Ropponen and Kalle Lyytinen: Components of Software Development Risk: How to Address Them? A Project Manager Survey. IEEE Transactions on Software Engineering, February (2000), 26(2): 98-112.
10. Brian Fitzgerald: A Critical Look at Open Source. IEEE Computer July (2004), 37 (7): 92-94.
11. G. Lawton: Open Source Security: Opportunity or Oxymoron? IEEE Computer, March (2002), 35(3): 18-21.
12. Padmal Vitharana: Risks and Challenges of Component-Based Software Development. Communications of the ACM, August (2003), 46(8): 67-72.
13. Michel Ruffin and Christof Ebert: Using Open Source Software in Product Development: A Primer. IEEE Software January/February (2004), 21(1): 82-86.

14. Jingyue Li, Finn Olav Bjørnson, Reidar Conradi, and Vigdis By Kampenes: An Empirical Study of Variations in COTS-based Software Development Processes in Norwegian IT Industry. Proceedings of the 10th IEEE International Metrics Symposium (Metrics'04), Chicago, USA, September 14-16 (2004) 72-83.
15. INCO project description, 2000, http://www.ifi.uio.no/~isu/INCO
16. Thomas A. Longstaff, Clyde Chittister, Rich Pethia, Yacov Y. Haimes: Are we forgetting the risks of information technology? IEEE Computer, December (2000), 33(12): 43-51.
17. Norwegian Census Bureau: http://www.ssb.no
18. M. Torchiano and M. Morisio, "Overlooked Facts on COTS-based Development", IEEE Software, March/April 2004, 21(2): 88-93.
19. Simula SESE tool: http://sese.simula.no

Managerial and Technical Barriers to the Adoption of Open Source Software

Jesper Holck, Michael Holm Larsen, and Mogens Kühn Pedersen

Copenhagen Business School, Informatics
Howitzvej 60, DK-2000 Frederiksberg, Denmark
{jeh, mhl, mk}.inf@cbs.dk

Abstract. In this paper we focus on managerial and technical decisions for acquisition of OSS and discuss potential approaches to a widespread adoption of OSS. Moving from mainly technical issues in procurement to corporate IS governance presents OSS with new challenges beyond outlining a business case for a particular OSS application. We draw parallels to the business case for commercial software products (COTS). Compared with COTS, OSS products seem to have several advantages, but based on existing literature and a case study, we develop and discuss the hypothesis that a major barrier may be the "customer's" uncertainty and unfamiliarity with OSS vendor relationships. We find that corporate governance and architecture needs to be accounted for in both COTS and OSS. This paper should be seen as a first step researching the fit between procurement and delivery models for OSS.

1 Introduction

Originally, Open source software (OSS) set out at the technical level of SW engineering communities but has recently gained interest at policy and managerial levels. In the face of a managerial demand for information about availability and accessibility of OSS publications on applications flourished in the beginning of the decade like O'Reilly's book series [1]. Today, OSS products are profiled against commercial products, e.g. Linux vs. Windows, OpenOffice.org vs. Microsoft Office, and Apache vs. IIS in performance measurements. Understanding OSS at policy and managerial levels reflects a need to cope with large application portfolios and increasing demands for interoperability. Attending to these new requirements we will take a look at OSS compared to COTS. We look at how a recent launch coped with policy and managerial issues indicating first steps toward a corporate governance and architecture policy that we expect OSS will be facing in the coming years.

2 Open Source Software Movement

In developing our understanding of the Open Source "movement" [1-3], a multi-perspective analysis needs to be undertaken in order to embrace the complexities of this phenomenon. As this research field is fairly young, mature bodies of theories such as

X. Franch and D. Port (Eds.): ICCBSS 2005, LNCS 3412, pp. 289–300, 2005.

economics [2] often set the development directions and research agendas of the research field. In our literature review we find a lack of research addressing Open Source Software (OSS) from a business perspective – not from a product, developer, community, or industry perspective [4-6].

Our focus will be the decision-making challenges for managers when confronted with OSS. Initial decision-making is of interest and highly important because even though the realized costs at this point in time are relatively small, costs derived from the decisions and dispositional mechanisms [7], will often be substantial.

This paper is a step in a larger research project on a series of research questions:

- What barriers and enablers do organizations experience considering adoption of OSS?
- Which measures do organizations take to acquire and deploy OSS?
- Are these measures different from measures taken when acquiring and deploying commercial software?
- Do these measures vary across different types of organizations?
- Can we identify a set of "best practices" for organizations when they consider, acquire, and deploy OSS within a governance and architectural framework?

The paper is organized as follows: After an overview in section three of OSS literature, we will in section four present our research question: why are OSS products not in more widespread use? In section five we describe our research approach, and in section six we outline our understanding of OSS. In sections seven to ten we discuss similarities and differences between COTS and OSS and the case of a Danish hospital migrating to OSS. In section 11 we discuss our results and further research.

3 Literature Study

Although the research area of OSS is relatively young, documented research contributions are coming at a rapid pace.

The one aspect of OSS that seems to have attracted most interest is the question of *why* individuals and organizations may choose to contribute to OSS projects, delivering time, work, and other resources, apparently without economic compensation. Focusing on the individual contributors, some authors [8, 9] suggest that OSS projects can be described as a "gift economy", where one gift (e.g. a source code contribution) must be paid back with other gifts. Ye et al. [10] suggest learning as the primary motivation; Hars and Ou [11] identify both internal (joy of programming, altruism, identification with a community) and external (self-marketing, building human capital, need for software solution) motivational factors, the external factors having most weight. In an analysis of the Apache project [12], Hann et al. found that active contributors received higher wages from the employers, also suggesting economic motives for their "voluntary" work.

Focusing on organizations, several authors [2, 13-19] have argued that contributing to and participating in OSS projects may under some circumstances be a viable economic activity. Dahlander [20], and Bonaccorsi and Rossi [21] have presented by case studies of OSS business models.

Another research question receiving much interest has been *how* OSS projects are organized, and what methods and techniques they use to produce software. Several case studies have been presented [4, 22-26], and the quality assurance models used in large OSS projects have been described in [24] and [27].

Scacchi [28] argues from a more technical perspective that OSS development is often faster, better, and cheaper than traditional software engineering. Paulson et al. [29] find that, compared with commercial projects, OSS projects show more creativity and faster location and removal of bugs; Kogut and Metiu [30] point to higher efficiency due to concurrent design and test, and avoidance of a strong intellectual property regime. Fitzgerald, on the other hand, identifies several weaknesses of the OSS development model [31], including limited interest in mundane tasks (documentation etc.), murky business models, and lack of strategic nous.

On an industry level, Wayner [5] investigates how the Free Software Movement and in particular Linux erodes market shares of established players in the field, and Mustonen [32] identifies circumstances under which OSS can influence the software markets, even when dominated by monopolies.

4 Our Research Questions

As mentioned above, one puzzling question has been why organizations and highly competent developers voluntarily invest resources in OSS development. In our research, we will look into the complementary question: why are OSS products not in more widespread use in companies and public institutions? Given that the products are available for free and often of high quality, this seems surprising from an economic view. Which are the barriers for managerial policy to include OSS products and which are the technical barriers to adoption of OSS?

Based on interviews with MIS managers, Dedrick and West [33] found that the most important driver for OSS adoption was cost, both direct savings (cheap software) and indirect savings (no upgrade fees, lower hardware requirements); barriers included compatibility with current technologies and skills, organizational resources and tasks, and the availability of external technological resources. (Fitzgerald and Kenny [34] has described a mostly successful adoption of OSS in a large organization, and case stories from German public organizations are presented by Terhoeven [35] and Müller [36]. Several authors have recommended use of OSS in the public sector, including Seiferth [37] (US Department of Defense), Schmitz and Castiaux [38] (public sector administrations across EU), and the Danish Board of Technology [39] (Danish public sector).

The increasing demand for application interoperability strengthens corporate approaches to architecture and IT investment priorities, replacing application-by-application approaches. In this new context of IT decision-making, how will OSS fare amongst infrastructure issues, standards, and specific needs for middleware, etc.? Will OSS meet the integration requirements with advantages (open source transparency) or liabilities (no vendor accountability), compared to COTS?

5 Research Approach

In our research we have combined literature studies with qualitative case studies, based on interviews with decision makers in Danish organizations who have considered the adoption of OSS seeing their concerns as first barriers for adoption of OSS. From the start we did not have very specific hypotheses regarding barriers and enablers of adoption of OSS at policy and implementation levels, but have asked quite open questions regarding concerns in past and current decisions on adoption of OSS; our research has been exploratory case studies [40]. We offer no complete case on corporate governance and architecture including OSS. Our cases provide insights into different types of organizations, both adopters and non-adopters. Space allows presenting only one case in this paper. Below, we discuss hypotheses regarding the limited adoption of OSS in commercial settings. First, however, we will discuss the notions of OSS and of being an OSS user.

6 Characteristics of Open Source Software and Open Source Software Users

Like many other terms, the exact meaning of "Open Source Software" is debatable. The definition offered by the Open Source Initiative (OSI) focuses on the software license. In contrast to proprietary software licenses, which mostly deal with restricting users' rights and limiting vendors' liabilities, OSS licenses, according to OSI, must provide users a number of rights, including

- Anyone is free to distribute and use the software
- The software source code is freely available

However, the license is not the only characteristic of "Open Source Software" as most people understand it. Another characteristic [16] is:

- Software developed and maintained through the "Open Source model," in which many developers contribute code to a common repository.

Our focus on organizations' adoption of OSS limits our interest to:

- Software distributed as application programs, excluding e.g. code libraries
- Software maintained and developed by a mature, active organization, including
  - Technological infrastructure: common software repository, website, mailing lists for users and developers etc.
  - Organizational infrastructure: hierarchy, procedures, etc.

This definition will cover all major OSS products, including Linux, Apache, MySQL, Mozilla, Eclipse, OpenOffice.org, and Samba.

Even though we may be able to identify a "vendor" organization that develops, maintains, and distributes the product, and a number of "customer" organizations that use the product, this is clearly not a complete picture of the many possible ways in which organizations can benefit from OSS products, including

- Software resellers or distributors, selling "packaged" OSS, possibly bundled with proprietary software, e.g. Red Hat's Linux distribution.
- Hardware vendors, bundling proprietary hardware products with OSS, e.g. IBM's computers with preinstalled Linux.
- Consultants, providing customer solutions based on OSS.

Even though all these categories of "users" have an interest in a widespread and high-quality supply of open-source software, we focus only on the direct users. We will explore organizational and managerial tools for providing a viable, adequate and robust platform for OSS users as a precondition for widespread adoption of OSS.

7 Comparing COTS and OSS

Even though OSS can be downloaded for free, and in this sense is neither commercial nor off-the-shelf, it shares several characteristics with COTS, Commercial-Off-The-Shelf Software. As mentioned in [41], several definitions of COTS exist, including the one offered by SEI [42], defining a COTS component as one that is:

- Sold, leased, or licensed to the general public
- Offered by a vendor trying to profit from it
- Supported and evolved by the vendor retaining intellectual property rights
- Available in multiple, identical copies
- Used without source code modification

We will briefly discuss each of these defining characteristics in relation to OSS.

Sold, leased, or licensed to the general public. According to our definition, OSS must be available for the general public for free, but this does not preclude that OSS products may also be sold or leased (e.g. Red Hat). The OSS license must always assure unlimited use and distribution to the general public.

Offered by a vendor trying to profit from it. OSS may also be offered by a commercial vendor trying to profit from it, but because OSS also is freely distributed, new business models must be found. Even when non-commercial communities offer OSS, providing money for servers and Internet access must be secured.

Supported and evolved by the vendor retaining intellectual property rights. According to our definition, OSS is also supported and evolved by a vendor or community; the intellectual property rights are maintained by the software author(s), but these rights are used to make sure that the software remains open (freely distributable etc.).

Available in multiple, identical copies. Because the source code is open, anyone can choose to produce his or her own software versions, but all major OSS products certainly exist in multiple, identical copies.

Used without source code modification. Again, users can choose to modify the source code, but as mentioned in [33], user organizations typically refrain from this.

Because of the many similarities between COTS and OSS it seems reasonable to draw upon the more established research field of COTS, when identifying managerial and technical barriers for adoption of OSS. Based on a large number of US case stories, a research group headed by Barry Boehm has collected a large number of "lessons learned" in relation to use of COTS. Some of the more interesting in relation to our present discussion [43]:

Avoid modifications. The reason for this is given in one of the cases as "Porting a COTS product generally implies code modifications to the COTS product. Such modifications, if not incorporated into the source by the supplier, means that every release of the source from the vendor has to be modified in accordance with the custom changes, thus losing some of the benefit from using a COTS product." As an alternative it is recommended to develop "glue code" in order to integrate the COTS product into the larger system. Interestingly, this code is assumed to be hard to write because of potential difficulties in obtaining necessary tools and information from the vendor; estimated 45 % of the total cost/effort associated with use of COTS products is used on glue code [44].

Unpredictable evolution of COTS products. The evolutionary nature of COTS products has a profound impact on program cost, schedule, and risks: "Decisions about COTS products … must anticipate that product change will be rapid." Of particular interest, when comparing use of commercial COTS and OSS products, is the suggestion that "the use of open systems concepts and interface standards and code escrow agreements may help. Also avoid lock-in to a particular vendor product and minimize the amount of customization and glue code."

Results from Boehm et al.'s research point to advantages of OSS:

- It is possible to modify the software and avoid re-doing this with new versions, if the modification is included in the OSS distribution.
- No need for source code escrow. If the customer is not satisfied with the direction or progress of the OSS project, the customer (or eventually another paid consultant) can "take over", if a wide OSS user community supports a market for consultants.
- All interfaces are public; glue code development is relatively simple.

Boehm et al.'s work provides arguments in favor of OSS both at the managerial policy level (keeping options open) and the technical level (lower costs of modifications) though lack of vendor accountability corrupt conditions to acquire these advantages.

At the same time, valuation of open standards where available remains a fragile and uncertain issue to cope with in both OSS and COTS since any system may still be constrained by proprietary systems in the corporate architecture. Presently, opportunities for an assessment of costs of alternative product portfolios remain an unfulfilled vision shared between COTS and OSS.

8 A New Perspective on COTS

Traditionally, products like spreadsheet or word processing applications were regarded as more or less stand-alone, technical products, not really a part of the organization's information systems. COTS components, on the other hand, were regarded as being embedded in the organization's information systems, e.g. the company payroll system as illustrated below:

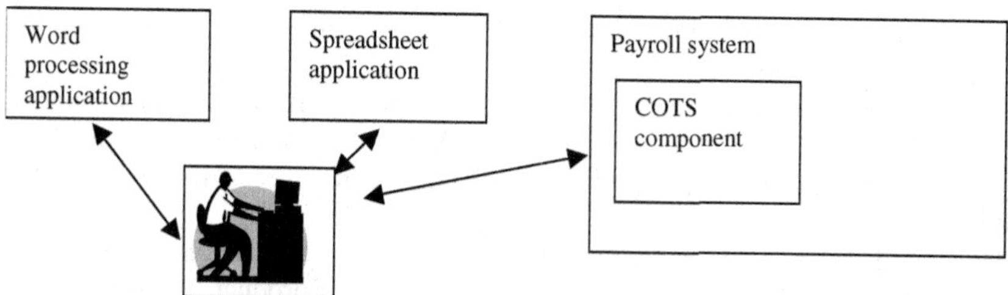

During the last decade(s), organizations have been integrating their various computer-based systems, so now the typical perspective is like illustrated below:

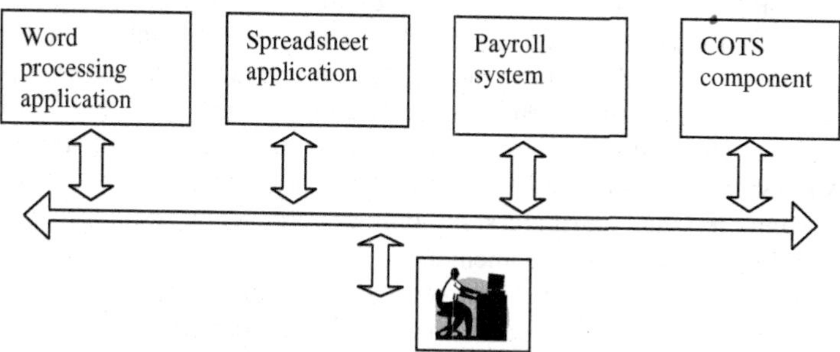

Applications like office suites can no longer be considered stand-alone products. They are components in an organization-wide IS architecture, heavily interacting with other application programs and software components. As a consequence, many issues previously considered relevant for COTS components (e.g. need for glue code, tailoring, and tuning) now become relevant for these applications. Also, because selection, acquisition and adoption of COTS components now have an influence on the organization-wide IS architecture, these decisions must be considered in a strategic perspective, including issues like corporate governance, vendor relationship, risk avoidance and lock-in, and they become elements of a corporate IS policy.

Developing corporate architectures face the problems of limited accountability from COTS vendors, leveling COTS and OSS products in this regard.

In order to develop a corporate architecture, customers place new requirements on COTS vendors, e.g. interoperability tests, interface specifications, and use of open document standards; requirements that OSS products often will satisfy almost by definition. This may bring COTS principles to OSS and the reverse, resulting in a convergence between the two. If this is the case the business models of COTS and OSS may also converge though this is yet to be seen.

9 Accountability Between Vendor and Customer

In our preliminary studies we have found support for a conjecture regarding accountability barriers for adoption of OSS. We will in this section develop the hypothesis:

that a major barrier is the unfamiliarity and uncertainty in regard to accountability in the relationship between OSS "vendor" and "customer".

Offering proprietary software, the vendor has an important, economic interest in attracting users: the more users, the more customers. This relationship is (ideally) also beneficial to the customer compelling the vendor to produce software that fits the customer's needs.

This relationship between "customer" and "vendor" is fundamentally different, when we consider OSS. Not being paid for the software product, the vendor has no immediate interest in keeping the customers satisfied. The customer may feel this new vendor relation quite unclear: If the product isn't paid for, what "guarantees" do the customer have for the product's quality and the future relation to the vendor? Also, the customer has to find other means than simply paying for the software, if he wants to persuade the vendor to pay attention to his interests.

One solution for the customer may be to buy the OSS product through a commercial company, in this way transferring to a third party the potential problems of cooperating with the OSS vendor. This can remove some of the uncertainties involved in being an OSS user, changing the role to one more like the familiar role of being a software product customer. Another solution for the customer is to engage in the OSS project. An OSS project may not be interested in "pure customers", but it has obvious and objective interests in contributors, not only as co-developers but also contributing error reports, localization, and documentation, etc.

As described in [45], it is also in a commercial setting important for a software vendor to establish good links to customers (bulletin boards, customer groups, pre-release demonstrations etc.), but they are of minor importance, compared with the relationship defined by the software acquisition.

In an open source setting, however, user participation in an OSS project is of major importance in the relationship between "customer" and "vendor", and will be on the initiative of and sponsored by the customer organization.

10 Case of Aarhus Psychiatric Hospital Migration

Regional authorities own Aarhus Psychiatric Hospital (APH); the IT department services over 2,000 users with access to some 170 applications.

In 2003, with a county council on a tight budget, being impelled by the government to shorten hospital waiting lists, and faced with a demand of new document formats, APH took interest in any means to reduce the IT budget. With no funds available for investments and yet with a pressure to migrate, the IT management of APH considered finding a solution using OSS products, promoted in the autumn of 2002 by the Danish Board of Technology [39]. The county council refrained formulating restrictive architectural policies, leaving it to each management to choose between OSS and proprietary Microsoft document formats.

At APH, StarOffice[1] was in February 2003 selected as candidate future office platform, followed by training of some IT staff and later of a select few users, to act first as testers and later as ambassadors and local instructors.

---

[1] Sun's commercial office suite, based on the OSS product OpenOffice.org

As StarOffice 7 was not yet available in Danish, the OSS product OpenOffice.Org (OOo) 1.1.1 was in February 2004 implemented for 2,000 users migrating from Corel Office (WordPerfect). Before launch, the IT-department translated all macros to OOo to ensure hassle-free use of the application from day one.

Overall IT department costs on preparing the OOo migration were 0,75 of a year's work, 35,000 DKK on external consultants, and 50,000 DKK on external training; as a result of the migration APH cut license fees over three years with 8,7 mill. DKK.

Previously, 40% of the IT budget was spent on licenses, with only 10% available for new projects and for development. After migration less than 10% is used for basic software with 40% released to development of new services (Jens Kjellerup, IT manager at APH, June 10, 2004).

A detailed account of the APH migration was prepared using total cost of ownership measures acquired before, during, and after migration in 2004. On behalf of The Danish Ministry of Science, Technology and Innovation a consultant found approx. 30% reduction in TCO with Ooo, tracing direct and indirect costs of the migration.

APH uses the following open source software besides OpenOffice.org: Zentrack, MySQL, Apache, Suse Linux, Debian, and LibWPD.

In this case migration was thoroughly prepared at board level and at user level whereas IT staff and support deliberately were used as change agents. More county institutions are preparing to migrate to OOo in the coming year expecting support from the "experts" at APH.

The Danish Ministry of Environment in October 2004 decided to launch OOo at the desktop. This ministry has a corporate IT governance and software architecture policy of *inter alia* interoperability and open standards. This is the first Danish case of OSS becoming a significant component in corporate IT policy and architecture.

11 Discussion

In large organizations, decisions regarding procurement of SW components are seldom taken on basis of the qualities of an individual component. Typically, top management has decided upon a common IT policy and enterprise architecture, constituting a strategic framework for future IT investments. If OSS, as is most likely today, is not part of this framework, it is unlikely to be adopted in any significant scale – not even if certain OSS products are highly competitive when compared with commercial alternatives. Exceptions may be certain "niche" areas, more or less invisible to company management, like software for researchers or for IT-departments' servers for SW development. Only at the time of IT policy revision will a reassessment of the present platform take place, and only if management invites an open IT-architecture will OSS find its way to the decision-making arena. If the organization has little competence in OSS, a migration to OSS will be perceived a high risk option with little or no support from the IT department. Only if decisions on IT strategy are taken at a corporate level, above IT operations management, will OSS become subject to serious evaluation in organization low in OSS competence.

This situation may be different in smaller organizations without constraining, strategic IT policies; these organizations might be expected to be more likely to experiment with platforms and new software vendors, including OSS. But, as one of our studies shows, even smaller organizations may be severely constrained in their decisions: legal obligations and large investments may make it unfeasible to change from commercial components to OSS. Further, smaller organizations will only have limited resources to develop competencies necessary for acquiring, deploying, and supporting OSS.

Procurement models and their "fit" with vendors' delivery models are essential when organizations formulate IT policies. Hence, an answer to our research question is that a major barrier for adoption of OSS is the lack of reliable procurement models, which must include technical (appropriation regarding functionality, security, interfaces, etc. within an architecture), legal (appropriation regarding license), and corporate policy and business elements (appropriation regarding vendor, customer support, software alliances, etc.). In the commercial market, satisfactory and well-proven procedures exist for these elements, but this has yet to evolve and mature for OSS.

It is our hypothesis that organizations will only adopt OSS (in a significant scale) if one of two conditions is met:

- OSS is bundled with hardware products, delivered through commercial vendors. This is what we are now seeing with IBM's and HP's distribution of computers with the Linux operating system. In this way, OSS is delivered as an included subcomponent that may not be activated.
- A credible combination of delivery and procurement models for OSS compatible with corporate IS governance and architectural policy is found.

So, for OSS to obtain a larger "market share" in the coming years, it will be an important challenge for both users and developers of OSS to establish credible and mutually acceptable combinations of OSS delivery and procurement models. We plan to continue our research into how organizations make decisions regarding OSS acquisition and deployment to detect viable models and best practices for adoption of OSS in organizations.

References

1. O'Reilly, T.: Hardware, Software, and Infoware. In DiBona, C., Ockman, S. and Stone, M. (ed.): Open Sources: Voices from the Open Source Revolution, O'Reilly & Associates, Sebastopol, California, USA (1999).
2. Lerner, J. and Tirole, J.: Some Simple Economics of Open Source. The Journal of Industrial Economics, L(2) (2002) 197-234.
3. Lakhani, K.R. and von Hippel, E.: How open source software works: "free" user-to-user assistance. Research Policy, 32(6) (2003) 923-943.
4. Nakakoji, K., Yamamoto, Y., Nishinaka, Y., Kishida, K. and Ye, Y.: Evolution Patterns of Open-Source Software Systems and Communities. Proc. Workshop on Principles of Software Evolution (IWPSE), Orlando, Florida (2002).
5. Wayner, P.: Free for All. HarperCollins (2000).
6. Wilson, G.: Is the Open-Source Community Setting a Bad Example. IEEE Software, 16(1) (1999) 23-25.
7. Olesen, J.: Concurrent Development in manufacturing - based on dispositional mechanisms Intitute for Engineering Design, Technical University of Denmark, (1992).

8. Bergquist, M. and Ljungberg, J.: The Power of Gifts: Organising Social Relationships in Open Source Communities. Information Systems Journal, 11(4) (2001) 305-320.
9. Raymond, E.S.: The Cathedral and the Bazaar: Musings on Linux and Open Source by an Accidental Revolutionary. O'Reilly & Associates, Inc., Sebastopol, California, USA (2001).
10. Ye, Y. and Kishida, K.: Toward an Understanding of the Motivation of Open Source Software Developers. Proc. International Conference on Software Engineering (ICSE 2003), Portland, Oregon, USA, 2003.
11. Hars, A. and Ou, S.: Working for Free? Motivations of Participating in Open Source Projects. Proc. 34th Hawaii International Conference on System Sciences, Hawaii (2001).
12. Hann, I.-H., Roberts, J., Slaughter, S. and Fielding, R.T.: Why do developers contribute to open source projects? First evidence of economic incentives. Proc. International Conference on Software Engineering (ICSE), Orlando, Florida, USA (2002).
13. Benkler, Y.: Coase's Penguin, or, Linux and The Nature of the Firm. The Yale Law Journal, 112(3) (2002).
14. Lerner, J. and Tirole, J.: The Open Source Movement: Key Research Questions. European Economic Review, 45 (2001) 819-826.
15. Johnson, J.P.: Open Source Software: Private Provision of a Public Good. Journal of Economics & Management Strategy, 11(4) (2002) 637-662.
16. Henkel, J.: Open Source Software from Commercial Firms -Tools, Complements, and Collective Invention, (2003).
17. Edwards, K.: An Economic Perspective on Software Licenses - Incentives in Open Source Software. Proc. 8th Annual CTI Conference, Copenhagen, Denmark (2003).
18. Haruvy, E., Prasad, A. and Sethi, S.P.: Harvesting Altruism in Open-Source Software Development. Journal of Optimization Theory and Applications, 118(2) (2003) 381-416.
19. von Hippel, E. and von Krogh, G.: Open Source Software and the "Private-Collective" Innovation Model: Issues for Organization Science. Organization Science, 14(2) (2003) 209-223.
20. Dahlander, L.: Appropriating Returns From Open Innovation Processes: A Multiple Case Study of Small Firms in Open Source Software, Department of Industrial Dynamics, School of Technology Management, Chalmers University of Technology, Gothenburg, Sweden (2004).
21. Bonaccorsi, A. and Rossi, C.: Altruistic individuals, selfish firms? The structure of motivation in Open Source software. First Monday, 9(1) (2004).
22. Fielding, R.T.: Shared Leadership in the Apache Project. Communications of the ACM, 42(4) (1999) 42-43.
23. Mockus, A., Fielding, R.T. and Herbsleb, J.D.: Two Case Studies of Open Source Software Development: Apache and Mozilla. ACM Transactions on Software Engineering and Methodology, 11(3) (2002) 309-346.
24. Holck, J. and Jørgensen, N.: Continuous Integration and Quality Assurance: a Case Study of two Open Source Projects. Australasian Journal of Information Systems (Special issue 2003/2004) (2004).
25. Holck, J. and Jørgensen, N.: Do not Check In On Red: Balancing Anarchy with Control in Two Open Source Projects. In Koch, S. (ed.): Free/Open Source Software Development, IDEA Publishing (2004).
26. Koch, S. and Schneider, G.: Effort, Cooperation and Coordination in an Open Source Software Project: GNOME. Information Systems Journal, 12(1) (2002).
27. Zhao, L. and Elbaum, S.: Quality Assurance Under the Open Source Development Model. The Journal of Systems and Software, 66(1) (2003) 65-75.

28. Scacchi, W.: When is Free/Open Source Software Development Faster, Better, and Cheaper than Software Engineering? In Koch, S. (ed.): Free/Open Source Software Development, IDEA Publishing (2003).
29. Paulson, J.W., Succi, G. and Eberlein, A.: An empirical study of open-source and closed-source software products. IEEE Transactions on Software Engineering, 30(4) (2004) 246-256.
30. Kogut, B. and Metiu, A.: Open-Source Software Development and Distributed Innovation. Oxford Review of Economic Policy, 17(2) (2001) 248-264.
31. Fitzgerald, B., The Mysteries of Open Source Software: Black and White and Red All Over? Retrieved May 19, 2004 from http://www.csis.ul.ie/staff/bf/bwr.rtf.
32. Mustonen, M.: Copyleft - the economics of Linux and other open source software. Information Economics and Policy, 15(1) (2003) 99-121.
33. Dedrick, J. and West, J.: An Exploratory Study into Open Source Platform Adoption. Proc. 37th Hawaii International Conference on System Sciences (HICSS), Hawaii, USA (2004).
34. Fitzgerald, B. and Kenny, T.: Open Source Software in the Trenches: Lessons from a Large-Scale OSS Implementation. Proc. International Conference on Software Engineering (ICSE 2003), Portland, Oregon, USA (2003).
35. Terhoeven, K.: Open-Source-Software am Büroarpeitsplatz: Erfahrungen der Endanwender aus der Migration der Geschäftsstelle der Monopolkommission. In Gehring, R.A. and Lutterbeck, B. (ed.): Open Source Jahrbuch 2004: Zwischen Softwareentwicklung und Gesellschaftsmodell, Lehmanns Media, Berlin (2004).
36. Müller, F.: Migration der Server- und Desktoplandschaft im Landesrechnungshof Meckelburg-Vorpommern. In Gehring, R.A. and Lutterbeck, B. (ed.): Open Source Jahrbuch 2004: Zwischen Softwareentwicklung und Gesellschaftsmodell, Lehmanns Media, Berlin (2004).
37. Seiferth, C.J.: Open Source and these United States. Knowledge Technology & Policy, 12(3) (1999).
38. Schmitz, P.-E. and Castiaux, S.: Pooling Open Source Software: An IDA Feasability Study, European Commission, DG Enterprise (2002).
39. Teknologirådet, Open-source software - in e-government. Retrieved May 2, 2004 from http://www.tekno.dk/pdf/projekter/p03_opensource_paper_english.pdf.
40. Yin, R.K.: Case Study Research: Design and Methods. Sage Publications, Newbury Park (1998).
41. Ben Sassi, S., Jilani, L.L. and Ben Ghezala, H.H.: COTS Characterization Model in a COTS-Based Development Environment. Proc. Tenth Asia-Pacific Software Engineering Conference (APSEC 2003), Chiang Mai, Thailand (2003).
42. Brownsword, L., Oberndorf, T. and Sledge, C.A.: Developing New Process for COTS-based Systems. IEEE Software, 17(4) (2000) 48-55.
43. Basili, V.R. and Boehm, B., COTS lessons learned. Retrieved April 14, 2004 from http://fc-md.umd.edu/ll/index.asp.
44. COCOTS. Retrieved Mar 26, 2004 from http://sunset.usc.edu/research/COCOTS/index.html.
45. Keil, M. and Carmel, E.: Customer-Developer Links in Software Development. Communications of the ACM, 38(5) (1995) 33-44.

COTS and Open Source Software Components: Are They Really Different on the Battlefield?

Piergiorgio Di Giacomo

European Software Institute,
Parque Tecnológico Edificio #204,
Zamudio, Bizkaia, Spain
Piergiorgio.DiGiacomo@esi.es

Abstract. When referring to Open Source Software (OSS) components, researchers, coders and managers do not feel comfortable in defining them as COTS. Many discussions have been aimed to decide whether or not OSS can be considered a COTS without reaching the unanimous consensus of the different international communities. This paper abandons any theoretical aspect of that question and focuses on the practical steps to follow when assembling component-based systems using also OSS components. All the activities normally performed when integrating COTS in a in-house built software are reviewed with the intention of underlining if the availability of the source code (and its possible exploitation) makes any difference. Moreover this article analyzes all the activities to perform when using OSS in a component-based system that are not necessary when using COTS. The purpose of this paper is to provide a guideline for the correct use of OSS within component-based systems, and not to answer whether OSS are considered or not COTS, leaving this task to the reader.

1 Introduction

The aggregation of different software components is nowadays a very common practice in the creation of complex systems. Not all the components in a system have to be inevitably built in-house. Outsourcing Commercial Off-the-Shelf (COTS) components can result convenient when an organization does not have time, internal competencies or resources to develop a particular functionality.

Outsourcing commercial components is often object of numerous debates and has produced different opinions among researchers, coders and managers. One of the main limitations when using COTS is the fact that the source code is not available. Consequently they cannot be entirely trusted and exploited. In fact, the unavailability of the source code is only one of the disadvantages the user has to face when using COTS. The impossibility to drive the evolution of the product, the obligations to upgrade the product and the conformity of the new version to the wrap code already written (and many others) are also aspects that often create discontent among the COTS users.

In many cases the adoption of Open Source Software (OSS) components can be a way of overcoming such problems. The first part of this paper summarizes the

X. Franch and D. Port (Eds.): ICCBSS 2005, LNCS 3412, pp. 301 – 310, 2005.

benefits and the disadvantages when using OSS components. It also clarifies the most common myths about OSS and OSS world. The second part analyzes the activities to be performed when outsourcing software components. After recalling the usual activities of software development, it compares the COTS vs. OSS activities and their similarities or differences. Moreover, the peculiar tasks of OSS component integration are exploited in deep detail.

2 OSS Myths and Mystifications: Why Management Do not Trust OSS

The confidence that coders have with the OSS world, their motivation when developing in communities and their enthusiastic view of the OSS, often supported by bad feelings against big corporations are making OSS to penetrate the industrial sector faster than initially thought.

Nevertheless, management is often more than reluctant to adopt OSS solutions. This cultural gap between coders and management is sometimes based on misinformation on the technical aspects of OSS.

The following sections analyze all the myths about open software and the truths in each of them. This clarification about the OSS and its implication is essential when deciding to implement on OSS solutions for both risk analysis and decision taking task.

2.1 The Money Factor

When Open Software solutions are exploited, their price is certainly attractive but it is also source of concern for the management. Total cost of ownership can be proven to be not equal to zero, as OSS components have to be integrated, tested and maintained just like COTS. When acquiring a COTS, managers go through a process that is not different by any other acquisition: they prepare requirements, select suppliers and their products, sign a contract and, most important, pay for what they buy.

The fact that a physical entity is providing the needed component provides indeed more assurances to the management. If the component does not work there is somebody to blame and the fee paid for the component is reassuring about the value of the component itself.

On the other side, a component acquired for free gives the impression of something created by amateurs. Even if in some cases this can be true, OSS has originated by the need to reach goals that can be achieved only by the cooperation of many parties:

1. An open group of developers and users who join their strengths to create an open software component since the ones already on the market are not suitable for them for economical or technical reasons.
2. A closed group of partners (normally SME[1]) establishing a small consortium for the creation of software which code is available only to the partners, with the double intention of decreasing the cost of the commodity software and opening of a new market in a short time period.

[1] Small-Medium Enterprise.

3. The last case is the one in which a commercial product becomes open because the company has no more interest in keeping it close because it is not enough competitive, the company goes out of business, the company needs external help to improve its component, etc.

Even though the source code is available, the lack of support, documentation and often, of a user friendly configuration/management environment makes the total cost of ownership increase dramatically.

In these cases the total cost of ownership of an OSS component tends to be equal to the one of COTS. But this is only one side of the matter. More than a study [1], [2], [3] reveals that in the long run OSS is not more expensive than commercial solutions:

- the licenses do not force upgrades;
- the license is cost effective if the same component has to be deployed on more than one system;
- when supported by a large community OSS are more stable, efficient and secure than their commercial counterparts: this leads to a more efficient overall system.

2.2 The Concerns About the Lack of Support

Support in the usage and maintenance of a COTS can be provided by:

- documentation and user manuals;
- customer care hotlines and installation support;
- patch releases every x months.

Such services require the existence of a dedicated team working on them. In the case of OSS components the situation is quite different and different are the risks for the user when help is needed.

As a matter of fact, the main problem of OSS is not the documentation (i.e. the installation and the user manual or the on-line help), since the quality of the manuals can be as good as in the commercial cases. Moreover, when acquiring an OSS they can usually be downloaded and evaluated before the acquisition. In any case it is not true that the documentation of commercial software is always good, especially if the extended support services are not free of charge.

No matter how good is the paper (or electronic) documentation, when the user has a problem the existence of a customer-care hot line can be helpful, especially if it is proved to be efficient: to obtain some help is as easy as writing an email or calling the given address/phone number. In case of OSS, it is different but not less functional. Every user is part of the community and can submit his questions and problems to the others. Communities are normally scattered all over the globe, so a question can be answered at any given time. Moreover, the service is free of charge, while COTS vendors can charge the user for using customer-line services after a limited period of free use or warranty, or simply refuse to give help if the used COTS is not the latest version.

Obviously there is the possibility that the community ignores the question of the user. This is normally due to social reasons: maybe the user is not active enough in the life and the activities of the communities and/or has refused to help other users in the past. This risk can be prevented during the acquisition phase, allocating resources to manage adequately the relationships with the community.

2.3 The Legal Implications Are Risky and Difficult to Understand

As summarized in [4], in the world of OSS exists a large variety of licenses and understanding their differences or their implications can be a good business for lawyers. The key-word in each license is "freedom" since mostly all of OSS licenses grant the freedom to use, copy, redistribute and modify the licensed software. Two different scenarios can be proposed. In the first one, a company simply modifies an OSS component: what are its obligations? In the second, the (modified) component is used in a proprietary system that will be sold to a third party: is proprietary code in the system to be released to the community?

Actually the main issue in this matter is the so called *copyleft*. In [5] it is defined as: "*a general method for making a program free software and requiring all modified and extended versions of the program to be free software as well*".

Not all OSS licenses impose restrictions about derived work and obviously not all of them do it with the same energy. In fact they can be divided in three big categories: copyleft licenses, mid-copyleft licenses, non-copyleft licenses.

For example, the world famous GNU General Public License (GPL) belongs to the first group. It actually imposes that the source code of every work derived from a GPL covered software should be made publicly available under terms that are compatible with the GPL. In other words every work derived from another one released under GPL, must be released under GPL conditions as well. This is known as the "*viral*" aspect of the GPL license i.e. everything gets in touch with GPL become GPL covered as well. This is because GPL considers a "modification" of the original OSS component as:

1) any new file in which there are parts of the original program;
2) any new original file in a bigger work based on a GPL-covered component.

In any case, mere aggregation of a work not based on a GPL protected program with GPL covered software (or with a work based on it) on a volume of a storage or distribution medium does not bring the other work under the scope of GPL.

The restrictions imposed by GPL are often considered too binding even by programmers who enthusiastically support OSS initiatives. Thus licenses have been created in which the meaning of the word "modification" has been changed and does not embrace any more the point 2) stated above. In this way it is possible to create new applications based on OSS component, without deliver proprietary code to the rest of the world. An example of programs using this license is the well known web-browser Netscape.

Finally, the licenses considered as non-copyleft do not force the user to deliver the improved code.

2.4 OSS Components and Security Related Aspects

"*Given enough eyeballs all bugs are shallow*". This is known in the OSS world as *Linus' Law*[2] and states that OSS is more secure than commercial software because its code can be reviewed by a huge number of coders. It is the OSS answer to the "Security by obscurity" philosophy in force in the COTS world.

[2] Linus Torvalds (creator of Linux, an OSS Operative System) is one of the most representative gurus of the OSS community

Hackers vs. SW Developers: they always compete who will be the first to discover security holes and make the two laws valid or not. When trying to attack proprietary software a hacker has to spend a lot of time in activities like collection of information, black-box testing, study of component behavior and reverse-engineering. When the source code is available, those activities do not have to be performed anymore, as the search for bugs can be done directly at code level.

Anyway, assuming that Linus' Law is true at least for the trivial bugs in the code, cyber terrorists have less opportunity to design minor attacks and at least less time to plan complicated ones. They are in fact competing against a large community of coders more than against a small team of programmers from a certain company and time is the key factor in hacker activities.

Furthermore when a community fixes a bug discovered *after* an attack, the patch normally fixes many other similar problems encountered and discussed while reviewing the code in search of the origin of the problem.

The availability of the source code also prevents the possibility of the insertion in the applications of backdoors that might undermine the privacy of the users/companies and the security of the data managed through the application. Similar situations have been discovered in real cases for example in Microsoft [13] and Borland [14] applications and are one of the reasons why OSS is especially penetrating the markets where the guarantee of the privacy is a key factor.

Finally, when a bug is reported it is normally fixed within days by the community or can be fixed by the user if he is competent enough. On the contrary, if a bug is found in a COTS there is not any guarantee about the fact that it will be fixed and when. COTS providers can simply refuse to fix a bug because it does not affect enough users. In this case, if the user having the problem is not a huge corporation (i.e. a really important client) there is no way to force the vendor to change its bad behavior.

One last word about security when talking about patches and bugs. The release of OSS components is not pressed by time-to-market and competition with other products. This means that they are presented in a fair manner to the user. If a component is not completely tested, it is presented as the beta version of what will be the final product. In commercial cases it happens more than often that users buy a product that is not 100% working. Market rules force COTS vendors to release a new version of their products even if they know they are not fully working. Later on vendors release patches to fix bugs that have in the meantime undermined the reliability and the security of the systems already using their COTS.

3 OSS Impact on the Project Life Cycle of a Component-Based System

The development of component based systems normally goes through a certain number of different phases performed in a sequential or recursive way. The adoption of external components to be assembled in a system affects all those steps, from the definition of the requirements until the maintenance of the main system. It also introduces a certain number of new activities to be performed and managed in order to acquire, integrate and maintain the external components as well. These activities can be conducted in a different way if the component to outsource is or it is not "open". The risks highlighted in the first part will be the main guide to perform these activities in the best possible way.

3.1 OSS Market Research

Market research is the first activity to performe when a company is willing to outsource SW components. It is carried out when selecting the possible candidates for the acquisition.

When outsourcing proprietary software, the acquiring company can check if any of its usual SW providers have any suitable COTS, move to known brands and finally can search for COTS through out the web.

Unfortunately, in case of OSS there is not a company advertising the product, so this task is more difficult. OSS communities do not approach companies advertising their OSS components and often there is not a brand to recall when starting the market research.

This does not mean that the research of OSS is more difficult than the research of proprietary COTS. In fact, there is a quite large number of portals that recollect almost all active OSS projects. Sourceforge.net or the more recent eCOTS.org are only a couple of good examples of such portals. They provide a recollection of the existing active projects providing their description, the evaluation of their work products (normally made directly by the users) and any kind of useful information about each component.

3.2 OSS Evaluation and Selection

Because of the peculiar nature of OSS components the evaluation criteria to adopt when selecting them are often quite different from the ones used to evaluate proprietary software components. Even if PECA[3], PORE[4], ISO 14598, MAUT[5] and other COTS evaluation frameworks can still be used to evaluate OSS components (especially in the case they are going to be used as black box anyway) with regard to the risks listed in the first part they do not fit OSS evaluation needs at 100%.

In the case of OSS, there are new factors to evaluate: the terms of the license, the structure and activity level of the developer community, the market acceptance and the compliance to the most used standards.

When deciding to acquire an OSS component, it is important to understand if its license is compatible with its future use in a (and of the) proprietary system. For example:

1. Component based systems, i.e. systems built by the aggregation of different components do not have problems with copyleft matters, especially if they are not going to be delivered to a third party;

---

[3] Process for COTS Evaluation, developed by National Research Council of Canada and the Software Engineering Institute, USA.

[4] Procurement-Oriented Requirements Engineering Method for the Component-Based Systems Engineering Development Paradigm, developed by the City University of London, UK.

[5] Multi-Attribute Utility Technique, developed by the Cambridge University, UK.

2. Proprietary applications based on a main OSS piece of work should instead consider the use of mid-copyleft or non-copyleft covering licenses. The company will avoid publishing parts of code that might be considered strategic if the application is delivered to a third party.

Compatibility among different licenses should also be considered. Some licenses do not admit the coexistence in the same system of their covered software components and the ones covered by some specific licenses [5].

To help companies and individuals in the selection of OSS, the Open Source Maturity Model [6], [7] has been released. It stresses not only the most valuable indicators (summarized in table 1) to consider when evaluating different OSS components, but also provides a way to compare the weak and strong points of each of them with the priorities and the business model of the acquiring company.

Table 1. OSS maturity indicators and their composing aspects

Product	**Integration**	**Use**	**Acceptance**
Age	Modularity	Standards	Ease of Deployment
Licensing	Collaboration with other products	Support	User community
Human hierarchies			Market penetration
Selling Points			
Developer community			

If a company is already using COTS (and consequently their dedicated evaluation methods) and is willing to adopt OSS solutions in a smoother way, it can choose to turn to a branded OSS component. Many companies have adopted business models that allow them to make money from the OSS. They assure a certain level of support, documentation, training and often some added features just like a normal COTS vendor would do. When choosing such OSS components many typical OSS problems disappear. The component can be considered almost a COTS and can be evaluated in a more classical way. Naturally, in this case the extra-service has a cost that should be carefully considered.

3.3 OSS Procurement

Physical OSS procurement is easy, it can be downloaded from the community web portal. Apart from the minimal fee the customer could get charged when using a download service, this task can be performed without any additional cost. Here the problem is still the same: the lack of a vendor makes difficult to understand how to manage the risks associated to the usage of the OSS component. Oberndorf and Myers [8] give five possible contracting strategies when acquiring software. Those strategies increase the portion of risks and responsibilities that fall on the customer or on the contractor at each stage of the development of the main system.

Since OSS is typically free of charge, it is given "as is" with no warranty of any kind [5]. This means that if the customer wants to increase the level of confidence in the OSS he/she is acquiring, has to turn to branded OSS. In this case, it can be possible to reduce the amount of responsibilities pending on the acquirer, but naturally, not all of them.

When acquiring an OSS component, the management should also choose a policy for the support of the community of developers that released the OSS component choosing an adequate strategy, for both political and social reasons. The user can simply become an economical sponsor or can take an active part in the community life participating to the discussions on the *fora*, where the decisions about component evolution are normally discussed and also release its own modification to the community (when the license does not oblige to do so anyway).

3.4 OSS Integration and Testing

The integration of an OSS component can be performed in two ways suitable for the different needs of the customer. If the exploitation of the source code is not a priority for the acquirer and the component has been chosen for its price, reputation, security, etc. it can be used as a mere COTS and integrated (and later on tested) as a pure black-box component.

In this case, the usual techniques of integration of COTS are still applicable and valid. When the specifications of the component are enough accurate, as described in [8] it can be integrated by implementation of glue code, by a common used standard or creating a shared platform interfacing all the components in the system.

However, the main advantage in this phase is the availability of the source code, which allows direct modifications. Such modifications can be performed directly by the user (if he has the competence to do it) or with the help of the whole of the developing community, especially if the user in need is socially accepted in it.

The main advantage of a direct modification is the fact that on the market there is not an off-the-shelf component that suits perfectly the need of an organization, not only in terms of lack of required features, but also in terms of their excessive number. If a feature is not required, instead of using some wrap code to mask it, the user can disable it by modifying the code. In [9] Hissam et al. claim this is not really an advantage because if the code is modified directly by the user, the so called "derived work" should be given back to the community and may expose parts of the code that can be considered strategic. This is in fact not always true (especially if the modified work will not be redistributed), because some licenses allow to keep the modifications covered and do not oblige to redistribute the source code. What is true is the fact that such behavior is in contrast with the open source philosophy.

The testing phase normally can be managed as the integration one. The OSS can be used as a black-box, but more likely it can also be tested as a white-box, especially when tracking bugs or when discovering a bad behavior of the system.

3.5 OSS Maintenance and Update

Maintenance and update of OSS is certainly an interesting part of the job when using OSS solutions in a proprietary system. In this phase, the freedom that OSS licenses give to the user is even more valuable than in other stages of the acquisition /development process. As mentioned before, the terms of the licenses covering OSS do not oblige the user to upgrade the component he/she is using if the user does not want to. This means that if the new versions are not interesting, or could undermine the stability of the overall system, the upgrade can be avoided. If instead the upgrade is considered valid, it does not cost anything to the user in terms of money. Of course a new version could need additional glue code or modifications to the underlying platform as for the COTS, but if the integration has been conducted watching the code, staff can evaluate the impact of a new version even more correctly and with less risk of performing an erroneous integration.

The evolution of the component can also be driven privately or publicly in the community. The user has more possibilities to influence the evolution of the software he is using.

In [10] Clapp and Taub give a summary of the highest risks of COTS maintenance. If OSS is used exploiting the code those risks are reduced by the availability of the code (easier configuration, more control over the quality, etc.).As usual, if the OSS is used as a black-box, since the user is more dependent from the community and its level of activity. In this case, the reliability of the community should be considered as one of the principal indicators of the maturity of OSS component to acquire.

4 Conclusions

The analysis conducted in this paper shows how the use of OSS is not completely different from the use of COTS. The tasks normally performed when outsourcing COTS are still valid, but because of the peculiar nature of OSS they have to be extended and carried out stressing different critical points. OSS solutions can be a real alternative to COTS anytime they cannot satisfy all the requirements an organization may have in terms of budget, security and privacy assurance, etc. Unfortunately, the lack of rigid methodologies and tools for OSS acquisition and integration, limit for the moment the successful exploitation of such components. This is impeding OSS to compete with COTS at the same level, as they can rely on a larger number of decision and risk-analysis models.

References

1. Carolyn Kenwood: A business Case Study of Open Source Software. MITRE, July 2001 pp.43-45 (http://www.mitre.org/work/tech_papers/tech_papers_01/kenwood_software/kenwood_software.pdf)
2. Linux vs. Windows: Total Cost of Ownership Comparison. Cybersource Pty. Ltd., 2002 pp. 2-7 (http://www.cyber.com.au/cyber/about/linux_vs_windows_pricing_comparison.pdf)
3. Total Cost of Ownership for Linux in the Enterprise. R. Frances Group, Jul. 2002 (http://www-1.ibm.com/linux/RFG-LinuxTCO-vFINAL-Jul2002.pdf)
4. http://www.gnu.org/licenses/license-list.html
5. http://www.gnu.org/copyleft/copyleft.html

6. C. Widdows, F.W. Duijnhouwer: Open Source Maturity Model. pp.6-10 (http://www.seriouslyopen.org/nuke/html/modules/Downloads/osmm/GB_Expert_Letter_Open_Source_Maturity_Model_1.5.3.pdf)
7. B. Golden: Succeeding with Open Source. Ed. Addison-Wesley, August 2004, Cap.4
8. Craig Meyers, Patricia Oberndorf: Managing Software Acquisition, SEI Series in Software Engineering, 2001
9. Scott Hissam, Charles B. Weinstock, Daniel Plakosh, Jayatirtha Asundi: Perspectives on Open Source Software. SEI, Nov. 2001, pp. 53-54
10. Judith A. Clapp & Audrey E. Taub: A Management Guide to Software Maintenance in COTS-Based Systems. MITRE Paper, November 1998
11. G. Geenberg et al.: Open Source moving into Enterprise. Cutter Consortium, 2003
12. A. Abella, J. Sanchez, M. A. Segovia: Libro Blanco del Software Libre en España. 2004
13. Joe Wilcox: Microsoft Secret File Could Allow Access to Web Sites. CNET news.com Apr. 2000 (http://news.com.com/2100-1001-239273.html?legacy=cnet)
14. Kevin Poulsen: Borland Interbase Backdoor Exposed. The Register Jan. 2001 (http://www.theregister.co.uk/2001/01/12/borland_interbase_backdoor_exposed/)

Author Index

Abramatic, Jean-François 2
Aldea-Montero, Fernando 258
Alves, Carina 146
Anderson, Wm B. 268
Andrés, Carlos Fernández 8
Aretxandieta, Xabier 3
Arias-Chausson, Carlos 5, 36
Avgeriou, Paris 248
Axelsson, Jakob 1
Ayala, Claudia P. 90

Barbier, Franck 3
Baron, Sally J. F. 101
Bastida Merino, Leire 25
Baxi, Pranjali 157
Benguria Elguezabal, Gorka 25
Beus-Dukic, Ljerka 77
Bhuta, Jesal 6, 132
Boehm, Barry 6, 9, 132
Botella, Pere 90
Brownsword, Lisa 13
Bunse, Christian 278

Carvallo, Juan P. 12, 146
Casquero, Oskar 191
Cechich, Alejandra 112
Chicote, Cristina Vicente 8
Choi, Myeonggil 11
Conradi, Reidar 278
Crnkovic, Ivica 1

Di Giacomo, Piergiorgio 301

Elgazzar, Shadia 43

Finkelstein, Anthony 146
Franch, Xavier 12, 90, 146

Ghosh, Sudipto 122
Gómez, Fernando Piera 2
González-Barahona, Jesús M. 2
González, Ignacio Delgado 5
Graf, Susanne 1
Grahn, Göran V. 144
Grunske, Lars 178
Guelfi, Nicolas 248

Han, Jun 54
Hansson, Elisabeth 144
Hirata, Fabio 157
Holck, Jesper 289
Hutchinson, John 212

Jefferson, Nigel 168
Jin, Yan 54
Juric, Radmila 77

Kaiser, Bernhard 178
Kamsties, Erik 223
Kark, Anatol 43
Katahira, Masafumi 4, 65
Kelly, John L. 122
Kim, Eunhye 11
Kim, Hyunwoo 11
Kim, Sehun 11
Kotonya, Gerald 212

Lang, Bernard 2
Larsen, Michael Holm 289
Larsson, Magnus 1
Lewis, Grace A. 236
Li, Jingyue 278

Mamiya, Hitoshi 65
Marcos, Marga 191

Moreo, Ana Toledo 8
Morisio, Maurizio 278
Morris, Edwin 268
Motes, Christina 4

Nakao, Haruka 4, 65
Nomoto, Hideki 65
Northcott, Mark 201
Norton, Barry 10

Pedersen, Mogens Kühn 2, 289
Piattini, Mario 112
Pohl, Klaus 223
Port, Daniel 4, 6, 65
Portillo, Javier 191
Putrycz, Erik 43

Quer, Carme 12

Reifer, Donald J. 157
Riddle, Steve 168
Rodríguez, Manuel 258
Rodríguez-Dapena, Patricia 258

Sagarduy, Goiuria 3
Schifman, Jonathan 157
Shankar, Roopashree P. 122
Silva, João Gabriel 258
Slyngstad, Odd Petter N. 278
Smith, Dennis 268
Smith, Jim 13
Strigini, Lorenzo 168

Torchiano, Marco 12, 278
Tsao, Ricky 157

Ulfat-Bunyadi, Nelufar 223

van der Meulen, Meine 168
van Loon, Han 258
van Ommering, Rob 1
Vigder, Mark 43, 201

Wallnau, Kurt 1
Ward, Mary Catherine 268

Yang, Ye 6, 9

Lecture Notes in Computer Science

For information about Vols. 1–3283

please contact your bookseller or Springer

Vol. 3332: K. Aizawa, Y. Nakamura, S. Satoh (Eds.), Advances in Multimedia Information Processing - PCM 2004, Part II. XXXVI, 1051 pages. 2004.

Vol. 3331: K. Aizawa, Y. Nakamura, S. Satoh (Eds.), Advances in Multimedia Information Processing - PCM 2004, Part I. XXXVI, 667 pages. 2004.

Vol. 3330: J. Akiyama, E.T. Baskoro, M. Kano (Eds.), Combinatorial Geometry and Graph Theory. VIII, 227 pages. 2005.

Vol. 3329: P.J. Lee (Ed.), Advances in Cryptology - ASIACRYPT 2004. XVI, 546 pages. 2004.

Vol. 3328: K. Lodaya, M. Mahajan (Eds.), FSTTCS 2004: Foundations of Software Technology and Theoretical Computer Science. XVI, 532 pages. 2004.

Vol. 3327: Y. Shi, W. Xu, Z. Chen (Eds.), Data Mining and Knowledge Management. XIII, 263 pages. 2004. (Subseries LNAI).

Vol. 3326: A. Sen, N. Das, S.K. Das, B.P. Sinha (Eds.), Distributed Computing - IWDC 2004. XIX, 546 pages. 2004.

Vol. 3323: G. Antoniou, H. Boley (Eds.), Rules and Rule Markup Languages for the Semantic Web. X, 215 pages. 2004.

Vol. 3322: R. Klette, J. Žunić (Eds.), Combinatorial Image Analysis. XII, 760 pages. 2004.

Vol. 3321: M.J. Maher (Ed.), Advances in Computer Science - ASIAN 2004. XII, 510 pages. 2004.

Vol. 3320: K.-M. Liew, H. Shen, S. See, W. Cai (Eds.), Parallel and Distributed Computing: Applications and Technologies. XXIV, 891 pages. 2004.

Vol. 3318: E. Eskin, C. Workman (Eds.), Regulatory Genomics. VIII, 115 pages. 2005. (Subseries LNBI).

Vol. 3317: M. Domaratzki, A. Okhotin, K. Salomaa, S. Yu (Eds.), Implementation and Application of Automata. XII, 336 pages. 2005.

Vol. 3316: N.R. Pal, N.K. Kasabov, R.K. Mudi, S. Pal, S.K. Parui (Eds.), Neural Information Processing. XXX, 1368 pages. 2004.

Vol. 3315: C. Lemaître, C.A. Reyes, J.A. González (Eds.), Advances in Artificial Intelligence – IBERAMIA 2004. XX, 987 pages. 2004. (Subseries LNAI).

Vol. 3314: J. Zhang, J.-H. He, Y. Fu (Eds.), Computational and Information Science. XXIV, 1259 pages. 2004.

Vol. 3313: C. Castelluccia, H. Hartenstein, C. Paar, D. Westhoff (Eds.), Security in Ad-hoc and Sensor Networks. VIII, 231 pages. 2004.

Vol. 3312: A.J. Hu, A.K. Martin (Eds.), Formal Methods in Computer-Aided Design. XI, 445 pages. 2004.

Vol. 3311: V. Roca, F. Rousseau (Eds.), Interactive Multimedia and Next Generation Networks. XIII, 287 pages. 2004.

Vol. 3310: U.K. Wiil (Ed.), Computer Music Modeling and Retrieval. XI, 371 pages. 2005.

Vol. 3309: C.-H. Chi, K.-Y. Lam (Eds.), Content Computing. XII, 510 pages. 2004.

Vol. 3308: J. Davies, W. Schulte, M. Barnett (Eds.), Formal Methods and Software Engineering. XIII, 500 pages. 2004.

Vol. 3307: C. Bussler, S.-k. Hong, W. Jun, R. Kaschek, D.. Kinshuk, S. Krishnaswamy, S.W. Loke, D. Oberle, D. Richards, A. Sharma, Y. Sure, B. Thalheim (Eds.), Web Information Systems – WISE 2004 Workshops. XV, 277 pages. 2004.

Vol. 3306: X. Zhou, S. Su, M.P. Papazoglou, M.E. Orlowska, K.G. Jeffery (Eds.), Web Information Systems – WISE 2004. XVII, 745 pages. 2004.

Vol. 3305: P.M.A. Sloot, B. Chopard, A.G. Hoekstra (Eds.), Cellular Automata. XV, 883 pages. 2004.

Vol. 3303: J.A. López, E. Benfenati, W. Dubitzky (Eds.), Knowledge Exploration in Life Science Informatics. X, 249 pages. 2004. (Subseries LNAI).

Vol. 3302: W.-N. Chin (Ed.), Programming Languages and Systems. XIII, 453 pages. 2004.

Vol. 3300: L. Bertossi, A. Hunter, T. Schaub (Eds.), Inconsistency Tolerance. VII, 295 pages. 2005.

Vol. 3299: F. Wang (Ed.), Automated Technology for Verification and Analysis. XII, 506 pages. 2004.

Vol. 3298: S.A. McIlraith, D. Plexousakis, F. van Harmelen (Eds.), The Semantic Web – ISWC 2004. XXI, 841 pages. 2004.

Vol. 3296: L. Bougé, V.K. Prasanna (Eds.), High Performance Computing - HiPC 2004. XXV, 530 pages. 2004.

Vol. 3295: P. Markopoulos, B. Eggen, E. Aarts, J.L. Crowley (Eds.), Ambient Intelligence. XIII, 388 pages. 2004.

Vol. 3294: C.N. Dean, R.T. Boute (Eds.), Teaching Formal Methods. X, 249 pages. 2004.

Vol. 3293: C.-H. Chi, M. van Steen, C. Wills (Eds.), Web Content Caching and Distribution. IX, 283 pages. 2004.

Vol. 3292: R. Meersman, Z. Tari, A. Corsaro (Eds.), On the Move to Meaningful Internet Systems 2004: OTM 2004 Workshops. XXIII, 885 pages. 2004.

Vol. 3291: R. Meersman, Z. Tari (Eds.), On the Move to Meaningful Internet Systems 2004: CoopIS, DOA, and ODBASE, Part II. XXV, 824 pages. 2004.

Vol. 3290: R. Meersman, Z. Tari (Eds.), On the Move to Meaningful Internet Systems 2004: CoopIS, DOA, and ODBASE, Part I. XXV, 823 pages. 2004.

Vol. 3289: S. Wang, K. Tanaka, S. Zhou, T.W. Ling, J. Guan, D. Yang, F. Grandi, E. Mangina, I.-Y. Song, H.C. Mayr (Eds.), Conceptual Modeling for Advanced Application Domains. XXII, 692 pages. 2004.

Vol. 3288: P. Atzeni, W. Chu, H. Lu, S. Zhou, T.W. Ling (Eds.), Conceptual Modeling – ER 2004. XXI, 869 pages. 2004.

Vol. 3287: A. Sanfeliu, J.F. Martínez Trinidad, J.A. Carrasco Ochoa (Eds.), Progress in Pattern Recognition, Image Analysis and Applications. XVII, 703 pages. 2004.

Vol. 3286: G. Karsai, E. Visser (Eds.), Generative Programming and Component Engineering. XIII, 491 pages. 2004.

Vol. 3285: S. Manandhar, J. Austin, U.B. Desai, Y. Oyanagi, A. Talukder (Eds.), Applied Computing. XII, 334 pages. 2004.

Vol. 3284: A. Karmouch, L. Korba, E.R.M. Madeira (Eds.), Mobility Aware Technologies and Applications. XII, 382 pages. 2004.